The Irish World Wide
History, Heritage, Identity

Volume 4 **Irish Women and Irish Migration**

The Irish World Wide
History, Heritage, Identity

Edited by Patrick O'Sullivan

The Irish World Wide
History, Heritage, Identity

Volume 4
Irish Women and Irish Migration

Edited by Patrick O'Sullivan

Leicester University Press
London and New York

Leicester University Press
A Cassell imprint
Wellington House, 125 Strand, London, WC2R 0BB

First published 1995
© Editor and contributors 1995

British Library Cataloguing in Publication Data
A CIP catalogue record for this book is available from The British Library

ISBN 0 7185 1425 4

Library of Congress Cataloging-in-Publication Data
Irish women and Irish migration / edited by Patrick O'Sullivan.
       p. cm. – (The Irish world wide ; v. 4)
  Includes bibliographical references and index.
  ISBN 0–7185–1425–4
  1. Women – Ireland – Social conditions. 2. Ireland – Emigration and immigration – History – 19th century. 3. Ireland – Emigration and immigration – History – 20th century. 4. Women immigrants.
I. O'Sullivan, Patrick, 1944 –. II. Series.
HQ1600.3.I7389 1995
305.42'09415 – dc20
                                               94–24613
                                                 CIP

Typeset by Saxon Graphics Ltd, Derby.
Printed and bound in Great Britain by Biddles Ltd of Guildford and King's Lynn

In memory of Dennis Clark

Contents

List of contributors

Dennis Clark was the author of eleven books on urban affairs, immigrant history and social issues. He had a special interest in the history of the Irish in Philadelphia and in the development of Irish Studies in the United States. He died in September 1993, whilst this volume of *The Irish World Wide* was in preparation. This volume is dedicated to his memory.

Marilyn Cohen is assistant professor of Sociology at Montclair State College, New Jersey, USA. Her work has appeared in journals, including *The Journal of Peasant Studies* and *The Journal of Family History,* and in collections like *Marxist Approaches in Economic Anthropology.* She is currently editing a volume on the Irish linen industry.

David Noel Doyle is based at University College, Dublin, Ireland. He is the author, co-author and editor of numerous volumes and articles on Ireland's relationship with America, including *Irish Americans, Native Rights and National Empires* and *Ireland, Irishmen and Revolutionary America.*

Gráinne Henry is a graduate of Saint Patrick's College, Maynooth, whose postgraduate overseas research was financed by the Royal Irish Academy's Eoin O'Mahony Award. Her book, *The Irish Military Community in Spanish Flanders 1586–1621,* was published in 1992. She now works as a teacher in County Kerry, Ireland.

Patricia Kelleher lectures in Women's Studies at the University of Wisconsin, USA, and is working on the history of Irish women in late nineteenth-century Chicago.

Mary Kells obtained an MA in Social Anthropology at St Andrews University, Scotland, and is currently engaged in research for a PhD in Social Anthropology at the London School of Economics, England.

Kate Kelly worked as an Education/Information Officer for Emigrant Advice, Dublin. She is a co-author of *Emigration Matters for Women.* She is now settled in Boston, USA.

Lynda Letford is a part-time research student at the Department of Geography, University of Lancaster. She is currently undertaking research on women in nineteenth-century Liverpool. She lives and teaches on Merseyside, England.

Dympna McLoughlin is a graduate of Saint Patrick's College, Maynooth who gained her PhD at Syracuse University, New York. She now teaches within the Geography Department of University College, Cork, Ireland.

Kerby A. Miller is Professor of History at the University of Missouri, USA. He is the author of *Emigrants and Exiles: Ireland and the Irish Exodus to North America*, which won the Merle Curti Prize for best book in US social history and the Theodore Saloutos Prize for best book in US immigration history. He is currently preparing an edited collection of Irish migrants' letters and memoirs for publication by Oxford University Press.

Tríona Nic Giolla Choille worked as an Education/Information Officer for Emigrant Advice, Dublin. She is a co-author of *Emigration Matters for Women*. She had previously worked for the Irish Society for the Prevention of Cruelty to Children, and she now works in Dublin, Ireland, with the European Anti-Poverty Network, a coalition struggling against poverty and social exclusion in the European Community.

Íde B. O'Carroll obtained her MA from Northeastern University, Boston, and her PhD from Harvard. Her book, *Models for Movers: Irish Women's Emigration to America*, drew on her MA thesis. She is a Research Associate at the Centre for Women's Studies, Trinity College, Dublin, Ireland, and works with Nexus (Europe), a research co-operative.

Colin G. Pooley is Senior Lecturer in Geography and Deputy Director of the Centre for Social History at the University of Lancaster, England. He has published widely on the social geography of nineteenth and twentieth century Britain, focusing especially on housing, health and migrant groups. He is the co-editor of *Emigrants, Migrants and Immigrants: a social history of Migration*.

Pauric Travers is head of the history department at Saint Patrick's College, Drumcondra, Dublin, Ireland. He is co-editor of *The Irish Emigrant Experience in Australia*.

List of figures

List of tables

Introduction to Volume 4:
Irish women and Irish migration

Patrick O'Sullivan

Women and migration

Every chapter in this, the women's history and women's studies volume of
The Irish World Wide, begins by remarking on the paucity of research into
the experiences of migrant Irish women and the paucity of comment on
women in earlier studies of the patterns of Irish migration. The editorial
shears have not lopped off what, at first sight, might seem like simple repe-
tition: for contributors use that starting point in a variety of ways, some to
explore complex methodological issues, others to reflect on personal experiences, and all to provoke thought. Cumulatively, when the opening
sections of each chapter are put side by side, we have a discussion of
evidence and experiences, and a demonstration of the ways that preconceptions can mis-shape our understanding of the past and the present, and
can shape our gathering of evidence.

In any case, the point is worth repeating. This ignoring of women is
extraordinary. Donald Harman Akenson has said, 'One half of the great
Irish diaspora was female. Between the Act of Union of 1800 and the independence of southern Ireland in 1922, about four million Irish females left
the homeland'.[1] Ann Rossiter, citing Hasia Diner, speaks of 'a mass female
movement without parallel ...' and 'a "defeminization" of the Irish countryside'.[2] And Bronwen Walter is able to show that for very significant periods
women formed the majority of Irish migrants, supporting Robert Emmet
Kennedy's thesis that, certainly for the period 1871–1971, greater female
emigration is the Irish norm.[3] Indeed, Akenson, Rossiter and Walter all
direct our attention back to Robert Emmet Kennedy's 1973 *The Irish:
Emigration, Marriage and Fertility*.[4] There are, surely to goodness, enough
signposts indicating the importance of women, and the importance of
issues of concern to women, in any serious study of Irish migration.

But it is not only histories of *Irish* migration that neglect women. In my
General Introduction to *The Irish World Wide* I directed attention to the 1966
migration theory of Everett S. Lee. There was something of a fashion in the
1960s for nice, tidy pencil-and-paper short theories in the social sciences.
There are many advantages to using Lee. You will find that, over the

decades, students of other migrating peoples have appealed, and still appeal, to Lee for their shaping ideas: so that seeing the fit between Lee and our own work on the Irish gives us a window onto the experiences of others, and allows us to share experiences.[5]

Lee, in 1966, in his turn, was attempting to clarify and tidy up the 'Laws of Migration' outlined in two papers in 1885 and 1889 by E.G. Ravenstein: and sometimes you find that migration theorists will appeal back to Ravenstein for insights. Ravenstein's first paper used census material from the British Isles (all the then United Kingdom, including all of the island of Ireland); his second paper used a variety of European and North American census materials. Writing towards the end of the nineteenth century he had before him a good run of censuses. Whatever the merits or demerits of each individual census, he could begin to see overall patterns.

Whilst Ravenstein is not be to accepted uncritically (he is, for example, a child of his time in his own uncritical acceptance of migration as a tool of imperialism), he is useful. In particular, I would look at his comments on the movement of Irish people: his research material allows him to see movement within Ireland and movement out of Ireland as a continuum. And Ravenstein's remarks on the migration of women are very much worth pondering: for they have had extraordinary *little* influence, on the study of Irish migration, and on the study of migration in general:

> Woman is a greater migrant than man. This may surprise those who associate women with domestic life, but the figures of the census clearly prove it. Nor do women migrate merely from the rural districts into the towns in search of domestic service, for they migrate quite as frequently into certain manufacturing districts, and the workshop is a formidable rival of the kitchen and the scullery.[6]

Because he was working with census material, mass data about virtually all the population, Ravenstein was able to see that pattern: he was not misled by impressionistic material, or 'ideals' of womenhood based on upper class and middle-class life. The question posed by Ravenstein's findings for Irish Migration Studies becomes then: why, in Ireland, did woman the migrant become woman the emigrant? Putting the question in this form has the merit of placing the apparent anomalies of Irish female emigration firmly within the patterns of Irish social, political and economic history.

We need, first, to think more calmly about those emotionally-freighted words 'emigrant' and 'immigrant': noting that, whenever possible in *The Irish World Wide*, we use the more neutral word 'migrant'.[7] It is not simply that the use of the words 'emigrant' and 'immigrant' makes for unclear narratives and untidy writing. The words 'emigrant' and 'immigrant' already contain their own narrative: they incorporate a point of view. The point of view may well be that of the nation state, or the would-be nation state, across whose borders the travellers have journeyed. It is nation states who jealously define and guard borders, and who help form views of the usefulness, or otherwise, of 'immigrants': we are thus plunged into the 'contribution history' approach to the study of migration.

The words 'emigrant' and 'immigrant' focus the narrative upon international boundaries, a focus which can be misleading: the two international boundaries that figure most in the narratives of Irish migration, the boundary between the United States and Canada, and the boundary between the Irish Free State (and its successor, the Republic of Ireland) and the United Kingdom of Great Britain, are the most porous on earth. For very significant parts of Irish history there was, of course, technically no international boundary between Ireland and the rest of the United Kingdom. Students of post-1922 Irish migration constantly find themselves in difficulties (statistical and nomenclative) when talking about movement of people from Northern Ireland to the sister island, Great Britain. Yes, such movement is part of the patterns of Irish migration. But is it 'emigration'? There is still a strong Irish tradition which regards any movement out of, or off, the island of Ireland as 'emigration'.

On the other hand, Everett S. Lee's working definition of 'migration' is strict and precise:

> Migration is defined broadly as a permanent or semipermanent change of residence. No restriction is placed upon the distance of the move or upon the voluntary or involuntary nature of the act, and no distinction is made between external and internal migration. Thus, a move across the hall from one apartment to another is counted as just as much an act of migration as a move from Bombay, India, to Cedar Rapids, Iowa, though of course the initiation and consequences of such moves are vastly different.[8]

As we shall see (in the chapter by Kelly and Nic Giolla Choille, for example), what happens in Ireland is that some crisis which might, in other circumstances, have been accommodated by a move 'across the hall', or across the city, becomes a cause of movement across the sea or the ocean. We should also note the recurring trope in histories of feminism whereby changes in the status of women are referred to as 'a migration'.[9] So that we should put 'migration' as a metaphor for change alongside migration as a process which is both a product and a cause of change.

Methodology

Thus all our contributors remark on the neglect of women in studies of migration. And the parallel neglect of women by standard history has often been commented on.[10] That neglect and Ravenstein's 1885 observation (migration theory in effect demanding that we study women) demanded that I should commit one volume of *The Irish World Wide* to *Irish Women and Irish Migration*. It might be more accurate to say that I wanted to see what would happen if I did commit one volume of the series to the study of women. What would be gained, and what would be lost, by this strategy? Every volume of *The Irish World Wide* is a report on 'the state of the art'. Would I be able to find or commission enough research to construct a meaningful volume about women? What patterns would emerge as that volume came together? Would the volume have its own coherence?

I decided to try for the 'long chronology', the pattern that had worked well in two earlier volumes of *The Irish World Wide*, Volume 1, *Patterns of Migration*, and Volume 3, *The Creative Migrant*. This volume, *Irish Women and Irish Migration*, thus stands in a relationship to those earlier volumes: in particular I would see this volume as acting as a critique of Volume 1, *Patterns of Migration*. Volume 2, *The Irish in the New Communities*, focuses on a series of cruxes in Irish migrations historiography, though its overarching theme is the search for work. As will be seen, a major focus of this present volume, *Irish Women and Irish Migration*, is women as workers (another theme predicted by Ravenstein).

The first aim of this volume, then, all our contributors agree, is to draw attention to the paucity of research into the experiences of women. Make the gap visible.[11] And then to do something to fill the gap. In constructing this volume I broadcast the usual appeal for suitable chapters. But I also personally approached a number of scholars who, I knew, were working on larger studies of which the experiences of women formed a part, or who were used to working with the kind of databases that would yield material. I asked those scholars to approach that wider material from a women's history/women's studies viewpoint. I asked the contributors, as I ask all contributors to *The Irish World Wide*, to make their research methodology crystal clear.

The fact that scholars seized these opportunities and that the results are so illuminating indicate that research about women is not so problematic as is sometimes made out. Such research is difficult (though the difficulties are institutional as much as conceptual). As our contributors demonstrate, it is not impossible. Indeed, I think the greatest achievement of our contributors here is that they have so clearly demonstrated the effort, ingenuity and subtlety needed to explore the real experiences of women, in the past and in the present. This volume, as well as adding substantially to our understanding of Irish migration, is itself a demonstration of subtle and sensitive women's history and women's studies methodologies.

Contributors were also asked to indicate paths towards wider reading and study, and I need not repeat their guidance here. My task in this Introduction, as in all the Introductions to the volumes of *The Irish World Wide*, is then an unusual and unusually interesting one. I must fill, within the limits of the space available, the gaps that remain, and I must make connections. Specifically, in this Introduction, I want to draw attention to research methodology issues in ways that illuminate the connections, and the differences, between Women's Studies and Irish Studies, and in ways that open research doors for Irish Migration Studies. I also want to give something of the flavour of the correspondence and the discussions that went into the making of this volume.

Women's Studies *vs.* Irish Studies

Let us look back to my General Introduction to *The Irish World Wide*, in

Volume 1, *Patterns of Migration*. There I suggested that it would be of help if we found a way of categorising pre-existing research into the Irish migrations: so that we could marshal research material even before it reached us, as it were. I adapted the categorisation of women's history by the feminist historian, Gerda Lerner. I suggested that much writing on the migrant Irish fell into the broad categories: oppression, compensation, contribution. In directing attention to the existence of these categories I made it clear that I did not, thereby, wish to belittle any particular way of studying the Irish, or to suggest, for example, that oppression did not exist. But I did draw attention to problems: the danger, for example, that some sorts of experience would not fall into any of those three categories, and would therefore not be studied. Further, I quoted Lerner on the tendency of women's history to start from the position of seeing women as victims, continually oppressed: this focus keeps women within a conceptual framework shaped by the oppressor, and does not allow us to build up a history of women 'functioning in that male-defined world *on their own terms*.'[12] I did not want our study of the Irish migrations to be shaped by oppressors. Even more so, in turn, in this volume, I did not want our study of Irish women migrants to be shaped by oppressors.

Why, it might be wondered, does writing on the Irish migrations fit into a pattern outlined by a feminist historian who looked at writing by women about women? That circle can now be closed, tidily, by quoting Renan's characterisation of 'the Celts': 'If it be permitted us to assign sex to nations as to individuals, we should have to say without hesitation that the Celtic race ... is an essentially feminine race.'[13] And that phrase, 'an essentially feminine race', becomes a chapter title in Cairns and Richards' *Writing Ireland*.[14] We can then go on to look at the other ways that 'the Celt' is constructed, reading *Writing Ireland* or Malcolm Chapman's *The Celts: the Construction of a Myth*. Chapman's book is a welcome application of the social anthropology of Edwin Ardener to 'Irish Studies' themes.[15] The male/female opposition is one of the oppositions through which 'the other' will be characterised by the powerful.[16]

My suggestion is that Lerner has noticed a pretty well universal pattern. When an oppressed group, any oppressed group, begins to explore itself and its own history, in defiance of the powerful but still within patterns defined by the powerful, the literature thus produced will tend to fall into the pattern: oppression, compensation, contribution. I do not want to labour this. But I do think that simply noticing this pattern gives us the power to step outside the pattern if we want to: which is what Lerner hoped for in women's history. At the very least it allows us to ask the question: who, or what, is shaping our research agenda?

This approach makes visible the similarities between those two areas of intellectual exploration and self-discovery, or self-creation: 'Women's Studies' and 'Irish Studies'. Women's Studies and Irish Studies approach more conventional, established academic disciplines at right angles, as it were. Our very subject matter takes us across a number of different academic disciplines, and demands that we approach each of those disciplines critically and syncretically. Specialists will be familiar with this approach, and the debates around it, in Women's Studies. This interdisciplinary, critical approach may not, for the moment, be so evident within Irish Studies: but to me, certainly in the field that I have called 'Irish Migration Studies', it is built in. 'Women's Studies' and 'Irish Studies' are paradigmatic of the critical, interdisciplinary approach. I will not here explore the *differences* between Irish Studies and Women's Studies. Let me simply say that you can certainly have, in turn, a critical Women's Studies approach to Irish Studies and to Irish Migration Studies. This volume, *Irish Women and Irish Migration*, is a contribution to that critique.

The temptation for the scholar is to study stereotypes, prejudices and preconceptions, simply because these are so well documented, and because they have real, painful consequences. (This repeats the argument developed in my General Introduction). But if any one thing shapes this volume it is that quotation from Gerda Lerner. This volume acknowledges oppression/ compensation/ contribution approaches to the study of Irish people, and to the study of migrating Irish women. But it does not allow those approaches to shape its research agenda: this is a volume about women functioning *on their own terms* in our male-defined world.

Muted groups

Yet another way of approaching that same knot of problems, similarities and dissimilarities, is to look at the concept of the 'muted group' as developed by Edwin Ardener and by Shirley Ardener.[17] In the 1970s, as history was being shaken out of its slumber by feminists like Gerda Lerner, another academic discipline, anthropology, became aware of its own gender biases. The collection *Perceiving Women*, edited by Shirley Ardener, included a paper by Edwin Ardener which looked at 'the Problem of Women':

> The methods of social anthroplogy as generally illustrated in the classical monographs of the last forty years have purported to 'crack the code' of a vast range of societies, without any direct reference to the female group. At the level of 'observation' in fieldwork, the behaviour of women has, of course, like that of men, been exhaustively plotted: their marriages; their economic activity, their rites, and the rest. When we come to the second or 'meta' level of fieldwork, the vast body of debate, discussion, question and answer, that social anthroplogists really depend upon to give conviction to their interpretations, there is a real imbalance. We are, for practical purposes, in a male world. The study of women is on a level little higher than the study of the ducks and fowls they commonly own — a mere bird-watching indeed.[18]

Thus, Edwin Ardener pointed out, it was perfectly possible for researchers to have visited a community and to return saying that they had studied that community, without ever having talked to women. 'The fact is that no one could come back from an ethnographic study of "the X", having talked only *to* women, and *about* men, without professional comment and self-doubt. The reverse can and does happen constantly.'[19] (All this is of more than academic interest to the migrant Irish. For it has often been remarked that the migrant must be an anthropologist).[20]

Thus, in Ardener's perception, entire groups, or peoples, can be rendered 'mute', their voices unheard, their histories unchronicled. The concept of 'mutedness' has by now been applied to a wide variety of groups.[21] The concept can be applied to the Irish. I must first (tedious as it is) acknowledge stereotypes: for it will seem odd to some to speak of a stereotypically loquacious group, the migrant Irish or women, as 'muted'. But even if some are loquacious, there is a difference between being loquacious, sociable or affable and being able to address matters of real concern, to the migrant Irish or to women, in public and in political forums, and in private. Indeed, affability and the desire not to offend may themselves be causes of 'mutedness'.

The concept of the muted group has also been applied to children.[22] That is illuminating: it draws attention to the patterned ways that dominant groups talk about women, 'the Celt', the 'native', as childish, unformed, needing guidance. This approach also has the merit of linking our discussion here with the strands in feminist critiques of language, feminist literary criticism and feminist art history that draw on the work of the Ardeners.[23]

Mind the gap

I must now place this volume in some relationship to the mass of women's studies and women's history material that has appeared over the past three decades. I must do this for the inexperienced scholar, coming new to this area of study and needing some signposts, and I must do it for the specialist reader (in the hope that you will speak to each other). Let me continue with the theme of 'gaps', focusing on areas where our contributors take much for granted.

First, there is a missing person, or rather personage. The symbolic woman, woman as ethereal ideal, woman as personification. Ireland as woman. It is a truism of dramatic criticism that when an audience settles down to watch an Irish play, any Irish play of the past one hundred years, it asks itself: All right then, which woman character represents Ireland?[24] The gap here is, in effect, the very gap noticed by Eiléan Ni Chuilleanáin in her book's title, *Irish Women: Image and Achievement*, and in her Introduction to that book: 'the study of the Irish woman's image through history is also the study of the gap, most easily appreciated for the last couple of centuries between that image and what many Irish women have experienced'.[25]

Our volume is about the experiences of Irish women. The contributors are only tangentially interested in 'images' and 'ideals' of women, and such images are perhaps best regarded as part of the oppression of women. Such images can certainly distort perceptions, as Ravenstein, reaching for the calm light of statistical enquiry, acknowledged in 1885. There are already problems with women's history, as it has emerged, problems which our contributors here are aware of, and try to counter. In women's history 'the patriarch's wife' has received more than her fair share of attention. And in the history of women's emigration it tends to be 'the emigrant gentle-woman' who has attracted study.[26] The song, 'Bread and Roses' pictures the two extremes: 'the drudge and idler — ten that toil where one reposes.'[27]

Women's history has been overweighted towards the study of the one that reposes. This volume, by contrast, is about the ten who toil. It is about women and work.

By the same token, because they construct creative methodologies to get at the experiences of real women, our contributors are interested only in passing in themes which have attracted great interest in previous women's history. Thus, there is interest in 'separate spheres' because there is interest in gender division in work and in the work place. There is interest in 'womanliness as masquerade' only as a survival strategy.

Classification systems, typologies, simple lists, form the essential base of many academic disciplines, and can be accepted as that. Typologies can be helpful: we have already seen that in the work of Gerda Lerner. But the classification systems that have been applied to women can be simply another tool of the powerful, and can contribute to processes that distort understanding and the collection of evidence. We are familiar with dyadic classifications, like 'madonnas and magdalens'.[28] Helen Haste, continuing the alliterative tradition, has suggested four categories: wife, waif, whore and witch.[29] Such categorisations tell us, perhaps, something about the 'male-defined world'. But they quickly break down when we look at the career, at the life, of any one woman. We can look at the lives of two migrant Irish women: we can imagine the standard response that would dismissively categorise Louison O'Morphi or Eliza Lynch. But awareness of the totality of their lives, the choices available to them, their 'careers' as women, immediately subverts dismissive categorisation.[30]

Much work has been done questioning the classification systems, typolo-gies and lists that specifically *exclude* women, and much work has been done renegotiating canons, constructing alternative anthologies, bringing to light creative women who had previously been ignored. A starting point here might be Christine de Pisan (*c*.1365–*c*.1430), the professional writer whose *Cité des Dames* imagines a mythical city peopled by the greatest women of all periods and social classes. Christine de Pisan is, of course, herself one of the women commemorated at Judy Chicago's Dinner Table.[31] Much of this work I greatly value.[32] Yet it usually falls, as you would expect, firmly within the 'compensation' and 'contribution' categories of Gerda Lerner.

It would be easy to imagine a book about Irish women and migration that is quite other than the book you now hold in your hands. That would be a book that accepted wholeheartedly the task of providing 'compensa-tion' and demonstrating 'contribution', whilst having space for the 'extraor-dinary' or 'notorious' women like Louison O'Morphi or Eliza Lynch. It would be a book to put alongside all those other compensatory books about

Irish *male* migrants. But that is not 'the state of the art'. That is not the book that our contributors wanted to shape.

Elsewhere in *The Irish World Wide* series I have drawn attention to other specific difficulties when we begin to study women. Thus in a section of the General Introduction called 'The lost Irish' I acknowledged that our eye and our ear are attracted by the familiar Irish family names. The current family-naming system within the English-speaking world means that a woman takes the husband's family name at marriage. If the new name is not one of the familiar names there is a danger that she, and her children, and her creative work, will become lost to us, to our research, to our thinking.[33]

The migrant woman and birth

Thus far in this Introduction we have seen how feminist critiques of two academic disciplines, history and anthropology, have opened up those disciplines in ways that are also of interest to Irish Studies and Irish Migration Studies. That strategy could be continued: there is space here to look at only one more discipline, philosophy. I know that some students are nonplussed by 'the race for theory', overwhelmed by the sheer quantity of feminist philosophical and theoretical writing that has emerged over the past three decades, and the complexity of the arguments offered. Is there indeed a feminist epistemology or ontology, is there indeed a feminist praxis, a feminist methodology?[34]

Mary O'Brien pauses, towards the end of *The Politics of Reproduction*, to acknowledge and reassure. 'What is being proposed is the development of metatheory from a feminist perspective, with the assumption that theory of this kind is essential to the dialectical tasks of understanding and changing the world. Yet women have been properly suspicious of metatheory, of systems of thought and the huge edifices of ideology and political practice which they have generated.'[35] These questions are of great interest to our contributors: they place themselves within the debates. Their interest is manifest in the practicalities of their research. The Ardeners would suggest that these are questions not of traditional methodology versus something else, but of good methodology versus bad methodology. Really, it is a matter of *appropriate* methodology. Scholars, in our fields, must be able to move confidently between different methodologies, aware of the issues and experiences that each methodology can get at.

There is a theme that is certainly around in studies of migrant women, but is often curiously inexplicit, as if researchers feared to find themselves marooned on the wilder shores of socio-biology: what, exactly, are the differences between women and men? Angela Carter gives us one starting point:

All archetypes are spurious but some are more spurious than others. There is the unarguable fact of sexual differentiation; but, separate from it and only partially derived from it, are the behavioural modes of masculine and feminine, which are culturally defined variables translated in the language of common usage to the status of universals.[36]

We could, with Margaret Mead, then track those culturally defined variables, 'constructing a paradigm in which some universal symmetrical or
complementary biological relationship, such as that between parents and
children, is shown to be linked in different kinds of behaviour, which may
itself become culturally modified'.[37] This is, after all, a perennial theme in
studies of migrating *families*, and in novels about such families. We could
look at 'the invention of motherhood'.[38] But let us pause, and look first at
'the unarguable fact of sexual differentiation', 'the biological relationship'.

Isabelle Bertaux–Wiame, noting the ways that studies of migration had
ignored women, is able, thanks to her research method, to take the discussion
further. 'Step by step, thanks to the life history approach, it became clear to
me that despite apparent similarities (women, like men, emigrate to earn
more) the method, conditions and significance of their migration were different. At its simplest, I would say that the difference is that, while men move
through the family network to find work, women move through job networks
to find a family.'[39] I suspect that this puts the matter too strongly, but I can see
how the specific group of women whose life histories Bertaux–Wiame listened
to would lead her to put the theme in that strong form.

Mary O'Brien ponders 'male-stream' philosophy's fascination with death.

> Death has haunted the male philosophical imagination since Man the Thinker
> first glimmered into action ... We have no comparable philosophies of birth. Birth
> was at one time important in a symbolic way to theological visions, mostly with a
> view to depreciating women's part, and rendering it passive and even virginal,
> while paternity took on divine trappings. Reproductive process is not a process
> which male-stream thought finds either ontologically or epistemologically inter-
> esting on the biological level. The human family is philosophically interesting,
> but its biological base is simply given.
>
> Women cannot be so dense nor so perverse ... [40]

Against a philosophy of death we place a philosophy of birth. O'Brien,
avoiding idealism but through a materialist reasoning, develops a philosophy of woman (and all human beings) centred on birth. Bertaux–Wiame
listened to the experiences of real women. Both make not only child-raising
but also *child-bearing* central to our concerns, in Women's Studies and in
Irish Migration Studies. This, more than any one thing, represents for me
the benefit of creating a volume which looked specifically at the experiences of women.

Bertaux–Wiame may have put the issue too strongly, but let us look
further at 'the unarguable fact of sexual differentiation'. It is women who
bear and give birth to children. That needs to be restated: for it is women
(not all women, but usually the majority of women) who can become mothers. And not all women choose to become mothers. Certainly one of the
interesting things about traditional Irish Catholic culture is that, through
women's religious orders, it allows a procedure whereby some women can
withdraw from the child-bearing role, and have respect, a role and a career
structure apart from the family.[41]

The evidence of the women we listen to in this volume is that 'woman the migrant' (searching, like men, for work) is not so much aiming to create a new family (though some of the women do put it in that way) as renegotiating her own individual role within child-bearing, child-raising patterns. O'Brien stresses that this is a process which changes historically: it changes over time. But it also changes over space. For the migrant woman a change of place can be the equivalent of a change of time. This approach has a number of merits, not least that it brings to the centre of our attention those women who have fallen foul of the socio-sexual norms.[42] Especially it refers to those women who travel out of Ireland to seek abortion.[43] It certainly places at the centre of our attention those women, described by our contributors below, who leave Ireland to escape physical and sexual abuse.

Women Wild Geese

Gráinne Henry's own book on the 'Wild Geese' appeared whilst this volume was in preparation.[44] Cumulatively, Gráinne Henry's patient researches, her use of records, her tracking of the Irish family names, 'Old English' as well as 'Old Irish', have already caused a rethink of our understanding of Irish migration in the sixteenth and seventeenth centuries, and of the ways that Irish identity was constructed in that period.[45] She now uses her knowledge to look at 'Women Wild Geese'.

It turns out that, for all these centuries, we have been talking about 'Wild Geese' when really we were talking only about wild ganders. As Henry makes clear, the very term 'Wild Geese' must be explored ideologically. The term not only encapsulates a perception of historical events: it also in effect decides what can be usefully studied. The martial men were of interest, but then only of real interest when, and if, they returned to Ireland, or if they could be made part of Ireland's national story. The economic and social realities of their lives outside Ireland were of little interest. The women were always there, of course, but, as it were, hidden behind the men. With the 'sideways step', the change of viewpoint, the change of perception, so typical of women's history, Henry reveals the women.

We next have five chapters that look at the 'long nineteenth century', the century of mass migration, the century in which those four million Irish women left Ireland. No name is more closely associated with Irish Migration Studies and the study of the patterns of Irish migration to North America than that of Kerby A. Miller, whose book, *Emigrants and Exiles* has been attacked, defended, and certainly cited, throughout *The Irish World Wide* series.[46] Kerby Miller's calm presence here is a model of true scholarship.

Irish women in the United States have been studied: there is a little cluster of studies which need now to be placed within the wider picture. This chapter by Miller and his colleagues should be regarded as the historiographic contribution to this volume, a summary of what has been said about Irish women and migration to America, with implications for the study of Irish women in other parts of the world.[47] The presence of the two courtesy authors means that we have a meditation by three scholarly minds on the nature of that existing research. One of Miller's courtesy co-authors, David N. Doyle, has already done much to clarify the history of the Irish in the United States.[48] Miller and his colleagues use an intriguing device to develop a critique of that research: letters.

Scholars of Irish history, women's history, working-class history and the histories of other 'muted groups', find themselves, again and again, working with hostile sources and reading through and beyond hostile sources. There cannot be a more hostile source for the exploration of the experiences of working-class Irish women than the material Dympna McLoughlin has made her special area of study, nineteenth-century Workhouse records.[49] McLoughlin embraces and overcomes the problems (note her subversive use of the Workhouse's own typologies) to find out something about real lives and survival strategies, and to lay bare some of the complex realities behind the often-discussed policy of 'exporting' Irish female paupers.

We now have tales of two cities: Liverpool, England, and Philadelphia, Pennsylvania. Lynda Letford and Colin G. Pooley here link the study of women with another dimension which looms large in Irish Migration Studies: Catholic/Protestant differences. I will let the conclusions of Letford and Pooley speak for themselves. I will draw attention to their methodology: they manoeuvre round the census material's fascination with the 'head of household' (usually male) by constructing alternative data sets. I have noted in *The Irish World Wide* the great, and still developing, contribution of the historical geographers to Irish Migration Studies: here we have more evidence of that contribution.

Dennis Clark died whilst this volume was in preparation. I have already recorded elsewhere in *The Irish World Wide* series my own appreciation of his work. He was a good friend to this project: I am grateful to Mrs Josie Clark for allowing me to dedicate this volume of *The Irish World Wide* to his memory. Clark, here in his last contribution to Irish Studies, reaches out across his beloved Philadelphia, reaches into the databases that he himself had done so much to create and encourage, and comes back with a descriptive overview of the main theme of this volume: a history of migrant Irish women and work, integrated into the history of one city.

The work of Marilyn Cohen is of great theoretical and methodological interest. Given that the nature of households looms so large in migration research we needed some picture of female-headed households: how are they formed, how are they different?[50] Cohen's chapter is a case study in the ways that 'woman the migrant' becomes 'woman the emigrant'. It is also (the themes are linked) a case study in the deindustrialisation of Ireland. Methodologically Cohen has set herself a difficult task, but a task that becomes more and more possible as databases become more usable and accessible: that of tracking individuals, or types, through different data sets: 'record linkage'.

The present day

Moving to the twentieth century, Pauric Travers' chapter forms a bridge between the five detailed studies of the experiences of Irish women in the nineteenth century and the three studies of Irish women in the present day which end this volume. Travers' chapter on the emigration of women in the mid part of the twentieth century begins with an image, a painting by Sean Keating. Keating was one of a group of early twentieth-century Irish painters who devoted their considerable talents to the service of the new Irish state, providing for Ireland those myth-fixing genre paintings that longer established states already had by the hundreds and thousands. Keating's paintings of the male heroes of the War of Independence, those 'Men of the West' (clustered unwisely around their machine gun) and the more relaxed 'Men of the South', take their place alongside the myriad Washingtons crossing Delawares or Deaths of Nelsons.[51] How interesting, then, that one of the myths that the painter Keating solidified for newly independent Ireland was the myth of the emigrant male and the stay-at-home woman.

Travers then explores the work of the Commission on Emigration and Other Population Issues. The work of the Commission has been strangely neglected. J.J. Lee brushes the Commission aside with one quotation from a minority, dissenting report, by one of the Commission's most conservative members.[52] And it is true that, as Travers demonstrates, the size and shape of the task that the Commission took on was most probably, in the end, more than its resources could cope with. Yet the Commission's statistical material is still steadily mined by scholars of Irish migration throughout the world. And its files, as Travers demonstrates, show the new nation, unsteadily and to an extent perhaps unwillingly, coming to a realisation that old shibboleths about emigration had served their purpose. The evidence presented to the Commission, by organisations not in the least radical, forced a recognition of the great numbers of women emigrating, and forced a recognition of the importance of issues of concern to women within the patterns of Irish migration. It may be that, for scholars like Pauric Travers, the importance of the Commission lies not so much in its (anodyne) conclusions as in the nation-wide exercise of research, debate and reflection that it initiated. How worrying then to note that Travers' own researches were hindered by the disappearance or the non-availability of Commission files.[53] Into his study of the findings and the work of the Commission Travers weaves his own, more human, research, interviews with women who migrated during that period. It is an interesting historical method, making visible the 'disjunction' between the official ethos and the realities of emigration.

Pauric Travers' interviews bring us to the present day, and to three chapters which cumulatively give a myriad insights into the migration experiences of Irish women. Though the chapters are very different, in style and in intellectual approach, they have in common contributors who listen to and learn from real women. History sometimes finds itself in the curiously isolated position of being the only academic discipline that does not learn from the present day: these chapters throw a light, sometimes a bleak light, back across the historical material already presented.

The Emigrant Advice agency was originally set up as long ago as 1942, by the then Archbishop of Dublin. The origins of the agency thus lie within the nation-wide debate analysed for us by Pauric Travers. Kate Kelly and Tríona Nic Giolla Choille worked for Emigrant Advice in the 1980s. They created their own book about Irish women's migration, a book of practical advice for the intending woman emigrant.[54] For us here they have created something much more personal. They make visible their own experiences.[55] (And, to continue their story, whilst this volume was in preparation one of these two contributors herself received one of the famed Morrison visas, and is now settled in the United States.[56]) And they make visible the experiences of the women who came to Emigrant Advice in the 1980s. The two contributors listen to and learn from the women. Perhaps the most poignant parts of their chapter have to do with the experiences of middle-aged women who find themselves forced to emigrate as families disintegrate (yet another piece of reality far removed from the image) and the experiences of older people left behind.

Important too are the accounts of women emigrating to escape from domestic violence and abuse. This connects with the next chapter. Íde O'Carroll's chapter certainly throws a bleak light back across the past: for we have already seen, in the work of Dympna McLoughlin, how the powerful sexually exploit the powerless. To develop her book, *Models for Movers*, about Irish women's migration to America, O'Carroll interviewed generations of Irish women who had made the move. In that book, I think it is true to say, O'Carroll wanted to paint a positive picture, of women taking control of their own lives. Yet, every person who listens to the experiences of women finds herself or himself, sooner rather than later, hearing of sexual abuse. In the period during which this volume was in preparation issues linked with the sexual abuse of children led to a constitutional crisis and a change of government in the Republic of Ireland: it is an issue worth having a constitutional crisis about. O'Carroll found herself hearing accounts of incest and sexual abuse within the family.[57]

O'Carroll's chapter places these experiences at the centre of the study of Irish women and Irish migration. If these experiences are not at the centre they are marginalised: and she will not have them marginalised. Íde O'Carroll ends her chapter with a personal appeal to the President of the Republic, Mary Robinson, as a President and as a woman, to make these experiences central to her concerns.

As is often the way Mary Kells' chapter has been cited and made use of even before it is published.[58] As part of a larger project which is based on the study of over fifty informants, Irish people living in London, Kells here talks and listens to four women. She is able to explore, in extraordinary detail, attitudes to ethnicity, politics, religion and integration. This is a classic example of 'women's studies' methodology.

Again, notice how the researcher herself is made visible. There is no other way of getting this amount of experience, this amount of thought, and these perceptions into our research. Yet something as simple as 'Caroline's' impressions of returning emigrants (those who returned from England were subdued, those returning from America were 'more noisy than when they went') can in itself create a whole research agenda. Kells constructs typologies, yes, but the typologies arise out of real, in-depth discussion with real women.

The future

If Maria Luddy and Cliona Murphy had not already used the title for their collection then *Women Surviving* would be an appropriate subtitle for this volume. I am content, then, to place the 'long chronology' of *Irish Women and Irish Migration* alongside the long chronologies of our own *Patterns of Migration* and of *Women Surviving*. The integrated study of women and migration is our aim.

Yet you cannot deconstruct only one half of the dyad, woman/man. If I can imagine a volume on Irish Women and Irish Migration quite other than the one you have in your hands, I can equally well imagine a volume on Irish Men and Irish Migration which would be the companion to this one. That volume would bring into Irish Studies and Irish Migration Studies the critical study of men and masculinities.[59] Certainly we now need studies of Irish migration which give the variable of gender its proper due. We need studies which place migration within the ensemble of Irish gender relations. As ever, even with so much done, there is much left to do. But at least women can no longer be ignored by scholars of Irish migration. Or by policy-makers.

Patrick O'Sullivan
Bradford
November 1994

Notes

1. Donald Harman Akenson, *The Irish Diaspora: a primer*, P.D. Meany, Toronto/The Institute of Irish Studies, Belfast, 1993, p. 157.
2. Ann Rossiter, 'Bringing the margins into the centre: a review of aspects of Irish women's emigration', in Seán Hutton and Paul Stewart, eds, *Ireland's Histories*, Routledge, London, 1991, p. 225.
3. Bronwen Walter, 'Gender and recent Irish migration to Britain', in Russell King, ed., *Contemporary Irish Migration*, Geographical Society of Ireland, Special Publication No. 6, Dublin, 1991, p. 11. Walter feels that amongst the 'exceptional events' which broke the pattern, of a norm of greater female emigration, were 'major British overseas wars when large numbers of Irish men joined the British army'.
4. Robert E. Kennedy, Jr., *The Irish: Emigration, Marriage and Fertility*, University of

California Press, Berkeley, 1973. Akenson, *Irish Diaspora*, p. 159, says: 'Although I am skeptical of some of his arguments, the book should be required reading for any student of the Irish diaspora or of Irish women's history.'

5. See my General Introduction, *Patterns of Migration*, p. xvii, citing Everett S. Lee, 'A theory of migration', *Demography*, 3(1), 1966, pp. 47–57. Lee offers something more dynamic than the usual push/pull migration theory (though in the Introduction to Volume 2, *The Irish in the New Communities*, I do look at Lucassen's creative use of push/pull). I like Lee's notion of 'stream and counter-stream': and in the Introduction to Volume 3, *The Creative Migrant*, I develop the idea of 'cultural counterstream'.

6. E.G. Ravenstein, 'On the laws of migration', *Journal of the Statistical Society*, Vol. XLVIII, Part II, June 1885, pp. 167–227: the quotation is from page 196. See also E.G. Ravenstein, 'The laws of migration, second paper', *Journal of the Statistical Society*, Vol. XLVIII, June 1889. In summarising Ravenstein on women Lee, p. 48, quotes only the second Ravenstein paper, p. 288, in a form which has the odd effect of diluting Ravenstein's observations about women: 'Females appear to predominate among short-journey migrants ...' A good survey of recent scholarship is the review article by Silvia Pedraza, 'Women and migration; the social consequences of gender', *Annual Review of Sociology*, 1991, Vol. 17, pp. 302–25.

7. In my original notes for the guidance of contributors to *The Irish World Wide* I recommended, for the reasons outlined here, that we standardise on the word 'migrant', granting a little leeway when dealing specifically with *images* of 'emigrants' or 'immigrants', or *attitudes* to them. Donald Harman Akenson, in 'The historiography of the Irish in the United States', his contribution to *The Irish in the New Communities*, Volume 2 of *The Irish World Wide*, p. 100, recommends the abandoning of 'emigrant'/'immigrant' because the words are simply confusing.

8. Everett S. Lee, 'A theory of migration', p. 49.

9. Sheila Rowbotham cites Liz Heron on Naomi Mitchison's symbolic Spring Queen who 'can only free herself by finding or inventing other cosmologies, other possibilities within which human beings can act. To do this she has to leave behind the familiar structures and setting of her domestic power.' Then Rowbotham herself comments, 'Our migration as a sex has been part of a wider process which has assumed some negative and disintegratory features.' Sheila Rowbotham, *The Past Before Us: Feminism in Action since the 1960s*, Pandora, London, 1989, pp. 295–6.

10. See, for example, Maria Luddy and Cliona Murphy, '"Cherchez la Femme": the elusive woman in Irish history', in Luddy and Murphy, eds., *Women Surviving*, Poolbeg, Dublin, 1989.

11. One consequence of making the gap visible in this way, by assigning one volume to *Irish Women and Irish Migration*, is that I have, paradoxically, made the gap seem greater: the chapters about women gathered here could have been placed in a different pattern, spread differently throughout *The Irish World Wide* series. Thus, Gráinne Henry's chapter on 'Women Wild Geese', Chapter 1 in this volume, would have fitted tidily between Patrick Fitzgeralds's chapter on the travelling Irish poor and John McGurk's chapter on the 'Wild Geese', the male soldiery, in *Patterns of Migration*, Volume 1 of *The Irish World Wide*.

12. Gerda Lerner, *The Majority Finds Its Past: Placing Women in History*, Oxford University Press, Oxford and New York, 1979, pp. 145–8. In general in this project, as you can see, my impulse is if there is a nice bit of theory already in existence, use it. It is far too easy in the social sciences to invent new theories

and new vocabularies that do not connect with anything else. For a fuller account of my use of Lerner's categorisations, oppression, compensation, contribution, see O'Sullivan, 'General Introduction' pp. xviii–xx, in O'Sullivan, ed., *Patterns of Migration*, Volume 1 of *The Irish World Wide*, where I also comment on the use of Lerner by Luddy and Murphy, *Women Surviving*.

13. Ernest Renan, *The Poetry of the Celtic Races, and Other Studies*, translated by William G. Hutchinson, Walter Scott, London [1897], p. 8.

14. 'An essentially feminine race', Chapter 3 of David Cairns and Shaun Richards, *Writing Ireland: Colonialism, Nationalism and Culture*, Manchester University Press, Manchester, 1988, shows how nineteenth century ideas about philology shaped and were shaped by nineteenth century ideas about race and empire. As Cairns and Richards show (p 49) the discourse shapes ways of understanding politics, and even choice of political activity: 'In Ireland, the implications of linking feminity as a racial trait with subservience were sufficiently recognised for nationalist writers to respond by emphasizing the manly and masculine aspects of the Irish character ...'

15. Malcolm Chapman, *The Celts: the Construction of a Myth*, Macmillan, Basingstoke, 1992, is a welcome application of the critical anthropology of Edwin Ardener and Shirley Ardener to 'Celtic' issues. Chapman's examples come mostly from his field research in Scotland and in Brittany, but he issues a general invitation to Irish specialists to make use of his work (p. xiv).

16. The specialist reader will at once make connections with the work of Albert Memmi and Edward Said. An interesting starting point, making the links between Women's Studies and 'ethnic studies' is Nancy Hartsock, 'Rethinking Modernism: Minority vs. Majority Theories' in Abdul R. JanMohamed and David Lloyd, eds, *The Nature and Context of Minority Discourse*, Oxford University Press, New York & Oxford, 1990, especially pp. 21–26.

17. Shirley Ardener, ed., *Perceiving Women*, J.M. Dent & Sons, London, 1975. The useful phrase 'muted group' was originally suggested by the social anthropologist, Charlotte Hardman, as Shirley Ardener records in her Introduction (p. xii). But the phrase, and the concept of 'mutedness', are now generally associated with the Ardeners. A similar volume from the same period is Dana Raphael, ed., *Being Female: Reproduction, Power, and Change*, Mouton Publishers, The Hague, 1975, which includes Judith–Maria Hess Buechler, 'The Eurogallegas: female Spanish migration'. Buechler's interesting chapter outlines (p. 209) the standard approach to the place of women within the patterns of migration: women 'make it possible for OTHERS, primarily men, to engage in wage labour which is often associated with migration'.

18. Edwin Ardener, 'Belief and the problem of women', in Shirley Ardener, *Perceiving Women*. This influential paper is now also available in Malcolm Chapman (ed.), *Edwin Ardener: the Voice of Prophecy and other essays*, Basil Blackwell, Oxford, 1989, a collection which brings together much Ardener material, including 'The "Problem" revisited', Ardener's reflections on feminist responses to the original paper. My page references here are to Shirley Ardener's collection.

There is something a little unsavoury about Ardener's 'bird-watching' image, but I leave it here for the reader to reflect on: how far have the study of women, and of migrating Irish people, got past the ornithological stage? Edwin Ardener himself did, at least once, write directly, if briefly, about Ireland. 'The cosmological Irishman', *New Society*, 14 August, 1975, relies, too uncritically it might be felt, on the geography of E. Estyn Evans.

19. Edwin Ardener, 'Belief and the problem of women', p. 3. Can Edwin Ardener's

strictures be applied to what are now classics within 'Irish Studies'? For example, in Hugh Brody's admirable, *Inishkillane: Change and Decline in the West of Ireland*, Penguin, Harmondsworth, 1974 (original edition 1973), the researcher speaks to women (p. 158), is aware of women, is aware of the *absence* of women (pp. 92–5). But the *companionable* parts of the book are the male parts: '... I went with a group of young men to the Inishkillane bog ... (p. 116). The invitation to attend church on Sunday is really an invitation to join in male companionship in the bar afterwards (p. 178). Compare Pnina Werbner, *The Migration Process: Capital Gifts and Offerings among British Pakistanis*, Berg, New York/Oxford, 1990, where the woman researcher is sensitively able to show the importance of women in re-establishing cultural patterns within the uprooted community.

20. 'As the research participants make clear, a key aspect of immigrant life, in developing survival and coping strategies, is to adopt a quasi-anthropological stance of observing the "native majority". In contrast to the English disinterest in the Irish, the latter know a lot about the former.' Máirtín Mac an Ghaill, 'Irish masculinities and sexualities in England: a working paper', unpublished paper given to the British Sociological Association Annual Conference, University of Central Lancashire, March 1994. To anticipate my argument, there are obvious links here with the 'standpoint epistemology' of feminist methodology.

21. Edwin Ardener encouraged the wider application of the concept in, for example, 'The "Problem" revisited', one of the Ardener papers collected in Chapman, ed., *The Voice of Prophecy*, p. 130. In Britain the concept of Irish 'mutedness' can be linked with Hobsbawm's phrase 'the invisible Irish' (see Rossiter, 'Bringing the margins into the centre', p. 223).

22. Keith Thomas, 'Children in early modern England', in Gillian Avery and Julia Briggs, eds, *Children and Their Books: a Celebration of the Work of Iona and Peter Opie*, Clarendon Press, Oxford, 1989. Thomas (pp. 47–8) criticises Lawrence Stone, who had said that 'the history of childhood is ... the history of how parents treated children.' Thomas goes on: 'Now the treatment of children is a vital subject and there is still a lot more to be found out about it. But it is not to be confused with the history of children proper, any more than the history of attitudes to women should be taken for the history *of* women. For children, like women, are what anthropologists like to call a "muted group". That is to say, their own values, attitudes and feelings are largely excluded from the official record and can only be discovered if they are excavated by the historian ... Some historians might very reasonably say that is impossible, because the evidence is not there ... This is unduly pessimistic ...'

23. Thus Dale Spender, *Man Made Language*, Routledge & Kegan Paul, London, 1980, has a chapter on 'the Dominant and the Muted'. The Ardeners and 'mutedness' also enter Marina Warner, *Monuments and Maidens: the Allegory of the Female Form*, Weidenfeld and Nicolson, London, 1985, p. 281. A further step takes us to the work of women poets, who see themselves (countering Baudrillard) as finding ways to counter imposed silence or mutedness: I think of Alicia Suskin Ostriker, *Stealing the Language: the Emergence of Women's Poetry in America*, The Women's Press, London, 1986.

24. It is one of the difficulties facing women actors in Irish plays that so often the women characters must carry this greater signification. Part of the audience's difficulty with O'Casey's *The Plough and the Stars* is that the search for the symbolic woman representing Ireland is frustrated, until the audience realises, with horror, that the only woman who can be taken to represent Ireland is Rosie Redmond, the prostitute.

25. Eiléan Ni Chuilleanáin, ed., *Irish Women: Image and Achievement: Women in Irish*

Culture from the Earliest Times, Arlen House, Dublin, 1985, 'Introduction', p. 2. She continues, 'And, coming from an awareness of the gap, it is also the history of the demand that Irish women be treated as human beings, that the freedom which many in fact exercised — if only by entering a convent or taking the boat to America or Australia — be recognised and institutionalised as part of the permanent structure of the society they lived in.' The importance of women's religious orders is studied in *Religion and Identity*, Volume 5 of *The Irish World Wide*.

26. Margaret J.M. Ezell, *The Patriarch's Wife: Literary Evidence and the History of the Family*, University of North Carolina Press, Chapel Hill, 1987, questions the use of only published literary evidence. A. James Hammerton, *Emigrant Gentlewomen: Genteel Poverty and Female Emigration*, Croom Helm, London, 1979, is an interesting study of some educated women who, for that reason, because they were educated, left evidence to be studied: some Irish women find them-selves amongst Hammerton's case studies.

27. 'Bread and Roses', words by James Oppenheim, music by Mimi Fariña, is sung by Judy Collins on the album, *Bread and Roses*, Elektra, 7E–1076.

28. *Madonnas and Magdalens: the Origins and Development of Victorian Sexual Attitudes* is the title of a book by Eric Trudgill, Heinemann, London, 1976.

29. Helen Haste, *The Sexual Metaphor*, Harvester Wheatsheaf, 1993. See also her arti-cle, 'The wife, the waif, the warrior & the warlock', *New Scientist*, Vol. 141, No. 1912, 12 February, 1994.

30. Marie Louise ('Louison') O'Morphi, or Murphy, was born in Rouen in 1736, the youngest of the five daughters of Daniel Murphy and his wife Margaret, née Hickey. Daniel may have been a soldier, displaced into France after the Treaty of Limerick. He worked as a shoemaker in Rouen and died in poverty soon after Louison's birth. Margaret Murphy took her daughters to Paris and established them as actresses or artist's models, finding rich protectors in the *demi-monde* around the palace of the King, Louis XV. Louison had enough cold sense to reject the advances of Casanova, was painted by Boucher and thus came to the attention of King Louis XV. She became one of the King's mistresses, bore him children, lived to see (and nearly die in) the French Revolution and the restora-tion of the monarchy.

That painting by Boucher (beautiful, pornographic, the perfect illustration for John Berger's theories about representations of women, *Ways of Seeing*, BBC/Penguin, London, 1972, p. 52) was used on the poster for the London production of Christopher Hampton's play based on Laclos' *Les Liaisons Dangereuses*. Everywhere we went in London we saw that image of this young migrant Irishwoman, the use of the image subverted by our knowledge of her history. See Desmond Clarke, *Louison: the Life and Loves of Marie Louise O'Morphi*, Blackstaff Press, Belfast, 1979. Casanova's version of the encounter with Louison appears in Casanova, Chevalier de Seingalt, *My Life and Adventures*, translated by Arthur Machen, Joiner and Steele, London, 1932, Chapter XXI, pp. 305 onwards.

Eliza Lynch was born in Cork in 1835. It has been suggested that her family were comparatively well-off people, ruined by the Famine crisis of 1845. In any case, by 1845 the Lynch family were established, in poverty, in Paris. After an unsuccessful marriage to a French officer Eliza Lynch drifted into the *demi-monde* and met Francisco Solano López, the son of the Dictator of Paraguay. When Francisco Solano, in turn, became ruler of Paraguay Eliza Lynch was by his side, and she was by his side throughout Paraguay's disastrous war with its neighbours. She died in Paris, in poverty, in 1886. López and 'Madame Lynch' are now part of Paraguay's nationalist hagiography. There are many accounts of Lynch's life, in Spanish and in English, popular or scholarly, appreciative (Henry Lyon Young, *Eliza Lynch: Regent of Paraguay*, Anthony Blond, 1966) or vituperative (Alyn Brodsky, *Madame Lynch and Friend*, Cassell, London, 1975), madonna or magdalen.

31. Judy Chicago, *The Dinner Party: a Symbol of Our Heritage*, Anchor Books, Garden City, 1979, is an account of the creation of this extraordinary work of art, a symbolic dinner table to which are invited great women of the past, previously neglected by mainstream/'malestream' culture. Georgia O'Keeffe has an honoured place at the table, of course. Irish-born women on Judy Chicago's lists include Morrigan, Saint Bridget, Brigh Brigaid, Ebba, Liadain, Lady Uallach, Petronilla de Meath (representing all witches), Failge, Finola O'Donnell, Cobhlair Mor, Margaret O'Connor, Grace O'Malley, Mary Bonaventure, Mary Monckton, Rose Mooney (the harpist), Eileen Gray. It is an impressive list, prompting (as was intended) a renegotiation of stereotypes. But specialists will see at once how the list was constructed: try as they might Judy Chicago and her team were restricted by the sieving processes that had already shaped then existing reference works.

32. I am thinking of works like Ann Owens Weekes, *Irish Women Writers: an Uncharted Tradition*, University Press of Kentucky, Lexington, 1990, or A.A. Kelly, *Pillars of the House: an Anthology of Verse by Irish Women, from 1690 to the present*, Wolfhound, Dublin, 1987.

33. See Patrick O'Sullivan, 'General Introduction', *The Irish World Wide*, Vol. I, p. xx, where I give some thoughts and examples. My example here is Dory Previn, *Bog–Trotter: an Autobiography with Lyrics*, Doubleday, Garden City NY, 1980. Only the title alerts us to the fact that this book begins with an exploration of the sensitivities of Irish–American Dorothy Langan (Engels' pig again), who under the name, 'Dory Previn', writes beautiful songs that continue the tradition of Thomas Moore.

34. See, for example, the discussions in Linda Alcoff and Elizabeth Potter, eds., *Feminist Epistemologies*, Routledge, New York and London, 1993; Liz Stanley and Sue Wise, *Breaking Out Again: Feminist Ontology and Epistemology*, Routledge, London, 1993 (a revision of the *Breaking Out* of 1983); Liz Stanley, ed., *Feminist Praxis: Research, Theory and Epistemology in Feminist Sociology*, Routledge, London, 1990. These are recent summaries of feminist reactions to what is called 'positivism' in the social sciences: what will intrigue the specialist is how much of that debate is repeated within Irish Studies and Irish Migration Studies. A brief, readable introduction to the arguments is provided in a review essay by Helen E. Longino, 'Feminist standpoint theory and the problems of knowledge', *Signs: Journal of Women in Culture and Society*, 1993, Vol. 19, no. 1, pp. 201–212.

35. Mary O'Brien, *The Politics of Reproduction*, Routledge and Kegan Paul, London, 1981, p. 185. O'Brien, like a good dialectician, develops her own thought through critiques of other theoreticians, including de Beauvoir and Millett.

36. Angela Carter, *The Sadeian Woman: an Exercise in Cultural History*, Virago, 1979, p. 6. She continues: 'And these archetypes serve only to confuse the main issue, that relationships between the sexes are determined by history and by the historical fact of the economic dependence of women upon men. This fact is now very largely a fact of the past and, even in the past, was only true for certain social groups and then only at certain periods. Today, most women work before, during and after marriage.'

37. Margaret Mead, 'End linkage: a tool for cross-cultural analysis', in John Brockman, ed., *About Bateson*, Dutton, New York, 1977, p. 172.

38. See, for example, Ann Dally, *Inventing Motherhood: The Consequences of an Ideal*, Burnett Books, London, 1982.
39. Isabelle Bertaux–Wiame, 'The life history approach to the study of internal migration: how women and men came to Paris between the wars', in Paul Thompson, ed., *Our Common History: the Transformation of Europe*, Pluto, 1982, p. 192. I have already drawn attention to the 'life history approach' of Isabelle Bertaux–Wiame and Daniel Bertaux in 'Introduction: patterns of migration' in Patterns of Migration, Volume 1 of *The Irish World Wide*, p. 12.
40. Mary O'Brien, *The Politics of Reproduction*, pp. 20–1. Mary O'Brien, born in Glasgow, Scotland, of Irish heritage (as her name indicates) worked for 25 years as a midwife and nurse in Scotland. In 1957 she emigrated to Canada, where a career change took her into philosophy: she is one of the most important philosophers of the twentieth century. When I met Mary O'Brien I asked her, 'Can it really be true that you are the first philosopher ever to place birth at the centre of her/his philosophy?' And she said, 'Extraordinary, isn't it?'
41 Discussion of the place of the women's religious orders within the patterns of Irish migration is continued in *Religion and Identity*, Volume 5 of *The Irish World Wide*.
42. See, for example, Jo Murphy–Lawless, 'The Silencing of Women in Childbirth: or Let's hear it from Bartholomew and the boys', *Women's Studies International Forum*, Vol. II, No. 4, 1988, pp. 293–8 (also published in Ailbhe Smyth, ed., *Irish Women's Studies Reader*, Attic, Dublin, 1993). See also Jo Murphy–Lawless, 'Images of "Poor" women in the writing of Irish men midwives', in Margaret MacCurtain and Mary O'Dowd, eds., *Women in Early Modern Ireland*, Edinburgh University Press, Edinburgh, 1991. My thanks to Mary Daniels, University of Liverpool, for help in thinking through this part of the Introduction.
43. 'Northern Ireland — like the Republic of Ireland — exports its abortions. A minimum of ten Irish women a day travel from North and South to have abortions in Britain. They do so quietly; more, given the repressive laws and attitudes in both societies, they do so secretly. Irish women are having abortions; they are just not having them in Ireland.' The Northern Ireland Abortion Law Reform Association, *Abortion in Northern Ireland: the Report of an International Tribunal*, Beyond the Pale Publications, Belfast, 1989, p. iv.
44. Gráinne Henry, *The Irish Military Community in Spanish Flanders 1586–1621*, Irish Academic Press, Dublin, 1992. See also, R.A. Stradling, *The Spanish Monarchy and Irish Mercenaries: the Wild Geese in Spain, 1618–68*, Irish Academic Press, Dublin, 1994.
45. See John McGurk, in O'Sullivan, ed., *Patterns of Migration*. See also, Brian Mac Cuarta, ed., *Ulster 1641: Aspects of the Rising*, Institute of Irish Studies, Belfast, 1994, and the appreciative review of that volume by Brendan Bradshaw, 'The Invention of the Irish', *The Times Literary Supplement*, 14, October 1994.
46. See the discussion, pp. 6–9, in Patrick O'Sullivan, Introduction, *The Irish in the New Communities*, and Donald Harman Akenson's chapter in that volume.
47. It should thus be put alongside Chapter 7, 'Women and the Irish diaspora: the great unknown' in Akenson, *The Irish Diaspora*. See also Sharon Morgan, 'Irishwomen in Port Phillip and Victoria, 1840–60', in Oliver MacDonagh and W.F. Mandle, eds, *Irish–Australian Studies*, Australian National University, Canberra, 1989.
48. I have already drawn attention, elsewhere in *The Irish World Wide*, to David Noel Doyle, 'The Irish as urban pioneers, 1850–1870', *Journal of American Ethnic History*, 10, Nos. 1–2 (Fall 1990-Winter 1991), and *Ireland, Irishmen and Revolutionary America, 1760–1820*, Mercier Press, London, 1981.
49. See Dympna McLoughlin, 'Workhouses and Irish female paupers, 1840–70', in Luddy and Murphy, *Women Surviving*.

50. Kate Young, Carol Wolkowitz and Roslyn McCullagh, eds, *Of Marriage and the Market: Women's Subordination Internationally and its Lessons*, Routledge, London, 1981, includes Olivia Harris, 'Households as natural units'. Under what conditions do female-headed households arise? 'Female headed households appear to be common in situations of migration, urban poverty, and chronic insecurity; nonetheless ideological elements also intervene' (p. 147).

51. The best work on Sean Keating is the unpublished MA thesis by Gemma Bradley: see L.-M. G. Bradley, 'John Keating: 1889–1977 – his life and work', University College Dublin, 1991. His work is mentioned in studies like Jeanne Sheehy, *The Rediscovery of Ireland's Past: the Celtic Revival, 1830–1930*, Thames and Hudson, London, 1980, pp. 179–181, and, of course, he figures largely in Bruce Arnold, *Orpen: Mirror to the Age*, Cape, London, 1981.

52. It is, in fairness, a quotation worth quoting, an extraordinarily plain statement of the providentialist, and 'possessing class', view of Irish emigration, by Alexis Fitzgerald: 'If the historical operation of emigration has been providential, Providence may in the future have a similar vocation for the nation. In the order of values, it seems more important to preserve and improve the quality of Irish life and thereby the purity of that message which our people have communicated to the world than it is to reduce the numbers of Irish emigrants ...' See the discussion in J.J. Lee, *Ireland, 1912–1985: Politics and Society*, Cambridge University Press, Cambridge, 1989, pp. 380–1.

53. See Travers' own Note 36 below.

54. Kate Kelly and Tríona Nic Giolla Choille, *Emigration Matters for Women*, Attic Press, Dublin, 1990.

55. For example, we recognise their classroom account of two of the autobiographies studied by Bernard Canavan, in 'Story-tellers and writers', in *The Creative Migrant*, Volume 3 of *The Irish World Wide*.

56. Our hearts go with her. For a discussion of the Donnelly visas and Morrison visas to the United States of America see Linda Dowling Almeida, '"And they still haven't found what they're looking for": a survey of the New Irish in New York city', in *Patterns of Migration*, Volume 1 of *The Irish World Wide*.

57. See also Kate Shanahan, *Crimes Worse than Death*, Attic Press, Dublin, 1992. Shanahan's accounts of rape and sexual abuse throughout Ireland give support to O'Carroll's accounts of emigration as the search for a safer place.

58. For example, Mary Kells' work is respectfully cited by Maurice Goldring, 'The Irish in contemporary Europe', *Irish Studies Review*, No. 6., Spring 1994.

59. There are obvious routes forward. Thus David H.J. Morgan, *Discovering Men*, Routledge, London and New York, 1992, mentions in passing, as if discovering something unexpected, the role of religion in 'the construction of masculinities', (p. 180). Guides to further reading include E. August, *Men's Studies: a Selected and Annotated Interdisciplinary Bibliography*, Libraries Unlimited, Littleton, 1985. My colleague, Jeff Hearn, at the University of Bradford, is developing a series of *Critical Studies on Men and Masculinities* for Unwin Hyman Publishers.

1 Women 'Wild Geese', 1585–1625: Irish women and migration to European armies in the late sixteenth and early seventeenth centuries

Gráinne Henry

First they took my brethren twain
Then wiled my love frae me:
O, woe into these cruell wars
In low Germaine. (Scottish folk-song)

As many as 10, 000 people left Ireland for Europe in the space of a forty-year period from 1585 to 1625. In a period when the populations of the two largest towns, Dublin and Galway, were 5,000 and 4,000 respectively, this was an astronomical percentage and it involved men, women and children from all levels of society. Leaving in response to economic devastation and immense political and social change in Ireland at the time, the destination of the so-called 'Wild Geese' was almost exclusively the armies of early modern Europe — principally the armies of Spain.

The term 'Wild Geese' is traditionally applied to those Irish who left Ireland to serve in the European armies of the seventeenth and eighteenth centuries. But the term also became an ideological concept that gave a specific historical identity to this group of Irish migrants to Europe. Within a concept of history that regarded the Irish past exclusively in terms of a conflict between English and Irish, Protestant and Catholic, the term 'Wild Geese' was used by Irish historians from the seventeenth century on to refer to a group of 'Irish' noblemen who, in the face of English and Protestant oppression, fled Ireland, thereby precipitating the collapse of Gaelic resistance to English rule in Ireland. Many readers, therefore, will associate the term, the 'Wild Geese', with the 'flight of the earls' in 1607 from Ulster or with the exodus of 11,000 Irish soldiers to France after the treaty of Limerick in 1691.

Within such a historical perception the only relevance of the 'Wild Geese' to Irish history lay in recounting this group's banishment to misery as martyrs or in their glorious return to battle against England as triumphant heroes. There could be little merit in examining the economic or social background of those that left Ireland for foreign military service or indeed in detailing too closely their lives in Europe. In short, the fate of this group of migrants in Irish history was to lead a shadowy existence, re-emerging in the pages of history only when such men as Owen Roe O'Neill and Thomas Preston returned to Ireland to make a rare dramatic impact on the course of the conflict between England and Ireland. Such a historical identity therefore not only limited our perception of the 'Wild Geese' but also prevented the construction of new roads of enquiry into the complex phenomenon of sixteenth and seventeenth-century migration to European armies from Ireland. My chapter aims both to establish the extent to which women formed a part of this military group and also to decide the economic and social function of their presence in a group which has until very recently been considered exclusively male.

The causes of migration from Ireland

Ireland in the late sixteenth century was a rapidly changing society in both the political as well as the socio-economic spheres. The second half of Elizabeth I's reign witnessed in Ireland the final military confrontation between the English Tudor administration and the powerful Anglo-Irish and Gaelic lordships. It was a clash that was being slowly won by a centralising Tudor and later Stuart monarchy and the process of conquest and colonisation was beginning to become effective at local level by the end of the sixteenth century.

This had many consequences. Political structures in Ireland were becoming increasingly dominated by New English planters. More and more land was being acquired by these English settlers or by Irish loyal to the English Crown, and the English legal system, language, dress and customs were introduced into all parts of Ireland for the first time. Such a process of colonisation alienated Old Irish and Anglo-Irish landed classes and particularly the professional 'swordsmen' or military men of the Old Irish and Anglo-Irish overlords. Their military function became obsolete within the framework of a composition settlement or planter community.[1]

On the one hand, the English administration embarked on a deliberate policy of 'ridding the country' of a redundant military class and other vagrant groups who could not be incorporated within the Tudor notion of an ordered and civilised society. State-funded foreign levies were organised for the Low Countries (modern-day Holland and Belgium) in 1586, and for Sweden between 1609 and 1613. Including both volunteers and some conscripts these state expeditions totalled roughly 7,000 men, while levies organised by Spanish authorities, and condoned officially by England, in 1605 and 1621–3, amounted to a further 4,500 for the Spanish Netherlands and Poland.[2]

On the other hand, thousands went independently of the English and Spanish levies and voluntarily joined foreign armies or went begging their way through England and continental Europe. In 1592 the lords of the council in England complained of the 'great numbers of vagrant and masterless persons of the Irish byrthe ... begging in and about the cittie of

London and the suburbs thereof', while according to William Lyons, Bishop of Cork, Cloyne and Ross, 4,000 to 5,000 members of his diocese were 'departed' either to France or Spain leaving tracts of countryside of up to sixty miles in West Cork totally devoid of inhabitants.[3]

The reasons for this wide-scale migration were twofold. Firstly, the major wars of the 1580s and 1590s in Ireland (the so-called Desmond rebellions and the Nine Years War) had wreaked economic havoc across the country. Describing the effects of the Nine Years War (1593–1601) on the Irish economy, Steven Ellis in his book *Tudor Ireland* wrote:

> Large parts of Ireland had been devastated, crops burned, cattle slaughtered, buildings razed: Ulster was almost a wilderness, Munster west of Cork almost uninhabited, trade disrupted, the coinage debased, towns ruined or declining by famine. The contrast with England could hardly have been starker.[4]

Secondly, bad harvest failures in 1585–7, 1600–3 and 1621–3 combined with a rapidly growing population to cause widespread famine and forced the price of wheat up. In 1602 the price was almost six times the 1589 level while famine was, of course, followed by disease. In 1604 and 1605, for example, 'plague' was reported in Kilkenny, Waterford and Dublin.[5] Thus all classes in society, both urban and rural, were affected by such disasters, and not surprisingly it was during the peak periods of war and famine in the mid-1580s, 1596 to 1603 and 1621 to 1623, that the Irish were reported to be leaving Ireland in their hundreds daily.[6]

Migration to foreign army service, then, was both a method promoted by the English administration in Ireland to create social and political stability and a response by many different groups of people to a political and economic structure which had failed to accommodate them.

Who migrated?

The make-up of this military group was remarkable. There appears to have been a tendency for the Irish both to migrate and be levied in family groups, or from specific areas. This resulted in a cohesive structure characterised by kin-groups. From the small amount of information we have relating to the names of the rank-and-file members of Irish companies abroad, nearly all names suggest that most members of companies were either related to one another or to their captains. Thus, Oghy O'Hanlon brought '50 persons' of the O'Hanlon and O'Doherty 'kinsmen and followers' with him to Sweden in 1609, while (between 1605 and 1610), in Henry O'Neill's Irish regiment in the Spanish Netherlands, 54 'groups' of soldiers having the same surname can be identified from the 250 soldiers overall receiving ordinary pay.[7]

Considering these family and kin ties among the Irish soldiers serving in European armies, it is perhaps not surprising to find that the womenfolk and children of these soldiers appear to have formed part of this military group in Europe. The Jesuit John Howlin spoke of this phenomenon quite incidentally in an account of Catholic martyrs in the reign of Elizabeth, noting how common it was for wives and female relatives to go with their menfolk as refugees abroad. Although John Howlin was referring to Spain and a merchant wealthy emigré circle, family migration seems also to have been common amongst those Irish in Spanish armies throughout Europe. Kathleen Barnwall, who was wife to a Captain Thomas Finglas in the vast 65,000-strong Spanish Army of Flanders, not only went with her husband to Flanders (modern-day Belgium), but seems to have been with him both in Brussels and in Antwerp where he had been posted. Similarly, John Daniel, who served in various companies of Spanish armies in both Spain and the Netherlands, noted in a request for leave of absence that he had a 'wife and children in Spain'. The petition of 1620 to the Archduke Albert from one Owen O'Riordain was typical of many such in the Army of Flanders. He claimed that 'the heretics banished him from his country, together with his wife and children'.[8]

Female relatives, other than wives, also formed a part of this Irish military group abroad. From amongst the upper ranks of military service, numerous examples can be cited. George Carew, governor of Munster, referred to 'Ellyne ny Donnough', late wife of Dermot Moel MacCarthy, who left Ireland in 1602 with her cousin Connor O'Driscoll and a group bound for service in the Army of Flanders. Owen O Loughye MacSweeney, captain of the gallowglass to Cormack MacDermott, had brothers in the Irish regiment in Flanders while his mother and sister were in Spain. A list of pensions for army dependents in 1635 noted several female relatives of soldiers, among them Captain Teig MacCarthy's sister, Elena, and the sister and daughter of Ensign Denis MacCarthy. Mothers, too, seem to have accompanied their sons who had come to serve on the continent, and their heartrending petitions were sometimes recorded by the Spanish and English bureaucracies. In 1589 a petition to the Privy Council of one Katherine Tehan, widow of Gubone MacShane, requested a pass and some money for herself and family to return to Ireland 'in commiseration of the loss of her husband killed in Ireland and of late, her son in the Queen's service, before Berghen Op Zoom'. A letter written almost twenty years later, by Rose Geoghegan, contained a similar plea. On 12 March 1607, she wrote to Philip III, requesting permission to leave Spain for Flanders as 'my brothers and my sons have gone to serve Your Majesty in Flanders and without them here in Galicia I am sad and lonely'.[9]

Some of these women were educated in religious institutions on the continent. A letter of one William Awes of Dublin to Fr. Thomas Deyse in 1605, referred to two daughters of a Mr James Stanihurst who were 'presently in a monastery at Louvain', while Dermot O'Mallun, who served on the Archduke's personal staff, placed his eldest daughter Maria in the abbey of Avesnes to be 'educated in religion and virtue'. The kind of studies pursued by these women is perhaps best indicated by the records of a convent for Irish Dominican nuns founded in Lisbon in 1639. These included reading and writing skills, the reading of Latin, plain chant and three vernaculars — English, Irish and in this case Portuguese.[10] Indeed the convent also provided career opportunities for women in the Irish military community. Elena O'Sullivan, whose three brothers died in the Netherlands fighting the Dutch, noted in a petition to the Infanta Isabella in 1627 that being now 'very poor and without protection' she desired to become a nun. Similarly, in 1618, on the death of their father Hugh O'Shaughnessy in the Army of Flanders, his two daughters requested and received permission to enter a convent in Brussels. It is noteworthy that two of the founder members of the Irish Poor Clares at Gravelines in 1625 were Cecilia and Eleanor Dillon, whose brother James later became a captain in the regiment of Colonel Owen Roe O'Neill, while four of the five other founder members, Magdalena Nugent, Maria-Petrus Dowdall, Maria Power and Bridget Eustace also had relatives in the Army of Flanders.[11]

The numbers of Irish women attending convents on the continent do not, however, seem to have been large. The Poor Clares were the first Irish order of nuns to be founded on the continent despite the blossoming of convents in Europe during the first two decades of the seventeenth century. Although Irish women might have gone to English convents, the first group of English nuns to settle in the Spanish Netherlands, for example, was not until shortly before 1598 in Brussels and Louvain, catering in that year for only twenty-five and forty-four women respectively. Private tuition was of course available to the upper-class women in schools attached to nunneries. Ursuline convents were a favourite haunt of Irish female boarders from the second half of the sixteenth century. Other women went to the White Ladies at Louvain or, like Mary O'Mallun, to the abbey of Avesnes near Arras in the Netherlands. For lower-class women the lack of an Irish order of nuns, and indeed any form of elementary classes for girls on the continent until Mary Ward's from 1619,[12] might well have indicated that the demand for such institutions was not high.

Were these women, then, the exception rather than the rule? Was family and female migration confined to those with wealth enough to pay their families' passages? The evidence would indicate that family migration was common among the lower ranks as well as the higher. In 1603, one Jacque Martin, 'ordinary soldier' serving with Captain John de Claramonte, was considered 'unfit for further service' but given a grant of a 'dead place' in the castle of Ghent 'to assist him to support his wife and family'. He was by no means the exception. In 1605 William Waad, lieutenant of the Tower of London, noted that there were 'many women' among the Irish levies on their way through London to Flanders, and women and children were consistently included in complaints against the Irish vagrants who flooded English ports and highways on their way to the continent. In October 1605, the lords of the council in England issued a formal complaint to the English administration in Dublin about the number of 'poor and miserable inhabitants' of Ireland, who, coming 'with their wives and children' had put the towns of England 'to continual charges' thereby 'greatly augmenting' the threat of plague. The 'blind and lame inmates of the hospitals of Middlesex' went as far as petitioning the 'King and Parliament' claiming that 'the roads near hospitals are infested with beggars, particularly Irish mendicants, men, women and children', thus, they stated, straining the channels of charity and support to the utmost.[13] The sight of Irish men and women was not uncommon in English towns. Seasonal migration to England was a long tradition among Irish agricultural labourers and weavers. However, the numbers of these Irish were unusually large and they went further than England. In particular, in the first decade of the seventeenth century, Irish beggars, including men, women and children, flooded France, only returning to Ireland under pain of an expulsion order.[14]

Women in the early modern army

The extent to which women were a customary sight on the battlefield of the early modern army was probably best exemplified by the Earl of Leicester's disciplinary code as early as 1585. Formulated for the benefit of the recently arrived Irish and English recruits to the Low Countries, rule five of this code stated clearly that due to the 'sundry disorders and horrible abuses committed' caused by the existence of 'many vagrant idle women in an armie'

> no man shall carrie into the fielde or deteine with him in the place of his garrison any woman whatsoever other than such as be known to be his lawful wife or such other women to tende the sicke and to serve for launders.

In 1609, according to William Trumbull, women were still causing 'sundry disorders' on the battlefield, this time in the Army of Flanders. He wrote to Thomas Edmondes that among the two Irish companies under Thomas Stanihurst ready to depart from Dunkirk, 'there were so many women belonging to the said companies as they would have proved very chargeable and noisome to the said ships'.[15] The women were abandoned to their fate ashore.

Whether as wives or as unlawful companions, women, certainly in the lower ranks of the army, appear to have had an important supplementary economic role in accompanying their menfolk to the wars. The pay of a soldier was both poor and irregular and H.J.C. von Grimmelshausen, who wrote in the context of the later wars with Sweden in the 1630s, spoke of the possible duties of a soldier's wife. He noted that many soldiers 'took to themselves wives ... for no other cause than to be kept by the said women's work, either with sewing, washing and spinning ... selling old clothes and haggling or even with stealing'. The work wives did was remarkably varied. While some worked as midwives, according to Grimmelshausen, 'others did sell tobacco and provide pipes ... others dealt in Branntwein; another was a seamstress, and ... another gained a livelihood from the fields' collecting 'snails ... salad herbs ... birds' nests, and ... fruit of all kinds ... anything to turn an honest penny which might augment the soldiers' meagre and overdue receipts'.[16] Apart from laundry-women and nurses, begging, as already noted in the English reports, was probably the prime duty of poor Irish women. Daniel Farrell, 'belonging to the company of Captain Cornelius O'Driscoll', claimed that after the *'reformación'*, i.e. reduction in army size of 1613, he had 'not more than five crowns, for himself, his wife and his three children'. He requested not only a licence for himself, but one also for 'his wife and children, to go about the country begging'. An interesting Spanish chronicle entitled *Memorial Histórico Español* and written between 1652 and 1660 probably gave an accurate picture of the poorer Irish women's role in army life. The following extract from this chronicle is not only relevant to Irish army life in Spain but can also probably be applied to all the armies of early modern Europe.

> The Irish came to Spain with their wives and families and they were numerous for their province was as extensive as Catalonia. Some were famous and handsome men and women ... others were forced to beg for alms around Spain. The women would do the begging dressed like gypsies with blankets or shawls over their heads. The men served in the army and there were some very good and brave soldiers among them but also robbers who did a great deal of damage in Catalonia.[17]

Women on their own

Many women had to survive on their own and as such deserve to be included on their own merits as part of any definition of the 'Wild Geese'. In an article on womenfolk among the 'Wild Geese', Micheline Walsh commented on the extraordinary number of women who went 'without money or possessions' to seek some form of income abroad.[18] Some of these, with more powerful connections, applied and received pensions or grants, particularly from the governor of Galicia, the Conde de Caracena. 'Catalina Geraldine' was a case in point. Described by Sir William Power, to Secretary Cecil in 1602, as one of 'four poor sisters' left behind by the Earl of Desmond, he wrote they are 'much distressed as the annuity allowed them by the Queen is very small' and they are 'friendless'. However by 1607 Catalina had obviously gone to Flanders and applied for a pension. On 24 November, she received a grant of forty escudos a month 'upon the castle of Antwerp' from the Spanish Secretary of War, where she was described as:

> a sister of the Earl of Desmond, who died in prison in London for his devotion to the Catholic faith and the service of his Majesty; she is herself an exile for the same cause and all her estate has been confiscated.[19]

The careers of Ellen, 'Countess of Clancarty', and Mary Stuart O'Donnell were particularly fascinating. Wife to Florence MacCarthy, who from 1607 was a prisoner in the Tower of London, Ellen, after an extremely colourful career in Ireland, applied in 1610 for a licence to transport 'certain tins of beer, into the Low Countries'. In 1612 she sought a pension in Flanders without obtaining the permission of her husband or, worse still, the permission of Don Alonso, the Spanish ambassador in England. Some months later she went to Madrid where she lived until 1621 returning again to Brussels in April of that year. Mary Stuart O'Donnell resisted attempts made by Charles I of England in 1627 to marry her to a Protestant in England, 'disguised herself as a man and fled with two other young girls and a male relation' to Flanders. Here she sought refuge with her O'Donnell cousins, who were with the Irish regiment in Brussels, and successfully sought a pension from the king of Spain.[20]

While these stories were perhaps dramatic, it was not uncommon for women in their own right to receive a pension or *entretenimiento* from the Spanish authorities out of army funds. However, the struggle to get a pension and keep it reasonably up to a date was difficult and a woman had to prove she was of noble birth and impeccable virtue to obtain a pension in the first place.

For poorer women, then, begging and prostitution were the chief means of survival, if one was without a husband or relatives. Mariana MacMahon, when her husband Hugh O'Shaughnessey was killed in Flanders in 1629, applied for a licence and a passport for 'her and another honest widow ... to go through the country asking for alms for three or four months, to enable her to find some support for herself and her children'.[21] The extent to which this practice was common amongst Irish women, particularly after the Nine Years War, was best reflected in the legal action taken to prohibit these activities. An English statute of James I in 1605 was designed specifically 'to restrain women and children (including Irish) to pass out of the realm without a special licence' though in 1606 the Lord Warden did suggest this 'statute should be extended to men'. Likewise in 1610, the city administration in Madrid issued a series of laws expelling both male and female Irish gypsies and vagabonds from the city. These measures appear to have been effective as Lord Deputy Chichester noted to the Earl of Salisbury in 1606 that great numbers of 'women and children of this country who had been in France and Spain were now returning'.[22]

Prostitution was certainly another option, though a far more difficult topic to research. In the Spanish armies of Europe an official number of prostitutes were allowed per company of two hundred men. This was at the discretion of the commander-in-chief of the army, so that in the Army of Flanders, for example, the figure allotted was eight per company under the Duke of Parma whereas under the more austere Archduke Albert this number was reduced to three! At the same time, the Archduke stipulated that prostitutes were to carry out their trade 'under the disguise of being washerwomen or some other servile task'. In reality there were probably many more 'companions', though the number of Irish women amongst these is completely unknown. Certainly Irish women appeared frequently before the courts in England on charges of prostitution in the seventeenth century, and in London the indefatigable Lieutenant Waad wrote in some disgust in 1605 that the Irish soldiers on their way to the wars in Flanders were frequently visiting a cluster of 'base tenements termed Knockfergus' where 'there were ... 20 children at least ... of which there is no father known'.[23]

The women left behind

Of course many of the soldiers who went to Europe left their families or womenfolk behind them. One Mrs Thickpenny, widow of a New English planter, John Thickpenny, wrote in 1586 to the English administration at Dublin that, as her sons were serving in Flanders under Colonel Stanley, she had no family income to live on. She was still receiving a grant from the English administration fourteen years later in 1600. Likewise, Peter Barnwall, in 1608, advised his sisters bluntly to remain in Ireland as he was in severe debt and their brother Patrick had been 'obliged to break off his studies' on the continent.[24] Among those who fled Ireland with Hugh O'Neill and Rory O'Donnell in 1607 only a few names of women appear. With O'Neill there was his wife, Countess Catherine Magennis, two ladies-in-waiting and three maidservants, while with O'Donnell there were two maidservants, two noblewomen acting as wet nurses, Nuala O'Donnell, her lady-in-waiting, a maid and Rosa O'Dogherty who had with her 'a woman attending on her son'. Of the ninety-nine claimed by O'Cianáin to be on board the ship this hardly represented a large proportion and, obviously, most of the wives and families of the men who undertook this journey in 1607 remained, at least for the time being, in Ireland.[25] Furthermore, in the 'Distribution of the goods of the fugitives' who left Ireland in 1607, most of the goods of these men, who were then serving in the Irish regiment in Flanders, went to their wives and children at home. Teig O'Kena's (Keenans?) wife got 'all her husbands goods', as did the wives of Murtagh O'Quin and Henry O'Hagan. In the case of Henry Hovenden's wife, she specifically received 'all her husband's goods ... to maintain her children at scholl', as well as 'for her relief'.

Probably, the greatest indication of the number of those serving in armies in Europe who had families in Ireland were the leave of absences frequently granted to Irish soldiers, to return to Ireland under what the Spanish termed *a negocios de su casa*, that is, on business relating to the family. Such leave was, for example, granted to Art and John O'Connor in 1609, and to Lieutenant Ferdinard O'Donnel in 1597. In fact, of the 130 leave of absences, or licences, granted in the Army of Flanders between 1587 and 1610 for Ireland, at least 17 were for reasons specifically related to family or property. The term *casa* in Spanish could relate, however, as easily to the house or extended kin of a soldier as to his immediate family, and such a licence did not prove a soldier's wife and children were not with him in Flanders. The licence of this nature granted to Edmund Wesley, for example, in 1591, concerned the death of his father.[26]

Without port records or census material it is impossible to speculate on the proportion of women who formed part of the Irish military community on the continent. The migration of this group of 'Wild Geese' was one, as we have seen, to a large extent imposed by circumstances beyond the control of the individual soldier, and therefore the migration was more likely to have consisted of a large number of women as part of family units. On the other hand, the numbers of women accompanying their menfolk to the European wars varied tremendously. In the state-organised levies, fewer women would have gone, at least initially, with troops, whereas they probably made up 40 per cent or more of those going independently to the army camps of Europe. It is also probable from the source material that it was more customary for women of the rank-and-file members of an army to brave the journey, as they had little to leave behind. But this is mere supposition. Despite the lack of detailed information, however, it is clear that it was certainly *not* a remarkable occurrence when women either went on their own or accompanied their menfolk. An analysis of 226 legatees who claimed the inheritance of a dead soldier in the Army of Flanders between 1604 and 1606 revealed 34 relatives, 39 comrades or fellow soldiers, 39 religious houses, charities or chaplains and 130 widows (see Figure 1.1).

The Scottish verse, quoted at the beginning of this chapter, bemoaning the departure of loved ones to war, was certainly relevant for some women. But many other women stayed with their husbands and male kin, forming an important part of their lives on the battle front.

Figure 1.1   The legatees of soldiers of the Army of Flanders

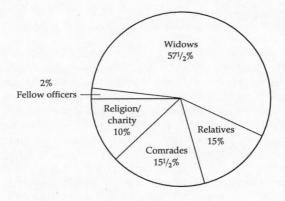

From a register of wills proved in the *auditoría general* of the Army of Flanders, May 1604–April 1606 (AGRB, *Tribunaux Miltaires*, 22). In all, 226 will were proved; all but six testators had nothing to bequeath except their wage-arrears, and in most cases there was only one beneficiary.

Source: Parker, *Spanish Road*, p.173 (with kind permission of Cambridge University Press)

The emergence of military communities

The greatest significance of family migration to the wars in Europe lay in the implication it had for the emergence of Irish military settlements or communities there. An examination of the parochial records of Flanders and Spain from 1585 to 1625 indicates clusters of Irish names in the parish registers of certain churches, particularly in the cities of Brussels and Bruges in Belgium and the cities of Barcelona, Madrid, Santiago de Compostella, Corunna, Bilbao and Seville in Spain.

The oldest and largest number of records of Irish interest in Flanders seem to be contained in the parish registers of St Michel et St Gudule and of St Catherine in Brussels. In Barcelona the Irish tended to settle around the harbour area and in Madrid the area of San Martin was a famous 'Irish quarter'. It is probable, then, that such Irish quarters existed in many cities around Europe and, although it is difficult to ascertain the backgrounds of many of the Irish names in these records, it is certain that many, particularly in Brussels, had military connections.

Perhaps the greatest single indicator of the existence of military communities was the marriages between Irish soldiers and Irish women. Such marriages frequently took place, pointing very much to the close interaction of Irish families. According to the testimony of Owen O'Loughye MacSweeney, Captains Cornelius O'Driscoll and Teig MacCarthy married two of his sisters in 1608, the ceremony having taken place in Rome. Rosa O'Dogherty and Captain Owen Roe O'Neill were married in Flanders sometime between 1613 and 1614, while for other members of the military circle, such as Thomas O'Connell and Helen O'Grady in 1614, actual marriage certificates survive.[27]

Baptismal records also indicated a father or mother as belonging to the Irish military circle in Brussels. Bonaventura, daughter of Captain Teig O'Sullivan and Maria Ketherbreghus, was born, for example, in April 1628 as recorded in the church of St Michel et St Gudule in Brussels, while a number of children of Irish captains, who obviously grew up on the continent, later served in the Army of Flanders. Captain Maurice Fitzgerald, for example, who served Spain for over forty years in various parts of Europe, had four sons, Peter, Richard, Marcellus and Gaspar, serving with him by 1630.

The age at which it was sometimes necessary for these children to begin service in the army was indicated in the case of Daniel Gallagher 'aged twelve years, eldest son of Juano Barri, widow of Hugo Gallocyur' [Gallagher] who received 'a place in the Irish infantry' of the Army of Flanders in 1625 on account of his father 'who had served his Majesty for 18 years and had left four children without means of support'.[28]

At first sight the number of marriages that took place within military circles does not appear to have been very large. Up to 1621 there is evidence of only 15 marriage certificates and 58 baptismal certificates of Irish interest in the two parishes of Brussels — the headquarters of the Irish regiment up to the 1620s. It is clear however that these parish registers are far from a complete record of military marriages, baptisms or deaths. Firstly, these registers are in themselves incomplete. Parish registers were not kept on a regular basis until well into the seventeenth century, while before the 1570s in Belgium and the 1550s in Spain they did not exist at all. Entire sections of parish records have also been destroyed due to fires or wars. Secondly, missing records can sometimes be found elsewhere. The existence of garrison churches, certainly at San Filippe in Antwerp and at other chief citadels both in Flanders and Spain, would lend credence to the theory that army records of marriages and deaths, particularly of the rank and file, may well have been housed here. Irish army chaplains were certainly asked to testify to the validity of the marriages of Irish soldiers and to take the orphans of Irish soldiers under their protection. It was undoubtedly this duty that prompted the colonel's secretary in Grimmelshausen's *Simplicissimus* sarcastically to describe the regimental chaplain as 'a fellow that gives wives to others but takes none himself'.[29]

If it is impossible to assess the size of these Irish settlements the trend towards their growth was very marked. Even given the fact that parish records were so incomplete and not representative of trends within the entire military community, there is a pattern of increase in the number of records of Irish interest. In the period after 1600 when registers were more complete, there were, for example, 48 Irish baptisms registered at St Michel et St Gudule for December 1605, whereas for October 1610 that number had increased to 86. Similarly, the period after 1600 saw the spread of these Irish settlements. Bruges was an example typical of many towns. Names of Irish interest appeared in the church registers of only Notre Dame and St Giles for the first decade of the 1600s, whereas by the 1640s Irish records were also turning up in the churches of St Salvador, St Donalus and St Anne. Likewise, in Spain, Irish names appeared for the first time in the town of Cadiz from 1623 and Valladolid from 1632.

Relations between the Irish military community and the local population

The concept of an Irish settlement in the Low Countries or Spain should not, however, be too closely identified with our modern-day perception of an Irish community in England or the United States. Spanish or Imperial armies, with which the Irish served, were made up of many different, what we would now call ethnic groups, including French, German, Italian, Burgundian and people from all parts of the British Isles, as well as of course Spanish. Records of Irish interest, while clustered in certain parish records, were listed among those of many other different groups including the local population, so that these quarters or parishes were by no means exclusively Irish. In fact, despite the interaction of Irish families there were surprisingly close links between the Irish military group and the local population.

Intermarriage between the Irish and local populace certainly occurred.

Flanders, or the Spanish Netherlands, again gives us the best examples of this. On 8 November 1601 the marriage of Luis Poolnia and Elizabeth Clerke took place in Brussels. He was a Walloon, or French-speaking native of Flanders, she was Irish and almost certainly a sister to Thomas Clarke, serving in Teig MacCarthy's company in the Irish regiment. Similarly, Benoit Feroilli of the Irish infantry and Mari Verrein, a Fleming, were married in 1606, while Thomas Preston (of 1641 fame) married the daughter of Charles Vander Eycken shortly before 1612.[30]

Such individual cases could hardly claim to be representative of all Irish in foreign service and it is extremely difficult to gauge the proportion of soldiers who married Netherland women. A case study done on the marriages of Spanish soldiers in the church of the Antwerp garrison from 1599 to 1658 pointed to a high and increasing level of intermarriage of up to 50 per cent between the soldiers and the Netherlanders. Such extensive information is not available on the marriages of Irish soldiers, but of 15 marriage records surviving in the parish registers of Brussels before 1621 10, at least, seem to have had Netherlands brides, while of the baptismal certificates where both parents' names are mentioned, 32 of the 41 children were of mixed marriages.[31] These figures would argue a high level of intermarriage between the Irish and Netherlanders, but they could be deceptive. The names on these registers seem to come mainly from the upper ranks of the military group and may not in fact be representative of the rank and file, while it has already been suggested that family migration was most common amongst the poorer sections. Nevertheless, from an army list of widows' pensions in 1635, including the wives of both soldiers and officers, about one-third of the marriages were mixed and it is noticeable that most of the rank-and-file widows had, in fact, Netherlands partners. An examination of the marriages among the various captains of Irish companies up to 1622 is equally interesting. Of 12 captains, for whom we have records of marriage, five and possibly six (Thomas Finglas, Hugh O'Gallagher, Henry O'Hagan, Christopher St Lawrence, Art O'Neill and possibly Thomas Stanihurst) married women in Ireland, four (Maurice Fitzgerald, Cornelius O'Driscoll, Owen Roe O'Neill and Teig MacCarthy) married 'Old Irish' women on the continent and two (Thomas Preston and James Gernon) married either Walloons or Flemings.[32]

Certainly it was probably in the interests of both Irish men and women to have local partners: it obviously gave them access to privileges and influence within the local communities otherwise denied them. Although Irish men and women were unique amongst those from the British Isles in being accorded equal rights to Spanish citizens, many Irish did improve their status on the continent by marriage. The Vander Eycken and Hannedor families, into which Thomas Preston and Dermot O'Mallun married, were two of the most powerful and wealthy families in Brabant. Many Irishwomen, like Maria Devine in 1587, and Joanna Barrett in 1608, married into the local business community while, on the other side of the coin, Adjutant John Kennedy and Thomas Preston both inherited estates through their wives.[33] On the whole, however, there would appear to be no particular pattern of marriage from the figures available, though within the upper ranks, Old English rather than Old Irish seem to have commonly married Netherlanders. Such figures could not be classified as statistics when the wives of at least 50 captains remain unknown, the widows' list by no means complete and while in countries like Sweden, where wives may not have accompanied their husbands as readily as to Flanders, the percentage of intermarriage may have been much greater. The real value of these examples lies in the indication they give that intermarriage between the Irish and the local population was by no means uncommon.

Even closer links between the Irish military and the Walloons and Flemings can be established from Irish baptismal certificates for this period. In accordance with the Council of Trent decrees, only two godparents were named for each child and these often appear to have been of local origin. From 32 complete baptismal certificates between 1585 and 1623 in St Michel et St Gudule in Brussels only 3, in fact, have not at least one Flemish or Walloon godparent. In the case of John, son of Cornelluis Kelly and Margareta Vander Gryge, both godparents were Netherlanders despite the fact that one parent was Irish and this appears to have been the case in at least eighteen certificates.[34] This system of choosing foreign godparents indicated the highest level of integration possible between at least some Irish with military connections and the local population. Given the important role of the godparent in European kin-groups even as late as the seventeenth century, this particular link signified a degree of intimacy and mutual acceptance between the two groups that was remarkable.

However such integration between Irish men and women and the local population must be seen in the context of the soldier's job. Relations between the soldier and the civilian population were far from harmonious particularly at the level of rank and file. The Irish soldier especially in the sixteenth century had a reputation for barbarity and wildness. Grotius called the Irish soldiers in the Low Countries strangers both to humanity and civility, while another contemporary writer, Le Clerc, described them as 'half naked and extraordinarily savage'. These were the remarks of men who were avowed enemies of Catholicism and Spain but there was some truth in their claims. During the horrific famine of 1587 to 1589 which decimated the population of the southern provinces of the Netherlands, Sir Ralph Sadler described the fate of Sergeant Major Simion Scurlocke with 'a group of Irish soldiers'. He wrote:

> While stragling with certain of the soldiers abroad, (Scurlocke) was incountred by the peasants and chased up into a church steeple, where finally both he and they refusing to submit themselves to the fury of the clownes [i.e., the peasants] were burnt alive.[35]

The very nature of a soldier's career, particularly in the armies of Spain, was transient and unstable. Apart from the high death rates during campaigns (2 per cent to 7 per cent every month), pay was often years in arrears, food in short supply while Irish soldiers were particularly affected by fever illness. The Irish regiment in Flanders was, for example, down to two-thirds of its force in 1607 due to this illness which seems to have been connected with the marshy location. Lord Deputy Mountjoy was probably accurate when he said that three out of every four Irish soldiers who went to foreign service would never return.[36]

Transience and movement, then, were the constant factors in a soldier's life that obviously form a background to any examination of an Irish military community and it is important not to overemphasise 'how settled' such a community could become. However, the years 1585 to 1625 certainly saw increasing numbers of Irish men and women migrate in family groups, saw women 'Wild Geese' who went under their own steam to join military communities, saw the growth and spread of Irish settlements and close links established with the local population. Ultimately the importance of the social development of the military group lay in its development towards a sense of community or belonging. This nineteenth-century verse by John Dalton captures the traditional image of the 'Wild Geese' perpetuated for so many years — 'In foreign fields it is their doom, to seek their fame — to find their tomb'. The traditional view of the soldier in exile which saw him purely in terms of a dispossessed and disillusioned wanderer from camp to camp was wholly inaccurate. The Irish in foreign military service were not simply all men. And not only did they (he or she) form a part of a cohesive collection of kin-groups and family units but they were also establishing certain links with their new world in Europe. The importance then of mapping the role of Irish women as part of this migrationary process to early modern European armies is twofold. Not only have women been excluded in the past from the history of this period of migration altogether but their existence as part of the 'Wild Geese' prompts us to redefine our perception of early modern migration to Europe.

Notes

1. The terms 'Old English' or 'Anglo-English' refer to a racial group in Ireland who were of English origin but had been, by 1600, resident in Ireland for a number of centuries. 'Old Irish' refers to the racial group settled in Ireland from before the Norman conquest.
2. Archives Générales du Royaume, secrétairerie d'Etat et de Guerre, regs 10–28 (hereafter referred to as AGR EG). *Calendar of State Papers Relating to Ireland* (hereafter *Cal.S.P.Ire.*) *1611–14*, p. 480; Brendan Jennings, *Wild Geese in Spanish Flanders, 1582–1700*, Irish Manuscripts Commission, Dublin, 1964 (hereafter referred to as Jennings, *Wild Geese*). Further notes on this subject in author's possession.
3. 7 August 1592, *Acts Privy Council, 1592*, pp. 99–100; March, 1607, *Cal.S.P.Ire.*, *1606–8*, p. 132. For an analysis of the exact number of Irish serving in the Spanish armies during this period see Chapter III of author's book entitled *Wild Geese in Spanish Flanders, 1586–1621*, Irish Academic Press, 1992.
4. Steven Ellis, *Tudor Ireland, Crown, Community and the Conflict of Cultures, 1470–1603*, Longman, 1985, p. 315.
5. See Raymond Gillespie, 'Harvest crisis in early seventeenth century Ireland', *Irish Economic and Social History*, xi, 1984, pp. 5–10.
6. For references to Irish migration for these periods see respectively *The Fugger*

Newsletters, 1568–1605, ed. Victor von Klarwill, trans. L.S.R. Byrne, 2nd series (documents relating to England only), London, 1926, No. 584, p. 281; 16 January 1606, *Cal.S.P.Ire., 1603–6*, p. 385, 29 May 1606, as before, pp. 486–7. For licences granted to Irish after 1621 to serve in the Army of Flanders, see AGR EG, reg.27/317 ff. See also, Jennings, *Wild Geese*, pp. 174 ff.

7. 31 October 1609, *Cal.S.P.Ire., 1611–14*, p. 305. For rank-and-file members of Henry O'Neill's regiment, see Appendix VI, Gráinne Henry, 'Wild Geese in Spanish Flanders — the Irish Military Community in Flanders, 1586–1610—an Emerging Identity', unpubl. MA thesis, N.U.I. Maynooth, 1986, pp. 382–4.

8. P.F. Moran ed., *Spicilegium Ossoriense ... being a collection of Original Letters and Papers illustrative of the History of the Irish Church from the Reformation to the year 1800*, I, Dublin, 1874, pp. 82–109; 1592, *Cal.S.P.Ire., 1592–6*, p. 65; 19/29 June 1591, *Cal.S.P.Ire., 1588–92*, p. 398; 15 February 1590, AGR EG, reg. 12/92; 11 May 1620, Archives Générales du Royaume, conseil privé, régime espagnol (hereafter AGR CPE), liasse 1357.

9. See respectively *Cal. Carew MSS, 1601–3*, p. 201; 20 March 1608, *Cal.S.P.Ire., 1606–8*, pp. 440–1; Jennings, *Wild Geese*, pp. 277–80; 1 December 1589, *Cal.S.P.Ire., 1588–92*, p. 287; Micheline Walsh, 'Some notes towards womenfolk in the Wild Geese', *Irish Sword*, V, 1961–2, p. 98 (hereafter referred to as Walsh, *Womenfolk*).

10. 1 September 1605, *Cal.S.P.Ire, 1603–6*, p. 309; O'Mallun to Archduke Albert, 1619, AGR, papiers d'État et de l'Audience (hereafter AGR EA), liasse 1895(2). For studies pursued see Margaret MacCurtain 'Women, education and learning in early modern Ireland', in Margaret MacCurtain and Mary O'Dowd, eds, *Women in Early Modern Ireland*, Wolfhound, Dublin, 1991, pp. 169–70.

11. Infanta Isabella to Philip IV, 18 January 1627, Jennings, *Wild Geese*, p. 212; 23 May 1618, AGR EG, reg. 26/60. For the Poor Clares see A. O'Flanders, *Toen Vlaanderen groat was: zantingen in Italie, Groat Brittannie en Ierland*, [*Calendar of the Carew Manuscripts*], Bruges, 1930, p. 235.

12. MacCurtain, see note 10 above, p. 163. Mary Ward's schools were established in St Omer, Liège, Rome, Naples, Cologne and Trier. See Peter Guilday, *The English Catholic Refugees on the Continent, 1558–1795*, London, 1914, pp. 15–16. In Bruges there were at least two schools maintained for the poor children of expatriates but we have no evidence on whether the Irish made use of them. See W.D. Phillips, 'Local integration and long-distance ties', *Sixteenth Cent. Jr.*, xvii, 1986, p. 43.

13. 29 June 1603, AGR EG, reg. 21/232v; 7 October 1605, *HMC Salisbury MSS*, xvii, p. 449; 12 October 1605, *Cal.S.P.Ire., 1603–6*, pp. 336–7;? James I., *HMC Salisbury MSS*, xxiv, pp. 254–5.

14. C.P. Meehan, ed., *Fate and Fortunes of Hugh O'Neill, Earl of Tyrone and Rory O'Donnell, Earl of Tyrconnel*, Dublin, 1886, p. 234; 4 July 1606, *Cal.S.P.Ire., 1603–6*, p. 512; 20 July 1602, *Cal. Carew MSS, 1601–3*, p. 276.

15. C.G. Cruickshank, *Elizabeth's Army*, Oxford, 1966, p. 298; 4 October 1605, *HMC Downshire MSS*, ii, p. 141.

16. H.J.C. von Grimmelshausen, *Simplicissimus the Vagabond*, trans. A.T.S. Goodrick, C. Routledge and Sons, London, 1924, p. 256.

17. Farrell to Archduke, 30 January 1614, Jennings, *Wild Geese*, p. 142; Dorothy Molloy, 'In search of the Wild Geese', *Éire–Ireland*, v, 1970, p. 6.

18. Walsh, *Womenfolk*, p. 98.

19. 17 January 1602, *Cal.S.P.Ire., 1601–3*, p. 288; 24 November 1607, AGR EG, reg. 24/85.

20. 23 July 1610, *Cal.S.P.Ire., 1608–10*, p. 482; 20 July 1602, *Cal.S.P.Ire., 1601–3*, p. 450; Walsh, *Womenfolk*, pp. 102–4; AGR EG, reg. 27/307; Jennings, *Wild Geese*, p. 567.

21. 18 December 1629, Jennings, *Wild Geese*, p. 242.
22. August 1606, *HMC Salisbury MSS*, xviii, p. 269; 4 July 1606, *Cal.S.P.Ire., 1603–6*, p. 512; Trinity College Dublin, MS, 9892.
23. Geoffrey Parker, *The Army of Flanders and the Spanish Road, 1567–1659*, Cambridge University Press, 1972, pp. 175–6 (hereafter Parker, *Spanish Road*); 7 October 1605, *HMC Salisbury MSS*, xvii, p. 449. For Irish prostitutes in English courts, see Jerrold Casway, 'Irish women overseas, 1500–1800', in Margaret MacCurtain and Mary O'Dowd, eds, *Women in Early Modern Ireland*, Wolfhound, Dublin, 1991, p. 115.
24. 15 May 1586, *Cal.S.P.Ire., 1586–8*, p. 58; *Acts Privy Council, 1586–7*, pp. 178–9; 26 October 1600, *Cal.S.P. Ire., 1600*, p. 500; 28 October 1608, *Cal.S.P.Ire., 1608–10*, p. 90.
25. Canice Mooney, 'A noble shipload', *Irish Sword*, ii, 1956–7, pp. 195–204. However no complete list of this group has survived.
26. 18 December 1610, *Cal.S.P.Ire., 1608–10*, pp. 543–4. For grants see respectively 14 August 1609, AGR EG, reg. 24/429v.; 15 February 1597, AGR EG, reg. 17/229; 4 October 1591, AGR EG, reg. 13/177v. All information on grants to soldiers comes from the records of the Army of Flanders housed in the Archives Générales du Royaume.
27. The only case study on Irish military records in parishes on the continent has been done by myself in Brussels from the Archives de l'Hôtel de Ville (hereafter AHV). However Micheline Walsh has given me tremendous help with regard to parish record sources in the rest of Belgium and Spain. She is probably the best authority on this subject and much of her research can be found in the Overseas Department, University College Dublin, Ireland. See also M. Walsh, 'The Handsors and some other Louth exiles in France and Spain', *Louth Archaeological Hist. Jr.*, xviii, 1976, p. 236; M. Walsh, *Womenfolk*, p. 101. See Phillips in note 12 above; pp. 33–49. For Owen MacSweeney's testimony, see Danvers to Salisbury, 20 April 1608, *Cal.S.P.Ire., 1606–8*, p. 479; Jerrold Casway, *Owen O'Neill and the Struggle for Catholic Ireland*, University of Pennsylvania Press, Philadelphia, 1984, pp. 25–6; 20 July 1614, AHV (Bruxelles), St Catherine, reg. 210/38.
28. 1 April 1628, AHV (Bruxelles), St Michel et St Gudule, reg. 87/217. For the Fitzgerald sons see AGR EG reg. 30/11v, reg. 31/103, reg. 32/196v. For Daniel see 15 November 1625, AGR EG, reg. 29/237.
29. For a study of the Antwerp garrison see Geoffrey Parker, 'Review essay: new light on an old theme: Spain and the Netherlands, 1550–1660', *European Hist. Quart.*, xv, 1985, p. 220. For an example of an Irish chaplain's testimonies see 17 December 1639, Jennings, *Wild Geese*, pp. 310–11; Grimmelshausen, *Simplicissimus*, p. 127.
30. 8 November 1601, AHV (Bruxelles), St Michel et St Gudule, AGR EG reg. 129; 25 May 1606, as above, reg. 130/31.
31. See note 29 above. From 1599 to 1638 20 marriages between Spanish and Netherlanders were recorded a year, rising to fifty per cent of such marriages between 1638 and 1647.
32. For the widows list see 3 January 1635, Jennings, *Wild Geese*, pp. 227–80. It is of course possible that those who had wives in Ireland before 1622 remarried at a later date on the continent. For details of names see Gráinne Henry, MA thesis as mentioned in note 7 above.
33. For an interesting discussion on the rights of Irish in Spanish territory, see John Mac Erlean, 'Ireland and world contact', *Studies*, viii, 1919, pp. 307–8. For Preston and O'Mallun see G. Steinman, 'Sepulchral memorials of the English formerly at Bruges', *Topographer and Genealogist*, ii, 1853, pp. 468–73; 9 June 1614, AGR EA, liasse 1887(3); 18 January 1587, AHV (Bruxelles), St Catherine, reg. 209/42r; 3

September 1608, reg. 130/70; Preston came into this estate by his second wife Marguerite de Namur. See 24 April 1647, *Cal.S.P.Ire.*, *1633–47*, p. 613; 16 March 1641, AGR EG, reg. 40/158v.

34. 24 June 1612, AHV (Bruxelles), St Michel et St Gudule, reg. 84/86. All notes on baptismal certificates in author's possession.

35. William Allen, *The Copie of a letter written by M. doctor Allen: concerning the yielding up of the citie of Daventrie*, ed. Thomas Heywood, Antwerp 1587, p. xviii; Arthur Clifford, ed., *The State Papers and Letters of Sir Ralph Sadler*, Constable, Edinburgh, 1809, p. 240.

36. By far the best account of conditions in an early modern army is to be found in Parker, *Spanish Road*, particularly pp. 158–84. For the Irish regiment see November 1607, *HMC Salisbury MSS*, xix, p. 313; 1 May 1601, *Cal. Carew MSS 1601–3*, pp. 50–1.

2 'For love and liberty': Irish women, migration and domesticity in Ireland and America, 1815–1920

Kerby A. Miller with David N. Doyle and Patricia Kelleher

Introduction

Fifteen years ago, scarcely any historians had studied women's roles in the history of Ireland, of Irish emigration, or of Irish America. However, since the late 1970s Joseph Lee, Mary Cullen, David Fitzpatrick, Rita Rhodes, Joanna Bourke and other scholars have written about women in nineteenth and twentieth-century Ireland, and Hasia Diner and Janet Nolan have published books about Irish women's emigration and their lives in the United States.[1]

Several major themes and debates have emerged from this new scholarship. First, with regard to the 'push factors' or Irish causes of female emigration, most scholars have concluded that the reason comparatively few women left Ireland between 1815 and 1844 was because their status in pre-Famine Irish rural society was relatively favorable. For example, although women's waged labor was less varied, extensive and remunerative after the Napoleonic wars than during the prosperous half-century prior to 1815, their economic contributions to their families' incomes and welfare were still very significant and highly valued. Thus, despite the rapid mechanization and urbanization of flax spinning, which sharply curtailed rural women's waged labor in cottage industry, spinning for local consumption continued to earn crucial shillings in many poor households. More important, female labor in waged field work and in dairying, pig and poultry-raising was vitally necessary on the multitude of small, semi-subsistence farms whose tenants engaged largely in the production of potatoes and other tillage crops. Among farm laborers, who comprised the largest classes in pre-Famine society, women's economic contributions were even more substantial. Mary Cullen estimates that laborers' wives' earnings from spinning, farm work and, in hard times, begging accounted for at least fifteen per cent of their families' incomes, rising to over thirty-five per cent when their husbands lacked steady employment — as was usually the case.[2] Also, prior to the Famine small farmers and cottier tenants usually practiced partible inheritance which, coupled with the high value placed on wives' wage-earning abilities, ensured ample opportunities for marriage — and at relatively early ages — for rural women among all but a small minority of affluent tenants, 'strong farmers' and graziers, who practiced impartible inheritance and restricted marriage through the dowry system. For instance, Kevin O'Neill's analysis of the 1841 census data from Killashandra Parish, County Cavan, an area dominated by smallholdings, indicates that on average farmers' wives had married at the age of 21.7, laborers' wives at 22.3.[3] Furthermore, although the average marriage age was rising during the depressed pre-Famine decades (David Fitzpatrick estimates that the average marriage age of Irishwomen born in 1821 was 26.2), celibacy rates were low, relative to post-Famine patterns. In 1841 only 12.5 per cent of Irish women aged 45–54 had never married.[4] The result, most historians conclude, was that rural women were generally able, encouraged and content to remain in early nineteenth-century Ireland, and so, prior to the Great Famine of 1845–50, Irish emigration to North America was predominantly (about two-thirds) male.[5]

However, nearly all scholars also argue that after mid-century, in the post-Famine period, 1850–1920, a great increase in female emigration occurred because the socio-economic status of rural Irish women deteriorated dramatically. High rates of mortality and emigration during and immediately after the Great Famine decimated the poorest classes which had practiced partible inheritance and to whose economic survival women had contributed most heavily. Likewise, after 1850 women's wage-earning opportunities contracted sharply because of the continued deindustrialization of the Irish countryside and because economic pressures and demographic change caused major shifts from subsistence to commercial agriculture and from tillage to pasture farming, both trends coupled with a fall in the production and consumption of potatoes, which were increasingly replaced by bread and other store-bought goods in the farmers' diets. Accompanying these economic changes was a shift among small farm families from partible to impartible inheritance which, linked to their declining wage-earning capacities, meant that women (and men) were not only obliged to marry less frequently and at later ages than in the pre-Famine past, but that their choices of marriage partners were determined and restricted by the dowry system, enforced by their fathers and reinforced by codes of female docility and sexual repression purveyed by a patriarchal Catholic Church. Thus, according to David Fitzpatrick, 'after the famine the daughters and wives of farmers steadily retreated from the process of production'; their socio-economic status declined commensurately, to the point where the dowry 'may be treated as a fine for the transfer of a redundant dependent female from one family to another'.[6] As a result, between 1845 and 1914 Ireland's annual marriage rate fell from seven to four per thousand; by 1926 the average marital age had risen to twenty-nine for women (to thirty-five for men), and nearly a quarter of Irish women aged 45–54 had never married.[7] In addition, by eradicating customary, magical and often female-centered features of popular religion, the increasing institutionalization of post-Famine Catholicism, within the confines of a male-dominated church, may have eroded rural women's traditional status in less tangible ways. The consequence of all these changes was massive post-Famine emigration by young, unmarried women, whose numbers equaled and eventually exceeded those of Irish emigrant males in the late nineteenth and early twentieth centuries.[8]

Second, with regard to the 'pull factors' in Irish women's emigration, all scholars agree that late nineteenth and early twentieth-century America's attractions — as advertised in emigrants' letters, for example — exacerbated Irish women's dissatisfaction with their limited economic and marital opportunities at home and accelerated their migration overseas. However, American historians disagree as to which specific motives and goals were paramount for Irish women emigrants. Hasia Diner argues that Irish females consciously rejected Irish male repression and emigrated as ambitious individuals seeking economic independence through waged labor, usually as domestic servants in American cities. In evidence, she demonstrates that Irish women in the United States had significantly lower marriage rates, and married at older ages, than did other immigrant women. According to Diner, these Irish–American marital patterns not only reflected cultural continuity with rural Ireland but, more importantly, indicated that 'economic motives for migration were paramount. Irishwomen did not migrate primarily to find the husbands they could not find at home'. Otherwise, Diner argues, Irish women would not have settled so often in eastern US cities where the gender ratios were so female-dominated as to inhibit their opportunities for endogamous marriage.[9] However, more recently Janet Nolan has contended that Irish women emigrated principally to recover overseas the lost opportunities for frequent, early marriage which their grandmothers had enjoyed in pre-Famine Ireland. Ironically, to support her own interpretation Nolan employs two assertions which Diner made but downplayed in her earlier work: that in the United States Irish immigrant women's marital rates were higher, and marriage ages and celibacy rates were lower, than among females who remained in post-Famine Ireland; and that Irish-American marital patterns were little different from those of native-born Americans.[10]

Remarkably, however, Diner and Nolan provide little or no evidence to prove either of those assertions. Diner's Irish–American data is fragmentary, often contradictory, and drawn primarily from studies of small north–eastern milltowns whose Irish-born populations were unusually female-dominated. For example, although Diner's evidence from late nineteenth-century Pittsburgh indicates that Irish celibacy rates in that city were much lower than in contemporary Ireland, and although she cites statistical surveys of Massachusetts in 1890–1900 which suggest the essential similarity of Irish-immigrant and native marital behavior, her data from other locales, such as Cohoes, New York, in 1880, suggest that in factory towns whose Irish work-forces were overwhelmingly female, Irish immigrant women married less often and at later ages than their sisters in Ireland.[11] Moreover, Nolan's argument for greater marital opportunities in America is scarcely supported at all, except by a dubious analogy with Irish practices in mid-nineteenth-century London and by a handful of personal reminiscences by elderly Irish–American women.[12]

Thus, despite their apparently universal acceptance, the assumptions that post-Famine Irish women married more often and earlier in the United States than in Ireland, and that Irish female immigrants' marital patterns were essentially similar to those of native Americans, must be considered highly likely but as yet unproven.[13] Rather than attempt the broad statistical study necessary to prove either hypothesis conclusively, this chapter will employ other kinds of evidence, primarily Irish female emigrants' letters and memoirs, to address and question both the accepted and the contested interpretations of the causes and goals of Irish women's emigration. This is still a novel field of study, and the following arguments are by no means definitive but will hopefully suggest alternative perspectives and new avenues of research.

Models and motives for emigration

The first and broadest point is that no single model or interpretation can apply to all female emigrants from Ireland, either before or after the Great Famine. Arguably, the ultimate determinants of gender roles and relationships are sexual divisions of labor, which in turn vary greatly among different socio-economic classes and cultures.[14] If Irish and Irish–American historians had access to the detailed documentation available to Scandinavian scholars, and could they trace large numbers of specific women from rural Ireland to the United States, it is highly probable they would discover that women from different class, regional and cultural backgrounds in Ireland had significantly different patterns of and motives for emigration and significantly different work and marital experiences in different regions of the new world. Lacking such evidence, historians have inadvertently homogenized the lives and attitudes of the daughters of commercial farmers in south Leinster, landless laborers in north Munster, mill workers in east Ulster, and Irish-speaking peasants in west Connaught — thereby obscuring these and other crucial distinctions which governed relationships and shaped outlooks in a highly localistic, family-centered and status-conscious society.[15] For example, even in the early 1900s marital rates remained higher, and marriage ages and celibacy rates were lower, in Ireland's impoverished western counties than in the rest of the island.[16] Thus, it is possible that women from those counties married abroad less frequently and later than females who remained in western Ireland, especially if they settled in the north-eastern United States where economic and marital prospects were comparatively poor. By contrast, females from eastern Ireland, where celibacy rates were highest, almost certainly improved their marriage opportunities by emigrating, particularly if they moved to midwestern or western US cities where both economic conditions and gender ratios favored matrimony. Also, it is very likely that important differences would emerge if scholars could determine the relative positions of emigrant women in the structures and dynamics of their respective Irish families. For instance, whether a woman was an older or younger daughter, or whether she had many — or any — male or female siblings, might determine her expectations and outlooks as to marriage and emigration. Equally crucial, such issues might determine her age at emigration, or her educational attainments and work experiences prior to emigration, which in turn would affect her economic and marital chances overseas.

Social status of women in pre-Famine Ireland

A more specific issue is whether rural women in the early nineteenth century indeed enjoyed a social status so favorable as to explain the relative paucity of female emigration from pre-Famine Ireland. Mary Cullen contends that no one paradigm of pre-Famine gender relations clearly applies — 'whether that of an oppressor-oppressed relationship between men and women or of a one-to-one relationship between economic contribution on the one hand and status on the other'[17]. However, much evidence suggests that the condition of rural women, married or unmarried, was far from advantageous. Contemporaries remarked repeatedly that both in agriculture and in cottage industry pre-Famine Irish women worked 'more like slaves than laborers', treated by their menfolk like 'beasts of burden'[18]. Judging from a variety of sources, ranging from parliamentary commission reports to William Carleton's short stories, it seems obvious that pre-Famine Irish women made major economic contributions to their households' survival because they had no other choice. Small farmers' and laborers' families, roughly 70 per cent of the rural population, were struggling for mere subsistence, and many Irish men were underemployed or unemployed and, by many accounts, often shiftless and drunken. Thus, a Famine emigrant, Ann McNabb from County Derry, later remembered that her father's alcoholism had obliged her mother to thatch the family's peat-walled cabin, a task normally considered 'men's work'; in addition, she recalled, 'My mother an' me an' [my sister] Tilly we worked in the field for Squire Varney ... plowin' an' seedin' an' diggin' — any farm work he'd give us. We did men's work, but we didn't get men's pay.'[19] Likewise, the evidence on the favorable character of pre-Famine marriages is very insubstantial. Contemporaries described the wives of small farmers and laborers as drudges and slaves, 'oppressed by their husbands and living in affectionless marriages',[20] and the era's emigrant letters reveal far more romantic sentiments among men and women in the urban and rural middle classes than among ordinary farmers and peasants, and far more cold calculations as to matrimony among the latter than the former. Also, among the latter alcoholism and its socio-economic consequences, including wife abuse and desertion, appear to have been common, which makes it unsurprising that pre-Famine Irish women enthusiastically embraced Fr. Theobald Mathew's temperance crusade, perhaps finding more consolation and protection in the institutional church than in popular religion's eroding folkways. Moreover, when poor, pre-Famine Irish women were unable to contribute positively to family incomes, they simply reduced their intake of food, allowing their husbands and sons to consume a disproportionate share of their families' meagre diets.[21] In short, most evidence indicates that women's status in pre-Famine Ireland was one of subjugation and that their economic contributions were inseparable from grinding poverty and backbreaking drudgery. If women in these conditions had any economic power, it was largely by default, and the only alternative power — that of Carleton's fictional 'big lump' of a peasant woman, who physically beat her husband in return for his abuse — was available only to an unusually strong and well-nourished few.

Female subordination and emigration in pre-Famine Ireland

The failure of pre-Famine women to emigrate in significant numbers may have been a direct or indirect result of their subjugated condition in early nineteenth-century Ireland, rather than a reflection of their allegedly high status and contentment. For example, in Irish experience there is a strong, positive correlation between literacy and emigration, and as late as 1841 Irish females (above the age of five) were over two and a half times more likely to be illiterate than were Irish males. Among those aged between fifteen and twenty-four, the most likely years of emigration, less than 27 per cent of Irish women were literate, compared to over 47 per cent of Irish men. Not until after 1850 would female literacy and emigration rise in tandem, eclipsing male rates in both respects by the century's end. Also, before the Famine there appears to have been a high, negative correlation between Irish-speaking and emigration, and as late as 1861 Irish women were twice as likely to be bilingual or monolingual Irish-speakers than Irish men.[22] Both illiteracy and Irish-speaking insulated Irish women from America's advertised attractions. Both also reflected women's markedly inferior educational opportunities in pre-Famine Ireland, and both probably reinforced a cultural conservatism which may also have inhibited emigration. In addition, illiteracy and ignorance of English may have made pre-Famine Irish women less marketable in America than were their menfolk, for whom such deficiencies mattered little when applying for jobs as unskilled laborers digging canals or loading cargoes. By contrast, except among southern slaves, female strength in rough, outdoor labour was less utilized in the United States than in Ireland, as one Irish-American farmer reported that 'it would be considered a wonder to see a woman in the States Carry water or milk Cows'.[23] Furthermore, early nineteenth-century America's urban-industrial economies were not yet sufficiently large or mature to generate the huge demand for great numbers of unskilled Irish female domestic servants and factory workers which would begin to develop around mid-century. And, finally, not until the 1840s and 1850s did massive Irish Catholic emigration and urban settlement begin to create the large and relatively stable Irish-American Catholic communities which could absorb great numbers of unmarried Irishwomen into familial and institutional networks.[24]

Family decisions and choice in pre-Famine emigration

That last point raises another, related issue. Save for runaways, Irish emigration was usually based on *family* — not individual — decisions: for example, choices by Irish parents as to which of their children to send or allow to go abroad first; and choices by Irish Americans as to which of their siblings, cousins, or other relatives to encourage and assist to emigrate and join them.[25] As indicated by the cautious tone of early nineteenth-century emigrants' letters, such decisions were more crucial in the pre-Famine era than later, because in these decades Catholic emigration from most parts of Ireland was just beginning, and most Irish families' first beachheads in America were just being established. Consequently, and given the female disabilities mentioned above, Irish parents or other relatives already settled in the United States were much more likely to send or bring over the strongest, most highly-skilled, best-educated and hence most marketable *male* emigrants — those deemed most likely to survive, succeed and, most important to those who remained in Ireland, send back the remittances which would pay rents, purchase necessities and establish the patterns of chain migration which would enable nearly all future Irish Catholic departures. From her parents' perspective, not only was it riskier to send a daughter to America from the standpoint of her limited economic marketability, but also the likelihood of her dropping quickly out of the marketplace by marrying into one of early nineteenth-century America's predominantly male Irish communities was very high. From the viewpoint of her parents and others waiting to emigrate at home, that might be disastrous, for marriage abroad usually would end a woman's willingness or ability to remit money to relatives in Ireland. Thus, as a later emigrant warned her mother, 'when I do get married I Suppose I will be like the rest [and] not write at all and as little as I send home now you will get nothing then'.[26] In the light of these circumstances, it is surprising that no scholars have interpreted the low rates of Irish female emigration in the early nineteenth century as evidence that pre-Famine Ireland was a *more* repressively patriarchal and male-dominated society than it later became — a society in which unmarried women and would-be emigrants like Margaret Wright, a poor spinster in County Tyrone, felt trapped by 'dependen[ce] on the[ir] mercenary and covetous [male relations] for a miserable and wretched support'.[27]

Reasons for post-Famine emigration

Conversely, it is questionable whether the massive emigration of young, unmarried women from post-Famine Ireland indeed reflected a marked deterioration in their status since the early nineteenth century. To be sure, Irishwomen's wage-earning opportunities and economic contributions to household incomes declined greatly after the Famine, both outside and inside the home, in agriculture and cottage industry alike. As a result, increasingly their contributions to the family economy were confined to unpaid housework and to the bearing and rearing of future heirs and emigrants. Certainly, also, the dearth of waged employment for women, coupled with the shifts among nearly all landholding families to impartible inheritance and the dowry system, made it much more difficult for rural women (and men) to marry, to marry early and to marry spouses of their own choosing. Likewise, it would be mistaken simply to reverse established interpretations by arguing that post-Famine women's emigration signified their liberation from pre-Famine repression. For in the late nineteenth century, as before, most decisions concerning emigration were made in the contexts of international labor markets and of Irish and Irish-American families' economic strategies, the terms of which now encouraged, as formerly they had discouraged, women's migration overseas.

Status of women: housewife and mother

However, whereas it may be fruitless to debate whether rural women's status was higher or lower, or their subordination greater or lesser, in pre or post-Famine Ireland, what is certain is that the parameters — and perhaps rural women's own definitions — of status and/or repression had been altered significantly. Thus, by applying to Ireland the insights of nine-teenth-century women's history in the United States and other 'moderniz-ing' societies, Joanna Bourke, a New Zealand scholar, argues persuasively that what most historians have regarded as post-Famine Irish women's increasing 'confinement' to a separate and inferior domestic sphere in fact enabled women — or at least married women — to exercise new and greater influence over their husbands and children than hitherto possible. Indeed, according to Bourke, women in post-Famine Ireland consciously and eagerly chose unpaid housework as wives and mothers precisely because it gave them greater status and authority than any form of paid labor available to them — or to their pre-Famine predecessors.[28]

Bourke contends that the concentration of post-Famine women in house-work reflected not only a decreased demand for female waged and/or rough outdoor labor, but, more importantly, it reflected rising rural incomes and the socio-cultural and psychological *embourgeoisement* of an Irish rural society which was increasingly dominated in all respects by affluent or aspiring farmers and village traders.[29] As farming became more commercialized (and mechanized) and as middle-class or 'Victorian' tastes and aspirations spread, the home became more separate, special and important. More capital was now available for investment in the home. Livestock and agricultural implements, formally quartered in the farmer's house, were relegated to barns and sheds. Thatched roofs were covered

with slate; new rooms were added and old ones were floored and wallpa-
pered; furniture became more ample and comfortable; and many families
built new stone houses to replace mud-walled dwellings. Perhaps most
striking were the new parlors which post-Famine farmers added to their
houses. In their elaborate furnishings, conspicuously displayed religious
objects and proverbially spotless cleanliness, the parlors embodied and
projected to visitors their owners' new pretensions to respectability and
gentility.

Contemporary literature describes post-Famine Irish women as dominat-
ing parlor activities, but they assumed primary responsibility for the functions and ethos of the entire domestic sphere, in the process marginalizing
their husbands' influence. To be sure, housework was tedious, even
exhausting, and many farmers' wives also raised poultry and performed
other chores outside the home.[30] For the most part, however, their new
duties required not physical strength but managerial skills and a ceaseless
attention to efficiency, order, cleanliness and decorum. For example, as
consumption and shop-purchases became more central to the household
economy, women played more active roles in managing the increased
proportion of the family earnings which was devoted to domestic needs.
Likewise, the housewife's tasks expanded as the farm family's diet became
more varied and elaborate. And the mother's role as nurturer of children
became more crucial due to the protraction of childhood and adolescence
caused in turn by the declining need for children's labor and by the new
trends toward delayed or averted marriage among both male and female
offspring. Indeed, emotional ties between mothers and children in post-
Famine Ireland were proverbially close, smotheringly so between mothers
and sons, allegedly because of the increasing age difference and consequent
emotional distance between husbands and wives — which in turn may
have reinforced both the ideal and the reality of separate spheres for
spouses, as well as the desexualized, 'passionless' image of the Irish mother.
As a result of these developments, housework in all its varied aspects
became more central to the life and self-image of Irish farm families than
ever before, and married women's status and authority were enhanced by
their dominion over the home and their guardianship of its values and
integrity.

Of course, only the wives of fairly substantial farmers were fully able to
create and rule a 'Victorian home'. Poor farmers could only approximate
that goal, and among landless laborers it largely remained elusive.
Nevertheless, although the new domesticity was imperfectly available, the
ideal was widely disseminated through all social classes and legitimated
through the cultural hegemony of the Catholic bourgeoisie, especially as
incorporated in education, employer-employee relations and religion.
Bourke and other scholars have demonstrated that after the Famine greatly
expanded opportunities for women's education accompanied their with-
drawal from the marketplace. The daughters of affluent farmers imbibed
order and refinement in new convent schools, often staffed by nuns from
France, but even girls from poorer families became literate and learned

domestic skills and bourgeois values from exposure to public education.[31] Likewise, domestic service in middle-class households was an important stage in the life cycle of many adolescent females in the Irish countryside.[32] This institution served at least two functions: it exposed the daughters of poor farmers and laborers to bourgeois norms and habits of domesticity; and the regulation of lower-class servants confirmed middle-class women's 'superior' status and values, especially through the enforcement of Victorian codes of sexual morality on their dependents.[33] Most important of all was the influence of the Irish Catholic Church. The bishops' goal was to create and defend a 'holy Ireland' against pernicious Protestant and secular influences. They conceptualized farm families as the foundation stones of their pious ideal, and their model of domesticity was the Sacred Family, in which Mary was the central figure. Tony Fahey suggests that 'it was primarily as wife and mother that the Irish Catholic Church drew on and utilized the support of laywomen, and that the church in return propped up and glorified those roles'.[34] By far the most numerous and important women's organizations in post-Famine Ireland were sodalities and other church-centered associations. Thus, whereas most Irish historians have viewed the post-Famine Church — with its emphases on women's purity and self-sacrifice — as an engine of female subordination, from these women's perspective the Church's ideology and institutional network reinforced by sanctifying their domestic hegemony. Their practical authority as housewives and mothers was fortified by a moral authority derived from the most powerful and pervasive institution in Irish society. It was no coincidence that when the priest came to visit an Irish farm family he was always entertained in the parlor: symbolic of the tacit alliance between the Church and the women to 'uplift' Catholic society, sacralize the home and guard against the potential immorality or irresponsibility of their menfolk — for whom the village pubs became a last retreat.

Unmarried women

Joanna Bourke contends that *all* women in post-Famine Ireland, even those who never married, were empowered to a degree by the increased importance and status of unwaged housework and the domestic sphere. Otherwise, she suggests, it is difficult to explain why so many single women remained in Ireland, instead of emigrating. However, other scholars have argued more persuasively that older, unmarried women in Ireland were generally objects of pity or scorn, despite the Church's ennobling of female self-sacrifice and exaltation of celibacy, as among nuns.[35] Unmarried women may have enjoyed some respect as homeworkers in parentless 'families' of middle-aged siblings, but as unmarriageable housekeepers who had forsaken emigration to care for elderly parents, awaiting the latters' deaths to release them from perpetual adolescence, their situations were commonly viewed as pathetic. Indeed, the failure of many unmarried women to emigrate should be considered, not as evidence of their empowerment at home, but rather as indicating their subordination to their male relatives' economic strategies and, more broadly, to a cult of family and domesticity which could entrap women as well as glorify their housekeeping roles. Thus, when west Kerrywoman Peig Sayers rejected an opportunity to emigrate by concluding she would be 'more favored with grace' if she stayed to comfort her parents' old age, she demonstrated that women's separate sphere could become a gilded cage for unmarried as well as for married women.[36]

The dowry system

Limited as it was, in order for a woman to exercise and enjoy the full status and authority of housework, it was essential for her to have the house and family of her own which could be acquired only through marriage and child-bearing. These were the goals to which nearly all women aspired — both because of the enhanced and sanctified roles of wife/mother/houseworker, and because the waged alternatives for women in post-Famine Ireland were so few and bleak. Hence, it is arguable that the dowry should be viewed in part as the *price* a woman's parents had to pay to secure for her a marriage and domestic sphere of her own — a price paid in part to compensate her new husband's mother and unmarried sisters, whose position and authority as houseworkers she would now supplant or, from their perspective, usurp.

For post-Famine Irishwomen, the greatest disadvantage of the dowry system was not the fact (if it is a 'fact,' for concrete evidence is sorely lacking) that marriages were more arranged or loveless than heretofore. Rather, the disadvantages were, first, given escalating dowry costs (itself perhaps a reflection of the increased value placed on housework),[37] most rural families could not afford the price of marriage for more than one of their several or many daughters; and, second, usually dowries or 'matches' could be arranged only between families of comparable wealth and reputation. If housework and family conferred status and authority on a woman, then the 'better' the house and family she could marry into, the more status and authority she would enjoy in a social system which linked hegemony, property and gentility. However, upward mobility under the dowry system was rare (although perhaps no rarer than in pre-Famine Ireland), as few laborers' daughters were allowed to marry farmers' sons, and few small-holders' daughters could wed the offspring of graziers or strong farmers.

Undowried women

It was the women whom the dowry system could not accommodate who poured overseas into American cities in the late nineteenth and early twentieth centuries: the non-dowried daughters of small farmers and the daughters of agricultural laborers, generally. However, did they emigrate primarily for economic opportunities, as Hasia Diner argues, or to secure husbands and families, as Janet Nolan contends?

In one sense, posing the questions in this way is misleading. As Rita Rhodes has written, economically-based decisions made by patriarchal Irish familes, and daughters' duties (to relieve financial burdens at home and to send back remittances from abroad) were conceived in traditional, self-sacrificial terms: these comprised the 'initial impetus' for female emigration from post-Famine Ireland. Thus, 'Go where you will earn good money, you have wasted your time too long here', was one Irish woman's typical injunction to her daughter. Nevertheless, Rhodes argues, additional reasons for female emigration derived from 'the gradual growth of a limited individualism on the part of daughters themselves' — reflected, for example, in the expressed desire of many young Irishwomen to escape the drudgery of unpaid, outdoor farm work. Ironically, emigration enabled young Irish women to reconcile traditional family obligations with new individual motivations. However, the latter were shaped in turn by familial values and goals which could no longer be realized in rural Ireland.[38]

In this light, Joanna Bourke's portrait of Irishwomen, of their motives and aspirations, suggests that Janet Nolan's hypothesis appears to be the more accurate: that young Irish women emigrated to establish families in which they could enjoy the status and moral authority of homemakers in the separate, domestic sphere which was eulogized in Victorian America, as in Ireland, and which was as idealized by the American Catholic Church and the emergent Irish-American bourgeoisie as by their native Protestant counterparts.[39] Although Irish women frequently migrated to eastern US cities and mill towns, where the preponderance of Irish-born females lessened their marital opportunities, such patterns do not necessarily reflect an indifference or aversion to matrimony, as Diner contends. Rather, they reflect continued patterns of earlier Irish settlement and the fact that nearly all post-Famine emigration was channeled by existing *family* networks, as uncles and brothers (not only aunts and sisters, as Nolan claims) sent remittances which brought Irishwomen (and men) to communities where employment opportunities for single Irish *males* (but not for females) were atrophying during the late nineteenth and early twentieth centuries. After arrival in such locales, Irish males tended to be more venturesome and mobile in search of employment or better wages, but female Irish immigrants tended to remain, under the protection of Irish relatives, unless they received specific invitations from other relations who had settled further west, in cities where Irish-American sex ratios were more favorable to endogamous marriage.

Marriage in America

Moreover, at least according to both Diner and Nolan, Irish women in the United States generally married more often and at younger ages than did those who remained in Ireland. Also, the most significant impression which emerges from their American data *c.* 1900 is not that Irish immigrants' marital rates and ages were so different from those of Italian, Polish, or French-

Canadian immigrants, but rather that they were increasingly so similar to the marriage patterns of native-born Protestants. This indicates the growing convergence of bourgeois life-styles and norms in Ireland and America, as already suggested, and also of native-Protestant and Irish-American societies in the United States. David Doyle and other scholars have already demonstrated that in the late nineteenth and early twentieth centuries Irish Americans had among the lowest rates of residential segregation and among the highest rates of suburbanization and home-ownership of all ethnic groups; furthermore, by 1900–20 Irish America's occupational structure and rates of school attendance and educational achievement were almost identical to those of native Protestants.[40] Likewise, the fact that nearly all post-Famine emigrants spoke English, were literate to some degree and adapted to American society through the medium of bourgeois-dominated and fervently patriotic associations (for example, the American Catholic Church, the Democratic Party, and Irish-American benevolent and temperance associations) also promoted Irish acculturation — as did unmarried Irish immigrant women's concentration in domestic service, to be discussed below.[41] Thus, it is little wonder that Irish women's marital patterns were similar to those of native Americans, or different from those of southern and eastern Europeans. Only in their patterns of marital fertility did Irish and native-born women still differ greatly — perhaps reflecting Irish women's view of large families as enhancing their domestic status and providing social insurance, as well as Church teachings regarding motherhood and the evils of contraception. Moreover, some evidence suggests that by 1900 even Irish-immigrant birthrates were converging toward native-American norms.[42]

Thus, according to Irish newspapers such as the *Cork Examiner*, during the post-Famine era 'Every [Irish] servant-maid thinks of the land of promise ... where husbands are thought more procurable than in Ireland'.[43] Likewise, the letters written by Irish immigrant women themselves indicate that the desire to marry, to marry men of their own choosing and to have families and households of their own was a primary motive for coming to the United States. After all, wrote one young Ulsterwoman in New York City, 'its the happiest time ever ... when under your own roof in [your] own house'.[44] Young Irish women such as Mary Ann Landy, Minnie Markey and Mary Brown were positively entranced by the liberal courtship patterns and romantic possibilities available in what the former called 'the free lands of America'.[45] 'You would not think I had any beaux but I have a good many', wrote the New York Irish servant, Mary Brown, to her envious cousin in County Wexford; 'I got half a dozen now I have [become] quite a yankee and if I was at home the boys would all be around me'.[46]

However, the distinction which Nolan and Diner have made between Irish women's marital and economic motives for emigration has been drawn too sharply. Female Irish emigrants desired what Mary Brown called 'love and liberty':[47] that is, they wanted both economic opportunity *and* domestic bliss in America — and they viewed the successful appropriation of the former as the key to the successful acquisition of the latter. That was one major reason why Irish women emigrated at an increasingly early age, usually in their late teens or early twenties: so they could work in the United States for six, eight, or even ten years — if as servants, as most of them were, honing their skills at domesticity; earning sufficient money to send remittances home; and, most important, accumulating the capital equivalents of dowries so they could attract and marry the most promising Irish immigrant males available and secure the status and moral authority of Irish-American homemakers and houseworkers before they passed beyond an age when matrimony and child-bearing became difficult or unlikely.

Examine, for example, the career of Julia Lough, a laborer's daughter from Queen's County, who emigrated in 1884 at the age of thirteen to Winsted, Connecticut, where she joined four of her older sisters, all of whom had already married in America. During her first several years in Winsted, Julia Lough worked as a seamstress for one of her sisters and in the neighborhood. At the age of nineteen she was an unpaid dressmaker's apprentice, as well as a member of the young women's sodality at St Leo's Catholic Church, and two years later she was a salaried employee in a dressmaker's shop. By the age of twenty-three she was an independent dressmaker, with an establishment of her own on Main Street, traveling frequently to New York City to purchase material and new patterns. However, three years later Julia Lough sold her business and married an Irish-born railway engineer (a 'good match' in socio-economic terms), bearing him six children in a home dominated by feminine piety and gentility until she and her husband died in 1959. Thus, although Julia Lough had exulted in the economic 'independence' which her hard work and business acumen had achieved, for her and most Irishwomen the 'good marriage' and the status and authority of wife/mother/houseworker represented their ultimate ambitions. Early emigration and successful economic strategies could make possible both capital accumulation and marriage, as in the case of Julia Lough who was still not quite twenty-six when she wed Thomas MaCarthy.[48]

Domestic service in America: preparation for marriage

Of course, most unmarried Irish women in America were domestic servants, not small entrepreneurs like Julia Lough. As late as 1900, over 70 per cent of employed Irish-born women in the United States were engaged in domestic and personal service, and in the late nineteenth and early twentieth centuries single Irish women dominated household service in most American cities outside the deep south.[49] Hasia Diner has argued that Irish immigrant women viewed domestic service, like other waged employment, as an alternative to marriage. However, in light of its central importance in the lives of *all* Irish female immigrants, including the great majority of those who eventually married, it would seem more pertinent to inquire into the conditions specific to that occupation which either encouraged or discouraged matrimony. First, both in Ireland and America, Catholic writers viewed domestic service for young women as a valuable preparation for housewifery, and at least some Irish women appear to have viewed it in that light.[50] As noted above, many Irish females had worked as household servants prior to emigrating, and most had been exposed to the cult, if not the reality, of bourgeois domesticity in Ireland. Thus, the criticism offered by James Reford, an Ulster Protestant immigrant, of newly arrived Irish Catholic servants 'from the bogs of Conoght', implies that they already expected and demanded middle-class comforts and conveniences from American employers: 'if you want a girl to do house work' in the United States, Reford complained, 'the[ir] first question is have you got hot and cold water in the house [and] Stationary wash tubs, wringer[?] is my Bed room carpeted [with] Bureau Table wash stand and chairs and what privaleges[?]'[51] On the other hand, many Irishwomen's letters indicate that domestic service in middle-class American households certainly increased and refined, if they did not create, bourgeois aspirations both material and socio-cultural. 'I would far rather live here than In Ireland,' wrote Mary Ann Sinclair, a house servant in San Francisco; 'The ways and customs of the people are so different the[y] are all so polite and for who will talk the prettiest'.[52] Similarly, another Ulsterwoman was almost overwhelmed by her first exposure to the comforts and manners of a Victorian home. '[I]t is a very nice place to live in,' wrote Annie Gass from Attica, Indiana:

> it seams to bee the nicest place that I ever sean ... [it] Contains 11 Rooms all carpeted with Ritsh Carpet all mehogny furniture also silver dishes nives and forkes and every thing in proportion you could have no idea how things looks ... the people are very Clean in their habits the[y] are all well bread and very fine dress ... [and] the Children ... are so nise in their manner ... [At dinner] there hands and fase must bee washed Clean and hair nicely Comed their Behaveour is very good.[53]

If only to keep their situations and increase their wages, Irish domestic servants had to conform to — and help maintain — such standards, and indeed the letters of many indicate clearly that they accepted and even internalized Victorian values of cleanliness, punctuality and efficiency.[54] Often, like Mary Clear of Utica, Maggie Hennessy of Hartford and Minnie Markey of Chicago, they criticized harshly the absence of such standards in rural Ireland or among their less 'respectable' Irish-American neighbors.[55] More importantly, as historian Colleen McDannell suggests, 'When these domestics married and started their own families, ... they sought to establish homes of similar quality'. Although they may not have 'consciously believed that Victorian domesticity was a way of inching into the middle class', they aspired to create 'the "right" kind of home ... which then would make them into the "right" kind of people'.[56] The results of such aspirations were described approvingly by visiting Irish priests, such as Fr. Pius Devine, who inspected working-class Irish-American neighborhoods and discovered as early as the 1870s that, despite their plain exteriors, 'the little wooden houses had each a parlor & a carpet into which nobody got entrance except very respectable visitors'.[57]

Also, domestic service provided an ideal economic as well as cultural foundation for achieving a 'good marriage' and a home in the United States. Although domestic service offered virtually no opportunities for occupational mobility, the possibilities of modest but significant capital accumulation were substantial. For domestic servants demand was greater, unemployment far less frequent and *real* wages — including room, board and often clothes and presents — were higher than in any other occupation available to unskilled (and most skilled) women in late nineteenth and early twentieth-century America.[58] Thus, in 1894 the Ulsterman Patrick McKeown, a streetpaver in Philadelphia, reported enviously that Irish domestic servants 'seem to be the most successful and save more money than any class of working girls, as they are at little or no expence, and get a great many presents if they are fortunate in getting into a good house'.[59] Indeed, Irish-American servants changed households frequently, much to their employers' displeasure, in search of higher wages, better working conditions, and kind mistresses who would bribe them to remain with gifts and other indulgences. Through such strategies, they often amassed savings of $1,000 or more before they quit work altogether for marriage.[60]

Of course, domestic service was an arduous occupation, and historians such as David Katzman and especially Faye Dudden have shown that over-work, long hours, constant supervision, demeaning treatment and profound loneliness and alienation were the lot of many unhappy servants.[61] In such respects, the record revealed by Irish immigrant servants' letters and memoirs is mixed. For example, Mary Hanlon, a servant in New York City, complained bitterly that her 'every act' was 'scrutinized & commented on' by her employers.[62] However, Ann Jane Sinclair's employer in Oakland, California, gave her free piano lessons; her sister in San Francisco received from her mistress 'a beautiful silver thimble for a christmas present'; and although Maggie Murphy's first employer in Jersey City was 'a perfect Devel [who] wanted every thing to perfection', she quickly abandoned her harsh mistress for another who gave her dresses and was 'as nice as you could get'.[63] Likewise, much evidence suggests that household service in America was less arduous or demeaning than the work to which small farmers' and laborers' daughters were accustomed at home, and many Irish servants in America remarked upon the relatively egalitarian treatment they received from their employers.[64] Thus, Mary Clear wrote that her 'rich' employer in Utica was 'nice to his help', and Annie Heggarty reported from Iowa that she had 'a good home' where her master 'makes no differ with me more than aney of his own daughters'.[65] In addition, the letters of Mary Clear, James Reford and others suggest that Irish-American servants did not shrink from confrontations with their employers, who often complained of their 'impudence'.[66] 'The cook is a very nice girl,' wrote Mary Clear of one of her fellow house servants; 'she is a Murphy, Irish-American, about the size of a doll, but as smart a piece as I ever saw. She makes the Boss think that she is just as good as him — she wouldn't take a word from the best of them, nor neither will I.'[67]

More importantly, for the great majority of Irish immigrant women domestic servitude was only temporary, a means to achieve another goal, and the extent to which Irish women resented its limitations only encouraged their escape to what they regarded as the shelters of husband and home-making. Thus, Catharine Ann McFarland of Philadelphia was so ashamed of 'liven at service' and so tired of what she had 'to put up with in ane ones kitchen' that she eagerly embraced 'an offer of Marige from a very respectable Man' — an Irish-born carpenter; 'you [k]now that i never had mutch plesur in my young days', she wrote to her mother in Derry, 'sow i hope to have som now'.[68] Likewise, although Mary Ann Rowe in Dedham, Massachusetts, admitted that she was employed in 'a very nice family', she, too, turned to matrimony to escape unbearable loneliness and longing for the home and family she had left behind in County Kilkenny.[69] Finally, Lizzie McCann, an Ulster Catholic and hotel servant in Minneapolis, confided to her sister in Belfast that 'it is pretty hard life for us to work out all those years we are just tired out with hardwork So i am not going to be so hard to soute in a husbant as i have been i am going to Make a home for my self this time. I will not wait any longer ... i Expect to get Married in May' — and she did so, in a sumptuous working-class wedding which, judging from her enthusiastic description, was the high point of her young life.[70]

Less fortunate Irish women

As far as can be known, Catharine Ann McFarland's and Lizzie McCann's experiences of immigration, like those of Julia Lough's, culminated happily according to their own aspirations. However, there were others who, by those standards at least, were less fortunate. First, there were those already mentioned whose situations or whose families' strategies allowed them neither to emigrate nor to marry nor to find a respected, 'independent' niche (for example, as nuns, teachers, or postal workers) in Irish society. Second, there were at least a few young immigrants whose overly-literal pursuit of 'love and liberty,' in defiance of bourgeois conventions, Irish traditions and religious sanctions, brought them only the disgrace of unwed motherhood and the likely poverty of prostitution. 'It was my fortune to witness an excommunication ... yesterday ... [of a] young girl', wrote one sanctimonious Irish-American, Hugh Harlin, from Jackson, Michigan:

> There is not a community of Irish in America but what there is always one or more houses where the lower class of servant girls associate. Of course they meet some company of the opposite sex and ... they frequently have a 'drop' by way of friendship. Of course such conduct will run to extremes, particularly at the satur-day night dances ... [So, i]s it to be wondered at that under the influence of the ... bottle or pitcher, their coarser natures are excited and they become passive to the fulsom adolations of the vilest scamps that ever left Ireland[?] When they reach this point they are *lost*.

In fact, the victim of Hugh Harlin's censure apparently escaped 'the fate worse than death': she married her lover and appears to have been excommunicated less for her sexual transgressions than because her husband was a Protestant and their wedding took place in an Episcopal Church![71] However, it is unlikely that this woman's problems ended happily at the altar, for third, and far more common than unwed mothers, were those immigrants whose eagerness to become Irish-American wives and house-workers blinded their judgements and led them to enter the abusive, drunken and often broken marriages which Hasia Diner describes in horrifying detail and which, sadly, became the fates of Mary Ann Rowe and Minnie Markey, blighting their dreams of romance and their hopes of ascent from drudgery to security and respectability.[72] Such pathological examples were evident everywhere in Irish America, but probably were most common in eastern cities and mill towns, where Irish women's endogamous marital choices were quantitatively fewer and, perhaps, qualitatively lower than further west.

Fourth were those female immigrants who never married in America, for although some became successful 'women of property' purchased with hoarded savings, others ended their lives in almshouses or asylums.[73] No doubt many unmarried Irish women consciously chose to remain single, and Diner may be correct in her contention that Irish socio-cultural patterns and/or Irish-American experiences made women from Ireland more hesitant to marry, or at least more aware of alternate survival strategies, than were females in other ethnic groups.[74] For example, if marriage postponement was a peculiarly Irish Catholic device to limit family size without recourse to birth control, as some scholars suggest, it is easy to imagine how the accompanying code of female chastity and sexual repression could discourage matrimony and make postponement permanent; indeed, at least one immigrant's letter implied that the lack of sexual instruction given by Irish mothers prior to their daughters' emigration may have inhibited the latters' sense of confidence regarding marriage and male-female relationships, generally.[75] Also, given the intimate connections among property, security and female self-identity in rural Irish and Victorian American cultures alike, perhaps it would not be surprising if, over time, steady employment and capital accumulation became ends in themselves for many Irish women abroad, especially for domestic servants who feared those achievements — as well as the genteel standards imbibed in their employers' households — might be forfeited, at least temporarily, through marriage to working-class Irish Americans.[76] At least a few Irish servants must have made quite rational decisions not to forsake their employers' comfortable homes and kind treatment for the uncertain bliss of matrimony.

In addition, as Faye Dudden and David Katzman point out, there were other aspects of domestic service which could discourage marriage. Perhaps fearful of the consequences Hugh Harlin described, some employers denied servants the leisure time and personal freedom necessary for social life and courtship rituals.[77] Furthermore, Katzman argues, 'many mistresses encouraged servants to express their nurturing and loving instincts on the employing family. In exploiting the emotional needs of the domestic, the employer might be winning a faithful and loyal servant, one who lost her own vision of an independent life and instead adopted the family she worked for as a substitute for her own.'[78] Such appears to have been the case with Ann McNabb, the laborer's daughter from County Derry, who, atypically, worked as cook and nurse for one family for twenty-two years and never married. 'Mrs Carr's interests was my interests,' she stated proudly; 'I took better care of her things than she did herself, and I loved the childer as if they was my own.'[79]

Irish immigrant spinsters

However, there were other Irish immigrant spinsters who had never enjoyed the opportunity or the choice of matrimony. For some, this may have been due to the gender imbalance which prevailed among the Irish in many American cities. Many others may have emigrated too late in life, obliged by their families' economic and inheritance strategies to postpone their departures until one brother married (since his wife's dowry might finance his sisters' emigrations) or until their parents' deaths.[80] Thus, Deirdre Mageean demonstrates that a high proportion of the unmarried, middle-aged and elderly Irish-born domestic servants in early twentieth-century Chicago had not emigrated until their late twenties or early thirties.[81] By the time they had labored five to ten years to accumulate much capital in America, they were pressing against the outer limits of marriage-ability and child-bearing. Also, the Irish cult of domestic duty could inhibit immigrants' marriage by burdening them with obligations to send home remittances, thus depleting their savings and stifling their social opportunities in order to finance their siblings' emigrations or to support their families in Ireland. Again, the greatest impositions may have fallen on older daughters who were the first of their siblings to emigrate: not only were they expected to pay their younger brothers' and sisters' passages, but also they would have to wait longest in America before their parents' deaths released them from obligations to the home farm. Such appears to have been at least part of the explanation for Annie Carroll's impoverished spinsterhood. Despite her often bitter complaints, she faithfully sent home large sums, earned at service in Chicago, to finance her brother's emigration and to pay the rent of her mother's farm. Unfortunately, Annie Carroll's mother did not die until 1891, eight years after her emigration; two years later she lost her only suitor to a younger rival; and in 1896 she developed the chronic foot ulcer which would terminate her employment. For a time she lived with her bachelor brother, but by 1915 she was residing in an asylum.[82]

Finally, it is likely that many Irish women who never married abroad had grown up in peasants' or laborers' households which were so poor and primitive that they had never been exposed to the new standards and skills of middle-class housework — which may have made them relatively unmarketable in America, both as domestic servants and as wives. One such case was Mary Malone from County Waterford, a 'lonesom and down harted' scrubwoman in Fairport, New York, who explained in a letter to her brother that 'my wages is so little' because 'I am not capable of earning big wages like other girls who can cook and [do] the large washings and fine ironings I cannot do this you know I was not brought [up] to any such thing [for] I was sent away frum my Mother when young to the farmers to work out in the fields and I never got much in sight about house keeping or to be handy to sew'.[83] To be sure, most young 'greenhorns' from similarly impoverished backgrounds, such as Ann McNabb, 'larned hand over hand' from their first employers how 'to cook and bake and to wash and do up shirts — all American fashion'.[84] 'America revolutionizes them', one observer wrote, referring contemptuously to Irish domestic servants' often pathetic early attempts to adapt to American bourgeois standards.[85] However, apparently some Irish women never overcame their initial deficiencies. Thus, Maggie Black, an Irish housewife in late nineteenth-century Chicago, described the plight of an inept or 'lazy' immigrant relative:

> Margaret has been rather unfortunate in her situation lately. She is likely to be out [of work] this week again. She was getting 3 dols per week in the last month. She was expected to do the *Shirts* but she cannot please the lady in doing them, so she loses a dollar a week for that & her mistress thinks she is not worth more than 2 dollars ... I think she is not worth *1 dollar a week*. She's awfully slow & that won't do here, & they won't wait on a girl here, just if she does not suit pay her off without much ceremony. I dont think she will ever be any better.[86]

Like Catharine Ann McFarland, the unhappy Mary Malone and Maggie Black's incompetent kinswoman might have been eager candidates for hasty matrimony. However, their lack of domestic skills and savings may have fatally reduced their marital prospects or, even worse, consigned them to 'unfortunate' marriages scarred by poverty, alcoholism and abuse.

Conclusion

In conclusion, emigration brought the Julia Loughs and Lizzie McCanns of Ireland all they had hoped for: economic achievement sufficient to secure 'respectable' marriages and the status and authority of homemakers. For Ireland's Annie Carrolls and Mary Malones, those goals were more elusive, and for Ireland's Ann McNabbs, the means to achieve matrimony ultimately became the ends in themselves. In the last analysis, it is difficult to say which were the most fortunate. Maggie Black, the lower middle-class wife of an Irish-born dry goods salesman, worked herself into a state of nervous exhaustion 'constantly cleaning & dusting' her nine-room house, attending missionary society and ladies' prayer meetings, and fretting over Chicago's moral dangers to her offspring.[87] Likewise, although Ellen Flinn, wife of a day laborer in Barrytown, New York, 'purchased a house and lot

that cost her fourteen hundred dollars' earned as a laundress, her
Sisyphean efforts to force her family up the road to respectability left her
'very thin and old looking'.[88] Perhaps 'love and liberty' was a dream only
for the young, and perhaps in old age even the Julia Loughs sometimes
wondered if they had sacrificed too much on the altar of domesticity.

Notes

1. The authors would like to thank Susan Porter Benson, Joanna Bourke, Malcolm
   Campbell, Hasia Diner, Deirdre Mageean and especially David Fitzpatrick for
   their helpful comments on earlier drafts of this essay.
       For a review of recent literature on Irish women's history, see David
   Fitzpatrick, 'Women, gender and the writing of Irish history', *Irish Historical
   Studies*, 28, 107, May 1991, pp. 267–73. Two excellent works, published too
   recently for inclusion in Fitzpatrick's survey, are: Rita M. Rhodes, *Women and the
   Family in Post-Famine Ireland: Status and Opportunity in a Patriarchal Society*,
   Garland, New York, 1992; and Joanna Bourke, *Husbandry to Housewifery: Women,
   Economic Change and Housework in Ireland, 1890–1914*, Oxford University Press,
   New York, 1993. On Irish-American women, see Hasia R. Diner, *Erin's Daughters
   in America: Irish Immigrant Women in the Nineteenth Century*, Johns Hopkins
   University Press, Baltimore, 1983; and Janet R. Nolan, *Ourselves Alone: Women's
   Emigration from Ireland, 1885–1920*, University Press of Kentucky, Lexington, 1989.
2. Mary Cullen, 'Breadwinners and providers: women in the household economy
   of labouring families, 1835–36', in Maria Luddy and Cliona Murphy, eds, *Women
   Surviving: Studies in Irish Women's History in the 19th and 20th centuries*, Poolbeg
   Press, Dublin, 1990, pp. 98–9, 106–11.
3. Kevin O'Neill, *Family and Farm in Pre-Famine Ireland: the Parish of Killashandra*,
   University of Wisconsin Press, Madison, 1985, pp. 178–84.
4. David Fitzpatrick, 'The modernisation of the Irish female', in Patrick
   O'Flanagan, Paul Ferguson, and Kevin Whelan, eds, *Rural Ireland, 1600–1900:
   Modernisation and Change*, Cork University Press, Cork, 1987, pp. 167–9.
5. On pre-Famine Irish society and emigration, generally, see Kerby A. Miller,
   Emigrants and Exiles: Ireland and the Irish Exodus to North America, Oxford
   University Press, New York and Oxford, 1985, pp. 26–101, 193–252.
6. Fitzpatrick, 'Modernisation of the Irish female', pp. 166–9.
7. Miller, pp. 403–4. Irish celibacy in 1926 computed from W.E. Vaughn, and A.J.
   Fitzpatrick, eds, *Irish Historical Statistics: Population, 1821–1971*, Royal Irish
   Academy, Dublin, 1978, p. 91.
8. On post-Famine Irish society and emigration, generally, see Miller, pp. 345–426.
   However, this is not to say that the ratio of female to male emigrants rose consistently after the Great Famine. David Fitzpatrick concludes that that ratio was 100
   in the early 1850s, fell to 74 by 1870, rose to 116 by 1900, and then declined to 90
   on the eve of World War I, which suggests that changes in sex-specific demands
   for immigrant workers were at least as influential as changes in post-Famine
   Irish women's socio-economic status. Fitzpatrick, letter to Miller, 12 February
   1992.
9. Diner, p. 50 and *passim*.
10. Nolan, pp. 74–5 and *passim*; Diner, pp. 46–7.
11. Diner, pp. 46–9.
12. Nolan, pp. 74–5.

13. The only detailed statistical comparison of Irish and Irish-American — and of Irish, German, and white native-American — marriage and celibacy patterns is Timothy Guinnane, 'Marriage, migration, and household formation: the Irish at the turn of the century', Stanford University, Ph.D. thesis, 1989. However, Guinnane focuses almost exclusively on *male* nuptiality, concluding that Irish celibacy in the USA (1900) was well below that for Ireland (1901), but significantly higher than for German or white native-Americans. According to David Fitzpatrick, in the USA in 1900 13 per cent of Irish-born women aged 45–54 were unmarried, compared with 22 per cent of those who remained in Ireland, but with 3 per cent of German-born women and 8 per cent of white native-born women in America. However, these statistics apply to women born shortly before and after 1850, who emigrated *c.* 1870, and the marital experiences of later cohorts of Irish-born women are still unknown. Fitzpatrick, letter to Miller, 12 February 1992.
14. Nancy A. Hewitt, 'Beyond the search for sisterhood: American women's history in the 1880s', in Ellen Carol DuBois and Vicki L. Ruiz, eds, *Unequal Sisters: a Multicultural Reader in US Women's History*, Routledge, New York, 1990, p. 11 and *passim.*
15. This point is also made by Rhodes, pp. 126–81, who distinguishes among the experiences and expectations of women in three types of rural families in post-Famine Ireland: those of commercial farmers; of subsistence smallholders, especially in the western counties; and of agricultural laborers.
16. Damian F. Hannan, 'Peasant models and the understanding of social and cultural change in rural Ireland', in P.J. Drudy, ed., *Irish Studies 2. Ireland: Land, Politics and People*, Cambridge University Press, Cambridge, 1982, pp. 150–1.
17. Cullen, p. 114.
18. Miller, pp. 58, 406.
19. 'The story of an Irish cook', *The Independent*, 58, 2939, 30 March 1905, p. 715.
20. Cullen, p. 112.
21. Rhodes, pp. 24–5.
22. Fitzpatrick, 'Modernisation of the Irish female', pp. 164–5, 174–6. Data on Irish-speakers compiled from the *1861 Irish Census*, Part 2, Vol. 1, p. 49.
23. Miller, p. 407.
24. Miller, pp. 263–79. Also see David N. Doyle, 'The Irish in North America, 1776–1845', in W.E. Vaughn, ed., *A New History of Ireland, V: Ireland Under the Union, I — 1801–1870*, Clarendon Press, Oxford, 1989, pp. 682–725.
25. Rhodes, especially in pp. 257–70, also argues that Irish emigration decisions should be viewed as strategic choices, made primarily by parents within the context of the rural family economy.
26. Julia Lough, 3 September 1893, Lough family letters, in collection of Kerby A. Miller, University of Missouri [hereafter cited as Miller collection].
27. Margaret Wright, 27 May 1808, in Kerr–McNish letters, Cornell University Library, Ithaca, NY.
28. Joanna Bourke, '"The best of all home rulers": the economic power of women in Ireland, 1880–1914', *Irish Economic and Social History*, 18, 1991, pp. 24–37. The authors wish to thank Dr Bourke for allowing them to see an earlier version of this article; unfortunately, time did not enable us to utilize her recently published book, *Husbandry to Housewifery*, for this article.
29. On post-Famine Irish society generally, see Miller, pp. 380–424.
30. Joanna Bourke, 'Women and poultry in Ireland, 1891–1914', *Irish Historical Studies*, 25, 99, May 1987, pp. 293–310.
31. Anne V. O'Connor, 'The revolution in girls' secondary education in Ireland, 1860–1910', in Mary Cullen, ed., *Girls Don't Do Honours: Irish Women in Education*

in the 19th and 20th Centuries, Women's Education Bureau, Dublin, 1987, pp. 31–54. Also see David Fitzpatrick, '"A share of the honeycomb": education, emigration and Irishwomen', in Mary Daly and David Dickson, eds, *The Origins of Popular Literacy in Ireland: Language Change and Educational Development, 1700–1920*, Department of Modern History, Trinity College, Dublin, 1990, pp. 167–87.

32. Fitzpatrick, 'Modernisation of the Irish female', p. 166.
33. For example, see Mary Carbery, *The Farm by Lough Gur*, Mercier Press, Dublin and Cork, 1973 edn. Also, Judith L. Newton, Mary P. Ryan and Judith R. Walkowitz, eds, *Sex and Class in Women's History*, Routledge & Kegan Paul, London, 1983, pp. 6–9.
34. Tony Fahey, 'Nuns in the Catholic church in the nineteenth century', in Cullen, pp. 27–8. Miller, pp. 463–5.
35. For example, Joseph J. Lee 'Women and the Church since the famine', in Margaret MacCurtain and Donncha O Corráin, eds., *Women in Irish Society: the Historical Dimension*, Arlen House, Dublin, 1978, pp. 37–45.
36. Miller, p. 475.
37. It must be noted that Cormac O Gráda has recently argued that dowry costs declined between 1870 and 1910. O Gráda, *Ireland before and after the Famine: explorations in economic history, 1800–1925*, Manchester University Press, Manchester, 1988, p. 167. However, O Gráda's conclusions are disputed, e.g. by David Fitzpatrick, 'Women, gender and the writing of Irish history', pp. 271–2.
38. Rhodes, pp. 257-77; quotation on p. 259.
39. Diner, p. 67. Colleen McDannell, *The Christian Home in Victorian America. 1840–1900*, Indiana University Press, Bloomington, 1986, pp. 52–76, 108–55.
40. Miller, pp. 492–501. David N. Doyle, *Irish Americans, Native Rights, and National Empires: the Structure, Divisions, and Attitudes of the Catholic Minority in the Decade of Expansion, 1890–1901*, Arno Press, New York, 1976, pp. 48–9, 59–63.
41. Kerby A. Miller, 'Class, culture, and immigrant group identity in the United States: the case of Irish-American ethnicity', in Virginia Yans-McLaughlin, ed., *Immigration Reconsidered: History, Sociology, and Politics*, Oxford University Press, New York and Oxford, 1990, pp. 96–129. With respect to post-Famine emigrant literacy, David Fitzpatrick's research indicates that merely 29 per cent of Irish emigrant females in 1851–60 (and 40 per cent of Irish emigrant males) were literate; however, by the end of the century literacy was nearly universal among the age cohorts most prone to emigration. Fitzpatrick, letter to Miller, 12 February 1992.
42. For example, see the suggestive data in 'Fecundity of immigrant women', *Reports of the Immigration Commission* (Dillingham Commission), 61st Congress, 2nd Session, Senate Documents, 65, Government Printing Office, Washington, DC, 1911, pp. 731–826.
43. Miller, *Emigrants and Exiles*, p. 408.
44. Mary Hanlon, fragment of letter [Autumn 1871], D.885/13, Public Record Office of Northern Ireland (hereafter cited as PRONI), Belfast.
45. Mary Ann Landy, undated letter [1884], Miller collection; Minnie Markey letters, 1889–94, in Carroll family letters, Miller collection.
46. Mary Brown, 11 March 1858, Mary Brown letters, in the collection of Professor Arnold Schrier, University of Cincinnati (hereafter cited as the Schrier collection).
47. Mary Brown, 20 January 1859, Schrier collection.
48. Julia Lough letters, 1884–1926, Miller collection. Biographical information from Mrs Jenny Rasmussen, Hartford, Connecticut.

49. Miller, *Emigrants and Exiles*, pp. 449–500; Nolan, p. 68; Rhodes, p. 299; Diner, pp. 80–105.
50. McDannell, p. 62.
51. James A. Reford, 9 April [1873], T.3028/B9, PRONI.
52. Mary Ann Sinclair, 3 June 1882, D.1497/2/2, PRONI.
53. Annie Gass, 8 January 1872, T.1396/7, PRONI.
54. For example, see the letters of Mary Ann Sinclair, 3 June 1882; Anne Jane Sinclair, ? December 1879 and 9 February 1881, D.1497/4/2 and 7, PRONI; Mary Clear, 14 May 1899, in 'Letters from Robert Eugene O'Neill', *The Past*, 1964, 115–18; and Maria Sheehan, 5 April 1921, M. Hayes Papers, Kinsale Regional Museum, Kinsale, Co. Cork.
55. Mary Clear, 14 May 1899; Minnie Markey, 23 October 1889, Carroll family letters; Maggie Hennessy, ? July 1882, Hennessy family letters, Miller collection.
56. McDannell, p. 73.
57. Fr. Pius Devine, CP, 'Journal of a voyage to America, 1870; and adventures and misadventures of a jolly beggar, 1872–75', Saint Paul of the Cross Retreat, Mount Argus, Dublin; unpublished MS courtesy of Fr. Declan O'Sullivan, CP, archivist.
58. Diner, p. 90; David M. Katzman, *Seven Days a Week: Women and Domestic Service in Industrializing America*, University of Illinois Press, Urbana, 1978, pp. 311–14.
59. Patrick McKeown, 22 April 1894, Schrier collection.
60. Katzman, pp. 3, 270; Diner, pp. 80–105.
61. Katzman, pp. 7–14, 267–69; Faye E. Dudden, *Serving Women: Household Service in Nineteenth-Century America*, Wesleyan University Press, Middletown, 1983, pp. 193–235.
62. Mary Hanlon [Autumn 1871].
63. Anne Jane Sinclair, 9 February 1881; Mary Ann Sinclair, 11 February 1880, D.1497/4/7, PRONI; and Maggie Murphy, 22 June [1924?], Murphy (Claregalway) letters, Miller collection.
64. Rhodes, p. 305, also makes this argument.
65. Mary Clear, 14 May 1899; Annie Heggarty, 19 July 1887, Heggarty family letters, Schrier collection.
66. Mary Clear, 14 May 1899; James A. Reford, 9 April [1873].
67. Mary Clear, 14 May 1899.
68. Catharine Ann McFarland, 5 March and 25 June 1855, D.1665/3/6–7, PRONI.
69. Mary Ann Rowe, 29 October 1888, Miller collection.
70. Lizzie McCann, 20 March and 17 July 1888, T.1456/7 and 4–6, PRONI.
71. Hugh Harlin, 19 April 1858, in Harlin family letters, Miller collection.
72. Diner, pp. 53–65. Biographical information on Mary Ann Rowe from Mrs Brid Galway, Barrowsland, Thomastown, Co. Kilkenny. Biographical information on Minnie Markey from Annie Carroll's letters, 1895–1898, Carroll family letters.
73. Dudden, p. 208.
74. Patricia Kelleher, letter to author, 16 July 1991.
75. Nan Lough McMahon, undated letter, Lough family letters.
76. Dudden, pp. 228–30.
77. Dudden, p. 211; Katzman, pp. 7–14.
78. Katzman, p. 269.
79. 'The story of an Irish cook', pp. 715–17.
80. Fitzpatrick, 'Modernisation of the Irish female', p. 174.
81. Deirdre Mageean, 'Irish women in Chicago', unpublished paper, conference on *Women in the Migration Process*, Worpswede, Germany, 4–7 November 1990.
82. Annie Carroll letters, 1883–1906; biographical information from Roberta Fosdal, Jefferson, Wisconsin.

83. Mary Malone, 24 January 1877, Schrier collection.
84. 'Story of an Irish cook', pp. 715–17.
85. James A. Reford, 9 April [1873].
86. Maggie Black, 12 February and 16 March 1891, D.2041/Bundle 13, PRONI.
87. Maggie Black, 25 September and 23 October 1890, D.2041/Bundle 13, PRONI.
88. Mary Quin, undated letter [1873?], and Arthur Quin, 18 September 1876, D.1819/3 and 6, PRONI.

3 Superfluous and unwanted deadweight: the emigration of nineteenth-century Irish pauper women

Dympna McLoughlin

Introduction

Over fifty thousand pauper women were assisted to emigrate from Irish Workhouses to North America in the period 1840–70.[1] Neither the lives of these women nor their involvement in large-scale emigration schemes has been previously documented. This chapter sets the context of these emigrations and then presents a case study of a scheme to remove thirty-three paupers from the South County Dublin Workhouse in Ireland to Quebec, Canada, in 1863.[2]

Workhouses and the Poor Law

Four years after the New Poor Law Act was passed in England and Scotland, the Irish Poor Relief Act came into effect in 1838. All existing structures of outdoor relief were abolished and one single institution, the Workhouse, was the only option now open to the destitute.[3] Accordingly, 130, later 163, Workhouses were built throughout the country. In keeping with the philosophy underlying the framing of the Poor Relief Act, utilitarian buildings without comfort or ornamentation were erected. Any one of these buildings could accommodate up to 3,000 paupers with separate rooms for the different sexes, an infirmary, schoolroom, courtyard and living quarters for the Workhouse functionaries.

In an age of *laissez-faire* individualism, poverty was perceived as an outward manifestation of the failure of individuals to secure work and support themselves because of idleness, laziness and other associated personal defects. Structural causes of widespread poverty in Ireland were completely overlooked. With the ending of the Napoleonic wars in 1815, the Irish economy was undergoing gradual but significant changes, the nature of which would not become evident until the Famine and the subsequent economic and class displacements of the 1850s. Individuals who were destitute through illness or misfortune were perceived as the 'deserving poor'. It was for this category of people that the Poor Law was intended. With a jaundiced view of human nature, the Poor Law administrators wished to offer only a minimal mode of relief, and only to the 'deserving poor': otherwise there was a fear that paupers (deserving and otherwise) would readily give up work, preferring to be supported by the state.

Workhouses were supervised by unpaid Poor Law Guardians. These were local men of substantial wealth, in effect representatives of those on whom a charge was levied for the upkeep of the destitute poor in their area. Any decrease in the Workhouse numbers resulted in a corresponding drop in the amount they had to pay. The Board of Guardians therefore had a vested interest in maintaining the minimum possible number of Workhouse inmates.

Physically the Workhouses were harsh and grim buildings. Food riots were common as a result of a minimalist and barely sustaining regime of bread, porridge, milk, gruel with the occasional meat soup.[4] The latter luxury consisted of two oxheads boiled in enough water to feed one hundred inmates.[5] The individuals in charge of running these institutions had little to recommend them. With the exception, perhaps, of the position of Master, few respectable persons sought employment as Workhouse functionaries. They were often accused of many irregularities, total lack of interest in their jobs and in the persons under their care, of professional incompetency, laxity and deliberate cruelty.[6] Charges levelled against the Master and his male assistants included filling out false entries on the admittance books and thus inflating the number of inmates in the house, theft, drunkeness and the sexual abuse of both male and female inmates. In the Tralee Union in 1844, sixteen schoolgirls issued complaints against the Master. It was established that his conduct towards them was 'most improper' and that the illness of the pauper Bridget Norton resulted from 'terror operating on the mind of the child and induced by the conduct of the master towards these children'.[7] Only occasionally were charges of violation and sexual violence brought to a court of law. In the Dublin Union in 1863 a wardsman was accused of being 'in the habit of getting boys into bed with him at night for the purpose of commiting unnatural offences'.[8] The sexual abuse of young boys was considered a serious charge and much more grievous than the rape of young girls and women. Women who complained of sexual assault were in many instances penalised for their outspokenness.

Considering the physical hardship of the Workhouse, the food scarcity, unremitting discipline and instances of cruelty and abuse, the question needs to be posed: why did paupers submit themselves to these institutions? The Workhouse system, despite all its limitations, did provide a buffer between life and death for the destitute.[9] Because of the well publicised and deliberately unattractive nature of life within the Workhouse, such as the splitting up of families, the surrendering of all personal resources, poor diet and strict discipline, the Poor Law Commissioners hoped that able-bodied labourers would keep themselves outside such an institution.

Whilst the Workhouses did house large numbers of the Irish poor, the

Poor Law Act of 1838 was never completely and uniformly enforced. In no instance did the provision of Workhouse relief correspond exactly with the Poor Law Act. Furthermore, no two unions carried out exactly the same relief procedures. Always there was variation between districts and this variation at local level and within micro-regional economies is the key to understanding the functioning of the Poor Law in the Irish context.

Admittance to the Workhouse

According to the Poor Law Act only those paupers born and resident within a clearly defined electoral area were entitled to poor relief within that area. Thus the tendency of the pauper class to 'wander about' and gain relief in other electoral areas would be effectively curtailed (or so it was presumed). Thus contained, their geographical mobility was also hampered. It was hoped that this would end begging, vagrancy and its associated social ills. In theory then, the Workhouse clerk would also have an accurate account of the number, ages and the condition of the poor within his circumscribed area. The very fundamental premiss of the Poor Law, in curbing the travels of the destitute, was challenged by the fact that geographical mobility was the essence of survival for many paupers. In practice, the institution of the Workhouse did not discourage pauper mobility. Many Workhouse functionaries saw nothing amiss in taking in pauper 'lodgers' and effectively ignored the instructions to provide only for paupers resident in their local area. In the Coleraine Union in 1848 a resolution was passed where 'the illegality of admitting casual tramps, ordinary vagrants and overnight lodgers was recognised and the practice ordered to be curtailed with the exception of cases of severe destitution of persons taken suddenly ill'.[10] The provision of relief was qualified for a time, but never totally withdrawn. In Dingle, female paupers were regularly sent off the premises to wash clothes in the local river and many took the opportunity to take a few days off from the Workhouse regime.[11] When a batch of women sent out from the South Dublin Workhouse to make their confirmation returned to the Workhouse late that evening under the influence of drink, the laxity of that particular house was temporarily at least brought to a halt.[12] Thus whilst the accessibility of Workhouse relief was periodically curtailed it was never totally denied to wandering paupers. Much depended upon the particular Workhouse Master. Some were characterised by a greater degree of flexibility and compassion than others. No Workhouse rigidly adhered to the strict principles of the Poor Law at all times.

If the Workhouse did little to curtail the mobility of paupers, neither was it perceived by them as a permanent abode. For the most part (omitting the aged and the infirm), the Workhouse was perceived by paupers as a place to be resorted to in sickness or in particularly pressing economic circumstances. It is inaccurate to project the modern notion of Workhouses — as loathsome places of confinement, degradation and eventual death — back in time. Too deep an immersion into official sources such as Parliamentary Papers, letters of the Poor Law Commissioners and other official proceedings, yields an understanding of the theoretical basis of the Poor Law but a very skewed impression of its actual operation.

The functioning of the system as perceived by Poor Law administrators and officials in both Ireland and England was altogether different from that perceived and utilised by paupers. At its simplest, instead of a uniform, centralised system of Workhouse relief, every Workhouse operated on a highly individualistic basis as the result of local economies, and to a lesser extent the personalities, foibles and values of Guardians and functionaries. Attention then should be placed not on the initial power in setting up these institutions but on the maintenance of power within the system and the negotiation of power and control between the government, Guardians, functionaries and inmates.[13]

The paupers of this study are firmly embedded in a micro-region or locality — the South County Dublin Union. The utilisation of the workhouse Minute Books as a primary source allows us to see how everyday life within the Workhouse intermeshed with ambitious schemes for pauper removal through emigration. Thus, in the Minute Books, ordinary daily happenings within the Workhouse such as quarrels, births and disturbances, are intermeshed with plans for the removal of female paupers. Through this detailed analysis of place, time and specific female emigration schemes, we can see that both the Poor Law Guardians and the paupers were aware of the larger world and possible migration strategies and destinations.

Why the emigration of women?

Able-bodied females constituted the largest category of Workhouse inmates. They tended to outnumber their male counterparts by a 3:1 ratio (see Table 3.1). There was a general belief that female paupers remained in the Workhouse as immovable deadweight — a permanent burden on the rates of the union. The proportion of aged and infirm males and females tended to be comparable though infirm females were slightly overrepresented.

Table 3.1 Categories of inmates in New Ross (1853), Cork (1860) and Dublin South (1854) Poor Law Unions

	ABLE – BODIED		AGED AND INFIRM		YOUTHS	
	Male	Female	Male	Female	Male	Female
NEW ROSS	185	559	149	153	252	253
CORK	170	562	229	575	163	104
DUBLIN	329	848	145	149	593	524

The large number of pauper women resident within the Workhouse undermined the contemporary assumption that all women functioned within a framework of stable domesticity. Evidence of the fact that these women were not tied to a single abode was their high rate of geographical mobility.[14] Further evidence of the absence of a rooted domestic existence was the frequent angry and frantic tirades of Workhouse functionaries against 'unfit mothers' and the constant problem of accommodating foundlings and abandoned children within the Workhouse.[15] Pauper women were also erroneously assumed to be prodigiously fertile. In the newly-sensitised Malthusian age, these women were perceived as recklessly bearing children outside the bounds of legal marriage. Furthermore the wages of sin (their offspring) were left in the Workhouse raising both the poor rate and the moral indignation of the self-declared 'decent and respectable citizens of the neighbourhood' who had to pay for the upkeep of these unwanted bastards.[16]

The Poor Law administrators acknowledged the remarkable capacity of pauper women to survive without the assistance of their men, by treating them as regular labourers for wages and equally as capable as men of their class of supporting themselves and their children. Romantic concepts of women as fragile and helpless creatures were exclusively reserved for the middle class. The then emerging concept of 'femininity' was, in effect, a class ideology of female dependency.[17] It might be thought that it would have been totally inappropriate to apply this social construct to female paupers, a class who had to be resourceful and independent in order to survive. The actual dependency that went with sickness and old age was, however, always feared by this group as these events posed a real risk to their very survival.

The reasons why pauper women entered the Workhouse were many. According to the Poor Law Act, relief was only to be given to individuals who were unable to support themselves or their families. Many women declared themselves to be incapacitated through injury or sickness or were rendered destitute and friendless on the death of a parent or relative. In a fewer number of cases they pleaded desertion by a husband. Most times they entered along with their children, not when destitute but when the subsistence level of the family economy was in crisis, as in winter weather when they could no longer travel, sell or beg. A significant number of admissions were of single women who had left the Workhouse to go into 'situations', as domestic servants, and had returned pregnant. Other reasons why women might enter the Workhouse temporarily were if they were rendered weak and unable to work, through illness or after the experience of childbirth. These women with valid reasons for seeking Workhouse admission were a major source of irritation to the Poor Law Commissioners. Nothing the Commissioners did reduced the number of female paupers and the Guardians were constantly seeking ways of removing this costly 'deadweight'. They made sporadic attempts to trace and prosecute husbands and fathers guilty of desertion. They tried also to send inmates to England where a relative or friend might have secured some work, but these inmates usually returned again. Finally, rather hamfisted attempts were made to offload inmates onto other institutions such as the prison, blind institute and lock hospital. None of these schemes offered a long-term solution to the perceived problem: an excessive number of destitute and fertile women lodged in Irish Workhouses.

Women of the Dublin Workhouse

The women who inhabited the Dublin Workhouse did not constitute an undifferentiated mudsill of nineteenth-century society. They constituted different groups with varying life experiences.

We should now look at two specific groups of women, whom I have characterised as 'the wretched' and 'the forsaken'. This will enable us to explore the nature of the 'problem' that the Poor Law Guardians perceived as being solvable through emigration, and only through emigration.

The wretched

Unfortunately the Workhouse Minute Books do not note the specific occupations of these women: however, these women are generally classified as destitute vagrants. The majority of these women were seasonal labourers who utilised the Workhouse during the winter months, pregnant women and those with young babies who were unable to travel and find work, elderly women who were sick and infirm, prostitutes, beggars, dealers and petty traders. Almost all these women entered the Workhouse alone or with their children: certainly without men. The women often claimed that they had been deserted by their husbands, a claim which must be treated with scepticism, as the Workhouse was often used as a family survival strategy. Women and children stayed within the Workhouse, maintained by the poor rate, until the husband had earned enough money to support them.[18] In other cases women had no intention of returning to live with their husbands.

These women can be easily categorised as the wretched. They drifted in and out of the Workhouse in times of penury, economic and seasonal scarcity, illness and general hard times. They utilised the Workhouse as a place of temporary refuge in lean times and left it when economic opportunities presented themselves outside, such as harvest work or other forms of seasonal agricultural employment. They had friends and relatives outside who kept them informed about prevailing economic conditions in Ireland, Britain and North America.

The forsaken

The 'forsaken' is the term used here to describe those women who were abandoned as infants and were brought up without parental or sibling bonds of affection. Prison wardens, Workhouse administrators, and Poor Law Guardians joined in unison in proclaiming that the most difficult class to deal with were the young girls who had been reared or had spent long periods in the Workhouse. These women were effectively institutionalised and were unable to carry out 'respectable' work. They were also subject to a moral classification based on 'repeated acts of indecency in language and demeanour'[19], which necessitated their separation from other inmates as

> much mischief must inevitably ensue if hardened profligates who disregard every moral tie and violate every serious duty are permitted to circulate without restraint amongst the young, the inexperienced and the weak minded of their own sex.[20]

Separate wards were set up for these women. Many were put to stone-breaking, in an attempt to control them and to bring some order into the running of the Workhouse. Such a punitive regime merely made matters worse. A prison warden proclaimed that these female pauper inmates

> seemed to be amenable to no advice, persuasion or punishment. When they are corrected even in the mildest manner for any breach of regulations they seem to lose all control of reason; they break the windows of their cells, tear up their bedding and in many other cases, when they have been secured before doing any more damage, they have torn the clothing with their teeth. Their language whilst in this state of excitement is shocking. They are not at all deficient in intelligence or capacity for better things. They learn quite as quickly or perhaps more quickly as the average of prisoners and when in school are generally very attentive.[21]

Seven women from the Workhouse were at that time in jail for behaving in a riotous manner and for setting fire to the Workhouse. This was not the first time in prison for any one of them. Of these women, Mary Kelly was first admitted to the Workhouse at the age of 16: in a three-and-a-half-year period she had been in prison five times, and had left and had been read-mitted to the Workhouse 13 times. Jane O Neill was also 16 when first admitted to the Workhouse. She had left and readmitted herself to the Workhouse up to 10 times in a nine-month period, along with numerous short spells in prison. The histories of Ellen Collins and Mary Weafer were similiar. Jane Kane had a different background in that she first entered the Workhouse at 14 years of age and was sent to jail 28 times between January 1852 and 9 June 1860. The freqency of her prison forays was probably due to the fact that her mother was a well-known Dublin brothel keeper and Jane took up residence in that establishment on quitting the Workhouse. The last young woman in this troublesome group was Mary–Ann Meehan, who was first admitted to the Workhouse on 13 January 1854 and had remained an inmate for three years before going out as a domestic servant.

She did not relish the work at all, preferring to return to the Workhouse. Her life since then had oscillated between prison and the Workhouse.[22]

The discharging of these young women from the Workhouse meant that they resorted to 'improper means of support': prostitution.[23] The concern of the Poor Law Guardians was not with their 'loss of virtue' but with the long-term repercussions of their careers. First of all, their careers were usually brief. The young women returned to the Workhouse pregnant or sought the Workhouse hospital to find relief from venereal maladies. The frequent issuing of permission slips to these women to spend time out of the Workhouse was seen as unwise. Their stay outside was too short to be a relief to the poor rates and contributed to what were regarded as two of the worst evils of the contemporary milieu—pregnancy and prostitution.

Workhouses were always overcrowded and children reared in them, most especially girls, were believed to continue in the vicious ways of their mothers. The extent of overcrowding in the Dublin Union was most alarming. The medical officer attested in 1854 that the Workhouse was in an excessively overcrowded state. There were 292 two-tier beds and 438 three-tier beds. The diseased and dying in the infirmary lay two to a bed, no doubt accelerating the death rate.[24] A further cause of concern was the rising number of syphilitic cases, with 51 females and 12 males suffering from the illness. The Master ruled that those so diseased were no longer to be admitted to the Workhouse but sent to the Westmoreland Street Lock Hospital, there to secure medical relief.[25]

Linked with overcrowding was the fighting, and in some instances riots, caused by troublesome women. In 1848 it was agreed that the Matron could inflict solitary confinement as a punishment on refractory females. She was subsequently criticised by the Roman Catholic chaplain of the house who stated that:

> her cruelty is beyond expression ... calls for the respectable Guardians to put an end to her tyranny as Bridget Murphy who had a child at her breast was confined to her cell for five hours and her child removed from her during that period.[26]

Despite this and similiar criticisms, the Matron continued with these punishments. However, the complaints mounted and the Master was asked to furnish the Board of Guardians with a report justifiying the excessive number of punishments meted out by himself, the Matron and the schoolmaster. He gave the following reply:

> an account of the universal degree of insurbordination that has existed in the Workhouse during the past year ... I may be permitted to state that the number of improper women submitted during that time average from 120–140 (while in the Rush Union the number of similiar characters did not exceed 11–12) to which may be added the fact that a large number of young females was selected for emigration and their minds buoyed up with the expectation of soon commencing a new and agreeable course of life whereby a resolution by the Board ... their departure was prohibited and the hope of permanently bettering themselves utterly destroyed from which time they have become discontented sometimes unmanageable.[27]

The Master was acquitted of all charges of excessive zeal in punishing female inmates.

Aside from the factors of female overcrowding, syphilitic illness and rumbustiousness whilst in the house, the Guardians were acutely aware of the tendency of pauper women to form temporary sexual alliances and then return and use the Workhouse as a lying-in hospital. Along with these social fears, the Poor Law Guardians, as ratepayers, were most vocal in complaining about the amount of rates levied for children left in the Workhouse when the mother absconded. The presence of so many undesirable inmates must have prompted the Guardians to reconsider schemes for removing such women permanently. Frequently the Master asked for special committees to be appointed to consider the

> best means to be adopted to improve the conduct of the refractory young female inmates.[28]

He declared that all the usual methods of submission and control had failed and that 'the training received in the Workhouse had not fitted them successfully for all the ordinary occupations of persons in their station of life'.[29] He was in fact acknowledging that all socially acceptable methods of control had failed with these women. They were troublesome to keep in the Workhouse and could not work outside except immorally. The only way to deal with them was to get rid of them permanently. He urged the Board to adopt a plan for the emigration of this group to the colonies. Significantly, the number of disorderly was here put at 30: earlier emigration schemes had been much larger, involving groups of between 70 and 200 women. It is therefore reasonable to suggest that this group of 30 were carefully selected troublemakers.

Forsaken pauper women were the most irksome, troublesome and costly of inmates. Fighting amongst each other and with their betters, dragging around herds of children after them, slipping out of the Workhouse to attend fairs and markets and returning after long intervals with long and complicated stories of hardship, they used a host of ploys to gain access to the Workhouse when ill with venereal disease, prior to the birth of a child or when seeking refuge in inclement weather. Finally, women reared in the Workhouse showed no taste for work as domestic servants or as agricultural labourers. Despite the best efforts of the Poor Law Guardians in all 163 Poor Law Unions, the Minute Books of these institutions testify that female inmates were perceived as 'unmovable deadweight'. Sending the inmates to England or giving them passes to roam around the country did nothing to reduce the problem. Sending them to the colonies was increasingly seen as an ideal solution. At least then there was a guarantee that they would not come back.

Life within the Workhouse and training for emigration

Paupers were set to work in the Workhouse mainly to relieve the burden of the poor rate, paid by the ratepayers of the district. Either the paupers would do work within the Workhouse, which would save the hiring of outside labour, or else they became actively involved in the labour market as agricultural labourers, thus relieving the ratepayers of the cost of their support.[30] A second reason why paupers were put to work was that it was a most effective mode of disciplining them and thus maintaining order within the Workhouse. It was also hoped that any training they received would equip them for the outside labour market, so that they would eventually leave the Workhouse and earn their own livings. How then were these pauper women equipped for their future work as domestic or agricultural servants in the Canadian outback?

Workhouses operated without kitchen utensils, crockery, or tableware. Pauper meals were served out of a large stirabout boiler and onto tin plates. The preparation of food was basic. Despite spending many years as 'cooks' within the Workhouse, pauper women never used a range or a stove. On entering domestic employment in the homes of the well-to-do in Ireland, England or North America they were confronted for the first time by a stove and a whole host of cooking utensils. The pauper quarters within the Workhouse were 'furnished' with the most rudimentary of beds, tables and benches, so that little time and care was needed for their maintenance. The sweeping out of rooms was the very limit of household work within the Workhouse and even then it was only sporadically carried out.[31] Perhaps of most significance was the fact that Workhouse paupers were not trained in the different codes of conduct appropriate to domestic servants and other forms of hired help. Not surprisingly then, Workhouse paupers were rarely sought after as domestic servants in Ireland. Their lack of training and spiritedness were well known. Whilst there was a widespread belief that all servants would steal from their employers, if an opportunity arose, pauper domestics were doubly suspect in this regard. Finally, militating against their employment in Ireland was the 'immoral' nature of some of these young women and the suspected dark designs they might have on the uninitiated men of respectable households.

In general, Irish domestic servants did not fare well in North America. The incompetence of the Irish Biddy has long been noted.[32] None have delved any deeper and asked whether these women might have had any other skills that could explain their great attraction to cities. Workhouse pauper women in particular had skills to market in the emerging urban industrial centres.

All women in Irish Workhouses received an industrial training. Inmates were engaged in spinning, weaving and various forms of needlework. The scale of these pursuits may be gauged from the fact that in the Ennistymon Union in 1857 the female paupers were engaged in the manufacturing of outfits for four hundred inmates.[33] This constituted a sizeable undertaking, as dresses, petticoats, shirts and chemises had to be made up for each individual. Other savings to the Union from this branch of needlework included the repair and upkeep of inmates' clothes, which constituted a sizeable economy. Women were also adept at the rough sewing needed for the repair of the houses' mattresses, to the extent that the administrators of the Killarney Union suggested that the female paupers be put to making the mattresses and bolsters of the Killarney Lunatic Asylum.[34] A section of the Poor Law prevented inmates from competing with outside labour: despite this, Workhouses actively engaged in manufacturing. In the Limerick Union, for example, the women manufactured shirts for profit,[35] in Dublin they made gloves[36] and many other Unions engaged in lace-making, embroidery, crochet, the knitting of stockings and the flowering of muslin. Other activities included the spinning and weaving of cotton, flax and wool and the working of leather. All these activities were the work of women, with the exception of the weaving which was sometimes carried out by young boys. The men were put to their own trades, such as tailoring, coopering, shoemaking and carpentry. An essential point to note, then, is that these female pauper inmates were skilled, but at industrial rather than domestic pursuits.

Assisted family emigration from the Workhouse

A frequent request to the Poor Law Commissioners was for them to grant a supplementary sum of money to individuals to whom a passage remittance had already been sent, to facilitate their emigration to a family member on the other side of the Atlantic. In a study of the Minutes of the Dublin South County Union there were fifty individual petitions for emigration in the period 1848–67. This was rather a small-scale movement without any dramatic repercussions. The Poor Law Guardians were only involved in facilitating this movement, not in promoting or organising it. This family emigration was not gender specific.

Remittances sent to Workhouse inmates illustrate the diversity and flexibility of family and kin bonds. By far the greatest number of remittances were sent to children left in the Workhouse while the parents or, most often, the mother emigrated. These children were left in the Workhouse for up to five years while the parent/mother settled in Canada or the United States and saved a sufficient sum to send for them.

The second most usual request for aid was to assist the emigration of whole families. Surprisingly few were for wives and children left in the Workhouse while the husband emigrated. In two instances it was the wives who sent for their husbands and children. In other instances, women were facilitated in their emigration by their sisters, friends and, in single instances, by a brother, father and uncle. There were also cases of sisters sending for brothers, and youngsters sending for aged parents. The Poor Law Guardians complemented these remittances with an outfit for the journey and sometimes with provisions, but the amount of money given in these assisted family emigration schemes never went beyond two pounds.

This family emigration would have gone ahead regardless of assistance. Financial assistance (by the Guardians) just made for a speedier departure.

Leaving children behind in the Workhouse was part of the emigration strategy of the very poorest individuals. The Workhouse was also used as a safe place to leave young children, who would have been unable to survive a long sea voyage and the initial harsh conditions encountered until their parent(s) secured steady employment. Therefore, the large number of children left in the Workhouse at any particular time does not necessarily reflect callousness on the part of the parent in 'deserting' them.[37] While Workhouse conditions were subsistence standard, with a high rate of child mortality, a child would have a better chance of surviving its initial years in the Workhouse, rather than facing an Atlantic crossing. The age at which the majority of children were sent for was between 8 and 11 years, an age when they had survived the Workhouse regime and had therefore proved both their strength and resilience. They were also now able to survive the Atlantic crossing and make an economic contribution to the family unit.

In many cases it was the mother who remitted a sum of money towards the emigration of her children. Ellen Walsh was listed as reared in the Workhouse when in 1856 her mother, who was in Australia, paid her passage out.[38] Ellen wanted an additional five pounds for sea stores for herself and her sister who was in a 'situation' (domestic service) in Tallaght. The young sisters intended to sail early in April and wanted the Board of Guardians to assist them, to ensure their departure. One mother concerned about a safe Atlantic passage for her two daughters saved up enough money not only for their emigration but also for a woman who would look after and protect them during the sea crossing.[39]

In addition to the independent emigration of single women leaving their children behind them, those sent in earlier group emigration schemes also left young children in the Workhouse. Such was the case of Mary Knight who was sent out in 1853, and, four years later, sent the sum of three pounds to the Guardians to take out her child, Richard O'Donnell.[40] Teresa O'Gara, also a participant in a group emigration scheme, sent for her sister, Eliza, who had been a Workhouse inmate for fourteen years.[41] In the following year, James Magee told the Poor Law Commissioners that 'his wife had emigrated some years since and sent him ten pounds to pay his passage to New York and that of their four children'.[42] Women thus made excellent primary migrators,[43] a fact that did not go unnoticed by contemporaries interested in promoting emigration, such as Vere Foster,[44] and indeed the Poor Law Commissioners.

However, a category which was poorly represented in these 'family' emigration schemes was that of unmarried women with children. These women were without an extended network of support. They fall into the broad group previously described as 'forsaken'. Having been orphaned or deserted, and living most of their lives within the institution of the Workhouse, meant that they did not have the opportunity to build up a network of close personal contacts which could manifest itself in the form of an American remittance. Thus, the failure of any of this group to be removed through spontaneous emigration meant that they became ideal candidates for the group emigration schemes.

Workhouse-sponsored group female pauper emigration schemes

The earliest documented female emigration scheme was in 1831, when 59 girls from the Cork Foundling Hospital were brought to New South Wales. In 1832, several contingents of girls were aided to sail to Australia. Given the very long and hazardous sea journey and the paltry attractions of what was still a penal colony, women were reluctant to emigrate to this place. It was with great difficulty that the emigration quotas were filled up. Complaints about the absence of women and the scarcity of labour were soon replaced with complaints about the unsuitable characters and scandalous morals of street women who, colonists believed, had been 'shovelled out' to them. As a response to these complaints, schemes for the emigration of Workhouse female orphans, young enough to be untainted and 'trained in the habits of useful industry' were implemented. The first of these groups set sail in June 1848, comprising 185 girls from 10 Poor Law Unions.[45] After 1850 the Australian colonists were no longer willing to build their country on the 'refuse' from Irish Workhouses. During the two years the scheme was in operation, 4,175 girls were sent out.[46] The South Dublin Union, the focus of this article, sent out small contingents to Australia. In November 1848 it sent out 31 orphans, in October 1849 it sent 7, in December it sent 4 and on 31 March 1860 it sent 7.

Fearing that they would be dragged into bankruptcy with the mounting costs of supporting what they saw as a destitute, exponentially increasing pauper population, Irish landowners and merchants who paid the poor rate were determined to protect their own interests. If Australia could no longer be relied upon as a landing place for Irish destitutes, then Quebec was an alternative, cheap, pauper destination. In many instances, the Master and vested local interests overrode the legal and administrative framework of the Poor Law and shipped out female paupers to Quebec without the knowledge or consent of the Poor Law Guardians.[47] These schemes for pauper emigration were quite ambitious, ranging from 30 to 400 inmates in any one shipment.

In those schemes which were documented (and how representative they were of the movement in general it is difficult to say) it was usual for a plan to be proposed and a committee appointed to inquire into the number of females 'suitable' for emigration. To avoid public notice, these emigrations were usually rather hastily carried out. Thus, in the Dublin Union in 1854, it was reported that there were 200 females aged between 16 and 30 who had been upwards of three years in the Workhouse and were keen to emigrate. The Commissioners urged that this scheme be carried out as quickly as possible and that tenders be placed in the newspapers for a loan to get the scheme running and to pay for provisions, conveyance to port and passage out.[48]

The haste with which this scheme was set up may have reflected a fear of unfavourable public reaction. The *Freeman's Journal*, the most widely read contemporary newspaper, fulminated about

> the heartless and inhuman system which gathers together the healthiest and most vigorous female emigrants because if retained at home they would prove the largest burden on the rates — dressed them up for a few shillings, packed them on board an emigrant ship and thought no more of the ship or its freight rejoicing only in the diminution of the workhouse numbers and rates.[49]

Similiarly some clergymen objected to 'the needless and indecent haste in which friendless and confiding emigrants are cast upon their own resources in a strange country'.[50] These schemes were viewed as leading to the loss of female modesty and virtue. Pauper women, of course, were generally deemed to be already lacking in female modesty and virtue but this point was conveniently forgotten in the ensuing debate. Despite public disapproval of the 1854 Dublin Union scheme, a tender was accepted from Mr Miley, at five pounds and ten shillings per adult voyage to Canada. The provisions were to include 'above the regular ship allowance of meat, sugar, tea and flour'. Fifty-four women on the scheme were provided with 2 gowns, a shift and gingham, a flannel petticoat, a stiff petticoat, 2 calico shifts, 3 pairs of stockings, 1 pair of shoes, 1 warm cloak, 1 pair of stays, 2 caps, 1 neck kerchief, a bonnet, a coarse and a fine comb and, finally, a bag into which to place all their belongings. An additional eight pounds was given to the Matron, Mrs Butler, to take charge of the women during the crossing.

The selection of suitable inmates

The length of a woman's residency in the Workhouse was the main criteria used in her selection for emigration. This period of time as an inmate was deemed to be closely related to the probability, indeed the danger, of her remaining in the Workhouse on a permanent basis. A second factor was the woman's state of health, this being closely linked to her capacity to work and maintain an independent life. The fittest, healthiest, and therefore the most eligible, women were those aged between 14 and 30. By no coincidence these were also the child-bearing years: the younger the emigrants selected, the less was the likelihood of their having children and increasing the poor rate in Ireland. The marketable skills these women possessed was the third criteria of their selection. The industrial training received in the Workhouse was completely ignored: the Guardians valued only the women's domestic abilities. The automatic assumption was that all women were able, or should be able, to cook, clean and keep house. The final element in this selection procedure was the character of the intending emigrant, which included her conduct whilst in the Workhouse, her 'morals' and whether she was judged to be 'reformed' in that she was no longer involved in prostitution or any type of sexual alliances outside marriage. This judgement of 'character' included an enquiry to ascertain whether the woman had relatives or kin inside the Workhouse. If the woman had kin inside the Workhouse there was every chance that she would assist her kin to emigrate by sending them remittances, thereby initiating a whole chain of Workhouse pauper emigration.

The concern with these women's characters and domestic abilities was a reflection of the demand for household and farm servants in Canada. The Colonial Land and Emigration Commission helped to promote this emigration not to rid Irish Workhouses of a surplus of inmates but to fill a labour shortage, particularly a demand for female labourers in rural Ontario. The Poor Law Guardians were primarily interested in getting rid of these troublesome women at the lowest possible cost. Both interests were therefore served in the voluntary removal of large numbers of pauper women to rural Canada. Pointing to the market for the respectable labour of these pauper women, the Poor Law Guardians then counteracted any public criticism of these schemes, firstly, by stressing the individuals' willingness to emigrate and, secondly, by stating that they had the emigrants' best interests at heart in sending them to places where they were assured of work.

Canada was viewed by the Poor Law Commissioners as a country where all who were willing to labour would be able to earn a good living. They seemed unaware of the selectivity of the North American labour market where only individuals with certain skills and crafts were sought after. For the most part it is valid to argue that the Poor Law Guardians' prime concern was with the burden of pauperism in Ireland and the ultimate fate of the paupers in North America was secondary. Implicit in their written proceedings was a belief that paupers were responsible for their own poverty: shifting some of the paupers to North America would not only reduce the poor rate but force the paupers to work. This type of thinking is evidence of the inability of the Guardians to see that the broader structures of nineteenth-century Irish society made for pauperism; land clearances and consolidation; shifts in the fundamental nature of the economy from arable to pastoral; and the real lack of employment opportunities in an undeveloped and dependent colony. The Poor Law Guardians in fact blamed the poor for their poverty and ignored the structural determinants bringing about this condition.

On 9 August 1862, a motion was put to the Board of Guardians of the Dublin South Workhouse suggesting a scheme which would allow the emigration of:

> such young female inmates of the Workhouse who have been inmates for at least two years and who may be found suitable and deserving from good character and industrial acquirements.[51]

In this case the motion was *not* well received by the Poor Law Guardians, as they believed that such schemes cost more than they were worth. Furthermore, the Guardians believed that the population of the country was stabilising, in that the country's natural resources, the waste and boglands, were about to be utilised. Taking all this into consideration they believed they 'would not require any forced system of emigration'.[52] The cost of maintaining a pauper was a penny and a half a week, whilst emigration schemes cost a minimum of five pounds a person. In the longer term, however, since the union had carried out previous emigration schemes, the advantages were well known. The initial cost was a small price to pay for the permanent removal of troublesome inmates who might also contribute to the process of pauper emigration at no additional cost to the poor rate.

Aside from careful consideration of the timing of their arrival, great care was to be taken in the selection of inmates. On 9 May 1863 the visiting committee viewed the young women selected by the Matron. Assisting them in their task was a gentleman from America who had

> a perfect knowledge of the sort of person suitable for servants in the Canadas and the US.[53]

This unnamed gentleman urged them to exclude girls of tender years, or those physically frail or weak in any way. It was generally agreed that they were looking for women of good character, up to thirty years of age, and who had been at least four years an inmate of the Workhouse. Various ages were put forward as the most desirable at which to send out the women. Up to forty years was considered initially but then thirty was more generally agreed upon. However, 'age', as a category, did not generally mean a lot as few paupers had any accurate idea of their own ages and others either underestimated or overestimated their ages in order to be eligible for the scheme.

The real criterion of selection was the fact that these women were the most troublesome of inmates who had spent at least four years in the Workhouse, with the strong possibility that they might remain indefinitely. An unusual feature of this scheme was that the Matron, Mrs Sullivan, was allowed to accompany the young women (her two daughters were also included in the group). It is probable that the reason why the Matron accompanied that group was to provide a shred of respectability to the scheme. Workhouse paupers were not sheltered, repining violets, and neither were they known for their virtue, dependency or diffidence. Mrs Sullivan as chaperone would hardly make a difference to pauper behaviour patterns: she, along with the combined Workhouse administration, had had no effect on conduct whilst in the Workhouse. For the unsuspecting Canadian employers it was necessary to give the impression that these were poor and unfortunate women, but that, at the same time, they were decent and respectable, and thus needed to be chaperoned and protected. The appearance of the inmates in Canada was thus a crucial factor in their reception. It was important for Canadian employers to see well-dressed and sturdy women: otherwise these immigrant women would remain in Quebec, destitute, and effectively bring all such emigration schemes to an end. Thus departing emigrants had to be properly provisioned, so that they landed in the best of health and were ready to proceed further inland and immediately take up work. Therefore carefully worked-out details as to emigrant outfits and provisions were not the result of a sudden burst of magnanimity on the part of the Guardians. In fact it was realised that these were the crucial factors determining the success or failure of these schemes.

The names of the selected 33 women were listed in the Minute Books but no other additional information was given as to their ages, whether they had children, or had any sort of relationship or union with a man.[54] They included:

1.	Bridget Hanlon	2.	Adelaide Winston
3.	Sarah Sullivan	4.	Susan Kavanagh
5.	Margaret O'Brian	6.	Lucy Clare
7.	Bridget Byrne	8.	Eliza Redmond
9.	Mary Hickey	10.	Abbey Deegan
11.	Catherine Finn	12.	Hannah Wood
13.	Eliza Gallagher	14.	Rose Doyle
15.	Margaret McCann	16.	Ellen McDonnell
17.	Margaret Cosgrove	18.	Sarah Reilly
19.	Mary Greene	20.	Sarah Tyne
21.	Mary Anne Keefe	22.	Catherine Delaney
23.	Mary McCarthy	24.	Eliza Johnston
25.	Jane White	26.	Mary Whire
27.	Bridget Gannon	28.	Mary Connor
29.	Emily Buckely	30.	Teresa Powell
31.	Anne Sullivan	32.	Mary Carey
33.	Ann Cody		

Once the thirty-three emigrants were selected they were then fitted with an outfit for the journey. It was particularly comprehensive and included 1 bonnet, 2 caps, 2 shifts, 2 towels, 1 handtowel, 1 pair of scissors, 1 prayer-book, 1 cape, 2 dresses, one a wrapper, 3 pairs of stockings, 1 bag, 1 hair-brush, needles and thread, reading book, 1 shawl, 1 petticoat, 2 aprons, a cap and marine soap. The dresses, petticoats, shifts and aprons were made by the women and girls themselves.

Having selected the emigrants, the Guardians then made arrangements with a shipowner for their transportation.[55] The availability of shippers willing to transport emigrants across the Atlantic was never a problem. The transatlantic trade in individuals was a lucrative business, the profits considerable and the competition fierce. The government emigration agent at Quebec was contacted with a view to providing these women with work. Accordingly, one pound per head was given to him to dispose of the women. This allowance was commonly referred to as 'landing money'. Making landing money available gave the emigrants some means of proceeding to areas in the interior, where they could secure 'respectable' employment as agricultural labourers. The provision of landing money was also in the best interests of the Poor Law Guardians. Firstly, because the emigrants had the means to leave the cities of the eastern seaboard, they did not incur the wrath of articulate and influential city dwellers, who resented the transportation of paupers. Secondly, emigrants who could secure immediate employment had the best chance of doing well, accumulating savings and sending remittances back to their kin or friends in Ireland. After 1850, Mr Buchannon, the Colonial Land and Emigration Commissioner based in Quebec, made the provision of landing money a precondition of his attending to Workhouse emigrants. The Poor Law Guardians believed that the scattering of inmates was the key to the successful continuation of Workhouse emigration schemes and the provision of landing money was a fair price to pay for this. It took some time for them to realise that no amount of inducements made these Workhouse women settle in the rural homesteads of Canada.

The Dublin contingent of 33 women, along with the Matron, left for Liverpool on 20 June 1863.[56] As was usual with many of these schemes some inmates changed their minds prior to departure. Thus Ellen McDonnell decided not to go and was replaced by Mary Downes, whilst Theresa Powell was rejected by the Medical Officer and replaced by Anna Moran. The Guardians estimated that the cost of their riddance was ten pounds and seven shillings per woman, which brought the cost of this relatively small scheme to three hundred and seventy-eight pounds.

A letter from Mr Buchannon, the Colonial Land and Emigration Commissioner, arrived in the Dublin South Union on 18 July.[57] He stated that the girls sent out to him had all arrived in good health, with the exception of Sarah Sullivan, the Matron's daughter, who had died of consumption shortly after her arrival. The Guardians wanted more detail on the success of the scheme and requested Mr Buchannon to furnish them with specific information on the employment of these women. On 6 February 1864, Mr Buchannon's letter to the Dublin Workhouse functionaries arrived. He testily pointed to the

> unsuitability of some of these young women to the work they were called upon to perform in this country ... a large proportion are not fitted for service in country districts.[58]

Buchannon pointed out that the fault was not entirely with the Guardians of the Dublin Union but was common amongst similiar institutions in Ireland.

R.J. Willis, the local agent for Buchannon who was stationed in Ottawa, was more specific and wrote, with weariness, that he had done his best and placed the Dublin paupers in service at wages from one dollar to three and a half dollars per month. Having gone to considerable trouble to place the women in different rural districts, the majority of them packed up and left in less than a week. Willis described them, kindly, as inexperienced girls, unaccustomed to any kind of household work. The subagent in the interior, Neil Stewart, was more honest and stated

> I found that they cannot do a turn of work such as farming requires. They are not the class of girls that suits farmers, as they were brought up in an institution

where no such work is proffered. I regret that I did not succeed with them, but girls who could milk cows, wash and iron clothes and do plain cooking would easily get into good employment in this village and neighbourhood.[59]

These Workhouse paupers had no desire for an agricultural life in the Canadian wilderness and many made their way to the large cities and towns of the south-east coast where they were deemed to be 'ill paid and exposed to many temptations'.[60] Cities and the opportunities they presented for single young women were far more attractive than isolation coupled with domestic and agricultural drudgery in the Canadian outback.

By the end of April that same year the ladies of the Dublin Workhouse Visiting Society suggested that a training school be set up in which girls could be taught common household tasks as well 'as moral discipline that will fit them for earning their bread'.[61] Did Mr Willis, the agent, go into greater detail than was mentioned in the Workhouse Minute Books as to what precisely these young women might be employed at in Canadian towns and cities? It would seem that the women were supporting themselves as he would otherwise have mentioned if they had become the objects of public charity. The question is how precisely were these emigrant women earning their bread and what was it about their method of earning it that was so distasteful as to prompt the speedy setting up of a training school?

Conclusion

Schemes for assisting female pauper emigration must be viewed as a conservative and not a radical expression of government policy. The aim of the government was to control a volatile, mobile, economically astute, labouring class, either by institutionalising them or by forcing them to emigrate, thus making for the continuity of the existing social order but without dealing effectively with the problem of a displaced labouring class.

The local Poor Law Guardians, who paid poor rates towards the maintenance of Workhouse paupers, also viewed these schemes as a qualified success. It was qualified in that although the poor rate was temporarily reduced, and troublesome paupers got rid of, the reduction of poor rates was short-lived. More paupers merely filled up the empty spaces left in the Workhouses, especially if there was any chance of emigrating from that particular union.

Why, considering all the expense and bother, did the Irish Poor Law Guardians persist with so many of these schemes? The first point to note is that these schemes were selective. The women chosen usually had lived much of their lives within the Workhouse and had every likelihood of remaining on as 'immovable deadweight'. Their removal, albeit at substantial cost, was viewed as worthwhile. Their riddance meant the automatic reduction of the poor rate and also a reduction of the fertility rate in a context newly sensitised to the dangers of Malthusian overpopulation. Moreover, assistance in the emigration of these women was viewed as an investment. The Guardians were aware that individuals so assisted in turn aided others. Thus, the high cost of the initial emigration investment was worthwhile, in that it paid dividends by setting in motion a whole series of chain migrations. These group emigration schemes must be viewed as the beginning of a process of continuing pauper emigration. The women were, then, pioneers of later movements. Their emigration brought about an awareness of America as a desirable place of habitation and employment and America was thus tacked on to the Irish paupers' mental list of accessible residences. Following the publicity given to many of these schemes, many paupers entered the Workhouse as a deliberate part of an assisted emigration strategy. By concealing their resources and their contacts in America, they presented themselves as destitute, thereby fulfilling the requirements necessary to be put on the emigration list.

Despite the contemporary negative reaction to these ventures, they were not, in fact, mere 'shovelling out' schemes. It is true that specifically *female* emigration was promoted. But adequate preparations were made for their outfits and for the transatlantic voyage. Selected emigrants were adequately dressed and provided for, and given passage on a reputable vessel. In their adequate provisioning of emigrants, the Guardians were ensuring that the Workhouse paupers appeared fit and healthy, and thus immediately employable, on their arrival in Quebec. They therefore anticipated colonists' objections to the arrival of famished and destitute paupers in their midst. Furthermore, an outfit was given to the emigrant which gave her a better chance of employment and thus of assimilation. Communication with the Colonial Land and Emigration Commissioner was undertaken to ensure that emigrants got immediate employment and at the same time filled the labour deficit in the Canadian interior. It was only in the final aspect of the emigration—the women's settlement in Canada— that the shortcomings of these schemes became increasingly apparent. Pauper women would not settle and work in agricultural areas in the interior of Canada. They preferred the large urban centres where they could utilise the industrial skills acquired whilst resident in Irish Workhouses. It took over ten years for Buchannon to ponder his previous automatic association of women with domesticity and to take cognisance of their former life and experiences in Ireland. He then had to specify that women intended for emigration should have basic household skills if he was to settle them. Unfortunately, the Guardians paid no heed whatever to Buchannon's instructions, and it was women who had been in the Workhouse for long periods, and who had no domestic accomplishments, who continued to fill these schemes up to 1860.

Finally, how may these schemes be evaluated from the point of view of the pauper women themselves? There can be no doubt but that the majority emigrated voluntarily. Indeed some used the Workhouse as the only way of getting to America; as a well thought-out and deliberate part of their emigration strategy. It is doubtful that they ever considered settling in rural Canada. The available evidence of the Workhouse Minute Books would suggest that they had no intention of taking up positions as frontier labourers in the isolated Canadian outback, as this type of 'farming' bore no comparison to any of their previous seasonal pursuits in Ireland. Instead these Irish women sought out and survived in the large urban industrial centres of North America.

Notes

1. For background information on the 1834 Poor Law Act see Sir George Nicholls, *A History of the Irish Poor Law*, printed in 1856, and reprinted 1967 by Augustus M. Kelley Publishers, New York. On the functioning of the English Workhouse system see M.A. Crowther, *The Workhouse System 1834–1929: the History of an English Social Institution*, Methuen, London, 1983. These however do not deal with the emigration of paupers. For specific information on assisted female pauper emigration see D. McLoughlin, 'Shovelling out Paupers — Female Emigration from Irish Workhouses to North America 1840–70', University of Syracuse Ph.D. thesis, 1988.
2. The South County Dublin Union was also known as the Rathdown Union and covered 40,768 acres. I am grateful to Paul Ferguson, Map Librarian, Trinity College Dublin, for this information.
3. For further details of the setting up of the Irish Poor Law system see Gerard O'Brien, 'The establishment of the Poor Law System in Ireland 1838–43', *Irish Historical Studies*, Vol xxiii, No. 90, November 1982, pp. 97–120. See also Helen Burke, *The People and the Poor Law in Nineteenth-Century Ireland*, WEB, Dublin, 1987.
4. Mary Cullen, 'Breadwinners and providers: women in the household economy of labouring families', in M. Luddy and C. Murphy, eds, *Women Surviving*, Poolbeg, Dublin, 1989, pp. 85–107.
5. Twelfth Annual Report of the Poor Law Commissioners, 1859.
6. The work of Joseph Robins, *The Charity Child In Ireland*, Institute of Public Administration, Dublin, 1982, is excellent in this respect.
7. Minute Books (hereafter Minutes), Tralee Union, 10 September 1844.
8. Punishment of inmates usually involved being placed in a small dark room, called the black hole, for a period of days at a time, or ejection from the Workhouse. For further documentation of the schoolmaster sent for trial see the Minute Book, Dublin South Union, 23 May 1863.
9. The Famine Years were the obvious exception where newly set-up institutions were unable to cope with the scale and absolute nature of destitution.
10. Minutes, Coleraine Union, 12 June 1848.
11. Minutes, Dingle Union, 13 September 1851.
12. Minutes, Dublin South Union, 7 February 1852.
13. For a better idea of the argument see Eugene D. Genovese, *Roll, Jordan Roll*, Pantheon, New York, 1974. He argues that the system of slavery as perceived and operated by the planter was altogether different from the system of slavery as lived by slaves. These opposing views lead to tensions within the system but, for the scholar, create the possibility of an analysis of institutions or systems which might otherwise be presumed to have triumphed totally.
14. For evidence of this geographical mobility see D. McLoughlin, 'Shovelling Out Paupers', Ph. D thesis, pp. 111–17.
15. For a more detailed treatment of the problem of unwanted children in nineteenth-century Ireland, see D. McLoughlin, 'Infanticide in nineteenth-century Ireland', unpublished manuscript in the author's possession.

16. Parliamentary Papers relating to Bastardy; The Royal Commission in Poor Laws and Relief of Distress Report of Ireland, 1909, Vol. xxxviii, p. 70; The Select Committee on the state of the poor in Ireland, 1830, Vol. vii, p. 1827.

17. Neilson Hancock, 'The Workhouse as a mode of relief for widows and orphans', *Dublin Statistical Society Journal*, Vol. 1, 1855–6, p. 84. Also by the same author, 'The effects of the employment of Women illustrated by the results of the Factory system at Bradford in 1857', *Dublin Statistical Society Journal*, Vol. 11, 1857–60, pp. 439–44.

18. The Poor Law Guardians had already acknowledged the remarkable ability of pauper women to survive without the assistance of a husband, and the plea of desertion did not gain automatic Workhouse admission.

19. Minutes, Dublin South Union, 24 January 1852.

20. Minutes, Dublin South Union, 23 April 1852.

21. Sixth Annual Report of Convict Prisons in Ireland and recorded in the Minutes of the Dublin South Union, 9 June 1860.

22. Minutes, Dublin South Union. It would seem then, that these young women, brought up within the Workhouse, could not live for any extended period of time outside the institutions of Workhouse or jail.

23. Minutes, Dublin South Union, 3 June 1848.

24. Minutes, Dublin South Union, 10 December 1853.

25. Minutes, Dublin South Union, 29 October 1853.

26. Minutes, Dublin South Union, 22 April 1848.

27. Minutes, Dublin South Union, 10 September 1857.

28. Minutes, Dublin South Union, 10 September 1857.

29. Minutes, Dublin South Union, 19 November 1857.

30. Many of the Workhouses had their own patch of land which the inmates worked. As well as engaging in this work young boys might be sent to a hiring fair, in an attempt to gain employment as agricultural labourers. Usually Workhouse inmates did not compete so boldly with outside labourers and instead interested farmers came directly to the Workhouse to hire a batch of able-bodied young men for seasonal work such as sowing or harvesting. The chief objective of these farmers was to extract the maximum of labour from these inmates at little or no financial cost.

31. For the infrequent nature of this cleaning see Minutes, Limerick Union, 27 December 1845.

32. There is an extensive literature on the Irish Biddy. These include Hasia Diner, *Erin's Daughters in America*, John Hopkins University Press, Baltimore, 1983; Faye E. Dudden, *Serving Women: Household Service in Nineteenth Century America*, Wesleyan University Press, Middletown, 1983; David M. Katzman, *Seven Days a Week: Women and Domestic Service in Industralising America*, University of Illinois Press, Champaign, 1981: Thomas Dublin, *Women at Work: the Transformation of Work and Community in Lowell, Massachusetts 1828–1868*, Columbia University Press, New York, 1976. Dublin's work is interesting in that he acknowledges the involvement of Irish immigrant women in mill and factory work.

33. Minutes, Ennistymon Union, 12 July 1857.

34. Minutes, Killarney Union, 9 February 1852.

35. Minutes, Limerick Union, 14 July 1853.

36. Minutes, Dublin Union, 20 August 1853.

37. On the week ended 5 May 1845 it was estimated that there were 128,799 young people under 18 years of age in Irish Workhouses.

38. Minutes, Dublin South Union, 17 March 1856.

39. Minutes, Dublin South Union, 22 November 1856.

40. Minutes, Dublin South Union, 24 January 1857.
41. Minutes, Dublin South Union, 1 July 1865.
42. Minutes, Dublin South Union, 24 June 1854.
43. Minutes, Dublin South Union, 25 June 1855.
44. Vere Foster was a nineteenth-century philanthropist and was well-known for his favourable views on assisted female emigration. For further information see Mary McNeill, *Vere Foster 1819–1900: an Irish Benefactor*, Institute of Irish Studies, Belfast, 1971 and Ruth–Ann Harris, '"Where the Poor Man is not Crushed Down to Exalt the Aristocrat": Vere Foster's programmes of assisted emigration', in Patrick O'Sullivan, ed., *The Meaning of the Famine*, Volume 6 of *The Irish World Wide*, forthcoming.
45. Minutes, Dublin South Union, 28 October 1848.
46. A total of 4,175 were acknowledged by the Poor Law Commissioners as having been sent to Australia in the two-year period 1848–50.
47. For example, in the Killarney Union, it was documented in the Minutes that 'emigrants have been allowed to embark without the Guardians having previously obtained the consent of the Commissioners'. No further details were given as to the extent and composition of that scheme.
48. Minutes, Dublin South Union, 11 March 1854.
49. *Freeman's Journal*, Dublin, 12 April 1848.
50. Minutes, Dublin South Union, 22 April 1848.
51. Minutes, Dublin South Union, 9 August 1862.
52. Minutes, Dublin South Union, 9 August 1862.
53. Minutes, Dublin South Union, 9 May 1863.
54. Minutes, Dublin South Union, 23 May 1863.
55. For further details on the competition amongst shippers for emigrants see McLoughlin, 'Shovelling Out Paupers', Chapter 9.
56. Minutes, Dublin South Union, 20 June 1863.
57. Minutes, Dublin South Union, 18 July 1863.
58. Minutes, Dublin South Union, 6 February 1864.
59. Minutes, Dublin South Union, 6 February 1864.
60. The city as a place of temptation especially for unaccompanied Irish women was the chief criticism Catholic clergymen had of these schemes.
61. Minutes, Dublin South Union, 30 April 1864.

4 Geographies of migration and religion: Irish women in mid-nineteenth-century Liverpool

Lynda Letford and Colin G. Pooley

Introduction

Most geographical studies of the Irish in nineteenth-century Britain make a number of important assumptions about the definition, composition and experience of the people involved. First, the ready availability of census evidence, which records place of birth for all those enumerated, leads inevitably to the definition of Irishness according to where a person was born. Thus all those recorded as born in Ireland are designated Irish, and all those born elsewhere are not Irish. This leads to obvious difficulties. It ignores those born in England of Irish parents who may feel strongly Irish, and it misclassifies those born in Ireland of English (or other) parents who may have no strong attachment to Ireland. It also ignores one of the most obvious divisions within the Irish population, as the census provides no evidence on religious affiliation. Thus Irish-born Catholics, Protestants and those with no strong religious affiliation are lumped together and are assumed to have the same experiences. Whilst some authors readily acknowledge these difficulties,[1] and a few have used other sources to examine the religious composition of specific populations,[2] all too frequently the experience of being Irish in Britain is seen through a single lens which fails to reveal the complexity and diversity of Irish communities in England.[3]

Secondly, geographical studies of residential location, segregation and the environment in which people lived are too often based on analyses of household heads, usually male. The experiences of women who were not household heads, of children, and of other family members, are often neglected. Given that women and children were likely to spend more time in and around the home than most men, it is important to examine the impact of particular residential environments on the lives of all family members.[4]

Thirdly, most geographical studies examine spatial variations and their environmental associations at a relatively large spatial scale. They clearly identify the major clusters of Irish residence, but fail to reveal more subtle variations in residential patterns between courts and from one end of a street to another.[5] Even less attention is paid to spatial and social relations within households. Who interacted with whom within particular households and how did the nature of household and family relations change in the process of migration?[6]

This chapter focuses on the experience of women in mid-Victorian Liverpool, examining in detail the relationships between residential location, employment, family, home environment, birthplace and religion. It centres particularly on one significant group in nineteenth-century Liverpool, Irish Catholic women, and asks how and to what extent their experience of life in Liverpool was different from that of other women. More specifically, we examine the hypothesis that the experience of Irish Catholic women in Liverpool owed more to the structural characteristics of the Liverpool labour and housing markets which affected all women, and to the male-dominated society in which all women lived, than it did to their Irishness or their Catholicism.

In general terms the history of Liverpool and its Irish community is well researched.[7] As a major port facing the Irish Sea, Liverpool had a long history of Irish settlement and a well-established Irish community in the early nineteenth century. Together with Glasgow it bore the brunt of Irish Famine migration, and by 1851 had the second largest Irish-born community in Britain. Numerically, London had more Irish, but proportionately the Liverpool–Irish community was much more important.[8] By 1851 there were 83, 813 Irish–born enumerated in the city, representing 22.3 per cent of Liverpool's total population. Liverpool was a large city (population 353, 313 in 1851), with extensive suburbs and a well-developed urban structure, and the Irish community was a distinctive feature of its internal geography. From the early nineteenth century Irish migrants had settled disproportionately in central and dockside areas, especially those to the north of the city centre. In these areas the Irish became associated with poverty, decayed housing, an unpleasant environment and a high incidence of disease. Such images of Irish Famine migrants became attached to most Irish, who experienced discrimination and violence in the city throughout the nineteenth century.[9] It is against this background that the experiences of Irish women in mid-nineteenth century Liverpool are examined.

Sources and methods

It is extremely difficult to gain reliable and comprehensive information on both migrant origin and religion. From 1841, decennial British census enumerators' books recorded place of birth[10] but, for those born outside their country of enumeration, this was usually only stated by country; thus it is not possible to identify systematically Irish migrants in Liverpool by their place of birth within Ireland[11] and a 100-year confidentiality rule prevents use of these data after 1891. Place of birth is the only comprehensive indicator of migrant origin for the mid-nineteenth century, but it must be re-emphasised that it does not necessarily equate with nationality, ethnicity or cultural affiliation and, of course, second-generation migrants who may have continued to have a strong attachment to their parents' place of origin are excluded.

Despite its drawbacks, this study uses birthplace data from the 1851 census enumerators' books for Liverpool to attribute migrant origin. In the analysis three broad categories are used: those born in Ireland; those born in Liverpool; and those born elsewhere in England, Scotland or Wales. Inevitably, some of those born in Liverpool and elsewhere may have had Irish parents, and thus be part of a second-generation Irish community. However, following the Famine, the majority of Liverpool Irish in 1851 were relatively recent arrivals, and thus this problem is less serious than it would be later in the century.

Information on religious adherence is only available through sporadic and, often, surrogate sources. Although the only census of religion to be taken in Britain was carried out in 1851,[12] this was a snapshot of church attendance and is no use at an individual level. Although membership lists do survive for some religious groups,[13] there is no record of who attended most places of worship. For most people their only recorded contacts with religion were when they were baptised, married and buried. Neither baptism nor marriage records consulted gave an address in Liverpool so they could not be used in this study. In addition, by no means everyone was baptised and it is a parental decision rather than one relating to the individual concerned; while marriage records are unreliable as indicators of religious affiliation as many people probably got married at the most convenient location.[14] In this research, burial records for parochial cemeteries, and other burial grounds where religious denomination was clearly recorded,[15] were used to provide an indicator of individual religious affiliation. These, of course, give no indication of the strength of belief, but presumably do reflect the wishes of the person buried or their close family. As all bodies had to be buried somewhere there should be few obvious omissions.

Details of all burials recorded in the registers of 17 churches and burial grounds were extracted for the period 1 April to 30 September 1851 (22 weeks after the day on which the 1851 census was taken).[16] This provided names and Liverpool addresses for 3,514 individuals for whom religious affiliation could be inferred. To ensure reasonable sample sizes these were divided into only two groups: Roman Catholics and Protestants. There was no attempt to differentiate between Anglican, Nonconformist and other Protestant sects. All burial registers available in Liverpool Record Office for the specified period were used. These 3,514 individuals were then traced back to the 1851 census enumerators' books, and 2,214 (63 per cent) were located at or near the address given. The remainder must have been absent on census night, have moved between the date of the census and their death or, for other reasons, were not traceable in the census.

As the focus of the study is on adult women, full details were recorded for all female members of each family where an individual was located, together with selected information on other household members. Adults were defined as those aged 12 years or over on the grounds that in 1851 all girls would have attained a degree of independence and responsibility by that age, and most would have entered the labour market or have been employed in responsible duties at home. It was assumed that all female members of a family took on the religious affiliation of the individual for whom the denomination of burial was known, and to whom they were related. Although this assumption can be questioned, it seems reasonable to assume that most related individuals living together in the mid-nineteenth century shared the same broad religious beliefs. Only a division between Roman Catholicism and Protestantism is assumed, so that related individuals attending different branches of the Protestant Church are of no consequence to the study; without this assumption it would have been impossible to get a sufficiently large sample. Of the linked burials only 282 (12.7 per cent) were adult women; the bulk of burials were of children. This procedure gave a final sample of 2,701 women aged 12 years and over for whom we have an inferred religious affiliation, address and full personal and household details. These were divided into six categories by birthplace and religion (see Table 4.1).

Table 4.1 Composition of the sample of women in Liverpool in 1851

Birthplace	Religion					
	Protestant		Catholic		Total	
	No	(%)	No	(%)	No	(%)
Liverpool	810	(30.0)	153	(5.7)	963	(35.7)
Ireland	188	(7.0)	679	(25.1)	867	(32.1)
Elsewhere in Britain	796	(29.4)	75	(2.8)	871	(32.2)
Total	1,794	(66.4)	907	(33.6)	2,701	(100.0)

Source: Census enumerators' books and burial registers, Liverpool, 1851

Apart from the untestable assumptions about religious affiliation made in this study, there are several other ways in which bias and error may have occurred. First, the sample may be biased towards families living in those areas of the city with a high mortality because these would produce the largest number of entries in the burial registers. Second, it could be skewed by the non-availability of registers for some churches; and, third, it may overrepresent the more stable population. Those who moved frequently stood the least chance of being linked. There is nothing that can be done about these problems, which are an inevitable consequence of the sources and methods used, but to some extent the biases may cancel each other out as high mortality areas containing a low-status population were also most likely to contain the most mobile population.[17] The sample also omits female servants living in their employer's house (and lodgers and guests in a household), as religious affiliation was only inferred for those related to the person identified in the burial records.

It is possible to compare selectively the sample with the total census population. The Irish-born population are overrepresented: 32.1 per cent of the sample of adult women were Irish-born (Table 4.1), but in 1851 22.3 per cent of Liverpool's total population had been born in Ireland. However, 28.6 per cent of those 20 years and over were Irish-born and, as there were probably more Irish-born women than men in Liverpool in 1851, the degree of overrepresentation does not seem too great. The sample is reasonably well distributed between the 16 wards of Liverpool, concentrated on the older and most densely populated residential areas, but compared to the total population there is an underrepresentation of higher-status suburban areas and an overrepresentation of most central wards (Table 4.2). Unfortunately, there were few available burial registers for Toxteth, Everton and Kirkdale while high mortality in central wards further inflated numbers in these areas. The broad occupational characteristics of the women recorded can also be compared to the census classification (Table 4.4). Domestic work is inevitably severely underrepresented due to the lack of living-in servants, but other categories are quite similar, although retailing and miscellaneous manufacturing are over-represented in the sample, probably due to their prominence in central wards. Given the difficulty of gaining information on religious affiliation, and then of linking it to census data, the sample can be considered reasonably representative of women in Liverpool.

Neighbourhood and home

Although male household heads, and sometimes family groups, usually dominated decisions about where to live, most women in mid-nineteenth century Liverpool spent more time than their menfolk in and around the home. For women with childcare responsibilities — be they mothers, elder sisters, aunts or grandmothers — the house, court, street and immediate neighbourhood took on much greater significance than it did for boys and men who worked long hours away from home.[18] Liverpool (unlike the textile towns) had few large factories that provided female employment, and those women who entered the labour market were most likely to be engaged in domestic, craft or retail work in the home or in nearby premises.[19] Those who moved out of their local area would most likely work in someone else's home. The home and the immediate residential environment thus took on especial significance for women.

The residential location of all women in the sample was examined both within wards and by plotting individual addresses. Although it was not always possible to determine a precise location for each address, most could with confidence be placed at one end of a street or another. This enabled both macro and micro-level segregation to be studied for all six groups, although in this chapter most emphasis is placed on differences between the Irish and non-Irish populations and between Catholic and Protestant Irish. Scotland ward, a large and densely populated area to the north of the city centre, contained more than 23 per cent of each of the sub-populations (Table 4.2). A substantial proportion of Irish and non-Irish, Catholics and Protestants shared the same general environment and should have had ample opportunity to meet and interact in shops and on the street. Catholics who had been born elsewhere in Britain were most concentrated in this ward (possibly due to the small sample size for this group); Protestants born in Liverpool and elsewhere in Britain were least concentrated in Scotland ward.

Table 4.2 Residential distribution of women in Liverpool by ward in 1851

Birthplace and religion of women in the sample population (1851)

Ward	Liverpool Protestants No (%)*	Liverpool Catholics No (%)	Irish Protestants No (%)	Irish Catholics No (%)	Migrant British Protestants No (%)	Migrant British Catholics No (%)	Total+ sample No (%)	Total women in 1851 census No (%)
Scotland	191 (23.6)	46 (30.1)	67 (35.6)	196 (28.9)	191 (24.0)	35 (46.7)	726 (26.9)	30,817 (16.9)
Vauxhall	41 (5.1)	31 (20.2)	16 (8.5)	237 (34.9)	25 (3.1)	6 (8.0)	356 (13.2)	13,552 (7.4)
St Paul's	58 (7.2)	3 (2.0)	5 (2.6)	25 (3.7)	45 (5.7)	7 (9.3)	381 (14.1)	15,478 (8.5)
Exchange	37 (4.6)	19 (12.4)	9 (4.8)	151 (22.2)	17 (2.1)	5 (6.7)	} 157 (5.8)	} 9,519 (5.2)
Castle Street	28 (3.4)	9 (5.9)	5 (2.6)	10 (1.5)	25 (3.1)	5 (6.7)		
St Peter's	28 (3.4)	4 (2.6)	6 (3.2)	8 (1.2)	28 (3.5)	1 (1.3)	} 159 (5.9)	} 16,988 (9.3)
Pitt Street	10 (1.2)	5 (3.3)	6 (3.2)	2 (0.3)	44 (5.5)	1 (1.3)		
Great George	31 (3.8)	7 (4.6)	13 (6.9)	10 (1.5)	29 (3.6)	1 (1.3)	} 271 (10.0)	} 23,577 (13.0)
Rodney Street	36 (4.4)	3 (2.0)	8 (4.2)	0 (0.0)	33 (4.1)	0 (0.0)		
Abercromby	83 (10.3)	5 (3.3)	5 (2.6)	8 (1.2)	89 (11.2)	1 (1.3)	} 351 (13.0)	} 21,193 (11.7)
Lime Street	48 (5.9)	8 (5.2)	8 (4.2)	8 (1.2)	64 (8.0)	2 (2.7)		
St Anne's Street	90 (11.1)	11 (7.2)	14 (7.4)	13 (2.0)	78 (9.8)	7 (9.3)	} 161 (5.9)	} 19,003 (10.5)
Everton and Kirkdale	40 (5.0)	0 (0.0)	14 (7.4)	2 (0.3)	34 (4.3)	1 (1.3)		
West Derby	29 (3.6)	2 (1.3)	4 (2.1)	7 (1.0)	26 (3.3)	2 (2.7)	} 139 (5.2)	} 31,845 (17.5)
South Toxteth	31 (3.8)	0 (0.0)	7 (3.7)	2 (0.3)	30 (3.8)	1 (1.3)		
North Toxteth	29 (3.7)	0 (0.0)	1 (0.5)	0 (0.0)	38 (4.8)	0 (0.0)		
TOTAL	810	153	188	679	796	75	2,701	181,972

Notes:
* Percentage of column total
+ By Registration subdistrict to allow comparison with the census population
Source: Census enumerators' books and burial registers, Liverpool, 1851; Census of Great Britain, 1851

All three Protestant groups were quite evenly distributed between the 15 remaining wards and no ward contained more than 12 per cent of any group. All Protestants were well represented in St Anne's Street ward and non-Irish Protestants were particularly found in Abercromby ward: both still contained substantial higher-status populations in 1851 despite their close proximity to the central area.[20] Irish Protestants were noticeably more concentrated in low-status central wards than non-Irish Protestants. In addition to Scotland ward, Irish Catholics and, to a lesser extent Liverpool-born Catholics (some of whom may have been of Irish origin), were especially concentrated in the low-status central wards of Vauxhall and Exchange. Although sharing some space with Irish Protestants in central Liverpool, they were much more concentrated than this group and whereas Protestants were quite well represented in Everton and Kirkdale ward, there were few Catholics in this area. There were statistically significant differences between the distributions of the six groups,[21] and in general terms Protestant women were more suburbanised than Catholic women and non-Irish women more suburbanised than Irish women.

These patterns are borne out at the micro-level, but some significant clustering and segregation is revealed by plots of individual addresses (Figures 4.1–3). Irish Catholics were especially densely concentrated in certain parts of the central wards — especially the streets between Vauxhall Road and Scotland Road — and even though they shared the same general space as other groups, at the micro-level they tended to be segregated into specific streets or courts. These differences were most obvious between Irish Catholics and the Irish Protestants who clustered around the edge of the main Catholic area but rarely penetrated it and, even then, lived in mainly non-Catholic streets and courts; but there was also micro-scale segregation between each of the three Catholic groups. Outside the central area Irish Protestants were markedly more clustered than the other two Protestant groups.

The implications of these residential patterns for women in mid-Victorian Liverpool can be explored on two levels. First, different residential environments affected such vital issues as housing quality, the availability of pure water or decent sanitation and access to open space for recreation and children's play. Second, although the distances between groups were relatively small, any strong contemporary perceptions of segregation could create more introverted communities, further restricting the mobility of women and leading to hostility between different groups. To some degree housing and sanitary conditions can be examined from empirical evidence, while assessment of perceptions and effects of segregation rely on a combination of speculation and contemporary comment.

Detailed evidence about housing conditions — including occupancy rates, access to facilities, privacy and the availability of space — is very hard to gather on a comprehensive basis for the mid-nineteenth century. However, by combining census evidence with a detailed analysis of large-scale plans, it is possible to make some appraisal of the quality of the home environment available to each group of women. For those who lived in courts and back-to-backs living conditions were harsh, often with one

Figure 4.1   Residential distribution of a sample of Irish-born Catholic women and Irish-born Protestant women in Liverpool in 1851
Source: Burial registers and census enumerators' books, Liverpool, 1851

Figure 4.2 Residential distribution of a sample of Liverpool-born Catholic women and Liverpool-born Protestant women in Liverpool in 1851
Source: Burial registers and census enumerators' books, Liverpool, 1851

British-born Migrant Catholics   +

British-born Migrant Protestants   •

Approximate extent of built-up area in 1851   — —

Figure 4.3   Residential distribution of a sample of British-born migrant Catholic women and British-born migrant Protestant women in Liverpool in 1851
Source: Burial registers and census enumerators' books, Liverpool, 1851

family occupying a single room. Houses were damp, lacked sanitation and a single water supply would be shared with all families in a court. The lack of space, privacy and adequate cooking and cleaning facilities meant that keeping a home clean and comfortable was an almost impossible task for many women.[22] It is clear that Catholics, and especially Irish Catholics, were overrepresented in poorer-quality court and back-to-back housing, and that this was not just a function of the greater suburbanisation of Protestant and non-Irish women (Table 4.3). Even in Scotland ward, which contained over 23 per cent of each group, Irish Catholics had the worst housing conditions, followed by Irish Protestants and Liverpool Catholics. Thus, even though Irish and non-Irish, Catholics and Protestants, often lived in similar parts of Liverpool, they did not always share the same housing conditions.

Table 4.3 The housing conditions of women in Liverpool in 1851

A All Liverpool wards

Housing type	Birthplace and religion							
	Liverpool Protestants	Liverpool Catholics	Irish Protestants	Irish Catholics	Migrant British Protestants	Migrant British Catholics	Total	
	No (%)+	No (%)	No (%)	No (%)	No (%)	No (%)	No	(%)
Cellars	2 (0.2)	0 (0.0)	5 (2.7)	11 (1.6)	0 (0.0)	0 (0.0)	18	(0.7)
Courts	286 (35.3)	71 (46.4)	77 (41.0)	395 (58.2)	199 (25.0)	25 (33.4)	1,053	(39.0)
Back-to-backs*	139 (17.2)	27 (17.6)	29 (15.4)	154 (22.7)	100 (12.6)	22 (29.3)	471	(17.4)
Small terraces	146 (18.0)	37 (24.2)	38 (20.2)	66 (9.7)	192 (24.1)	16 (21.3)	495	(18.3)
Medium terraces	199 (24.6)	13 (8.5)	37 (19.7)	42 (6.2)	260 (32.7)	9 (12.0)	560	(20.7)
Large terraces	13 (1.6)	0 (0.0)	0 (0.0)	3 (0.4)	24 (3.0)	1 (1.3)	41	(1.5)
Commercial property	25 (3.1)	5 (3.3)	2 (1.0)	8 (1.2)	21 (2.6)	2 (2.7)	63	(2.3)
TOTAL	810	153	188	679	796	75	2,701	

B Scotland ward only

Cellars	0 (0.0)	0 (0.0)	1 (1.5)	11 (5.6)	0 (0.0)	0 (0.0)	12	(1.7)
Courts	69 (36.1)	23 (50.0)	33 (49.3)	113 (57.7)	62 (32.5)	13 (37.2)	313	(43.1)
Back-to-backs	72 (37.7)	10 (21.7)	17 (25.4)	53 (27.0)	46 (24.0)	12 (34.3)	210	(28.9)
Small terraces	34 (17.8)	11 (23.9)	9 (13.4)	11 (5.6)	42 (22.0)	8 (22.9)	115	(15.8)
Medium terraces	16 (8.4)	2 (4.4)	7 (10.4)	8 (4.1)	41 (21.5)	2 (5.7)	76	(10.5)
Large terraces	0 (0.0)	0 (0.0)	0 (0.0)	0 (0.0)	0 (0.0)	0 (0.0)	0	(0.0)
Commercial property	0 (0.0)	0 (0.0)	0 (0.0)	0 (0.0)	0 (0.0)	0 (0.0)	0	(0.0)
TOTAL	191	46	67	196	191	35	726	

Notes:
* Includes houses backing on to a court
+ Percentage of column total
Source: : Census enumerators' books, burial registers, maps and plans, Liverpool 1851

The extent to which residential separation was carried over into everyday perceptions and action spaces can be deduced from both contemporary comments and later research. For instance, Denvir commented both on the segregation of Catholics and Protestants and the hostility which Catholics faced from the Protestant community.[23] Neal has analysed the distribution and organisation of Orange Lodges in Liverpool.[24] However, such organisations were almost exclusively male, and most associated comments were based on male perceptions and activities. It is not known whether the acute social segregation of Catholic and Protestant Irish men infused the daily lives of women to the same degree.[25] In a male-dominated society it might be assumed that most women followed the dominant values of the community to which they belonged. However, it can be suggested that some interaction between different groups of women on the streets and in shops and markets would have been inevitable, although the extent to which such women used avoidance strategies to combat unpleasantness and discrimination in their daily activities is not known.[26]

Though a crucial part of the geography of mid-Victorian Liverpool, residential and social segregation was no more than the result of a number of processes acting on both Irish and non-Irish women. Two of the most important causes of Liverpool's distinctive residential structure were the operation of the labour market (and the resulting pattern of poverty and inequality), and the attitudes of society at large, particularly those (mainly male) with power, towards both women in general and Irish women in particular. The relevance of these factors to the experience of Irish women will now be examined.

Work

Access to work and associated income was a vital factor affecting residential location and the quality of the home environment experienced by women. As the disposable income of most women was inextricably bound up with the work of their husbands, the operation of the labour market for both men and women is relevant to this study. The Liverpool labour market had a number of distinctive characteristics. First, it was heavily dependent on the docks and associated industries and services. Because the volume of trade passing through the docks fluctuated wildly over short periods, this led to a mainly casual labour force for whom short periods of unemployment were common and resulted in massive variations in weekly income.[27] Second, opportunities for female employment in Liverpool were distinctly limited. Dock and dock-related work was mainly a male preserve, and women were very heavily concentrated in low-paid and often casual service, retail and domestic work (Table 4.4). Although some single women worked as domestic servants in the homes of the rich, most married women had much less regular employment. The availability of work affected residential location in two obvious ways: first, through the income that a family could regularly commit to housing and, second,

Table 4.4   The occupations of women in Liverpool in 1851

Occupation	Birthplace and religion of women in the sample population (1851)*							
	Liverpool Protestants	Liverpool Catholics	Irish Protestants	Irish Catholics	Migrant British Protestants	Migrant British Catholics	Total Sample	Total women in 1851 census
	No (%)⁺	No (%)	No (%)	No (%)	No (%)	No (%)	No (%)	No (%)
Dressmaking and Sewing	64 (29.4)	14 (28.6)	10 (24.4)	41 (22.0)	44 (24.9)	7 (43.8)	180 (26.2)	11,461 (23.0)
Domestic cleaning	51 (23.4)	15 (30.6)	6 (14.6)	29 (15.6)	30 (16.9)	5 (31.3)	136 (19.8)	21,406 (42.8)
Cleaning clothes	16 (7.3)	2 (4.1)	4 (9.8)	11 (5.9)	10 (5.6)	0 (0.0)	43 (6.3)	2,768 (5.5)
Housekeeping	22 (10.1)	1 (2.0)	6 (14.6)	24 (12.9)	25 (14.1)	2 (12.5)	80 (11.6)	2,586 (5.2)
Cooking	0 (0.0)	1 (2.0)	0 (0.0)	1 (0.5)	11 (6.2)	0 (0.0)	13 (1.9)	1,219 (2.4)
Childcare /teaching	9 (4.1)	1 (2.0)	0 (0.0)	3 (1.6)	16 (9.0)	0 (0.0)	29 (4.2)	2,210 (4.4)
Miscellaneous non-manual	5 (2.3)	0 (0.0)	0 (0.0)	0 (0.0)	3 (1.7)	0 (0.0)	8 (1.2)	670 (1.3)
Miscellaneous Manufacturing	25 (11.5)	2 (4.1)	7 (17.0)	10 (5.4)	12 (6.8)	1 (6.3)	57 (8.3)	1,673 (3.4)
Retailing/ hawking	25 (11.5)	13 (26.5)	8 (19.5)	67 (36.0)	26 (14.7)	1 (6.3)	140 (20.4)	5,575 (11.1)
Other	1 (0.5)	0 (0.0)	0 (0.0)	0 (0.0)	0 (0.0)	0 (0.0)	1 (0.1)	444 (0.9)
TOTAL	218 (31.7)	49 (7.1)	41 (6.0)	186 (27.1)	177 (25.8)	16 (2.3)	687 (100.0)	50,012 (100.0)

* Data refer to all women in the sample with paid employment recorded in the census
⁺ Percentage of column total
Source: : Census enumerators' books and burial registers, Liverpool, 1851; Census of Great Britain, 1851

through the need for those in casual work (especially on the docks) to live close to their place of employment.

Although the inaccuracies of census occupational descriptions for women are well known,[28] these are the only data available. Labour-force participation was low for all women in the sample (only 25.4 per cent of all women were recorded as having any form of paid employment) with only small variations between the groups. Liverpool-born Catholic women were most likely to be in paid employment (32.0 per cent) and Catholics who had migrated to Liverpool from elsewhere in Britain least likely (21.3 per cent). Irish Catholic women were more likely to be employed (27.6 per cent) than Irish Protestant women (21.8 per cent). These figures emphasise the importance of the home environment for most women.

The most common employment for all women was dressmaking and other forms of sewing (26.3 per cent), much of which was likely to have been carried out either in the home or in small workshops nearby. Other common occupations were various forms of retailing (20.0 per cent) and house cleaning as a domestic servant (19.9 per cent). Domestic service among women is underrepresented in the sample because live-in servants were excluded. Although sample sizes are small, there were some differences between groups (Table 4.4). Irish Catholics were overrepresented in retailing trades (including hawking), Irish Protestants in various manufacturing occupations, migrant British Catholics in dressmaking, Liverpool-born Catholics in cleaning and retailing and migrant British Protestants in childcare. Of the most important sectors, retailing tended to be dominated by Liverpool and Irish-born Catholic women, cleaning by non-Irish born Catholics and dressmaking by the non-Irish.

When classified by socio-economic group (albeit using a classification better suited to male occupations), almost half of all women were in skilled manual work (48.8 per cent) with 22.7 per cent in unskilled manual jobs and 12.5 per cent in non-manual work. Irish Catholics and Liverpool-born Catholics were overrepresented in both unskilled manual and non-manual occupations (including retailing), while migrant British and Irish Protestants were overrepresented in skilled manual work (Table 4.5). Whilst Irish Catholic women were more likely to fill low-skill jobs than Irish Protestants, they were no worse off than other Catholics.

Table 4.5 Socio-economic group of women* in Liverpool in 1851

Socio-economic group of occupation	Birthplace and religion						
	Liverpool Protestants	Liverpool Catholics	Irish Protestants	Irish Catholics	Migrant British Protestants	Migrant British Catholics	Total
	No (%)+	No (%)	No (%)	No (%)	No (%)	No (%)	No (%)
Professional and intermediate	1 (0.5)	0 (0.0)	0 (0.0)	0 (0.0)	0 (0.0)	0 (0.0)	1 (0.1)
Non-manual	23 (10.6)	8 (16.3)	3 (7.3)	27 (14.5)	24 (13.6)	0 (0.0)	85 (12.4)
Skilled manual	114 (52.3)	18 (36.7)	24 (58.5)	64 (34.4)	106 (59.9)	9 (56.3)	335 (48.8)
Semi-skilled manual	40 (18.3)	6 (12.2)	8 (19.5)	36 (19.4)	18 (10.2)	2 (12.5)	110 (16.0)
Unskilled manual	40 (18.3)	17 (34.7)	6 (14.6)	59 (31.7)	29 (16.4)	5 (31.3)	156 (22.7)
Total	218 (31.7)	49 (7.1)	41 (6.0)	186 (27.1)	177 (25.8)	16 (2.3)	687 (100.0)

Notes:
* Data refer to all women in the sample with paid employment recorded in the census
+ Percentage of column total
Source: Census enumerators' books and burial registers, Liverpool, 1851

For most women their husbands' (or fathers') occupation was more important than their own paid work. Even among single women only 43.4 per cent had an occupation recorded in the census, with slightly more single Irish and Liverpool-born Catholics in the work-force than other groups. The lack of opportunity to take paid work in Liverpool, whether due to social constraints or the structure of the labour market, thus affected all women and variations between different categories were relatively minor. Among those women who did work, although there were small differences between groups, most clustered in the same sorts of trades, again reflecting labour market constraints that affected all women.

In contrast, variations in the employment characteristics of the husbands of married women were much more significant (Table 4.6). Overall, around one-third of husbands were in unskilled work and 46.1 per cent were in skilled manual work; but no fewer than 61.5 per cent of husbands of Irish Catholic women were in unskilled jobs compared with only 36.0 per cent of Irish Protestants and 19.7 per cent of Liverpool-born Protestants. The husbands of Irish Catholic women, and to a lesser extent those of Liverpool-born Catholics, clearly fared much worse in the labour market than all Protestants (including the Irish) and other Catholics. Irish Catholic women, mainly dependent on a male household wage to feed, clothe and house a family, were likely to be considerably worse off than most other women in Liverpool. This must have had a major effect upon their residential choice and the quality of their home environment.

Table 4.6 Socio-economic group of husbands* of women in Liverpool in 1851

Socio-economic group of husbands' occupation	Birthplace and religion of women						
	Liverpool Protestants	Liverpool Catholics	Irish Protestants	Irish Catholics	Migrant British Protestants	Migrant British Catholics	Total
	No (%)+	No (%)	No (%)	No (%)	No (%)	No (%)	No (%)
Professional and intermediate	7 (1.7)	0 (0.0)	0 (0.0)	0 (0.0)	8 (1.5)	0 (0.0)	15 (1.0)
Non-manual	44 (11.5)	3 (4.8)	8 (7.0)	41 (10.3)	92 (18.1)	6 (15.0)	194 (12.9)
Skilled manual	218 (57.2)	29 (46.0)	62 (54.4)	100 (25.0)	270 (53.1)	16 (40.0)	695 (46.1)
Semi-skilled manual	37 (9.7)	4 (6.3)	3 (2.6)	13 (3.3)	34 (6.7)	5 (12.5)	96 (6.4)
Unskilled manual	75 (19.7)	27 (42.9)	41 (36.0)	246 (61.5)	104 (20.5)	13 (32.5)	506 (33.6)
Total	381 (25.3)	63 (4.2)	114 (7.6)	400 (26.6)	508 (33.7)	40 (2.7)	1,506 (100.0)

Notes:
* Data refer to men in paid employment married to women in the sample
+ Percentage of column total
Source: Census enumerators' books and burial registers, Liverpool, 1851

Many of the women not recorded as having a paid occupation in the census may well have taken part-time casual work when it was available. This is borne out by contemporary descriptions of life in the courts. Shimmin, for instance, describes women in Crosbie Street employed as 'oakum pickers, chip choppers or sandsellers'[29], occupations that rarely occur in the census, and it is clear that a whole range of petty retail and other activities were carried out in and around the courts.[30] However, the main employment of most of these women was probably in the home, and many of those women who were in more regular paid work outside the home environment no doubt also spent a large part of their time in household and childcare duties.

The quality of their work environment and the arduousness of their toil were mainly affected by the size and regularity of family income — influencing both the quality of their home and their ability to engage paid domestic help — and by the size and composition of their household, although the willingness of other family members to assist with chores must also have been important. If, as suggested above, the family income of married Irish Catholics was likely to be lower than that of other groups, then the task of running the home would have been that much more difficult. The position of all widowed women running a household and providing an income would have been especially hard.

There were relatively few differences in the family and household composition of the six groups of women. Those born in Liverpool were most likely to be single, usually young girls still living in the parental home, while migrants from elsewhere in Britain were most likely to be widowed. In this respect there were no significant differences between Irish Protestants and Catholics.

The majority of all women lived in nuclear family units (Table 4.7) with relatively few differences between groups. Protestants were marginally more likely to live with kin outside the nuclear family while Irish Catholics and migrant British women were most likely to live in households with lodgers. Few households had servants, but they were most common in households of migrant British Protestants. Irish Catholics were overwhelmingly more likely to live in multi-family houses, emphasising the poor home environment experienced by many Catholic Irish women.

It can thus be suggested that the experiences of Liverpool women working in the home and in the labour market were surprisingly similar. Regardless of birthplace or religion most women spent most of their life in domestic work, and those that did gain paid employment were mainly forced into low-paid and low-skill domestic work, sewing or petty retailing. Although Irish Catholic women were marginally more likely to be in paid employment (perhaps reflecting the lower income of their menfolk), and to be in lower-skilled work than Irish Protestant women, they were not necessarily different from other groups. The husbands of Irish Catholic women were, however, in noticeably lower-status and more poorly paid work than other men. This must have had a major impact on the quality of life of their wives and families.

Attitudes and values

Irish women in mid-Victorian Liverpool were likely to be constrained by two sets of values within contemporary society. First, there were those attitudes that affected almost all women in a male-dominated society and which excluded women from much economic, political and social life.[31]

Table 4.7 Family and household structure of women in Liverpool in 1851

Family and household structure[6]	Birthplace and religion of women													
	Liverpool Protestants		Liverpool Catholics		Irish Protestants		Irish Catholics		Migrant British Protestants		Migrant British Catholics		Total	
	No	(%)[7]	No	(%)	No	(%)	No	(%)	No	(%)	No	(%)	No	(%)
Nuclear family	498	(61.5)	111	(72.5)	117	(62.3)	488	(71.9)	516	(64.8)	58	(77.3)	1,788	(66.2)
Nuclear[1] family with kin	170	(21.0)	21	(13.7)	36	(19.1)	97	(14.3)	147	(18.5)	5	(6.7)	476	(17.6)
Extended family[2]	109	(13.5)	17	(11.1)	28	(14.9)	44	(6.5)	103	(13.0)	10	(13.3)	311	(11.5)
Multi-family[3]	25	(3.1)	4	(2.7)	6	(3.2)	49	(7.2)	23	(2.9)	0	(0.0)	107	(4.0)
Single person family[4]	8	(0.9)	0	(0.0)	1	(0.5)	1	(0.1)	7	(0.8)	2	(2.7)	19	(0.7)
Households with lodgers[6]	121	(14.9)	23	(15.0)	46	(24.5)	240	(35.3)	223	(28.0)	25	(33.3)	678	(25.1)
Households with servants[6]	73	(9.0)	8	(5.2)	12	(6.4)	38	(5.6)	138	(17.3)	8	(10.7)	277	(10.3)
Single households	575	(71.0)	90	(58.9)	117	(62.2)	318	(46.8)	568	(71.4)	55	(73.3)	1,723	(63.8)
Multiple households[5]	235	(29.0)	63	(41.1)	71	(37.8)	361	(53.2)	228	(28.6)	20	(26.7)	978	(36.2)
Total	810		153		188		679		796		75		2,701	(100.0)

Notes:
1. Nuclear family plus a mixture of kin
2. Three generations but no other kin
3. More than one related whole family unit
4. But not necessarily living alone
5. More than one household in same housing unit
6. The number of women living in households of a particular type
7. Percentage of all women in group

Second, there were contemporary attitudes towards the Irish — especially the Catholic Irish — which led to discrimination and persecution.[32] In such a situation Irish Catholic women may have been doubly disadvantaged. Together with economic factors outlined above, such attitudes and perceptions played a major role in determining the neighbourhood, home environment and quality of life of many Irish women.

While census evidence provides a comprehensive, if sometimes flawed, picture of the residential and occupational structure of the population, attitudes and values in the past can only be inferred from sporadic (usually male-generated) written records. The typicality, context and meaning of such sources are often difficult to establish. They must be interpreted with care, and the ways in which contemporary values permeated women's lives can be little more than speculation.

All women were subject to the pressures produced by patriarchal authority in the home and work place. Such pressures were characterised by generalisations concerning the nature of women and their consequent role. It was assumed that women, being biologically, intellectually and spiritually weaker than men, were in need of male protection provided within the family and household. This was characterised by the dominance of the husband and/or father, and his rights over female kin. The primary sphere of a woman's life was the home, and the highest role to which she could aspire was motherhood. A rewarding and fulfilling life was to be found in the nurturing and education of children, and the efficient and frugal organisation of the household budget. Work outside the home was against the natural order and was to the detriment of family responsibilities.[33]

Such attitudes were strongly reinforced by the Christian Churches, both Protestant and Catholic. The Bible was instrumental in promoting the stereotypes of woman as virgin, mother or whore, and gave authority to the natural right of men to dominate women.[34] Contrasts between images of the female temptress and the ideal mother come through in some of Shimmin's comments on Liverpool slum life. Of one man who frequented the 'salle de danse', probably on London Road, he says:

> He had been in this place with this broadfaced, foulmouthed girl hundreds of times. He had spent his money, wasted his substance in this riotous mode of life, had loved this vile woman ... She is here laughing at his folly ... loud and brazen in her lewdness.[35]

Yet of another family he comments:

> One house is particularly striking, and shows what can be done under adverse circumstances if a woman has a right notion and a will to do her work. We saw in the court a little girl at play. Her clothes were extremely neat and becoming; her hair was carefully brushed and combed; the true colour of her skin could be seen; and in these respects she stood out from her playmates and attracted attention ... The steps, floors, walls, stairs — the arrangement of all the little household ornaments — told forth the praise of the clean housewife ... here was a home of which any working man might well be proud ... Long may she live to brighten the home and cheer the heart of her husband.[36]

For those women who worked outside the home a patriarchal hierarchy structured most employment,[37] widening the gap between male and female wages and excluding women from apprenticeships. Elder daughters, in particular, were pressurised to remain at home to help with domestic work and childcare and were then often pushed into marriage for economic reasons. Irish women suffered the additional disadvantage of being the subject of English stereotypes and exploitation in contemporary media and literature.[38] The Liverpool Medical Officer of Health would have reflected the views of many non-Irish Liverpudlians when he used vivid prose to describe an Irish wake:

> The three houses were crammed with men, women and children, while drunken women squatted thickly on the flags of the court before the open door of the crowded room where the corpse was laid. There had been, in the presence of

death, one of those shameful carousals, which, to the disgrace of the enlightened progress and advanced civilization of the nineteenth century, still lingers as dregs of ancient manners amongst the funeral customs of the Irish peasantry.[39]

The attitudes of those in authority (such as the Liverpool MOH) were frequently recorded and probably had most impact on the lives of ordinary women. The attitudes and behaviour of the police to different categories of crime and different groups of people were particularly important. Although evidence is limited, Watch Committee statistics suggest that the Irish were consistently arrested more often than other groups for all classes of crime: in 1855 the Irish-born represented 42 per cent of all arrests, whereas in 1851 those born in Ireland accounted for only 22.3 per cent of the city's population (Table 4.8). Women were particularly arrested for drunkeness, disorderly behaviour or prostitution and a large proportion of these arrests must have been of Irish women.[40] Although many English contemporaries would have argued that these figures showed the lawlessness of the Irish, they can equally easily be used to suggest that the Liverpool police were more eager to arrest Irish men and women than other groups.[41] The stereotyping of the Irish as dirty, feckless and violent must have affected the perceptions of those, such as the police, who came into daily contact with Irish women in Liverpool.

Conclusion

Evidence assembled in this study suggests that Irish Catholic women were disadvantaged in a number of ways relative to other women, but that the causes of this disadvantage were not straightforward. In many respects the problems and experiences they faced were similar to those of all women. At home, on the street, in the labour market and in society in general all women were constrained and disadvantaged relative to men. But Catholic Irish women experienced two additional difficulties. First, their menfolk also fared particularly poorly in the labour market and thus family incomes in Catholic households were probably lower than many elsewhere. Second, they experienced double discrimination because they were both female and Irish.

This combination of factors helped to establish Irish Catholic families in relatively well-segregated residential districts in Liverpool, and forced many such families into acute poverty. In most cases it was women who had to handle the consequences of poverty, overcrowding, disease and decaying housing on a day-to-day basis. Men, more likely to have work outside the home and more easily able to shrug off the demands of cold or hungry children, could most readily escape from these conditions. In this respect, at least, the geographies of Irish Catholic women in Liverpool were not only different from those of Protestants but also from those of Irish Catholic men.

While it has been suggested that the general experiences of all women were roughly similar in mid-Victorian Liverpool, it can also be postulated that those factors which separated Catholics from Protestants and Irish from non-Irish were due more to the activities of men than of women. Not

Table 4.8 Offences recorded in Liverpool in 1855 by sex and birthplace

Offences*	All males No (%)+		All females No (%)		Males and females born in:								Total No
					Liverpool No (%)		Britain No (%)		Ireland No (%)		Overseas No (%)		
Common assaults	783	(69.2)	348	(30.8)	291	(25.7)	328	(29.0)	456	(40.3)	56	(5.0)	1,131
Assaults on Police Officers	813	(93.1)	60	(6.9)	224	(25.7)	261	(29.9)	329	(37.7)	59	(6.8)	873
All offences against the person	1,792	(78.6)	487	(21.4)	574	(25.2)	673	(29.5)	879	(38.6)	153	(6.7)	2,279
All offences against property with violence	179	(84.0)	34	(16.0)	50	(23.5)	59	(27.7)	91	(42.7)	13	(6.1)	213
Robbery from the person by prostitutes	0	(0.0)	800	(100.0)	192	(24.0)	252	(31.5)	335	(41.9)	21	(2.6)	800
All offences against property without violence	3,472	(55.0)	2,842	(45.0)	1,598	(25.3)	1,892	(30.0)	270	(42.8)	122	(1.9)	6,314
Disorderly persons	318	(41.5)	449	(58.5)	162	(21.1)	149	(19.4)	427	(55.7)	29	(3.8)	767
Drunk and disorderly persons	5,438	(60.1)	3,617	(39.9)	2,428	(26.8)	2,768	(30.6)	3,550	(39.2)	309	(3.4)	9,055
Drunk and incapable	2,561	(68.0)	1,203	(32.0)	994	(26.4)	1,155	(30.7)	1,572	(41.8)	43	(1.1)	3,764
Vagrancy	369	(54.3)	310	(45.7)	145	(21.4)	91	(13.4)	429	(63.2)	14	(2.1)	679
All miscellaneous offences	10,786	(63.9)	6,097	(36.1)	4,384	(26.0)	4,884	(28.9)	7,112	(42.1)	501	(3.0)	16,883
Total offences	16,229	(63.2)	9,640	(36.8)	6,606	(25.7)	7,508	(29.2)	10,784	(42.0)	791	(3.1)	25,689

Notes:
+ per cent of row total
* offences are divided into 4 major categories: offences against the person; offences against property with violence; offences against property without violence; miscellaneous. Within these categories offences accounting for over 2 per cent of the total are shown
Source: Report of Liverpool Watch Committee, 1855

only was the economic position of most women dependent on men, either relying on a male wage in the home or dependent on a male boss in the work place, but the attitudes which shaped society and especially disadvantaged some women tended to be perpetuated by men. The churches, Orange Lodges and other Catholic and Protestant Irish organisations were all dominated by men, and street violence was almost certainly mainly perpetrated by men.[42]

There is little direct evidence for mid-Victorian Liverpool, but the role of women in the peace movement in general suggests that most women prefer to break down barriers rather than erect them.[43] Living each day in similar or adjacent neighbourhoods, meeting on the street and in shops and markets, sharing the same concerns about children, home and family, it seems quite probable that many women were less clearly socially and economically segregated than their menfolk. Perhaps the common experiences of being female in mid-nineteenth century Liverpool were more important than any differences created by origin or religion.

Notes

1. See especially several essays in the two volumes edited by Roger Swift and Sheridan Gilley, *The Irish in the Victorian City*, Croom Helm, London, 1985, and *The Irish in Britain, 1815–1939*, Pinter, London, 1989.
2. There are many studies which examine the influence of religion on the Irish community in general, but few which explore religious affiliation within specific communities. In a Liverpool context see F. Neal, *Sectarian Violence: the Liverpool Experience, 1819–1914*, Manchester University Press, Manchester, 1987. Also J. Klapas, 'Geographical Aspects of Religious Change in Victorian Liverpool, 1837–1901', unpublished MA thesis, University of Liverpool, 1977.
3. Relevant geographical studies include R. Lawton, 'Irish immigration to England and Wales in the mid-nineteenth century', *Irish Geography*, 4, 1, 1959, pp. 35–54; C. Richardson, 'Irish settlement in mid-nineteenth century Bradford', *Yorkshire Bulletin of Economic and Social Research*, 20, 1968, pp. 40–57; R.D. Lobban, 'The Irish community in Greenock in the nineteenth century', *Irish Geography*, 6, 1971, pp. 270–81; C.G. Pooley, 'The residential segregation of migrant communities in mid-Victorian Liverpool', *Transactions of the Institute of British Geographers*, NS2, 3, 1977, pp. 369–72; C.R. Lewis, 'The Irish in Cardiff in the mid-nineteenth century', *Cambria*, 7, 1980, pp. 13–41.
4. One of the few studies dealing explicitly with Irish women in Britain is B. Walter, *Gender and Irish Migration to Britain*, Geography working paper 4, Anglia College, Cambridge, 1989. See also L. Lees, *Exiles of Erin*, Manchester University Press, Manchester, 1979. Elsewhere see H. Diner, *Erin's Daughters in America*, Johns Hopkins University Press, Baltimore, 1983.
5. For a discussion see C.G. Pooley, 'Segregation or integration? The residential experience of the Irish in mid-Victorian Britain', in Swift and Gilley, *The Irish in Britain*, pp. 60–83.
6. But see L. Lees, 'Mid-Victorian migration and the Irish family economy', *Victorian Studies*, 20, 1976, pp. 25–43.
7. For instance R. Lawton, 'The population of Liverpool in the mid-nineteenth century', *Transactions of the Historic Society of Lancashire and Cheshire*, 107, 1955,

pp. 89–120; F.E. Hyde, *Liverpool and the Mersey: the Development of a Port 1700–1970*, David and Charles, Newton Abbot, 1971; I.C. Taylor, ' Black Spot on the Mersey', unpublished Ph.D. thesis, University of Liverpool, 1975; R. Lawton, and C.G. Pooley, *The Social Geography of Merseyside in the Nineteenth Century*, Final report to the SSRC, Liverpool, 1978; C.G. Pooley, 'Migration, Mobility and Residential Areas in Nineteenth-century Liverpool', unpublished Ph.D. thesis, University of Liverpool, 1978; J. Papworth, 'The Irish in Liverpool 1835–72: Segregation and Dispersal', unpublished Ph.D. thesis, University of Liverpool, 1981; P.J. Waller, *Democracy and Sectarianism: a Political History of Liverpool, 1808–1939*, Liverpool University Press, Liverpool, 1981; Neal, *Sectarian Violence*.

8. For more details of the distribution of the Irish in nineteenth-century Britain see Pooley, 'Segregation or integration'.

9. C.G. Pooley, 'The Irish in Liverpool, 1850–1940', in M. Engman, F. Carter, A. Hepburn and C. Pooley, eds, *Ethnic Groups in Urban Europe, 1850–1940*, Dartmouth, London, 1992.

10. In 1841 there was only a crude classification (which does separate Irish from English) but from 1851 precise place of birth is given for those born in their country of enumeration. See M. Drake, 'The census, 1801–1891', in E.A. Wrigley, ed., *Nineteenth-century Society: Essays in the Use of Quantitative Methods for the Study of Social Data*, Cambridge University Press, Cambridge, 1972, pp. 7–46; D.E. Baines, 'Birthplace statistics and the study of internal migration', in R. Lawton, ed., *The Census and Social Structure*, Frank Cass, London, 1978, pp. 146–64.

11. Some census enumerators did give more detailed information and this can be used to identify partially the more precise origins of Irish migrants. See P. Laxton, 'Social structure of the Irish in English cities', paper presented at the University of Liverpool, 1987.

12. See D.M. Thomson, 'The religious census of 1851', in Lawton, *The Census and Social Structure*, pp. 241–88.

13. In Liverpool these survive for some Welsh Presbyterian chapels. Jewish synagogues also kept membership lists. See B. Williams, *The Making of the Manchester Jewry, 1740–1875*, Manchester University Press, Manchester, 1976.

14. Marriage records have been used to study spatial interaction. See R. Dennis, 'Distance and social interaction in a Victorian city', *Journal of Historical Geography*, 3, 1977, pp. 237–50.

15. In 1851 the majority of burials were in parochial cemeteries which, although linked to Anglican parish churches, were also used for burials of other denominations with the service performed by the appropriate minister. Other, smaller, burial grounds were attached to local Anglican and Roman Catholic churches, often established as the population grew, while the Necropolis was a central burial ground specifically for Nonconformist churches. Corporation cemeteries were developed after 1856.

16. The cemeteries used and numbers of burials recorded were: Necropolis (Protestant) 767; St Martin's in the Fields (Roman Catholic and Protestant) 741; St Anthony's (Roman Catholic) 683; St James' (Protestant) 448; St Mary's (Roman Catholic and Protestant) 431; St John's (Protestant) 228; St Michael's (Protestant) 84; St Nicholas' (Roman Catholic) 39; St Oswald's (Roman Catholic) 33; Ancient Chapel (Protestant) 19; Holy Trinity (Protestant) 8; St George's (Protestant) 7; Christ Church (Protestant) 6; St Paul's (Protestant) 6; St Mary's (Protestant) 5; St Thomas (Protestant) 3; St Anne's (Protestant) 2.

17. Several studies have demonstrated that residential mobility in British Victorian cities was highest amongst the lowest social classes. See R. Dennis, 'Inter-censal mobility in a Victorian city', *Transactions of the Institute of British Geographers*, NS2,

1977, pp. 349–63; C.G. Pooley, 'Residential mobility in the Victorian city', *Transactions of the Institute of British Geographers*, NS4, 1979, pp. 258–77.

18. Many studies have shown that even today women with young children have a restricted action space. See for example J. Tivers, *Women Attached: the Daily Lives of Women with Young Children*, Croom Helm, London, 1985; L. McDowell, 'Women, gender and the organization of space' in D. Gregory and R. Walford, eds, *Horizons in Human Geography*, Macmillan, London, 1989, pp. 136–51.

19. For general discussions of women's work in the past see: E. Roberts, *Women's Work, 1840–1940*, Macmillan, London, 1988; J. Rendall, *Women in an Industrializing Society: England 1750–1880*, Blackwell, Oxford, 1990; S. Pennington and B. Westover, *A Hidden Workforce. Homeworkers in England*, 1850–1985, Macmillan, London, 1989; L. McDowell, and D. Massey, 'A woman's place?', in D. Massey and T. Allen, eds, *Geography Matters!*, Cambridge University Press, Cambridge, 1984.

20. For a detailed analysis of the social geography of Liverpool in 1851 see Taylor, 'Black Spot', and Lawton, 'The population of Liverpool'.

21. Where relevant all tables were tested for statistical significance using the Chi Square test. In all cases there were significant differences between the six groups at the 99 per cent confidence level.

22. On housing in Liverpool see I.C. Taylor. 'The court and cellar dwelling: the eighteenth-century origin of the Liverpool slum', *Transactions of the Historic Society of Lancashire and Cheshire*, 122, 1970 pp. 67–90; J.H. Treble, 'Liverpool working-class housing, 1801–51', in S.D. Chapman, ed., *The History of Working-Class Housing*, David and Charles, Newton Abbot, 1971, pp. 167–220; C.G. Pooley, 'Choice and constraint in the nineteenth-century city: a basis for residential differentiation', in J.H. Johnson and C.G. Pooley, eds, *The Structure of Nineteenth-century Cities*, Croom Helm, London, 1982, pp. 199–233.

23. J. Denvir, *The Life Story of an Old Rebel*, Irish University Press, Dublin, 1910, reprinted 1972.

24. Neal, *Sectarian Violence*.

25. There is very little documented evidence of female involvement in Irish organisations in mid-century Liverpool, but this is as likely to reflect the status of women in Liverpool in general as it is to indicate that women did not support such activities.

26. Oral studies of present-day communities have certainly suggested that such strategies are important for some Irish women. See Walter, *Gender and Irish Migration*, p. 33.

27. For more information see Hyde, *Liverpool*; R. Williams, *The Liverpool Docks Problem*, Liverpool Economic and Statistical Society, Liverpool, 1912.

28. See Roberts, *Women's Work*; Rendall, *Women in an Industrializing Society*.

29. H. Shimmin, *The Courts and Alleys of Liverpool*, Liverpool, 1864. Reprinted by Garland Publishing, New York, 1985, p. 48.

30. See also H. Shimmin, *Liverpool Life*, Liverpool, 1856. Reprinted by Garland Publishing, New York, 1985. For a slightly later period see C. Black, *Married Women's Work*, G. Bell, London, 1915. Republished by Virago, London, 1983.

31. See for example C. Dyhouse, *Feminism and the Family in England, 1880–1939*, Blackwell, Oxford, 1989; S. Walby, *Patriarchy at Work*, University of Minnesota Press, Minneapolis, 1986; J. Lown, *Women and Industrialization: Gender at Work in Nineteenth-century England*, Polity Press, Oxford, 1990; M. Simey, *Charitable Effort in Liverpool in the Nineteenth Century*, Liverpool University Press, Liverpool, 1951. For a contemporary view see J. Butler, ed., *Women's Work and Women's Culture*, Macmillan, London, 1869.

32. See for example: S. Gilley, 'English attitudes to the Irish in England, 1780–1900', in C. Holmes, ed., *Immigrants and Minorities in British Society*, Allen and Unwin, London, 1978, pp. 81–110; M.A.G. O'Tuathaigh, 'The Irish in nineteenth-century Britain: problems of integration', *Transactions of the Royal Historical Society*, 5th series, 31, 1981, pp. 149–74.

33. Dyhouse, *Feminism and the Family*; Walby, *Patriarchy at Work*; Lown, *Women and Industrialization*; Rendall, *Women in an Industrializing Society*.

34. K. Harris, *Sex, Ideology and Religion. The Representation of Women in the Bible*, Barnes and Noble, New Jersey, 1984.

35. Shimmin, *Liverpool Life*, p. 44.

36. Shimmin, *The Courts and Alleys*, p. 20.

37. Walby, *Patriarchy at Work*; Lown, *Women and Industrialization*.

38. See for example evidence in H. Mayhew, *London Labour and the London Poor*, Cass, London, 1967. First published, 1861–2.

39. W.S. Trench, *Report on the Health of Liverpool*, Liverpool, 1866. p. 23.

40. For more general discussions of female crime see D. Philips, *Crime and Authority in Victorian England*, Croom Helm, London, 1977, p. 148; D. Jones, *Crime, Protest, Community and Police in Nineteenth-century Britain*, Routledge, London, 1982, pp. 167–8. More generally see C. Emsley, *Crime and Society in England, 1750–1900*, Longman, London, 1987. For an analysis of crime in nineteenth-century Liverpool see J. Tobias, 'A statistical study of a nineteenth-century criminal area', *British Journal of Criminology*, 14, 1974, pp. 221–35.

41. This would parallel the experience of many Black youths in present-day Britain. See G. Ben Tovim *et al.*, eds, *Racial Disadvantage in Liverpool — an Area Profile*, University of Liverpool, Liverpool, 1981, pp. 71–85; Lord Scarman, *The Scarman Report*, Penguin, Harmondsworth, 1982, Part 4; J. Benyon, ed., *Scarman and After*, Pergamon, Oxford, 1984, Part 3.

42. This assertion is based mainly on negative rather than positive evidence for the mid-nineteenth century. It is an area in need of much more research.

43. See for example: R.J. Evans, *Comrades and Sisters: Feminism, Socialism and Pacifism in Europe 1870–1945*, Wheatsheaf Books, Brighton, 1987; S. Oldfield, *Women against the Iron Fist: Alternatives to Militarism, 1900–1989*, Blackwell, Oxford, 1989; A. Cook and G. Kirk, *Greenham Women Everywhere: Dreams, Ideas and Actions from the Women's Peace Movement*, Pluto, London, 1983; P. Smoker, R. Davies and B. Munske, eds, *A Reader in Peace Studies*, Pergamon, Oxford, 1990, especially Section 5, 'The contribution of feminism to the understanding of peace'.

5 Irish women workers and American labor patterns: the Philadelphia story

Dennis Clark

Various studies have detailed the slow and unsteady course of the absorption of Irish male workers into the American labor force.[1] Such research throws light on the broad and intricate issue of the adaptation of immigrants to the economic realities of the American economy. A key consideration with respect to Irish workers is the fact that their extensive engagement with the American labor force began earlier and lasted longer than that of almost all other ethnic groups with the exception of English workers and Blacks. The immigrant ethnic infusions of the period after 1850 tend to obscure the longevity of the Irish labor patterns. The scope of this ethnic work history is a formidable challenge to study. It ranges across whole developmental stages of American economic growth.

One of the most obscure and intriguing components of this long sequence of work life is the part played by women, and this subject has really only become accessible for analysis because of the intellectual revolution stimulated by the study of women's history in recent years. It is not possible to address more than a fragmentary portion of the panorama of Irish–American female work life in this chapter, but the present study is devoted to an illustration of the great span of this female work experience. The focus on three quite different periods of labor history should serve to remind us of the difficulties of exploring a terrain so new and extensive as women's studies. Each of the periods of economic development treated is sufficiently distinctive so that generalizations about the lives of immigrant women and their daughters must remain tentative. The extraordinary diversity of American society is a basic condition influencing such inquiries.

The major city of Philadelphia, where the American experiment was launched in the eighteenth century, became one of the most dynamic segments of the Atlantic seaboard economy. It offers, therefore, an advantageous locale in which to explore the history of immigrant women workers. Beginning as a colonial port, the city was soon the second largest English-speaking city in the British Empire. Its eighteenth-century growth due to shipping, a rich agricultural hinterland and a thriving craft economy endowed it with central political importance as the American Revolution approached. The persistent need for more labor made it a magnet for immigrants. In the 1830s a new formulation of production in the factory system benefited from the city becoming a transportation nexus of great strategic importance. A base of heavy industry and widely diversified manufacturing made Philadelphia the nation's premier industrial center, and its prominence in this respect lasted until the 1920s. After that a new diversification ensued and light industry, scientific production and service industries accumulated, especially in the rich suburban belt around the old city. These successive mobilizations of economic activity were each distinct settings for the employment of Irish females, and represented a clear difference of social situations in which they had to adapt to labor conditions.[2]

Historian Jean R. Soderlund has provided a critique of the picture of female status that has been available to us prior to the period of broadened historical study of female life. She documents the narrowness of the depiction because of the dominance of upper-class sources and other biases in portrayals of the eighteenth century, and notes the gender role differences from one ethnic group to another that are seldom reflected in the portrayals.[3] Certainly the Irish in the eighteenth century, whether Protestant or Catholic, labored under distinctive disabilities. Alice Kessler Harris and Virginia Yans McLaughlin state that generally, 'The Irish seem to have experienced more overt economic and legal discrimination than any other group, partly because they were the first large ethnic group entering the nation to present the triple threats of religious, class and ethnic differences.'[4]

Indentures and inferiority

An examination of the indentured female labor of the eighteenth century in Philadelphia permits some insight into the pre-industrial work-force at the bottom of the occupational scale among white immigrants. An advertisement in *The Pennsylvania Gazette* in 1769 for a runaway indentured servant suggests the invidious view of such workers at the time:

> Between the Ninth and Seventh day,
> Mary Nowland ran away;
> Her age I know not but appears
> To be at least full twenty years;
> The same religion with the Pope,
> Short neck, scarce room to fix a rope;
> Brown hair, red face, short nose, thick lips,
> She's large and round from neck to hips;
> Short, thick and clumsy in her jog
> As neat as any fattened hog.
> Upon her tongue she wears a brogue,
> And was she man would be a rogue ...
> Whoever takes her up, don't fail
> To lay her fast in any jail ...[5]

The two main stimuli of emigration of Irish indentured labor to America were outright poverty and the need to pay for passage across the Atlantic. Labor agents went to Ireland to seek out redemptioners, and there was an unsavory trade in Irish ports in which officials sold passages for redemptioners to ship captains and agents for a good fee. The agents were known at the time as 'soul drivers'. A great many of the bound servants from British ports were also Irish, and their careers in America were far from enviable. In Philadelphia the Guardians of the Poor had the power to indenture Almshouse inmates, but officials and the courts were empowered to indenture criminals and debtors, orphans and runaway children as well.[6]

As the Philadelphia economy developed, the increase in some crafts and the decline of others created dislocations among craftsmen with resulting disruption of indenture relationships. As handweaving declined in the face of textile factory growth, for instance, those indentured to handweavers were placed in an occupational limbo. Old skills became redundant. Many of the females indentured, however, were never destined to learn a valued skill. A review of the Indenture Book of the Moyamensing Commissioners, who presided over a raucous area south of the city proper, shows that the females with distinctively Irish names bound to service were usually under ten years of age and were bound to 'housewifery'. These child workers taken into American households were bound for terms of seven, fourteen or twenty-one years. They were usually in family work situations where they were to work from sun-up to sundown, subject to both family and occupational discipline, practically excluded from schooling and expected to observe the religion of the family to which they were attached.[7]

Although the growth of the factory system had gradually eroded the indenture system by the second half of the nineteenth century, its long persistence carried with it a record of abuse that stimulated a steady absconding by the bound people. In colonial times the great majority of the runaways were Irish and English.[8] One study found that fifty-four per cent of all runaways in the Philadelphia area were Irish. They fled long hours, monotonous labor, poor living conditions, stern masters and harsh punishments. Thus, the indentured drawn from the ranks of beggars, orphans or families in which the parents could not support them, toiled or fled. As late as 1857 the Children's Asylum of the Guardians of the Poor was still indenturing children as young as three years into such tasks as serving in tavern kitchens, tending hogs and the drudgery of laundering.[9]

One result of this indenture work predicament and the escape of the Irish workers involved is that it stimulated an image of the Irish as unreliable workers that became widespread. Dale Knobel shows that this image was a major factor in thinking about the Irish in the first half of the nineteenth century long before the great Famine influx of the 1840s.[10] The courts and officials were active in pursuing fugitives who broke their indenture, just as they pursued runaway slaves, so that the rancor engendered by escapes and recaptures can be imagined. Hence, this labor condition early in the history of the country helped to shape the occupational setting for

Irish women workers in a period when exploitation of labor generally was largely untrammeled by complex considerations of social justice or governmental responsibility for the welfare of working people.

Famine refugees

In the generation that experienced the Famine calamity of the 1840s, the occupational world of the United States was a bewildering refuge for Irish emigrants. One of the Quaker philanthropist Vere Foster's informants, writing back to Ireland from the state of Virginia stated, 'Many is the poor woman I have seen on bended knees and (with) uplifted hands called [sic] the curse of God on Irish Landlords and the British government who have driven them from their homes to be risked in a foreign land where there is but little compassion for the poor.' Although this correspondent reported that servant girls could earn six or seven dollars a month, he also confirmed that prices for housing, clothes and necessities were very high, and that milliners and tailoresses were poorly paid.[11] The jobs commonly open to Irish women in Philadelphia were street vending, domestic work, needle trades, sifting and sorting work and laundering. There was, too, begging, and *The Philadelphia Bulletin* editorialized in 1858 with respect to one beggar 'There is the fat and saucy Irishwoman, who always steers with a peculiarly insolent slide, so as to intercept one's progress, something as a pirate craft which has got the wind of a wealthy merchantman, bears down on the latter and sticks close to it'.[12] The intolerance implicit in the characterization is obvious. A sampling of the Female Vagrant Register in the Philadelphia Archives from 1874 gives evidence of scores of Irish-born women who were jobless and homeless. Their average ages being about forty-three years, they were in all probability women used up by that period of their lives and bereft of employment opportunities.[13]

In 1879 the Report of the Superintendent of the Twenty-Fourth Ward of the Society for the Organization of Charitable Relief and Repressing Mendicancy listed over a thousand females requiring charity, and some one-third of these were Irish-born.[14] An organization for 'Suppressing Pauperism' meeting in 1878 was publicized in *The Public Ledger* newspaper, and a letter in response to its proceedings from a hard-pressed woman stated:

> It is very true that the woman who makes seersucker coats for six cents apiece or does other sewing at the same rate, and has to work eighteen hours of the twenty-four cannot spare a minute to take care of her child and all the time she takes to wash, dress and feed it is so much stolen from the effort to keep a roof over its head or get it bread.[15]

In the decades after the Civil War, however, the situation changed for Irish working women. Their presence even became desirable in the burgeoning factory system for they could be hired at cheaper wages than men. Conditions in Ireland conspired to continue the flow of female labor to cities such as Philadelphia. Janet Nolan states that 'by 1880, when all of Ireland had been transformed from a subsistence into a cash economy, fully two-thirds of all women over age fifteen in the country were unmarried and unable to find a man to "protect" them from the harsh reality of their diminished social and economic status'.[16] Hasia Diner notes that the unfavorable position of rural women with respect to inheritance and land arrangements in Ireland left them little alternative but to leave their island homes. Against this background, female emigration exceeded male emigration from 1880 to 1920 by 82,000, with the largest female exodus clustered around 1880.[17] The need for factory 'hands' and domestic servants expanded as the economy surged. In a St Patrick's Day editorial in *The Philadelphia Times* in 1875, a provocatively patronizing tone was mixed with some sympathetic thoughts about Irish women:

> But what are we to say of the daughters — compelled to be the drudges of our households and the victims of a social aristocracy and of outrages utterly at variance with democratic notions and often cruelly unjust? ... they too have their compensations ... They are secure from competition and can afford to laugh at their detractors ... And they have fewer faults, too, than are charged to them. Tidiness seems their natural state, and no people are more obedient, affectionate and faithful when kindly used.[18]

Mill-hands and slavies

The great expansion of the industrial mass labor market had changed employment patterns irrevocably. Examination of Irish female immigrant occupations based on the materials of the Philadelphia Social History Project gives a picture of employment distribution using a sample of data from the 1880 US census. The sample contained 1,033 persons whose household heads were Irish-born. The resident females in the sample were 54 per cent Irish-born.[19] The first American-born generation in these households, we can have little doubt, would have considered themselves Irish-Americans. Given what we know about the high endogamous patterns of marriage among the Irish, and the cohesiveness of family and community ethnic bonds at the time, it is not an exaggeration to characterize the females as 'Irish', for culturally and ethnically they were part of the city's very large Irish community. First names characteristic of the Irish at the time, the residence of the women in heavily Irish enclaves and the kinds of jobs the women held also mark them as part of that portion of the population that formed a largely self-contained cultural system in the second half of the nineteenth century. It should be noted in this respect that between 1860 and 1910 there were never less than 100,000 Irish-born people residing in the city.

The economy into which the immigrant women in the sample were introduced was complex and active. By the 1870s, Philadelphia had become a vast hive of labor and technology. It encompassed 125,000 buildings, 300 miles of paved streets, 86,000 gas lights, 8,339 businesses turning out 335 million dollars worth of production annually. By 1880 this huge expanse of docks, warehouses, mills, stores and transit facilities had a population of 875,000. The Irish were both segregated in older areas around the central business district and scattered throughout the city in communities formed by railroad construction, textile factories and various processing centers. There were 100,000 Irish-born people in the city and great numbers of American-born Irish from previous generations of immigration. The city economy was emerging from the deep Depression of 1873, and women in the labor force were caught up in the expansion of manufacturing, the emergence of expanded retail marketing and the need for service workers at various levels of urban life.[20]

Within this economic structure there was a strong demand for female servants and for mill workers. The relation of Irishwomen to the work-force was conditioned by endogamous marriage patterns that carried with them religious constraints about female family roles and cultural expectations about fertility and household duties. The Irish were subject to widespread discriminatory practices and social disadvantages in recruitment for jobs and in access to education. The presence of large numbers of Irish immigrants in the city for generations had led to their concentration in such labor areas as textile manufacture, garment manufacture and servant categories.

The following is a listing of the occupations recorded for 1,033 women residing in households in the sample employed in this study:

Keeping house	585
Factory or mill work	152
Needle trades	105
Servants	86
Clerks and sales	31
Weavers	23
Washerwomen	15
Teachers	11
Milliners	11
Book manufacture	5
Hairdressers	3
Boarding house keeper	2
Presser-starcher	2
Corsetmaker	1
Nurse	1

Some comment upon this listing may provide further insight. In the census designations women are listed both as 'Keeping house' and 'Housekeeper'. This could be a source of major confusion. Colloquially, 'keeping house' implied being at home and caring for a household. 'Housekeeper' was usually a woman who acted in a servant capacity in a household, boarding house or hotel. Factory and mill workers were employed in establishments making shirts, shoes, boxes, umbrellas, cigars, matches and soap. Only one supervisory forelady was among them. Among those in the needle trades there were tailoresses, dressmakers, seamstresses and those listed as doing 'sewing', perhaps piecework or 'outwork' clothworkers. Among the clerks and sales personnel were those working in stores selling drygoods, candy, groceries, cigars and 'variety' items. The lack of listings for food preparation work is perhaps related to the fact that much food preparation was done by servants, or to the dominance of males in commercial cooking and food preparation. Only one woman baker and a market stand seller were listed as food workers. Women in the needle trades were buffeted in the 1880s by the changes wrought by the sewing machine. Proportional drafting systems and production of patterns on paper were part of a revolution in sewing that was bringing about more and more cheap clothing, and that was also downgrading the traditional skills of needle workers.[21]

In addition to these working women, there were a number of females listed in the processed census schedules examined with no occupation and with the designation of simply being 'At home'. The oldest was seventy and the youngest fourteen years old, and there were forty-six such names. Possible reasons for females being at home would include illness, pregnancy confinement, unemployment, old age or affluence that exempted them from the work-force. What the distinction was between 'At home' and 'Keeping house' must remain a mystery of enumerator's jargon. There were, as well, numerous student females designated as being 'At school'. These two categories of females were not included in the occupational sample although they were distributed throughout the census listings.

The Philadelphia Social History Project tabulations did include marital status designations, so that it was possible to determine that only a very few of the married women were in the work-force outside the home. Single women at home included dependent daughters or relatives and widows as well as those suggested above. Married women who worked were subject to criticism, particularly by trade unionists, because they were believed to be taking jobs rightfully belonging to men, and were invidiously regarded because they supposedly already had men to 'support' them. Since by 1880 only three per cent of females were in 'white–collar' positions nationally, many jobs outside the home were seen as unladylike, full of moral temptations and otherwise unsuitable for females.[22] Catholic clergy often opposed female labor in factories, and the Papal encyclical *Rerum Novarum* in 1891 declared that 'woman is by nature fitted for home-work'.[23] The significance of this opinion bias in society for working women was trenchant, for it stigmataized not only those married women forced into the labor force, but cast moral aspersion even upon those single women who had to earn their bread by daily work. An added feature was the stratification imposed by the kind of labor itself and attitudes toward it. Factory girls were viewed as more independent than servants, and servants were regarded as those with the least status.[24]

A look at the family situations of some of the Irish women workers puts the statistical information into some human perspective. The women workers were concentrated heavily in the various working-class districts that by 1880 had become traditional havens for immigrant families. Cheap red brick row housing was the dominant dwelling type, and it was frequently located amid mills, railroad yards, noisome stables and commercial premises jumbled together in the mixed land-use pattern of the urban landscape. In the Kensington area, a district with huge textile factories, Elizabeth McDevitt, 51, kept house for her husband, James, a laborer, and her daughters, Mary and Lizzie, who worked in cotton mills. Charles Lafferty operated a dye house in the same area, and his daughter, Mary, had a millinery store, while son, Peter, was a 'digger'. In another semi-industrial district in North Philadelphia, Kate and Maryann McCarty 'kept house' for 'hotel keeper' Dennis McCarty who had five laborers as tenants. Sarah Nevill in this neighborhood was still at work as a spooler in a mill at age 80. She was similar to Agnes Craig, who was 70 and still winding bobbins in a Kensington mill. More fortunate were the Dunn sisters who lived near old Sarah Nevill. All four sisters, Maggie, Mary, Mattie and Lillie, aged nineteen to thirty, were teachers, quite an achievement for a family of Irish girls whose parents were not with them in 1880. In the Schuylkill area, the city's most concentrated Irish neighborhood, Mary Lecky kept house for daughters Jane and Kate, who worked as shirtmakers. Thus, the Irish immigrant female work-force was distributed across the factory-filled city, working in carpet and hosiery mills, cleaning, cooking and sewing, a population of laboring women from largely rural backgrounds, adapting to the economy and the work life of urban society.

Calculating the ages of the labor force workers contrasted with those of the women keeping house is problematical. The mores of the time for females led to understatements of age as a minor fetish of behavior. For employed females there could be misleading ages given for those who were in the work-force very young in order to avoid some early child labor strictures. The average age of those keeping house in this sample was 34 years, and for those employed outside the home 24.7 years.

Daughters of the City

Some comparisons of this Philadelphia data with that from other studies provide indications of how much a large city differed from smaller communities. In studies of women in servant employment the US census as late as 1900 shows 54 per cent as Irish-born as a national figure. In Kingston, New York, virtually all Irish women were servants, and in Buffalo two-thirds of those 18 to 21 years old were servants.[25] In this Philadelphia sample, those designated servants made up only 19 per cent of the females in the work-force. Although Irish women were said to prefer servant jobs because they were more stable than lay-off prone factory jobs, and hence permitted steadier remittances back to Ireland, in Philadelphia this was apparently less so. Factory and other jobs probably offered better wages and more autonomy despite harsh conditions. There was in the large Philadelphia labor market a broader range of employment available, for the city economy was highly diversified. Although native-American women commonly rejected servant work as demeaning, many Irish women had less latitude to do so considering their economic needs and lack of other kinds of experience.

Kleinberg found that by 1880 16 per cent of all women were in the labor force nationally. This contrasts with the situation of the women in this Philadelphia Irish data set, 43.3 per cent of whom were in the work-force outside the home.[26] The position of immigrant women and their daughters in the industrial environment meant not only that they had to work because of economic necessity, but that occupational practices afforded them jobs, albeit at lesser wages than men and in occupational structures where there was less opportunity for upward mobility and where protection by labor organizations was rare. It was not until 1885 that the intrepid Mary Hannafin was appointed even to collect data on female workers for the Knights of Labor in Philadelphia.[27]

A notable absence in these statistics is evidence of the keeping of boarding houses by women. Alice Kessler–Harris remarks that census takers did not even bother to note boarding house operations, and she sees this as a factor in the underestimation of female economic contributions. Similarly, there is little evidence of child employment in these figures, but Claudia Goldin in an intensive analysis of the Project data on children found that 45 per cent of the female children over eleven years were employed.[28] This is another factor pertaining to the earning capacity of the families involved.

Kessler–Harris found that three or more mill workers per family were required to be at employment to provide a sufficient family income in textile labor.[29] In the female sample used in this article textile employment was the largest single form of occupation outside the home, since 152 women worked in mills and factories, many of them hosiery and cotton mills of various kinds, while 23 women were listed as weavers, and many of the 105 women in the needle trades would have been involved with textile fabrication as well. In Philadelphia, Michael Haines calculated that the lowest quartile of families by income contained a disproportionate quotient of Irish, and that the males in these families had the lowest wage occupations.[30] The occupational pattern, therefore, was one that placed families in a vulnerable position in view of the interrupted work cycles common for men and women at the time. The fact that such a high proportion of women in this sample were in the work-force outside the home in itself testifies to the economic necessity to work.

Although there were many textile workers, the job market did offer diversity. Factory skills were often varied, or at least involved with different kinds of products. Teaching and nursing had not yet emerged as extensive occupational choices for such women, and they would require educational progress to gain access to such jobs. Still, the job market in a large city did offer more choices than the avenue of work as a servant.

Of the women who kept house for the families in this sample, almost all of whom were married or widows, there is no information in the data set used about how many of them earned some money by forms of labor beyond housekeeping. Carol Groneman found that in New York at an earlier period between one-fourth and one-third of immigrant Irish women earned some income to supplement the family budget.[31] The role of the household-maintaining women as supporters of the immigrant social fabric was a central factor in sustaining ethnic cohesion. It was in the home that personal and family identity and ethnic consciousness were cultivated, and the presence of female figures anchoring the household through daily supportive work to produce order, cleanliness and food strongly enhanced Irish domestic and community stability. Still, according to the customs of the time, these women had to forego increased family income to carry out the responsibilities they assumed for household labor and child nurture.

These findings underscore the distinctive patterns of a large city environment. Research into work life has often been undertaken by social historians in smaller cities such as Lowell, Massachusetts, or Paterson, New Jersey, where the compactness of the labor market and the availability of records in manageable form made study practical. The Philadelphia Social History Project afforded an opportunity to examine job holding among women in a complex urban setting, and the contrasts are notable, showing the generalized character of statistics compiled from national census materials and the more discrete nature of data from a specific but larger community.

The Philadelphia data also show the limited labor market opportunities available to these women at the time, and the vulnerability they experienced being concentrated in areas of occupation notorious for low wages, factory health hazards and unsteady employment patterns. The Irish women made a disadvantageous bargain in their new environment: dead-end jobs were taken in a large and impersonal labor market, and in return for long hours and assignment to low social status, wages and some degree of independence were obtained that contributed to the support of families or the setting up of one's own household. It was only slowly that the daughters and granddaughters of these women freed themselves from that bargain.

A new technology

Beginning in the 1890s, the employment market for women began to change again. The pre-industrial era in the first part of the nineteenth century faded with the rise of the factory system, but the change was massive, so absorption of immigrant women was gradual. The diversification following full industrialization that began in the 1890s was also gradual. It was accompanied by a 'schooling to order' in parochial and public schools, and a succession of temperance and moral campaigns with active female participation. As a projection of nineteenth-century phenomena into the twentieth century, the field of domestic service remained extensive, and Irish rural women flocked to it. Interviews with women in Philadelphia provide ample evidence of the advantages over Irish rural life that they found in American domestic service.[32] At the same time, nursing and teaching careers rapidly expanded. Records of the Philadelphia General Hospital School of Nursing and the Girls Normal School for training teachers show the rising entry of young women with Irish names. The emergence of female clerical jobs and such networks as telephone company employment brought tens of thousands of females into new roles in work life.[33] The passing of Victorian restrictions on women, especially the swift tide of change in the 1920s, made the acquisition of new educational and employment opportunities possible.

Although World War I meant employment in factory jobs of a different kind in war industries as the American Leviathan produced materials for the Allied battles against the Germans, patterns of sex discrimination were extended into the fields of new opportunities. Sex segregation in the labor market changed little in the following decades. Women were given preference for low-wage factory jobs and the expanding white-collar clerical jobs, but were excluded to the greatest extent possible from wide areas of skilled and semi-skilled industrial and management positions.[34] There was ethnic segregation that persisted in the labor force as well. In 1890 more than 90 per cent of the clerical work-force was born in the United States.[35] Irish-born women were still confined to factory, servant and petty retail work, and this changed only slowly over the next half century. So strong were the lines of sex segregation that in 1930, after a booming decade of 1920s prosperity, of every ten women in the work-force, three were domestics, two worked in low-wage garment labor and one was either a school teacher or nurse. The field of domestic service, though, was rapidly shrinking, for between 1880 and 1920 the number of domestics had fallen by one half.[36]

The transformation of housework due to the introduction of household appliances and electricity did create a different and less arduous domestic realm, and the evolution of the 'companionate' family with less patriarchal control permitted women much more freedom. Still, many women found the prospect of wifely responsibilities to be more intimidating than they cared to tolerate. High religious idealism and the prospect of higher ethnic social status and education led large numbers of Irish women into religious orders of nurses and teachers. In Philadelphia there were by 1920 114 Catholic churches, five hospitals and a whole network of charities, and these institutions were served by 3,560 nuns, the great majority of whom were Irish-born or Irish–American. This career option was strongly attractive to women who sought to find a life of ordered commitment as an alternative to a city working-class environment that was often tawdry and shallow, beset with drab domesticity and unfulfilling diversions.[37]

The situation of women in the work-force in new areas of technology often meant that they were more closely supervised than ever. Scientific management was one of the dominant themes of early twentieth-century business organization, and this meant the application of rationalizing techniques that were a stark contrast to the work patterns and setting in a still largely rural Ireland. Time was budgeted to the minute in these new labor settings where people were paced to machines. Insurance companies gave their clerical workers a scant thirty minutes for lunch. Women in assembly line positions in light industry had to match the speed of the conveyor belts beside which they worked. Time clocks to mark the minute of arrival and departure from work were standard features of factory and office life, and workers were docked of pay for minute lateness or departure infractions. Instead of the common nineteenth-century adjacency of worker housing and factories, cities like Philadelphia expanded so that long commutes by bus and subway were now required to reach work locations. Some employers still insisted on hiring only unmarried female workers, and pregnancy brought dismissal for women in many jobs. Although the brutal regimes of textile and other machine tending jobs were somewhat relieved by unionization and legislation curtailing the length of the work day for females, the intensity of labor in service to more technical and managerially sophisticated technology was a draining regimen for thousands.

An instance of this situation is reflected in the new telephone industry that arose with remarkable rapidity as the twentieth century progressed. The job of telephone operator was a popular one for Irish-American women in Philadelphia in the early decades of the century. Hundreds of women trooped daily to the big telephone exchange buildings where they would tend the switchboards that handled a myriad of telephone calls daily. The telephone exchanges functioned around the clock, so that women with children to raise could often work at night while the children slept. Irish-born women as native speakers of English did not face the barriers of many foreign-born women in entering the communications field. Irish-American women, having attended parish schools, were usually well grounded in their basic literacy and education, and employers also thought them amenable to authority because of the code of respect for teachers and school discipline in which they had been tutored. For these reasons the Irish women were thought to be well adapted to the telephone tasks. The mammoth telephone companies, all but monopolies in their field, also wanted a work-force shielded from strong trade unionism, and the Catholic background of the overwhelming majority of the female 'telephone girls' was believed to be a safeguard against militancy and an assurance of docility. When labor organization threatened, the telephone companies were quick to form company unions and to create managerial coddling that outflanked the more active kind of labor unions. The companies created a cult of 'telephone girl' propaganda that romanticized the switchboard labor and glamorized such work for women whose horizons had previously been limited to factory jobs and domestic service.

The technology of the early decades of the twentieth century in the telephone industry required constant attention by human minds and hands. Long aisles of switchboards tended by female operators thrived with the electronic messages of the new age. Hour after hour the operators had to respond to the callers and calls, and the supervision was omnipresent. The operators had to be familiar with technical rules for their work and the switchboard rooms were policed with a sharp oversight.[38] The glamor of the job eventually faded as the rigors of the routine took hold. The Communications Workers of America began organizing drives in the workforce and strikes for better wages and working conditions ensued.[39] The telephone companies, with a full mastery of communications and persuasion techniques, were difficult opponents of the labor organizers, but the labor groups independent of the company unions gradually gained strength. Better conditions were secured, but ultimately changing technology bringing about fully automated systems with few direct human interventions made 'telephone girls' an anachronism. Most Irish-born and Irish-American females moved on to broader job fields.

In the first half of the twentieth century the educational disparity between Irish-born women and their American counterparts with respect to schooling that oriented them toward the American labor market ordained that women emigrants from Ireland's rural areas were at a distinct disadvantage in employment in cities like Philadelphia, despite the fact that this city was highly diverse.[40] Patterns of low-wage employment persisted through 'chain reference' of women into accepted areas of labor. The traditional family ties that continued through the emigration trajectory led thousands of women to work in jobs that previous emigrants had filtered into, and concentrations of Irish women workers abounded in certain unskilled fields. One of these was the job of waitress. Major restaurant chains such as Schraffts, Lintons and especially Horn and Hardart had large forces of table-serving women, and Irish women became fixtures in these chains in the decades from 1920 to 1970. Again, round-the-clock service hours often permitted women with children to work at night. The ruddy faces of matronly servers behind the steam tables filled with hearty food, and the smiling waitress, bantering in her brogue, became one of the pleasant features of eating in these big and popular restaurants over the years. The coming of competition from black women seeking these jobs was a disrupting factor toward the end of the lifetime of these restaurant chains.[41] But, the invention of the 'fast food' industry with its simpler packaged menu was the influence that finally subverted this whole area of low-wage, low-skill work that had been a province of Irish immigrant women.

The age of feminism

It was only in the 1960s, when an ideology of feminism began to assert itself in growing campaigns for employment equality for women, that attitudes and practices showed signs of notably changing. The increased entry of women into the labor market, with over half of the white women over sixteen years of age in the labor force, has meant a profound change in work life. The traditional male dominance and female disabilities are being challenged on every hand. Hence, the prospects for female Irish immigrants in American economic settings, though still hampered by inequities, are historically altered to a great degree. The increase in second and third-level education in Ireland has meant that women coming to America are much better prepared to compete for well-paying jobs. This is fortunate because many of the older forms of employment that required only limited education are now wiped out by automation and the need for higher qualifications. There is, however, a changed demographic character for all of the United States, and large black, Hispanic and other minorities are actively pressing for advantages for their own groups, so that Irish newcomers face strong competition for employment.

There continues to be a wage gap faced by women in relation to male earnings in the 1990s. Women make only 66 per cent of male wages. Sixty per cent of professional women are confined to teaching and nursing. As Alice Kessler-Harris has pointed out, the impact of women on work life outside the home has challenged gender controlled patterns of self-esteem and social organization. With women owning 30 per cent of all businesses in Pennsylvania, cities like Philadelphia are committed to responding to pressures for changing the disparities of status affecting employed women.[42]

For young Irishwomen coming into the United States legally under liberalized immigration laws in the 1990s, educational and employment trajectories are greatly extended. Illegal entrants will still face the problem of earning their support through relatively low-level, and frequently exploited, tasks such as housecleaning, childminding and waitress service. For those with full legal status, however, earnings depend upon the ability to prepare for employment and press against outmoded gender roles. A survey of women appearing in the pages of the Philadelphia *Irish Edition*, a monthly newspaper, revealed the following occupations during 1990 as part of the listings of personalities in its coverage of women in Irish community activities:

County Commissioner
School Board Member
Laboratory technician
Business proprietors—4
Professional musicians—6
Attorneys—3
Youth worker
College professors—2
Museum guide
Environmental scientist
Television actress
Newspaper columnist
Artist
Real estate manager
Veterinarian
Athlete
Author
Dance teacher
Radio announcer

Social worker
Labor union executive
Horticulturist
Librarian
Nuns[43]

Although these occupations may be accessible to only a portion of the Irish-born and Irish-American women in the area, they do reflect the diversity of a metropolitan economy and the attainments of a wide range of females from this community. There is in all probability an even broader spectrum of occupational differentiation represented within this ethnic group.[44]

The foregoing has traced the employment worlds of Irishwomen in pre-industrial, industrial and post-industrial settings. The long perspective reminds us of the protracted length of the social experience of the group in America. The engagement with industrial employment was obviously the most transforming experience for Irish immigrant females. It transcended the life-style and work that had gone before, and it prepared, at times very harshly, the working women for the educational and vocational changes that lay beyond the industrial economy. The entire human drama of the transition from a traditional Irish rural economy to a metropolitan industrial and technical economy is one of the astonishing historic departures of modern times. We have only just begun to interpret what it has meant for the women who took part in it.

The documentation of the dispersion of Irish females throughout various countries, part of a vast international emigration and resettlement, challenges us to examine the assumptions of our historical writing. The biological role of these women as child bearers alone is a subject of momentous significance in an era of population explosion. The diffusion of female-supported familism from a rural Irish base into metropolitan societies with their developing urban patterns has constituted a notable source of social stability amid tides of economic disruption and spiritual dislocation. The previously prevailing historical perspective with its political and patriarchal orientation must now yield to the elevation of that female half of society that has been submerged in previous studies. In the course of the revelation of this new human testament of female social participation, the history of those Irish women who left their island's shores will certainly revolutionize our understanding of the past of Ireland's people.

Notes

1. See R.A. Burchell, *The San Francisco Irish, 1848–1880*, University of California Press, Berkeley, CA, 1980, pp. 52–72; Alan Dawley, *Class and Community: The Industrial Revolution in Lynn*, Harvard University Press, Cambridge, MA, 1976, pp. 129–49; Dennis Clark, 'The Irish in the American Economy', in P.J. Drudy, ed., *The Irish in America: Emigration, Assimilation and Impact*, Cambridge University Press, New York, 1985, pp. 231–52; David M. Emmons, *The Butte Irish:*

Class and Ethnicity in an American Mining Town, 1875–1925, University of Illinois Press, Urbana, IL, 1989, pp. 180–220; Theodore Hershberg, ed., *Philadelphia: Work, Space, Family and Group Experience in the Nineteenth Century*, Oxford University Press, New York, 1981, *passim*; Bruce Laurie, *Working People of Philadelphia*, Temple University Press, Philadelphia, 1980, pp. 33–106; Stephan Thernstrom, *Poverty and Progress: Social Mobility in a Nineteenth Century City*, Harvard University Press, Cambridge, MA, 1969, pp. 57–192; Stephan Thernstrom, *The Other Bostonians: Poverty and Progress in the American Metropolis, 1880–1970*, Harvard University Press, Cambridge, MA, 1973, pp. 111–44.

2. Sam Bass Warner, Jr., *The Private City: Philadelphia in Three Periods of Its Growth*, University of Pennsylvania Press, Philadelphia, 1968, pp. xi–xii.

3. Jean R. Soderlund, 'Women in 18th century Pennsylvania: toward a model of diversity', *Pennsylvania Magazine of History and Biography*, Vol. 116, No. 2, April 1991, pp. 164–79.

4. Alice Kessler–Harris and Virginia Yans McLaughlin, 'European immigrant groups', in Thomas Sowell, ed., *American Ethnic Groups*, The Urban Institute, Washington, 1978.

5. *The Pennsylvania Gazette* (Philadelphia), 29 June 1769.

6. Lewis R. Harley, 'The Redemptioners', Address to the Montgomery County Historical Society, 31 May 1893, p. 1.

7. Moyamensing Commissioners Indenture Book, Archives of the City of Philadelphia, RG. 214.2.

8. Karl F. Geiser, *Redemptioners and Indentured Service in the Colony and Commonwealth of Pennsylvania*, The Tuttle, Morehouse and Taylor Co., New Haven, CT, 1901, p. 81; Ian M.G. Quimby, 'Apprenticeship in Colonial Philadelphia', MA dissertation, University of Delaware, 1963, p. 153.

9. Cheeseman Herrick, *White Servitude in Pennsylvania*, John J. McVey, Philadelphia, 1926, p. 265; Guardians of the Poor, Committee on the Children's Asylum, Minutes, November 1856–July 1857, Archives of the City of Philadelphia, RG 35.2; Gibson Bell Smith, 'Footloose and Fancy Free: the Demography and Sociology of the Runaway Class in Colonial Pennsylvania', MA Paper, Bryn Mawr College, 29 April 1971, pp. 6–17.

10. Dale T. Knobel, *Paddy and the Republic: Ethnicity and Nationality in Antebellum America*, Wesleyan Univeristy Press, Middletown, CT, 1986, pp. 165–82.

11. Ruth Ann Harris, 'If there be no chance of marriage then many shall cross the pond: new perspectives on the American letters from Vere Foster's emigrants' Paper for the American Conference for Irish Studies Conference, Washington, DC, November 1990, pp. 8–10.

12. *The Evening Bulletin* (Philadelphia), 5 January 1858.

13. Female Vagrant Register, 21 October 1874, Archives of the City of Philadelphia.

14. Report of Superintendent of the 24th Ward of the Society for the Organization of Charitable Relief and Repressing Mendicancy, Archives of the City of Philadelphia.

15. *The Public Ledger* (Philadelphia), 13 June, 1878.

16. Janet Nolan, *Ourselves Alone: Women's Emigration from Ireland, 1885–1920*, The University Press of Kentucky, 1989, pp. 37, 98.

17. Hasia Diner, *Erin's Daughters in America: Irish Immigrant Women in the Nineteenth Century*, The Johns Hopkins University Press, Baltimore, 1983, p. 33.

18. *The Philadelphia Times* (Philadelphia), 16 March 1875.

19. Theodore Hershberg, ed., *Philadelphia*, p. 505. The sub-sample used to examine occupations was drawn from a data set of 2,000 households headed by Irish-born males that was compiled by the Philadelphia Social History Project. The

household data was then classified into groupings of occupational lists of the male household heads by Mr Henry Williams, a project specialist, in 1984 at the request of the author. The occupations of the women household members were tabulated by hand from this listing.

20. Dennis Clark, ed., *Philadelphia, 1776–2076: a Three Hundred Year View*, Kennikat Press, Port Washington, NY, 1975, pp. 43–59.

21. Joan M. Jensen, 'Needlework as art, craft and livelihood before 1900', in Joan M. Jensen and Sue Davidson, eds, *A Needle, A Bobbin, A Strike: Women Needleworkers in America*, Temple University Press, Philadelphia, 1984, pp. 10–14.

22. S.J. Kleinberg, 'Women in the American economy', in S.J. Kleinberg, ed., *Retrieving Women's History*, Berg Publications, New York, 1988, p. 21.

23. Alice Kessler–Harris, *Out To Work*, Oxford University Press, New York, 1982, p. 135; Diner, *Erin's Daughters*, p. 81.

24. Faye E. Dudden, *Serving Women: Household Service in 19th Century America*, Wesleyan University Press, Middletown, CT, 1983, pp. 60–2.

25. Kleinberg, ed., *Retrieving Women's History*, p. 201.

26. Kleinberg, *Retrieving Women's History*, p. 201.

27. Judith O'Sullivan, *Workers and Allies: Female Participation in the American Trade Union Movement*, Smithsonian Institution Press, Washington, 1975, p. 75.

28. Kessler–Harris, *Out To Work*, pp. 124–5; Dennis Clark, 'Woman of the house', in Dennis Clark, *The Irish Relations: Trials of an Immigrant Tradition*, Associated University Presses, Cranbury, NJ, 1982, pp. 36–45; Claudia Goldin, 'Family strategies and family economy in the late nineteenth century: the role of secondary workers', in Hershberg, ed., *Philadelphia*, pp. 277–310 and Table 2.

29. Kessler–Harris, *Out To Work*, p. 122.

30. Michael R. Haines, 'Poverty, economic stress and the family in a late-nineteenth century American city: Whites in Philadelphia', Hershberg, *Philadelphia*, ed., pp. 240–76.

31. Carol Groneman, 'She earns as a child — she pays as a man: women workers in a mid-nineteenth century New York City community', Richard L. Ehrlich, ed., *Immigrants in Industrial America, 1850–1920*, University Press of Virginia, Charlottesville, VA, 1977, pp. 33–46.

32. Dennis Clark, *Erin's Heirs: Irish Bonds of Community*, The University Press of Kentucky, Lexington, KY, 1991, pp. 14–15; David Nasaw, *Schooled to Order: a Social History of Public Schooling in the United States*, Oxford University Press, New York, 1979, pp. 66–72.

33. Register of the Training School for Nurses, the Philadelphia Hospital, 1897–1901; Sixty-Second Annual Report of the Board of Education of Philadelphia, pp. 78–82, Archives of the City of Philadelphia; Stephanie A. Stachniewicz and Jean K. Axelrod, *The Double Frill: the History of the Philadelphia General Hospital School of Nursing*, George F. Stickley Co., Philadelphia, 1976, p. 216.

34. Women's Alliance for Job Equality, WAJE Earner Notes, July–August 1991, p. 1; Alice Kessler-Harris, *A Woman's Wage: Historical Meanings and Social Consequences*, The University Press of Kentucky, Lexington, KY, 1991, Introduction.

35. Marjery W. Davies, *Woman's Place is at the Typewriter: Office Work and Office Workers, 1870–1930*, Temple University Press, Philadelphia, 1984, pp. 74.

36. Steven Mintz and Susan Kellogg, *Domestic Revolutions: a Social History of American Family Life*, The Free Press, New York, 1988, p. 124.

37. Revd William J. Lallou, 'Catholicism in Philadelphia', in C.E. McGuire, ed., *Catholic Builders of the Nation*, Continental Press, Inc., Boston, 1925, p. 268.

38. 'Rules for operating employees', *American Telephone Journal*, Vol. XVII, No. 2, 11 January 1908, pp. 18–96; Philip S. Foner, *Women and the American Labor Movement*

from Colonial Times to the Eve of World War II, The Free Press, New York, 1979, pp. 467–9.

39. Richard Stembert, *The Telephone Book*, Riverward Publications, Croton on Hudson, 1977, p. 178.

40. See the column 'The Greenhorn' by Maureen Benzing in *The Irish Edition* (Philadelphia), 1981 to 1988. As late as 1961 only 29 per cent of all women in Ireland were in the work-force outside the home. Frank Litton, ed., *Unequal Achievement: the Irish Experience, 1957–1982*, Institute of Public Administration, Dublin, 1982, p. 49; Gráinne Flynn, 'Our Age of Innocence', in Mary Cullen, ed., *Girls Don't Do Honors*, pp. 78–9.

41. Clark, *Erin's Heirs*, pp. 91–2.

42. Kessler-Harris, *A Woman's Wage*, Introduction.

43. Files of *The Irish Edition* (Philadelphia), 1990, the Balch Institute for Ethnic Studies, Philadelphia.

44. The employment prospects for contemporary Irish emigrants are discussed by Frank Shouldice, 'On the emigration trail', *The Irish Voice* (New York), 9 July 1991.

6 The migration experience of female-headed households: Gilford, Co. Down, to Greenwich, New York, 1880–1910

Marilyn Cohen

Introduction

It is well known that women comprised a large proportion of Irish migrants to textile centres in north-east Ireland, Great Britain, and the American North-east.[1] These women were part of a larger process of rural to urban migration in which a largely rural Irish population left its native country to live in various cities and towns on both sides of the Atlantic.[2] However, there has been little focus on these women's particular demographic characteristics, residential patterns, household survival strategies, or opportunities for vertical mobility.[3] This chapter attempts partially to fill this gap by linking and comparing female-headed households in two factory towns built by the paternalistic McMaster family and dominated by the production of linen yarn: Gilford, County Down, and Greenwich, New York, between 1880–1910. It will present both a methodological approach for analysing this large minority of Irish working-class migrants and substantive findings.

The two towns chosen are ideal for such a case study in comparative methodology. The older town of Dunbarton, adjacent to Gilford in the parish of Tullylish, dates from the late 1830s and grew astronomically throughout the period between 1841 and 1871.[4] The enormous profits earned by the McMasters and their partners in the second half of the nineteenth century prompted them to build another yarn spinning mill called Dunbarton Mill and a factory village at Greenwich, New York, in 1880. Due to the onset of an economic depression in the Irish linen industry, many Gilford residents migrated to work in Greenwich.

This chapter will concentrate specifically on the female-headed households who migrated from Gilford to Greenwich between 1880 and 1910. Male-headed households will serve as a reference group for comparative purposes. Several issues relating to female-headed households will be addressed. The first focuses upon demographic characteristics including age, marital status and occupation, to see if there was a 'typical' female migrant from Gilford. Second, the association between migration and the formation of female-headed households in Gilford and Greenwich will be examined. Third, I will discuss continuities and changes in household strategies regarding composition, employment patterns and various indicators of social mobility. Following the lead of feminist scholars, a distinction will be made between widow-headed households and households headed by single women.[5]

Methodology

Kamphoefner has discussed several methodological approaches based upon linking migrant lists with the US census which facilitate the analysis of migration as a process or 'a complete sequence of experience'.[6] He suggests that studies of migrants, both in their European and American social contexts, can shed light on a number of important questions relating to social mobility. I will follow this approach and argue further that record linkage can facilitate comparison of such strategic aspects of social life as household composition, and employment patterns, and shed light on the formation of female-headed households in Gilford and Greenwich.

Data for this study were derived from linking three sets of records: the 1901 Irish Census Enumerator's Schedules for Gilford Town, the 1900 and 1910 US Federal Census for Greenwich Town and Village, and ships' passenger lists between 1897 and 1902. Record linkage is a historical methodology whereby the researcher attempts to ascertain that an individual recorded on one nominal list is the same as that on another. There are numerous criteria used to establish links including surname, given name, age, religion, occupation, residence and birthplace.

The criteria used in this study for linkage between the US Federal Census and Irish Census Enumerator's Schedules were in order of importance: name, age and occupation. Unfortunately, the US census did not list specific birthplace information beyond country of origin. Therefore, I selected only those households from Ireland who migrated after 1880 and whose occupations were linen industry related. By concentrating on this group I had the best chance of identifying previous Gilford residents. These household members were then linked by surname and given name to either the 1901 Irish Enumerator's Schedules or to school attendance registers for the Gilford Mill National School or to the Gilford No. 1 National School which predated the census. The 1910 US census was used to establish additional links and to obtain a ten-year longitudinal view of migrating households.

The criteria used to establish a link between an individual listed in the US and Irish censuses to ships' passenger lists were name, age, previous residence, destination and date of arrival. Ships' passenger lists were quite specific regarding the previous residence of a migrant and linkages were clear. The problem with this source is that information on migrants to New York begins in June 1897. Since the majority left Gilford in the 1880s, only a tiny minority of those migrating to Greenwich were traced.

Historical backdrop: the linen industry in Gilford

Technological innovation in many industries is often coupled with a femi-
nisation of the work-force, and linen cloth production was no exception.
Technological advances in bleaching linen cloth during the late eighteenth
century did not alter the domestic production system to any significant
degree. However, the impact of the wet spinning process on domestic
handloom weaving and handspinning households was profound. Irish
handspinners were female and the small amounts of cash earned by them
were vital to the economic survival of their households.[7] The mechanised
production of linen yarn eliminated this enduring female occupation since
wet spinning frames could produce yarn far more cheaply and in greater
quantities than spinning wheels.

More than a century ago, E.G. Ravenstein argued that the major causes
of migration are economic.[8] In the Ulster context, one result of this technological revolution in yarn spinning was the migration of many young male
farmer-weavers. While large numbers of farmer-weavers migrated to
America in 1816–17 to take advantage of higher wages in the textile industry, estimates are that up to one-third of all those born between 1801 and
1810, and up to one-fifth of those born between 1810 and 1821 emigrated in
the 1820s and 1830s.[9] These petty-commodity producers had previously
earned their livelihood by combining small-scale agriculture with spinning
yarn or weaving linen cloth. Those who did not migrate were forced to
accept lower wages and reduced independence since the yarn needed to
supply weavers was now controlled by manufacturers through the
'putting-out' system.[10]

In the short term, handloom weavers everywhere in Ulster felt the effects
of the transition to mill-based spinning, but adaptations varied by region.[11]
In West Ulster, handspinning households simply lost a vital cash-earning
occupation, increasing their dependence upon marginal agriculture. In the
rapidly industrialising regions of East Ulster, options were broader allowing
for alternatives to long-distance migration. In the parish of Tullylish in
north-west County Down, migration to America was reported in 1836 to be
'very trifling in comparison with others'.[12] Here women frequently became
handloom weavers, winders of yarn for manufacturers and filled the many
operative occupations in the new spinning mills.

One significant reason why migration from Tullylish was 'trifling' was
the opening of a new spinning mill, Dunbar McMaster & Co., in Gilford.
The impact of this mill is representative of the industrial development of
the region as a whole between 1825 and 1860. Hugh Dunbar, the original
owner, and his partners met the challenge posed by British mill-spun yarn
by building both a large yarn spinning and thread twisting mill and a
factory village. The new mill, which opened in 1841, was one of Ireland's
largest, and readily absorbed the technologically displaced population. By
1846, its work-force had grown to over 2,000, and in the decade which
reflects the impact of the Great Famine between 1841 and 1851, the population of Gilford grew from 643 to 2,814.[13]

Female-headed households in Gilford/Dunbarton

The vast majority of the new factory labour force in most branches of linen production were young and female, resulting in more females than males living in Gilford/Dunbarton and its surrounding townlands. For example, in 1841 there were nearly equal numbers of males and females in Gilford (300 and 343 respectively). By 1851, the proportion was 55.7 per cent female and by 1861 females comprised 56.7 per cent of Gilford's population.[14]

While the typical female mill worker was young, single and living with her parents, many female workers did not conform to this norm. A significant minority of wives worked, many single women lived on their own as boarders and an even larger proportion of women lived in female-headed households headed by widows, or single women. In 1851, female-headed households were in the majority comprising 55.3 per cent of Gilford's households. The predominance of female-headed households at this time can be explained partly by the migration, death and desertion of many married men during the Great Famine years, and partly by the expanding labour force of Dunbar McMaster & Co.[15]

During the 1860s, when the population of Gilford/Dunbarton peaked, many single women came in search of work. In 1867, the paternalistic mill owners stated that young single women 'whose employment necessitates their leaving home' were 'comfortably lodged with long resident and respectable families and placed under the immediate supervision of their respective clergy'.[16] Finally, in 1901, 31.3 per cent of Gilford's population were living in female-headed households with 60 per cent of this total headed by widows and 36 per cent headed by single women. The remaining 4 per cent were married women who were not currently living with their husbands for unknown reasons.

As in Belfast, where female-headed households comprised more than 20 per cent of the population, the high proportion of female-headed households in Gilford can largely be attributed to the availability of employment for women in the linen industry.[17] In spite of employment opportunities, female-headed households nevertheless faced considerable economic hardship for several reasons. First, the linen industry was notoriously low paying. Second, women earned about half the wages of men. Finally, female-headed households were smaller, averaging 3.3 persons or potential wage earners compared with 5.4 persons in male-headed households.[18]

This formidable challenge to economic survival was met in a number of ways. First, it was necessary for all members to contribute to the household budget. Of the 236 female heads of household in Gilford in 1901, 60.2 per cent were employed, a figure far exceeding the 20.7 per cent figure for wives with resident husbands. Among widows, 41.7 per cent were employed, with the majority still attempting to rely on the wages earned by their children or through taking in boarders. Among children, 61.7 per cent of daughters under thirty-five were employed, 10 per cent of daughters were over thirty-five and employed, 49.7 per cent of sons were under thirty-five and employed, and 6.6 per cent of sons were employed and still residing at home after the age of thirty-five. This large proportion of unmarried children in widow-headed households suggests a strategy of postponed marriage ensuring a prolonged contribution to the household budget. In households headed by single women, nearly all (88 per cent) members over the age of twelve were employed, suggesting an even higher level of economic interdependence.

Female-headed households in Gilford also 'tended to have markedly different demographic characteristics from households headed by men'.[19] In addition to their smaller size, members were older, averaging 30.8 years of age as compared with 25.3 years in male-headed households. They were also more likely to be single with only 7.9 per cent married, and female with only 26.9 per cent male members.

The vast majority of widows (84.8 per cent) lived in nuclear family units augmented at times with descendent kin or boarders. Single women who headed households usually chose to live with kin such as sisters, brothers, cousins or nieces. Very few widows and single women lived alone since state assistance for the poor was both minimal and stigmatised.

Finally, while most of the population in Gilford by the turn of the century could read and write, literacy rates were lower both among female heads of household and their co-residing members. In the population at large only 10 per cent were totally illiterate and another 9 per cent could read only. Among female heads of household, 27 per cent were illiterate, and 30 per cent could read only. Fifteen per cent of those residing in female-headed households were illiterate as compared with 10.7 per cent in male-headed households. Both the ability to read only and illiteracy were more common in female-headed households because of the increased need for the wage contributions of school-aged children.

Female migration from Gilford

After the 'linen boom' years in the Irish linen industry during the late 1860s and 1870s, a period of stagnation ensued. Both the output of linen yarn and cloth fell during the 1880s resulting in high rates of unemployment.[20] The opening of Dunbarton Mill at Greenwich, New York, in 1880 coincided with this recession. Dunbarton Mill, valued in 1885 at £31,647, attracted a number of Gilford residents who are reflected in the comparative population figures for Gilford and Greenwich.[21] In Gilford, the population fell from 1,324 in 1881 to 1,199 in 1901 while the population of the village in Greenwich rose from 1,231 in 1880 to 1,663 in 1890.[22]

Lees has argued that sustained migration from Ireland to urbanising regions in America and England during the nineteenth century should be understood in the context of a wider developing Atlantic economy.[23] One of the social consequences of an emerging industrial capitalism during the nineteenth century was the creation of female-headed households on both sides of the Atlantic. By 1900, there were 1,071 total households in Greenwich with 16.9 per cent of these headed by women.[24]

Several processes were at work in the creation of these female-headed households. First, migration often takes place in stages with one member initiating the migration chain and subsequently sending for other family members.[25] In Greenwich, 2.7 per cent of the households were headed by males who migrated prior to sending for their wives. During the interim period, the household in Ireland was female-headed, and dependent upon wages earned by remaining members and remittances sent. For example, in the Poor Law Union of Banbridge which included Gilford, for three consecutive decades between 1871–91, both the number and relative proportion of married women were greater than those of married men. In 1871, 14 per cent of the total population were married men, and 14.5 per cent married women. By 1881, 13.7 per cent were married men, and 14.1 per cent married women. In 1891, 13.6 per cent were married men, and 13.9 per cent married women.[26] Finally, it is reasonable to assume that migration partly accounts for the 4 per cent of female-headed households in Gilford listed as married with no resident husband in 1901. This data suggests that proportionately more males than females were migrating out of Banbridge Union which offered far greater employment opportunities for females.

Kerby Miller has demonstrated that, in the post-Famine period, Irish migration patterns also included large proportions of single men and women.[27] These single individuals are reflected in the census in a number of ways: as boarders, servants, or when a wife's entry into the United States predated that of her husband. In 1900, 8.7 per cent of the total households in Greenwich were augmented with boarders and 9.1 per cent with servants. Both servants and boarders were unmarried and relatively young, usually in their twenties and thirties. This suggests that individuals chose these options at a particular stage in their life cycle prior to marriage.

For the purposes of this study, boarders are of greater interest. There were 118 male boarders in Greenwich, 11.9 per cent of whom were from Ireland. Since only five had linen mill occupations we can conclude that the spinning mill was a weak pull factor for the vast majority of male boarders. Instead, we find among males a variety of occupations including agricultural labourers, skilled workers, salesmen and professionals. A larger proportion (27.8 per cent) of the seventy-six female boarders were Irish and many more of these women were operatives in the local linen (17.1 per cent) and knitting mills.

While female boarders did not initially form separate female-headed households, they are of considerable interest to an analysis of both female migration patterns and the survival strategies of female-headed households for several reasons. First, they represent a category like other single women who were largely self-supporting. Second, boarders often resided in female-headed households diversifying their composition and contributing to their economic survival. Finally, many female boarders after a period of time formed female-headed households of their own.

The reasons why female migrants initially lived as boarders are complex. Focusing first on economic reasons, women's wages between 1880 and 1890 were about 70 per cent of those paid to adult men, making it far more difficult for them initally to afford a separate residence.[28] Wage statistics for the period do not include linen industry workers. The closest industry for which there are related data is cotton. Male workers in cotton mills in 1890 would have earned a median wage of $1.33 a day while a female would have earned $0.91 a day or 68 per cent of the male wage.[29] Thus, it would have taken a period of time for a single female migrant to afford her own accomodations. A case is provided by Lizzie Shillcock who migrated in 1892 at the age of thirty-two to work in Dunbarton Mill. She initially boarded with a household headed by Joseph Chambers, but, by 1910, she was a self-supporting winder in the mill.

Turning to socio-cultural reasons, at the turn of the century, Ireland was a patriarchal society with adult men assuming control over both women and the younger generation. Consequently, both single men and women characteristically remained at home until marriage. This socio-cultural context may have prompted a young migrating woman to prefer residence with others rather than living alone. The overlap between boarders and extended kin is impossible to determine. However, it is reasonable to assume that many boarders were related, preferring to live with and contribute to the households of kin until they could afford to make a residental change. Even when Irish boarders were unrelated, they overwhelmingly chose to reside in Irish households. It is reasonable to assume that many chose to live with former Gilford residents, sustaining old Irish networks while developing new ones in Greenwich.

Thus, it was a rational strategy for young single women and men to live with a family for a period of time after arriving in the United States. Boarding most frequently occurred in the period between leaving one's family of origin and establishing a separate household. Established household members could help ease the transition by helping to secure employment, by providing shelter and much needed social networks, services and companionship.[30]

A third indicator of the prevalence of single female migrants is the proportion of households (3.0 per cent) where a wife's migration predated that of her husband or where the wife was born in Ireland while her husband was born in the United States. It is impossible to determine from the census the initial occupations of these wives or their residence patterns prior to marriage. What can be determined is that they did not remain single for long. The data suggest that marriage patterns among migrants to Greenwich followed urban rather than rural Irish patterns with an average age of 21.7 at first marriage for women and 23.8 for men.

Thus, evidence from the 1900 census suggests that the typical female migrant to Greenwich was in her twenties and single. What can we learn about these female migrants by linking them to their households of origin in Gilford? Did the migration patterns of members of male-headed households differ from female-headed households? Nineteen Greenwich households in the 1900 US Federal Census were linked to households in the 1901 Irish Census Enumerator's Schedules for Gilford. A further five in the 1910 US Federal Census were linked.

Seven of the linked Greenwich households had members who were originally from female-headed households in Gilford. When we concentrate on
the migration patterns of members of female-headed households, we find
first that the female head of the household was rarely the first link in the
migration chain. In no case did the female head migrate first followed by
her children or siblings. Instead, we find the sons (four) and daughters
(three) of widows, and the brothers (two) and sisters (four) of single women
migrating to Greenwich either on their own or with siblings. We also do
not find children subsequently sending for their widowed mothers.

For example, in 1901 at the age of twenty-four, Owen Murphy migrated
from Gilford leaving behind his widowed mother and two sisters. His
passage was paid by his uncle John McCann, and with $4.00 he made his
way to Greenwich. Owen was previously employed as a bleacher in one of
the several bleachgreens located along the Bann River near Gilford, but in
1910 he is listed as a labourer. While Owen migrated single, he did not
remain so for long. By 1910, he had been married to his wife Alice for seven
years and had a two-year-old son.

In two cases women migrating from female-headed households in
Gilford re-established female-headed households in Greenwich. The other
four became members of male-headed households. An example of the
former was the household headed by Mary Mullan, a sixty-year-old widow
who worked as a bobbin carter at Dunbar McMaster & Co. in Gilford. In
1883, she said farewell to her daughter Anne who migrated to Greenwich at
the age of twenty-one to work as a thread twister. At the age of thirty-eight,
Anne had remained single, sharing her rented home with a twenty-eight-
year-old boarder named Katherine Livery who arrived in 1884 and also
worked as a twister in Dunbarton Mill.

A contrasting example is provided by the Gilford household of Jane
Chambers, aged sixty-two. Her son Joseph, his wife Kate and his sister
Hannah all migrated in 1881 at the ages of nineteen, eighteen and twenty-
one respectively to work in Dunbarton Mill. They were followed the next
year by sister Jane at the age of twenty-three. By 1900, Joseph and his wife
had been married for eighteen years with four children. However, both
Jane and Hannah followed a pattern common to the children of widows. In
1910, they were still single contributing their earnings to the household
purse as did their two unmarried brothers and one sister in Gilford.[31]

Migration patterns in male-headed households were significantly different. First, it was common for the male head to initiate the migration process
either alone or with a son or daughter. Given that male linen industry
workers in Gilford earned twice the wages of women, they were in a better
position to migrate first and subsequently send for other members of the
family. Also, there is scant but suggestive evidence that fewer daughters of
male-headed households migrated alone, choosing instead to migrate with
siblings.

For example, between 1896 and 1901, five of the nine children of William
McCann, a forty-six-year-old widower and shoemaker, migrated to
Greenwich. His two oldest sons Arthur and Thomas initiated the migration

chain arriving in Greenwich in 1896 to work in the linen mill. In 1900, Arthur paid the fare for his sister Rose, aged nineteen, and brother Patrick, aged fourteen. They arrived with $7.50 and $10.00 respectively and presumably lived for a time with Arthur and his wife Mary. In 1901, Rose paid for her two sisters, Mary aged nine and Sarah aged seven, who arrived with no additional money to be schooled further and work in Greenwich. Between 1900 and 1910, Arthur and his wife Mary had six children. Prior to migrating, Mary had resided in Dunbarton with her widowed mother and two sisters. In 1900, her sister Elizabeth also migrated to work as a spreader in Dunbarton Mill living for a time with Mary and Arthur.

Survival strategies in Greenwich: employment patterns

I argued above that among female-headed households in Gilford, it was imperative for all members to work. Were there any changes in the employment patterns of female-headed households in Greenwich? When we examine female-headed households in Greenwich we find that employment patterns remained virtually unchanged: all members who were of age worked. This suggests that the necessity for a continuous pattern of employment among all categories of co-residing women due to asymmetrical wage scales remained unchanged.[32] In contrast, only one wife in seventeen male-headed households was employed.

Even in male-headed households in Greenwich at the turn of the century, the wages paid to linen industry workers were rarely sufficient enough to allow a household to rely on the male head alone. The annual earnings for a cotton goods worker in 1890 were $302, for a woollen goods worker $340. Assuming that the earnings of linen industry workers were similar, households required the wages earned by children who were the principal supplemental contributors to the household budget followed by extended kin such as unmarried siblings, or boarders.

This reliance upon child labour was more pronounced in female-headed households and necessarily affected children's schooling. Evidence from Gilford suggests that the schooling patterns of children in female-headed households diverged significantly from those with resident fathers. On the average, they remained in school one year less and they attended school more erratically due to greater pressure to begin earning wages. While this study does not include data from school attendance registers in Greenwich, census data suggest that the average age of male children in school was 10.9, a year older than the 9.9 for female children. In addition to greater importance placed upon the schooling of males during this period, employment opportunties for females in Dunbarton Mill would have drawn daughters into wage-earning sooner than sons.

Indicators of social mobility

Lees has argued that the analysis of vertical mobility needs to expand beyond occupational terms to include many small but meaningful indicators in working-class communities.[33] I will follow this suggestion by focusing upon the proportion of working wives, the ages of children in school, ownership of a home versus rental, and a comparison of the occupations of parents and children within Greenwich households and between Greenwich and Gilford households. Looking first at working wives, in Gilford, 20.7 per cent of wives were employed. In contrast, the data from Greenwich suggests that nearly all wives whose husbands worked either in the linen mill or elsewhere were listed as having no occupation. It should be stressed, however, that because the census does not include supplemental wage-earning activities by wives, it underrepresents their income-earning contributions.[34] The presence of boarders is an important case in point.

In Gilford, both documentary and oral evidence suggest that a working mother was an indicator of poverty and an object of pity. Because women were fully responsible for the domestic domain, a working wife had to accomplish her domestic duties after working hours and on weekends, virtually eliminating leisure time.[35] The fact that so few wives with resident husbands in Greenwich were employed is significant, especially since women formed the bulk of the labour force in Dunbarton Mill. There are two possible explanations for the low proportion of working wives in Greenwich. One is that the wages earned by husbands and children were sufficient to allow wives to remain at home. Another is that the ideology of a better life in America was partly interpreted to include wives being spared double-duty.

Female-headed households were rarely able to keep a woman home to attend solely to domestic duties. In widow-headed households some were able to rely on the wages earned by children. However, all members living in households headed by single women worked. It is unclear in these households who functioned as housekeeper. Whether these duties fell to one woman or were shared, housekeeping was time-consuming and reduced available leisure time.

There is a growing literature which argues that home ownership confers a greater sense of personal identity, control, autonomy and security than renting.[36] In Gilford, none of the working class owned their homes or property free. Rents paid either to Dunbar McMaster & Co. or to other principal landlords in and around Gilford were relatively low, but all households needed to include rent payments in their budget. In contrast, ten of the eighteen male-headed households in Greenwich owned their homes entirely or were in the process of paying off a mortgage. Most of these male heads were skilled workers in Dunbarton Mill such as flaxdressers, engineers or overseers. The possibility of property ownership by members of the working class in Greenwich represents a tangible increase in their standard of living and is a small but meaningful indicator of vertical social mobility.

It is significant that only one of the households headed by a single woman was able to obtain a mortage for a home. Scholars are beginning to address the relationship between lower incomes, housing costs and access to housing among widowed, divorced and single women.[37] These studies have concentrated on access to housing by female heads of household in contemporary urban regions; however, their findings are equally applicable to the past. Since the wages paid to women in Greenwich were substantially less than those paid to men, they were rarely able to obtain mortgages on their own, and were effectively barred from this form of vertical social mobility.

In Ireland, at the turn of the century, a combination of Factory and Education Acts ensured that children remained in school until the Fourth Standard or until the age of twelve when they could begin full-time work. Younger children could work part-time at the age of eleven as half-timers. In the United States, prior to 1889, children under the age of thirteen were prohibited from employment in a factory. By 1889, the age limit was raised to fourteen years.[38]

Evidence from the 1900 US census suggests that most children did not begin earning wages until the age of fourteen. There were no cases of twelve-year-old children employed and only two thirteen-year-olds were listed as having linen mill occupations. Still evidence suggests that Greenwich households relied heavily upon the wage contributions of children since the vast majority of fourteen-year-olds are listed as employed. If we assume that one indicator of social mobility is a decreasing reliance upon child labour, the economic strategies of migrant households in Greenwich in 1900 suggest that most households heavily relied upon the wages earned by children. Most of the children of linen industry workers continued to leave school to begin earning wages at the earliest possible age.

However, by 1910, census data suggest that Greenwich parents were able to keep their children in school longer. All fourteen-year-olds are listed as in school and many, especially girls, between fifteen and nineteen are listed as in school with no occupations. Given the strength of the working-class family economy throughout the nineteenth century, and the opportunties for female employment in the spinning mill, this is a significant change. Since the census only provides us with a snapshot we cannot obtain a processual view of the household throughout its cycle. Therefore, it is probable that older children began working earlier and helped make possible the longer schooling of their younger siblings. Nevertheless, the ability fully to support unemployed teenaged children while they remain in school may represent a new strategy by working-class migrant families to provide their children with the opportunity for social mobility in the future.

Finally, did migrants or their children in Greenwich obtain occupations which were higher paying, higher skilled, or of a higher social class than either their parents or family members in Gilford? The evidence from both the 1900 and 1910 census suggests that in both male and female-headed households they did not. In most cases the occupations of migrants were of a similar skill level as family members in Gilford suggesting that they filled similar niches. In only two cases did a son have a job requiring a higher level of skill than his father, and in only two cases did a son have an occupation (clerk) indicating a higher social class. In no cases did daughters have jobs requiring more skill or associated with a higher social class than their parents. Thus, by 1910, the overwhelming majority of working-class children were still being tracked into the same types of working-class occupations as their parents in Greenwich or family members in Gilford.

Conclusion

Although much is known about the migration patterns of the Irish, significant gaps in our knowledge remain. Modell and Lees have argued that 'because of Ireland's pattern of economic and political development, the Irish became an urban people unable to remain in their predominantly rural homeland'.[39] Irish migrants from rural areas migrated to a variety of urban areas, moving essentially from cities at the top of the urban hierarchy to smaller towns 'as the American urban hierarchy spread into the hinterland'.[40] They also point to Ireland's overall economic and urban stagnation in the nineteenth century with Dublin and Belfast as exceptions proving the rule.[41]

This study has attempted to broaden their general picture by focusing on migration from a rural industrial town in north-east Ulster which formed part of an atypical yet 'well-articulated and growing urban hierarchy consisting of towns and villages of varying sizes ... linked by transportation, marketing and communication networks'.[42] Unlike rural Ireland, in north-east Ulster, due to significant industrial development 'a regional system of urban options' did exist which provided alternatives to long-distance migration even during the Famine years.[43] However, this urban hierarchy was overwhelmingly dependent upon the linen industry, and when opportunities for employment decreased in the 1880s, long-distance migration from Gilford to Greenwich became a more rational choice than short-distance migration to other towns or to Belfast at the top of Ireland's urban hierarchy.

This chapter has also used record linkage to provide evidence useful in the analysis of the migration patterns and survival strategies of Irish women and female-headed households. Individual-level tracing allows us to examine the processes of chain migration, residence strategies, employment patterns and indicators of vertical social mobility amongst categories of people who otherwise have left little historical documentation. In spite of their numbers, single women and female-headed households are among the least understood segments of Irish working-class migrants. Evidence presented here suggests that a full explanation of the migration process and experience must account for the sharp divergence in adaptive strategies along gender lines.

Comparisons between Greenwich and other nearby textile centres with large Irish populations such as Troy or Cohoes suggest that such gender distinctions were widespread. Historians of these urban regions have also pointed to the large proportion of female-headed households among the Irish.[44] The town of Greenwich in 1900 was comparable, with 24.3 per cent of its female-headed households of Irish descent. The full explanation for these high proportions of female-headed households is complex. However, in the case of Greenwich, it is clear that the push factor of declining employment opportunities for women in Gilford and the pull factor of abundant employment opportunities for women in Greenwich both attracted single female migrants and provided the material base for female-headed households.

The hope of a better life is usually a key motivation for migration. However, evidence presented here casts doubt about the realisation of such aspirations for members of female-headed households. In male-headed households, there is some indication of an improved standard of living in the very low proportion of working wives, the increasing ability to keep teenaged children in school and the ability for many to own a home. Still, even in male-headed households, intergenerational mobility based upon occupation was infrequent since child labour remained vital.

When we turn to female-headed households, we find little evidence for an improved life since low wages heightened economic interdependence and denied them such tangible rewards as home ownership. Instead, evidence points to similar material constraints faced by female-headed households in Gilford and Greenwich. Households headed by women both in the past and present are persistent symbols of the poverty often faced by women living without men.

Notes

1. Brenda Collins, 'Families in Edwardian Belfast', unpublished paper presented to the Urban History Group of the Economic History Society annual meeting, University of Aberdeen, 1982; Hasia R. Diner, *Erin's Daughters in America*, John Hopkins University Press, Baltimore, 1983; Thomas Dublin, *Women at Work*, Columbia University Press, New York, 1979; Daniel J. Walkowitz, 'Working-class women in the gilded age: factory, community and family life among Cohoes, New York cotton workers', *Journal of Social History*, 5,4, 1972, pp. 464–90; Daniel J. Walkowitz, *Worker City, Company Town*, University of Illinois Press, Urbana, 1978; and Carole Turbin, 'Beyond dichotomies: interdependence in mid-nineteenth century working-class families in the United States, *Gender and History*, 1, 3, 1989, pp. 293–308.
2. John Modell and Lynn Lees, 'The Irish countryman urbanized: a comparative perspective on the Famine migration', in Theodore Hershberg, ed., *Philadelphia*, Oxford University Press, Oxford, 1981, p. 358.
3. The principal exceptions are A.C. Hepburn and Brenda Collins, 'Industrial society: the structure of Belfast, 1901', in Peter Roebuck, ed., *Plantation to Partition: Essays in Honour of J.L. McCracken*, Blackstaff Press, Belfast, 1981; and Collins, 'Families'.
4. For an analysis of industrial and demographic growth in Gilford see Marilyn

Cohen, 'Proletarianization and family strategies in the parish of Tullylish, County Down, Ireland: 1690–1914', The New School for Social Research Ph. D. thesis, 1988.

5. Carole Turbin, 'Beyond conventional wisdom: women's wage work, household economic contribution, and labor activism in a mid-nineteenth century working-class community', in Carol Groneman and Mary Beth Norton, eds., *To Toil the Livelong Day*, Cornell University Press, Ithaca, 1987; and Turbin, 'Beyond dichotomies'.

6. Walter D. Kamphoefner, 'Problems and possibilities of individual-level tracing in German-American migration research', in Robert M. Taylor, Jr. and Ralph J. Crandall, eds., *Generations and Change: Genealogical Perspectives in Social History*, Mercer University Press, Macon, Georgia, 1986, pp. 311–321.

7. Emily J. Boyle, 'The Economic Development of the Irish Linen Industry, 1825–1913', Queen's University of Belfast Ph. D. thesis, 1977; Brenda Collins, 'Proto-industrialisation and pre-Famine emigration', *Social History*, 7, 2, 1982, pp. 127–46; and Cohen, 'Proletarianization'.

8. D.B. Grigg, 'E.G. Ravenstein and the "Laws of Migration"', *Journal of Historical Geography*, 3, 1, 1977, p. 43.

9. Lynn H. Lees, *Exiles of Erin*, Cornell University Press, Ithaca, 1979, pp. 37–8; and Brenda Collins, 'Outworkers in the Ulster linen industry in the nineteenth and twentieth centuries', Paper presented at a conference on textile regions in Western Europe, Munster, July 1991, pp. 8–9.

10. William H. Crawford, *Domestic Industry in Ireland: the Experience of the Linen Industry*, Gill & Macmillan, Dublin, 1972.

11. Collins, 'Proto-industrialisation', pp. 138–9.

12. *Reports From Commissioners, Poor Laws (Ireland)*, Appendix (F), 1836, XXXIII, pp. 335–6.

13. *Reports by Inspectors of Factories* (Brit. Parl. Papers) IUP ser., Industrial Revolution: Factories, 1842–47, Report by James Stewart; Public Record Office of Northern Ireland (PRONI), *Census of Ireland, 1841–51*.

14. PRONI, *Census of Ireland, 1841–61*.

15. PRONI, BG.22/G/1–21, Lurgan Board of Guardians, Workhouse Registers, 1841–1901.

16. *Reports from Commissioners: Paris Universal Exhibition*, (Brit. Parl. Papers) 30, Part III, pp. 28, 47.

17. Collins, 'Families', p. 4.

18. *Board of Trade Report by Miss Collet on Changes in the Employment of Women and Girls in Industrial Centres, Part I: Flax and Jute Centres*, (Brit. Parl. Papers) 88, 1989; *Report of an Enquiry of Trade into the Earnings and Hours of Labour of the U.K. Part I. Textile Trades in 1906* (Brit. Parl. Papers) 80, 1909; Hepburn and Collins, 'Industrial society', pp. 216–17; Collins, 'Families', p. 4; and Mary Daly, *Dublin: The Deposed Capital*, Cork University Press, Cork, 1984, p. 307.

19. Hepburn and Collins, 'Industrial society', p. 216–17; Collins 'Families', p. 4.

20. Boyle, 'Economic development', Chapter 5.

21. PRONI, D.1769/8/1A, Dunbar McMaster & Co., L'Estrange & Brett Papers.

22. PRONI, *Irish Census of Population, 1880–1900*: US Federal Census 1880–90.

23. Lees, *Exiles*, p. 42; Modell and Lees, 'The Irish countryman urbanized', p. 351.

24. Lees, *Exiles*, p. 130, found a nearly equal proportion (17 per cent) of female-headed households in her 1851 London sample.

25. Lees, *Exiles*, p. 50.

26. PRONI, *Census of Ireland, 1871–91*.

27. Kerby A. Miller, *Emigrants and Exiles*, Oxford University Press, Oxford, 1985, pp.

352, 581–2, citing the *Commission on Emigration and Other Population Problems*, see also Lees, *Exiles*, p. 48.

28. Clarence D. Long, *Wages and Earnings in the United States, 1860–1890*, Arno Press, New York, 1975, p. 106.
29. Long, *Wages*, pp. 95, 105–6.
30. Tamara K. Haraven and John Modell, 'Urbanization and the malleable household: an examination of boarding and lodging in American families, *Journal of Marriage and the Family*, 35, 3 August 1973, pp. 467–79; Lees, *Exiles*, p. 124.
31. Olwen Hufton, 'Women without men: widows and spinsters in Britain and France in the eighteenth century', *Journal of Family History*, Winter (1984), pp. 362–4; Turbin, 'Beyond conventional wisdom', 1987, p. 52.
32. Lees, *Exiles*, pp. 102, 106, 113, found that because female wages were below those of male labourers, most would have lived below Rowntree's poverty line. This resulted in 75 per cent of Irish female heads working as compared with 22 per cent of wives with resident husbands.
33. Lees, *Exiles*, p. 118.
34. Cohen, 'Proletarianization', pp. 592–600.
35. Cohen, 'Proletarianization'.
36. Ruth Madigan, Moira Munro and Susan J. Smith, 'Gender and the meaning of the home', *International Journal of Urban and Regional Research*, 14, 4, December 1990, pp. 625–47.
37. Susan J. Smith, 'Income, housing, wealth, and gender inequality', *Urban Studies*, 27, 1, February 1990, pp. 67–88; Madigan *et al.*, 'Gender', p. 633.
38. L. 1889, c. 560. White v. Wittemann Lithographic Co., 1892, 131 N.Y. 631, 30 N.E. 236.
39. Modell and Lees, 'The Irish countryman urbanized', p. 351.
40. Modell and Lees, 'The Irish countryman urbanized', p. 358.
41. Modell and Lees, 'The Irish countryman urbanized', p. 355.
42. Modell and Lees, 'The Irish countryman urbanized', p. 357.
43. Modell and Lees, 'The Irish countryman urbanized', p. 357; Grigg, 'E.G. Ravenstein', pp. 43–7; Cohen, 'Proletarianization', pp. 307, 361–6.
44. Dublin, *Women at Work*, pp. 170–3; Turbin, 'Beyond dichotomies', pp. 300–1.

7 'There was nothing for me there': Irish female emigration, 1922–71

Pauric Travers

Sean Keating's beautiful painting, 'Economic Pressure', completed in the early 1950s and now in the Crawford Municipal Gallery, Cork, depicts what is probably for most people a 'typical' emigrant scene: as the emigrant ship waits in the harbour, the departing Irish peasant (a young man) embraces a sorrowing female. Mother, sister or girlfriend, the painting suggests that it is the woman who stays. If art were true to life it is more likely that it would be a young woman who was emigrating, and that young woman would be unlikely to shed tears for the ageing bachelors she was choosing to leave behind.

The migration process has generally been seen in male terms: the destitute or adventurous male who leaves his homeland, driven out by poverty or attracted by the prospect of economic improvement in a new land. In so far as women are considered it is as dependents who accompany or later join their menfolk.[1] The reality belies this view. For example, female immigration in the United States has exceeded male since the 1930s. In the case of Irish emigration, the preponderance of female emigrants is even longer established.

Keating's painting is important because it perpetuates a common misconception about Irish emigration (and indeed emigration generally): that it was/is predominantly male. In fact, between 1871 and 1971, Irish female emigration exceeded that of male. When the painting appeared the rate of net female emigration per thousand population was 9.7 as compared to 6.9 for males.[2] Despite this, historians have paid remarkably little attention to Irish female emigration, particularly in the period after 1922.[3]

My main intention here is to examine the extent and causes of Irish female emigration in the fifty years after political independence in the south of Ireland in 1922. A fundamental question which arises immediately is whether Irish female emigration can or should be seen as separate from male. Should it be seen as a subheading of emigration generally or as a distinct phenomenon? In her splendid review of recent work in the field of Women and Migration[4] Silvia Pedraza argues persuasively that ethnicity, class and gender interact in the process of migration. Until recently, migration studies have concentrated on the first two and virtually ignored the third. It is not simply a question of female migration having been ignored or underrated. The exclusion of gender has produced a flawed understanding of the wider process of migration, both male and female.[5] Thus female emigration warrants study in its own right and at the same time contributes to a more accurate picture of the whole.

What follows is structured in three sections: the first is concerned with establishing the extent, composition and nature of female emigration. The second and largest section, seeks to explain the extent of female emigration and in the process to throw some light on the position of women in Irish society. The final section raises some of the implications of female emigration and suggests areas in need of further research. It includes brief reference to the cultural and psychological baggage which these women brought with them to their new homes and the importance of that for the host society.

Extent and composition of female emigration

There has been no more profound and durable influence on Irish society in recent centuries than emigration. The Irish were arguably an emigrant people even before the Famine but emigration then took place in the context of a growing population. After the Famine, it was associated with a steady decline in population which continued even after the achievement of political autonomy in the Irish Free State. The strong component of female emigration which was such a feature of the late nineteenth century also continued, unaffected by self-government. Irish women continued to emigrate in large numbers. It is this post-independence female emigration, until now largely ignored by historians, which is the main focus of this chapter.

As Table 7.1 illustrates, in the century from 1871 to 1971, female emigration outnumbered male overall and in six decades. For the century as a whole, the annual average emigration for males was 15,707 whereas for females it was 15,983. This excess of females is small but it is of some importance, not least in the context of the assumption that emigration is a predominantly male phenomenon.

These aggregate figures mask a considerable amount of variation from decade to decade. In the last three decades of the nineteenth century, the balance between males and females was even. Thereafter it fluctuated considerably in both directions, with significant female predominance in 1901–11, 1926–36, 1946–51 and 1961–71. During the period of the two World Wars, the outflow of female emigrants lessened considerably while that of men increased because of military recruitment and the outflow of men to Britain to fill the vacuum left by British recruitment.

During the 1950s, a sharp decline in male employment in Ireland (male employment fell by 135,000 whereas female declined only by 35,000) contributed to a substantial excess of male over female emigration. The

Table 7.1 Net Irish emigration by sex 1871–1971

Intercensal Period	Males	Annual Average Females	Total	Females per 1,000 males
1871–81	24,958	25,314	50,172	1,010
1881–91	29,257	30,476	59,733	1,042
1891–1901	20,315	19,327	39,642	951
1901–11	11,764	14,390	26,154	1,223
1911–26	13,934	13,068	27,002	938
1926–36	7,255	9,420	16,675	1,298
1936–46	11,258	7,453	18,711	662
1946–51	10,309	14,075	24,384	1,365
1951–61	21,786	19,091	40,877	876
1961–71	6,236	7,215	13,451	1,157

Source: Commission on Emigration and Other Population Problems 1948–54 Reports, (CEOP), Stationery Office, Dublin, 1954, p. 23; Economic Implications, p. 68 [see Note 6]

economic improvement of the 1960s benefited men more than women thus helping to reverse the balance. In the 1970s, there was a net inward migration with male emigrants returning to Ireland in greater numbers than females, itself an interesting phenomenon. With resumption of large-scale emigration in the 1980s, the initial outflow was strongly male rather than female.[6]

Age

Irish emigrants since the famine have always been predominantly young, the vast majority falling within the 15–24 age-group. This was the case before and after 1922, with over 50 per cent falling into this category during the period from 1924 to 1939. Ten to fifteen per cent were under 15, giving some indication of the extent of family emigration. This is much smaller than the immediate post-Famine period but in line with the pattern in the late nineteenth century.

During the 1940s, emigration was largely to Britain to work in war industries. It was necessary to acquire a travel and employment permit with emigrants being required to arrange employment through the employment exchange before departure. This has facilitated more detailed and accurate analysis (Table 7.2) In terms of age, the majority continued to fall into the 15–24 category but there was a noticeable increase in the emigration of older males. This was not true of female emigration which remained decisively youthful. For obvious reasons, family emigration dried up but it reappeared in the 1950s whereas emigration among older males declined.[7]

Overall, it is clear that during the period covered by this chapter, female emigrants were on average younger than male while fewer older women than men emigrated.[8] A surprisingly large proportion of women emigrated

Table 7.2 Age distribution of recipients of travel employment permits 1943–51

	15–19	20–4	25–9 %	30–4	35 & over
Males	12.6	33.4	19.9	12.1	22.0
Female	31.1	37.9	14.8	6.8	9.4

Source: Conflated from *CEOP*, p. 129

between the ages of 15 and 19. The most likely reason for this is the large numbers of women who went to work in domestic service. Average age of employees in domestic service was lower than in the unskilled employment which most Irish male emigrants gravitated towards. While the discrepancy can be easily explained, it should not be underestimated. Emigration at the best of times is a disorientating experience: it was all the more so for the very young girls who composed such a large proportion of Irish emigrants.

Geographical origins

Emigration was a phenomenon which affected all parts of Ireland but some areas suffered disproportionately. In the decades after the Famine the flow was particularly strong from Munster. Connacht and the North–west were worst hit later in the century with County Mayo in particular faring badly. This pattern continued after 1922.

The pattern for female emigration corresponds roughly with that of men with the exception that male emigration from urban centres, especially Dublin, was higher while that in rural areas was lower. It would seem that women were more eager to leave rural areas than urban perhaps because of availability of employment or more conducive social conditions. Of the 122,954 women who sought travel permits to go to work in Britain, 15,419 lived in Dublin county or borough, 23,944 came from other urban districts, while 83,591 came from rural districts.[9] Many women initially migrated from the country to the towns and then moved on. Others stayed and effectively took the place of town women who emigrated. (Internal migration was much more popular with women, especially better educated women, than it was with men.)

Destination

It is difficult to establish the number of emigrants to Britain with any degree of certainty but Britain always attracted large numbers of both male and female emigrants. After 1929, Britain became the most popular destination for emigrants followed by the USA, Canada, Australia and other 'overseas' destinations. Between 1926 and 1951, approximately 180,000 female emigrants went from Ireland to Britain whereas just over 52,000 went to the

United States (Table 7.3). Until 1929–30, the United States was the preferred destination but this changed dramatically during the 1930s.

Table 7.3 Net female emigration by destination 1926–51

	1926–36	1936–46	1946–51
Britain & Europe	45,791	74,530	59,534
Overseas	48,397	c4200	9482

Source: Conflated from *CEOP*, pp. 116 and 317

Male emigrants dispersed in roughly similar proportions with the difference that the men were slightly less likely to go to Britain. Of the 101,338 female migrants between 1924 and 1952 who went to 'overseas' destinations (i.e. outside Europe), 87,103 went to the United States, 5,398 to Canada, 4,012 to Australia and 4,825 to other countries. The USA was the most popular of the 'overseas' destinations with both sexes but a smaller proportion of women went to Canada and Australia. Again, within these aggregate figures, there is a good deal of variation from decade to decade. Emigration to the United States and Canada dried up during the 1930s and recovered only somewhat after World War II. But throughout the period the proportion of female overseas emigrants going to the United States (as opposed to Australia, Canada or other destinations) remained very high.[10]

The decision to emigrate

It is considerably easier to delineate the extent and composition of Irish female emigration than to disentangle the reasons for it. How can one determine the reasons people emigrated? And what conclusions, if any, can be drawn about Irish society in the period? Undoubtedly, male and female emigration were both largely a product of the same general factors but these often affected one sex more than the other and, in the case of women, there were a range of additional factors relating to the nature of Irish society, women's inferior status and the late age of marriage, which all played a part in the decision to emigrate.

Having examined this question for six years, the Commission on Emigration concluded in 1954 that the fundamental cause of emigration was economic. However, it added that the decision to emigrate arose from an interplay of factors, social, political, economic and psychological.[11] This conclusion was based partly on surveys of emigrants conducted for the Commission. A later survey of intending emigrants in County Cavan during the 1960s found that a majority of girls with secondary school education would emigrate even if a job was available in Ireland.[12] For some women, it was as much the attitude to work which prompted emigration as its scarcity. As one female emigrant remembered:

There were no opportunities for women in my day. If a woman got married and then started to work in the 1930s, she'd be criticised all over the place. 'God, she didn't make much of a match, he can't even keep her.' It never dawned on anybody that a person might like to go out to work. You couldn't take up a decent job, because you'd be expected to leave the minute you got married.[13]

The preliminary results of an as yet incomplete survey of Irish female emigrants begun by the present author as part of this research bear out all these findings. The vast majority of respondents cite employment as a major determinant of their decision to emigrate but most also cite other factors including restlessness, dissatisfaction with their lot, poor or unattractive social conditions, marriage and the influence of an emigrant network. A minority admitted to unhappiness within their extended family or frustration with social or religious aspects of Irish society.[14]

The high rate of Irish female emigration is undoubtedly related to the low rate and late age of marriage.[15] Throughout the period under review here, the marriage rate in Ireland was one of the lowest in the world. Nor was this feature of Irish society of recent origin: a side effect of the Famine, it emerged clearly when marriage statistics were first compiled in 1864 and peristed until the 1960s. From an annual average rate of 5.10 per thousand population in the late 1860s, it declined to 4.02 in the 1880s but increased again, reaching 5.11 in 1911–20. During the first decade of the Irish Free State, it declined to 4.76 but then increased gradually, reaching 5.59 in the decade spanning World War II before declining again during the 1950s.

These variations are of some importance but, even at its highest, the Irish marriage rate still fell short of comparable countries. In 1936, the number of married women under 45 in the Irish Free State was 73 per thousand as compared with 96 in Finland, 97 in Northern Ireland, 105 in Scotland, 123 in England and Wales, 120 in Australia and 145 in the USA. One in four women remained finally unmarried as compared with one in eight in 1841. By the 1950s, Ireland had both the lowest marriage rate and the highest celibacy rate in Europe with one woman in four and one man in three over the age of 55 unmarried (see Table 7.4). The Free State had the lowest marriage rate of twenty-three countries investigated by the Commission on Emigration.

While the Irish marriage rate as a whole was lower than other countries, there was a particular problem in rural areas where farmers and their sons showed a remarkable tardiness in the nuptial stakes. During World War II, one senior Land Commission official described the typical marriage practices among farmers in rural Ireland:

What invariably happens in the case of these people is the eldest son is retained at home say at 18 years of age to assist the father on the farm who is say now 50 years of age. The son's term of service, usually ending when the last member of the family has been done for, can be taken to be anything from 20 to 25 years. He is then anything from 40 to 45 years of age, a settled middle-aged man, careless about marriage and with ambition failing. If he does happen to marry he will probably choose a partner about his own age, oftentimes ending in a childless marriage.[16]

Table 7.4 Single males and females as a percentage of total population in 1951

Age-group	Ireland	France
25–29	76.6	31.0
30–34	57.9	17.6
35–39	44.9	13.6
40–44	35.9	11.9
45–54	31.0	10.5
55–64	28.0	9.7
65–74	28.6	8.8
>74	22.4	8.3

Source: Report of Interdepartmental Committee on the 'Question of Making Available on Farms of Second Dwelling Houses, with a View to Removing Certain Difficulties in the Way of Early Marriage' (Dower House Report), November 1944, NA, D/T S13413/1, p. 10; *CEOP*, pp. 74–6; Patrick Clancy *et al.*, eds, *Ireland: a Sociological Profile, Institute of Public Administration*, Institute of Public Administration, Dublin, 1986, p.157.

The low rate and late age of marriage was not simply a problem afflicting small farms. Large farms suffered even more than small. The larger the farm the greater the number of sons and daughters who remained unmarried. In 1936, for instance, 53 per cent of all daughters in the age-group 20–34 on farms 30 acres and under were single, whereas the figure was 57 per cent for farms 30–50 acres or more, 60 per cent for farms 50–200 acres and 62 per cent for farms over 200 acres. The Land Commissioner already cited concluded:

> I am of the opinion resulting from my observations and experiences throughout the country of the family life of the better class of farmer that something is wrong with the natural sequence of marriage by these people. Whether the cause can be ascribed to selfish or conservative motives by the parents or the lack of living facilities on the farm is a matter of conjecture.[17]

While sons and daughters of larger farmers were less likely to be married, there was less variation between the farmers themselves, as Table 7.5 shows. However this table does confirm the underlying reluctance of all Irish farmers to marry.

Table 7.5 Conjugal status of farmers by size of holding

| | Size of farm in acres | | | |
	1–30	30–50	50–200	over 200
Total farmers	135,792	53,730	60,657	5,834
Number single	30,051	12,060	13,400	1,324
Percentage	22.1	22.4	22.1	22.7

Source: Dower House Report, p. 9

These figures confirm that poverty and poor social conditions alone do not explain the late age of marriage in rural Ireland. Although it was declining, the dowry system was still widespread. It contributed to the problem by restricting choice and giving the parents undue influence. Above all, as a government report on the subject concluded in the 1940s, 'the most important single factor causing the postponement of marriage among farmers is the unwillingness of the head of the household to retire from his occupation with advancing years'.[18] One rural clergyman described as 'debilitating and stagnatory' the effect of this state of affairs which led to frequent absurdities such as a twenty-five year old son having to ask for the price of a smoke or the price of a ticket to the cinema or a dance.[19] The inevitable frustration goes a long way towards explaining the high rate of emigration among daughters and non-inheriting sons. (If one excludes inheriting sons from the calculations, there is little significant variation among male and female emigrants.)

Marriage, albeit long delayed, was central to the maintenance of the Irish rural economy. The new wife provided labour and the heir to whom the farm would ultimately be transferred. As K.H. Connell remarked in 1962, marriage was likely to be contemplated 'not when a man needed a wife but when the land needed a woman'.[20] With due respect to the official state commitment, popularised initially by Sinn Féin but articulated most frequently and eloquently by Fianna Fáil, to create a self-sufficient Ireland and in the process establish as many people as possible on the land, emigration was a permanent, almost essential, feature of Irish life in the forty years after independence. Political rhetoric or official government policy never acquired sufficient force to counterbalance the central features of the rural economy. The deeply entrenched commitment to land ownership and maintenance of the family inheritance, and the concomitant of these, the avoidance of subdivision, proved more than a match for de Valera's hazy visions of frugal sufficiency and communal values. The latter aimed implicitly, if ineffectually, to end emigration while the former depended on it. Paradoxically, as we shall see, emigrants, particularly female emigrants, were victims of both.

Despite its policies, the number of agricultural jobs in Ireland declined steadily during Fianna Fáil's period of political dominance from 1932 onwards. This decline is as much an index of the strength of the existing rural system as of the failure of de Valera's economic policy. In the absence of viable alternative employment locally, emigration was an inevitable result of large family size and impartible inheritance. The size of the flow depended to a large extent on economic circumstances elsewhere, although in the case of female emigrants, the force of push factors was probably stronger than for men.[21] The economic depression of the 1930s and the popularity of protectionist policies kept emigration in check and helped de Valera pursue his economic experiment. But when, in the 1940s and 1950s, the floodgates opened and the stream became a flood, the crisis which developed threatened not only to submerge de Valera's vision but to undermine a rural economy which had tolerated if not demanded emigration.

An interesting feature of the public debate on emigration in Ireland in the period 1945–60 is the extent to which it focused on female as well as male emigration. Whatever the impression conveyed by Keating's painting, the extent of female emigration was the subject of regular public comment, particularly in the local press. Indeed, in the context of marriage the flight of Irish women in such numbers was a cause of particular concern. In January 1948, Daniel Morrissey TD told his constituents in a public letter that Ireland had

> failed to retain any percentage of the cream of young Ireland to build up the nation. From our universities and secondary schools, thousands of brilliant graduates and students have had to seek employment in Britain. Worse still, sons and daughters of farmers have gone across the channel so that rural Ireland is slowly bleeding to death and the government has lamentably failed to staunch the outflow.[22]

In Morrissey's analysis, which was widely shared, some emigration was inevitable and the loss of some emigrants was to be more lamented than others, not least if it threatened to deplete the 'brood stock'. Dr T.F. O'Higgins in Westmeath in August 1947 articulated an unspoken fear: 'Could anybody', he asked, 'contemplate a more serious national situation ... [with] a steady outward flow of young women so that many parishes have not a single young girl left'.[23]

The necessity for drastic remedial action was widely accepted. In the wider political sphere the new expansionist economic policies adopted by Lemass and Whitaker in 1958 were not so much a watershed as a culmination of the painful reappraisal under way since at least 1948. But elsewhere too there was evidence of the recognition of the necessity for changes in social mores if the crisis was to be averted. Such changes were altogether more difficult to achieve.

Successive governments between 1922 and 1958 considered piecemeal schemes aimed at improving social conditions and particularly at making life in rural Ireland more attractive for young women. One way of achieving that, which was widely discussed in government circles for many years and which bears directly on the emigration issue, was the promotion of earlier marriages. In 1937, the year in which de Valera introduced his new constitution *inter alia* sanctifying the role of women in the home, the Executive Council of the Irish Free State received a depressing account of social conditions among small farmers in West Cork. The report itself was depressingly familiar but it was accompanied by a proposal from a local parish priest for the introduction of a marriage bounty to encourage young women to marry into small holdings rather than emigrate. Fr. O'Leary argued that it would give an incentive to young men to marry and would encourage young women

> to settle down at home rather than to emigrate. At present the girls refuse to marry into holdings because of the poor prospects. On the other hand, as they have no prospects, they are not looked for by the older people.[24]

O'Leary felt that, even if the scheme proved expensive to implement, the state would be getting good value as 'the young girls would be kept at home and would settle down with the young men, working the small hold-ings that were at present not cared for'.

Such an outcome was eminently desirable from de Valera's point of view but the scheme did not get beyond the drawing-board. However, similar proposals for what would in effect have been a state dowry surfaced peri-odically. In 1954, when Robert K. Flynn of Chicago wrote to de Valera proposing a bold new remedy for Irish reluctance to marry early, his scheme was merely an ingenious variation on O'Leary's. On the basis that 'the raging fires of young love were more productive than the flukey flames of advancing age', Flynn suggested a graduated scheme under which the younger the groom the larger the bounty (with a maximum of $1,500 for a twenty-one year old). He anticipated that the huge cost would be met by the increased volumes of taxation produced from a growing population while Irish farmers would also benefit from an expanded market for their produce.[25]

Flynn's scheme received only a polite acknowledgement from de Valera who by the 1950s had grown increasingly disillusioned about the possibility of stemming emigration by changing marriage practices. His attitude was shaped in large measure by the abysmal failure of a pet project of his own, the provision of dower or second houses on farms to encourage the marriage of sons who normally postponed marriage until they inherited the farm on the death of their father.

De Valera was convinced that there was a direct link between emigra-tion and the late age of marriage. He also came to accept that the success of his party's policy of establishing as many families as possible on the land was dependent *inter alia* on persuading young women to marry into small farms. He displayed a considerable interest in proposals to deal with this situation. One approach which he favoured strongly was the notion of the state subsidising the building of dower houses. He raised that possibility in the late 1920s and again in the 1930s. In 1943, following a speech by de Valera, an interdepartmental committee was established to prepare such a scheme. Not surprisingly, the idea was popular with farmers. One, from near Youghal in East Cork, wrote to de Valera encouraging him to proceed:

> I would be most interested in a scheme of this sort, as my son who is to get this farm is now eligable [sic] for marriage, I myself being 65 next month.[26]

What followed was to prove how deep-rooted certain mores were in the Irish situation. Despite the continued sponsorship of de Valera for many years, the dower house scheme got nowhere.

It quickly became clear to the members of the dower house committee that, although the aims of de Valera's scheme were laudable, there were enormous difficulties in the way of its implementation. Remarkably, given de Valera's total domination of his government and his almost mystical status, an attempt was made to have the terms of reference of the committee changed to allow it to recommend other solutions, but de Valera refused to budge. The committee was forced to produce a scheme along the lines desired by the Chief, but to minimise the danger of subdivision they restricted it to holdings more than twice the size regarded by the Land Commission as an economic holding. In practice, this excluded the most needy farmers and precisely those in whom de Valera was most interested. The committee also included an alternative scheme based on enlarging and improving existing dwellings which it was felt had more chance of success and might be more socially desirable.[27]

Disappointed with the failure of his civil servants to endorse enthusiastically his approach, de Valera reluctantly shelved their report. However, the upsurge in emigration after World War II encouraged him to reopen the issue. In July 1947, when an opposition TD suggested a dower house scheme as a way of stemming the rush to the emigrant ship, de Valera responded with some bitterness about the lack of support he had received earlier. He accepted that it might not be possible on small farms but felt that the scheme could work.[28] With party supporters warning de Valera that the late age of marriage was a 'danger to the race', he received encouragement to revive his scheme from an unlikely source. The *Irish Times* hailed the idea as 'a further revelation of Mr de Valera's resourceful and ingenious mind' and one which, 'unlike some of his visions' might actually work. Despite this strong support, the scheme was shelved because of what it might cost.[29]

The idea was revived again on Fianna Fáil's return to power in 1951. When Dr Barton, the Protestant Archbishop of Dublin, called for such a scheme, de Valera established a new committee. To ensure that he would get a result more to his own liking, he entrusted the task to a group of Fianna Fáil TDs rather than civil servants. The group rapidly produced a grants scheme to promote the building of dower houses. However, despite the support of farm organisations such as Macra na Tuaithe and Muintir na Tíre, the scheme foundered because in their haste the politicians underestimated the financial implications and the practical difficulties.[30]

The failure of the dower house scheme to get beyond the drawing-board despite the strong support of de Valera illustrates the way in which key elements of the rural economy outweighed government policy or the desire to end emigration. The main objection to the dower house proposal was that two houses on a holding might lead to subdivision of the holding. This was specifically forbidden in various land acts and ran counter to the policy pursued by the Land Commission almost since its foundation. When the 1944 committee sought the views of agricultural inspectors from different parts of the country as to the possible impact of such a scheme, this point was made repeatedly. F.W. Stock from Galway suggested that if there was only one son and one daughter-in-law in each family, a dower house would be the 'most ideal arrangement on earth' but as it was, the provision of a dower house would be a 'direct and irresistible incentive to permanent subdivision of the holding'. For that reason it was 'too dangerous an experiment to be fostered by the State'. Although late marriage was a 'most vital social defect', Stock opposed the scheme as a 'first step to congestion'.[31]

Stock's unusual forthrightness was repeated in the responses of many of his colleagues. So also was his preoccupation with property rather than people and his identification of the maintenance intact of the family holding as the supreme value in rural Ireland, a priority outweighing all other considerations, including the fight against emigration and the preferences of his Taoiseach. J.F. Glynn from Tipperary thought that the scheme would 'strike at the foundations of family life as lived heretofore in Ireland'. He dismissed even the notion that the scheme might lead to earlier marriage: it would, he thought, lower marriage rates because with the older brother out of the way in the dower house, the younger sons would be under less pressure to move out. The only 'advantage' he could see in the scheme was as a 'love nest' for the newly weds so that they 'could spend a protracted honeymoon billing and cooing until such times as they realised that they had also to earn a living'.[32]

Glynn's forthright views betrayed an old-fashioned impatience with the expectations of a new generation, and the new expectations of women. The responses of many of his colleagues provide a revealing if not always very sensitive insight into the problems of women in rural areas and the growing impatience with backward social conditions which led so many to choose emigration as a form of escape. R.M. Duncan accepted that there was a general distaste for the drudgery of life on small farms: women were influenced by the lure of jobs in the towns where conditions were better and the added attractions included the cinema which provided a glimpse of a different kind of life. Again and again in these reports, the cinema is identified as a significant factor in luring women away from rural areas and increasing their expectations.

Even relatively properous farmers who were willing to marry had difficulty finding wives because of the reluctance of women to embrace the farming life. Duncan insisted that the late age of marriage was not simply a product of poor conditions. Many women were unwilling to marry a farmer even where the standard of comfort on the farm left nothing to be desired. In the case of better class farmers,

> the girls have generally been sent to good secondary schools and will not contemplate becoming farmers wives even where an adequate staff of servants is available.[33]

The dower house proposal was never a realistic proposition for small farms which could not support two families, but it did help to highlight the frustration and friction which could be generated within extended families living in overcrowded and substandard accommodation in rural areas. Many of the officials consulted were quick to endorse the extended family as the most desirable family model from a social point of view but they were forced to accept the problems it created. M.J. Curley admitted that 'a normal married woman still able to work demands a home of her own'. A woman who chose to marry into a farm had to contend with enormous difficulties. There was liable to be

> continual friction due to the overlap of the spheres of two queen-bees confined to the same hive. In such a conflict of interests, precedence should pass to the younger woman who must take the responsibility for the future and each day's humiliation makes the mother-in-law more aware of the social eclipse.

Curley quoted the saying popular in south Connemara:

> An tsean bhean ar a tealach, tá sí 'sa mbealach
> An sean-fhear 'sa doras, tá sé sa solas
> (The old woman on the hearth is in the way;
> the old man in the doorway is blocking the light.)

In fact, however, the balance in the relationship was more likely to be in favour of the older couple as they normally retained ownership of the holding rather than signing it over. Thus, as Curley admitted, 'the clash of wills can become almost intolerable when fostered by a suspicious, mean mind ... it also comes sore on the most valuable citizens, that is people of unusual assiduity and enterprise'.[34] It was precisely these people who were likely to seek the escape offered by emigration.

The strong evidence, presented in the reports of the Land Commission inspectors, that women in rural Ireland were frustrated and unhappy with their lot, was supported a decade later by the Commission on Emigration and Other Population Problems established in 1948. This was the most ambitious and extensive attempt by the government of the Irish Free State to investigate the roots of emigration. Chaired by Dr James Beddy, an economist and later head of the IDA, the twenty-four-member Commission included four statisticians, two economists, a sociologist, two distinguished medical doctors, two trade union officials, a number of central and local government officials, writers, social critics and clergymen. Despite the fact that the majority of emigrants at the time were women, the Commission contained only two women, a fact strongly condemned by the Irish Housewives' Association.[35]

The Commission met 115 times and received submissions from and interviewed a vast range of individuals and organisations. Intending emigrants were interviewed and surveys were undertaken of social conditions in different parts of the country. Unfortunately most of the unpublished records of the Commission cannot be traced, but what survives provides a remarkable insight into social life in Ireland at the time and into the state of mind of emigrants.[36] In his survey of County Clare, Fr. Counihan tabulated the causes of emigration offered by the people themselves. The reasons cited ranged from general poverty to restlessness and absence of freedoms, from the impossibility of getting farmers to marry to the poor social conditions, the monotony of rural life and the attractions of life in urban centres abroad. The remedies offered by the people included planning, decentralisation, running water and lavatories. Clare emigrants cited hardship as a reason for emigration but they also cited the opportunities offered by emigration. A strong thread of pragmatism and realism ran through all county social inquiry reports: nationalist rhetoric or the call to frugal sufficiency were no longer sufficient.[37] The playwright M.J. Molloy told the Commission that everything 'went back to education, wrong psychology, wrong outlook on life. Practical patriotism is extinct, and there was no use preaching patriotism to a girl without a fortune'. His solution was the introduction of a ban on emigration and a state dowry for marriage.[38]

The high rate of emigration among single women inevitably focused a good deal of attention on the position of women and the late age of marriage. The Irish Housewives' Association argued that the main causes of female emigration were the inferior status of women in Irish society, poor conditions on small farms and the fact that women were dismissed from public appointments on marriage. These views met with a mixed response from the Commission. They were vociferously rejected by Bishop Lucey, who also rejected a suggestion that late marriage was the Irish form of birth control. In his minority report, Lucey argued that urban society by its nature was corrupt and sterile and the only hope for the future was to go back to the land. Another member of the Commission, speaking strictly off the record, told the *Irish Times* that the real reason women emigrated was to get married:

> they were mostly attractive country girls who are striving to get away from the late marriage prospect in this country and also, perhaps, from the prevalent mother-in-law difficulties.[39]

Hardly surprisingly, the Commission did not produce any miracle cure for emigration but it did contribute to a more realistic understanding of its causes. It confirmed that more women than men were emigrating; that most of them were going to Britain rather than the USA, unlike before the war, and that most were in the 20–25 age-group. As we have seen, it concluded that while the fundamental cause of emigration was economic, the decision to emigrate arose from the interplay of a variety of motives. The decision was affected by conditions in Ireland and elsewhere. Not all emigration was bad. What was a matter of acute concern was when emigration was involuntary or unnecessary or when it contributed to a falling population, as in Ireland in the 1950s.[40]

The claim by the Irish Housewives' Association that female emigration was partly a product of the inferior position of women in Irish society was well established by the early 1950s. De Valera's 1937 constitution encapsulated that position well and generated a significant debate which throws considerable light on the position of Irish women and the perceptions of at least some of them. No clauses in the constitution attracted more attention at the time than those which related to women. Indeed such was the intensity of the reaction against his initial proposals that de Valera was forced to drop some of the more contentious provisons.

The constitution enshrined the Fianna Fáil aspiration that 'there may be established on the land in economic security as many families as in the circumstances shall be practicable' (Article 45.2). It also seems likely that the idealisation of the family in the constitution partly reflected the persistence of emigration and the threat it posed to families. In both cases, the reality stood in stark contrast to the aspiration.

The constitution enshrined a particularly nineteenth-century, Victorian view of the role of woman as the homemaker. In the section on fundamental rights, Article 40.1 declared all citizens to be equal before the law. In a move widely criticised by women's groups, de Valera initially omitted the phrase 'without distinction of sex' which appeared in the Free State constitution of 1922 but added a new qualification which alarmed many women: 'This shall not be held to mean that the state shall not in its enactments have due regard to differences of capacity, physical and moral, and of social function'. It was rightly feared that it was particularly gender differences which de Valera had in mind.

The articles which followed stated *inter alia* that the state recognised that 'by her life within the home, woman gives to the State a support without which the common good cannot be achieved ... The State shall, therefore, endeavour to ensure that mothers shall not be obliged by economic necessity to engage in labour to the neglect of their duties in the home'. In the Dáil debate on the constitution, one critic pointed to the reality that, with so many women emigrating, these sections were little more than 'pious resolutions', while another suggested that they might as well put the Book of Proverbs into the constitution.[41]

The strength of the female reaction against the constitution is remarkable. There were three women TDs in the Dáil at the time but they made no real contribution to the debate, earning for themselves the nickname 'silent sisters'. However, there was a considerable public and private campaign.[42] The campaign was spearheaded by the National University Women Graduates' Association, the Irish Women Workers' Union, the Standing Committee on Legislation Affecting Women and the Joint Committee of Women's Societies, and Social Workers representing more than fourteen women's groups. A mass meeting of women graduates chaired by Mary Hayden deplored the omission of the principle of equal rights and opportunities enunciated in the 1916 proclamation and reiterated in the 1922 constitution as 'sinister and retrogressive'. Articles 41, 42 and 45 were condemned as leaving the way open for reactionary legislation.[43]

Mary Hayden claimed that women's rights as citizens, their civil status and their right to work was to be left to the whim of government ministers. Mary S. Kettle of the Joint Committee alleged that the government was striking at the rights of women under the cloak of the constitution. So vociferous was the attack that the *Irish Press* was forced to come to de Valera's defence in a series of editorials which accused some of his critics of 'gratuitous libel'.[44] Even after de Valera met delegations from the Joint Committee and the Women Graduates' Association, and promised to consider their reservations, the storm continued. A joint committee representing republican women's groups including Cumann na mBan, Mná na

Poblachta, Cumann na Poblachta and Sinn Féin added their voice to the protest. A campaign was organised to lobby TDs and to get women's groups in Ireland and abroad to take up the issue. Telegrams were sent from different parts of the country and abroad and a women writers' petition was signed by, among others, Kate Cruise O'Brien and Dorothy Macardle. Dublin University Women Graduates' Association, the Irish Women Citizens' Association, the Six Point Group led by Lady Balfour in London, and the International Alliance of Women for Suffrage and Equal Citizenship all objected to the draft constitution.[45]

Gertrude Gaffney accused the constitution of sounding the death-knell of the working women. De Valera, she said,

> had always been a reactionary where women were concerned. He dislikes and distrusts us as a sex, and his aim ever since he came into office has been to put us in what he considers is our place, and to keep us there.

She went on to accuse de Valera and his predominantly male government of being remote from the experience of women. De Valera, she said, had

> never been in contact with, and will never descend to, the realities of life. He lives in a remote and distant political world of his own where his plans look exceedingly well on paper ... If he had more contact with the average working man and woman he would know that ninety per cent of the women who work for their living in this country do so because they must.[46]

Gaffney forcefully reminded de Valera of the role played by women in the independence movement, in return for which they were now being harshly treated. She also raised the contribution of women in the social area:

> It would do well to recall, too, that all the social services which we enjoy today were achieved by the fight women made for them, and not by men. Do you think we should have school meals, free milk, school medical inspection, organised welfare help for mother and child, old age pensions, and so forth, if it were not that the demand for these things came from women pioneers who organised the agitation for them. If it were left to men our social services would be in a sorry state and welfare work non-existent.[47]

The problem was that in the main the provision of welfare services were in the hands of men and by 1937 the provision of such services in Ireland had fallen behind the rest of Europe.

Perhaps most influential of all were the strong positions adopted by two women for whom de Valera had considerable respect. Dorothy Macardle wrote from London telling him that she could not see how anyone holding advanced views on the rights of women could support the new constitution, and the persistent lobbying of Louie Bennett of the Irish Women Worker's Union helped persuade the normally unyielding de Valera to include a reference to 'without distinction of sex' and to omit a reference to the 'inadequate strength' of women. However that was as far as he was willing to go.

Although the women's campaign against the provisions of the constitution was only partially successful, at best, it does provide evidence of a considerable level of organisation and politicisation on the part of middle-class, professional women in Ireland. Indeed, some conservative critics who urged de Valera not to give in to the 'clamour of these suffragettes' saw the campaign as evidence of the wisdom of the constitutional provisions and the need to make the articles on the family and women in the home mandatory by guaranteeing a family wage. That, argued the influential Jesuit, Fr. Cahill, was the only way to deal with depopulation and female emigration.[48]

Many of the organisations which orchestrated the campaign against the constitution had been active on issues of concern to women in earlier years and they continued their involvement afterwards. The Joint Committee of Women's Societies was particularly active under the formidable leadership of women such as W.R. O'Hegarty. Issues on which the committee campaigned included pervasive state censorship, equal pay for women, the marriage bar in the civil service which forced women to retire on marriage, the exclusion of women from key positions in the civil service, Garda Síochána and Prison Service, the inadequacy of welfare provisons, and maternity and health issues. The bureaucratic response was invariably condescending and evasive, as when, on the eve of World War II, O'Hegarty argued forcibly that as police were regarded as the 'custodians of civilisation', the Garda Síochána would not be a properly constituted police force until it included women. In fact, this had been recommended in 1931 by the Carrigan committee on Criminal Law. Yet, although the Joint Committee had won the support of forty public bodies including Dublin Corporation, the Taoiseach and Minister for Justice refused even to meet them. As his secretary reported, the Minister for Justice was disinclined to meet a delegation, for he was assured that the agitation was 'an artificial business without any real roots in the country'.[49]

The issue of women in the police force was first raised with the Minister for Justice in 1926. In 1930, the Cork Council of Women raised it with the President. Two years later the League of Nations pursued the issue. In 1936, the Joint Council met the Deputy Commissioner of the Garda and pressed the case. In the same year, the Minister for Justice refused requests to meet a delegation from the Joint Committee and the Irish Women Citizens' Committee. Undaunted, the Joint Committee drew up a scheme and another delegation met the Assistant Commissioner in 1938. In 1939, 1940, 1945, 1953, 1954 and 1955, they raised the matter again. In 1951, an official inquiry recommended the appointment of women police officers and in 1955 the issue reached the floor of the Dáil. What was involved initially was the recruitment of a small number of women officers who would handle mainly sensitive women's issues. Provision was finally made for women police officers in 1958 but on a lower rate of pay than their male counterparts and with compulsory retirement on marriage.[50]

It is not likely that exclusion from the police service persuaded many or any Irish women to emigrate. But the issue does typify the unfriendly nature of Irish society and particularly the state apparatus as far as many women were concerned. At a time when the expectations of women were increasing, the state remained insensitive if not hostile.

Implications of female emigration

The implications of the loss of such large numbers of young women for Irish society can only be guessed at. The implications for the host society lie beyond the scope of this chapter. However some tentative suggestions can be made and markers laid for further research.[51]

The relative youth of the female emigrants, their rural background and their undoubted frustration with rural life must certainly have shaped their experience. So too did the fact that so many emigrated as individuals rather than as part of a family, a fact which makes them somewhat different from female emigrants from other parts of Europe. Little or no effort was made to prepare emigrants for their new life. As the Commission on Emigration admitted, there was a reluctance to argue in favour of pre-emigration education lest it appear that emigration was being condoned or encouraged. A proposal by the Commission for the establishment of emigrant advice centres was largely ignored.[52] Emigrants continued to make do as best they could. Just how ill-prepared they were may be guessed from Gertrude Gaffney's book *Emigration to England: What You Should Know About It; Advice to Irish Girls* published in the same year as de Valera's constitution. Gaffney was a brave advocate of the rights of women and wrote with some sensitivity about the need for practical education for emigration, the work of rescue societies and the plight of destitute Irish girls in London and Liverpool. However, some of her advice was of doubtful value: among other pitfalls, she warned her readers against foreign Jews, low boarding houses and bars.[53]

There was a disjunction between the reality of large-scale emigration and the official Irish ethos. The latter saw emigration as evil, dangerous, even anti-social. The Catholic Church, in particular, highlighted the moral danger posed to young women who, as the *Irish Press* put it, preferred the 'kitchens, factories and dancehalls of other lands' and fled from 'the green fields of Ireland to the grey streets of an alien underworld'.[54] How many of the female emigrants really considered London or New York an alien underworld is a matter worth investigating. More detailed study is also required on issues such as their marriage patterns after they had emigrated, their attitude to the extended family, their social outlook generally and how many continued in paid employment after marriage.

It is hardly surprising that Irish female emigrants congregated in cities in even larger proportions than male emigrants. Only a small fraction settled in rural areas. What is perhaps ironic is that such large numbers found themselves in domestic service in Britain and the United States, especially in the pre-war period, at a time when domestic service in Ireland was on the decline. For many migrant women, domestic service was the only employment available. The assumption that these women, or Irish female emigrants generally, were docile, subservient or deferential and brought these attributes to their new societies is at least questionable.

Maureen H., one of the respondents in my own survey, left a small Midlands farm in 1934 and took a job in a draper's shop in Dublin in preference to entering domestic service locally. Three years later she emigrated to New York without telling her parents. Here she found herself in domestic service where she remained until she married six years later. Asked why she was willing to enter service in America but not in Ireland, she insisted that it was different. By her own account, she insisted from the outset that she was an employee not a servant and would eat what the family ate and accompany them on vacation and so on. Such assertiveness is probably unusual, but it does seem likely that Irish female emigrants who entered service abroad were more independent and strong-willed than their counterparts at home.[55]

Well over half the Irish female emigrants entered domestic service but the proportion declined steadily after World War II. Others worked in shops, restaurants, pubs and factories. It would be wrong to assume that they were all unskilled or uneducated. As the period progressed, a growing proportion enrolled as nurses in Britain. This reflects a trend towards their being better educated. Throughout the period, the educational qualifications on average were superior to those of their male counterparts. As the Land Commission inspectors testified, for many farmer's daughters secondary school education was a significant catalyst in the decision to abandon the farming life. It is also well to remember that, among the female emigrants, there were more than a few professional women, many of them graduates.[56]

A study of Irish emigrants living in London in the early 1970s confirmed that the women emigrants were better educated and that a higher proportion cited reasons other than employment as a reason for emigration. Dissatisfaction with their life and status in Ireland was identified as a more important factor for men than for women. Arising from this, a larger proportion of women than men indicated that they did not intend to return to Ireland. No doubt, partly because of this, women were found to have integrated better than men into their new society. These findings accord with my own, although it will require more extensive study of the gender issue in different countries to establish the case beyond doubt. It certainly seems probable that emigrant women would be less likely to embrace the 'Erin's children in exile' interpretation of emigration so beloved of Irish politicians, at home and abroad.[57]

The recent NESC investigation of the causes of contemporary Irish emigration concluded that gender alone is not a good indicator of a likelihood to emigrate but that it is a factor of some significance. My conclusions support that view and confirm the validity of Pedraza's argument that ethnicity, gender and class interact in the process of emigration. Irish women emigrated in relatively greater numbers than their European sisters. Poverty and employment were important factors. However, the high rate of emigration among the daughters of larger farmers points to the necessity for a broader approach which includes gender as one of the key interacting causes.[58] I leave the last word to one female emigrant who left a small holding in Achill in the late 1940s. Faced with the choice of an arranged marriage or emigration, she chose the boat-train to Britain. Forty years later, she described her feelings:

> I didn't think much of it at the time. I'd worked with my sister in Scotland from when I was fourteen [as a seasonal worker]. Still I missed home and cried every night for a year ... But I never dreamed of going back. There was nothing for me there.[59]

Notes

1. See M.F. Houston, R.G. Kramer and J.M. Barrett, 'Female preponderance of immigration to the United States since 1930', *International Migration Review*, XVIII, 1983, p. 908; E.S. Lee, 'A theory of migration', *Demography*, III (1966), p. 51.
2. See Table 7.1.
3. Recent decades have seen a growing interest in Irish female emigration but mainly in the period before 1921. See for example, H.R. Diner, *Erin's Daughters in America: Irish Immigrant Women in the Nineteenth Century*, Johns Hopkins University Press, Baltimore, 1983; P. Jackson, 'Women in nineteenth-century Irish emigration', *International Migration Review*, XIX, 1984, pp. 1004–20. For the period after 1922, see Mary Lennon *et al.*, *Across the Water: Irish Women's Lives in Britain*, Virago, London, 1988.
4. Silvia Pedraza, 'Women and migration: the social consequences of gender', *Annual Review of Sociology*, 1991, **17**, pp. 302–25.
5. For a useful general discussion of the current debate on women's history and gender history, see Cliona Murphy, 'Women's history: feminist history or gender history?', *Irish Review*, XII, 1992, pp. 21–7.
6. J.J. Sexton *et al.*, *The Economic and Social Implications of Emigration*, NESC, Dublin, 1991, pp. 67–9 (hereafter *Economic Implications*).
7. *Economic Implications* pp. 70–1; D. Hannan, 'Emigration 1946–71', unpublished Thomas Davis lecture, October 1972.
8. See *Economic Implications*, Table 3.5, p. 73.
9. *Economic Implications*, pp. 75–6; *Commission on Emigration and Other Population Problems 1948–54 Reports (CEOP)*, Stationery Office, Dublin, 1955, pp. 321 and 7; Mary Daly, 'Internal migration', unpublished Thomas Davis lecture, December 1972.
10. *CEOP*, pp. 25 and 317.
11. *CEOP*, p. 153.
12. See D. Hannan, *Rural Exodus: a Study of the Forces Influencing the Large-Scale Migration of Irish Youth*, Geoffrey Chapman, London, 1970; C. O'Gráda, 'On two aspects of post-war Irish emigration', Centre for Economic Research, UCD, Working paper No. 31; Mary Daly, 'Internal migration'.
13. Quoted in Mary Lennon, *et al.*, *Across the Water*, p. 33.
14. The value of the findings of this survey are circumscribed by the facts that the research is taking place at least thirty years after the decision to emigrate was made and that virtually all of the respondents so far have retained a close

connection with Irish communities in their new homes. Therefore the sample may be unrepresentative.

15. For a good discussion of marriage in rural Ireland, see K.H. Connell, 'Peasant marriage in Ireland: its structure and development since the Famine', *Economic History Review*, XIV, (1962), pp. 504–23.

16. T.P. O'Cathán, January 1944, NA, S13413/1. In fact, the eldest son did not invariably inherit. And if he married, he was as likely to take a younger bride, thus skipping a generation.

17. Report of Interdepartmental Committee on the Question of Making Available on Farms of Second Dwelling Houses, with a View to Removing Certain Difficulties in the Way of Early Marriage (hereafter Dower House Report), November 1944, NA, D/T S 13413/1, p. 7; T.P. O'Cathán to the Land Commission, January 1944.

18. Dower House Report, pp. 11–12.

19. Revd T.H. McFall, Piltown, County Waterford, to Taoiseach, 4 Dec. 1943, NA, D/T 13413/A.

20. K.H. Connell, 'Peasant marriage', p. 503.

21. Joy Rudd, 'The emigration of Irish women', *Social Studies*, IX, 1987, pp. 10–26.

22. *Midland Tribune*, 10 Jan. 1948.

23. *Westmeath Independent*, 2 Aug. 1947.

24. 'Small farmers in West Cork: economic conditions', 23 Feb. 1937; 'Marriage bounty', March 1937, NA, D/T S9696 and 9645.

25. Robert K. Flynn to de Valera, 17 March 1954, NA, D/T S9645.

26. *Irish Press*, 4 Dec. 1943; *Farmer's Gazette*, 11 Dec. 1943; D. Glavin to de Valera, 13 Dec. 1943, NA, D/T S13413/A.

27. 'Early marriage: encouragement among Farmers', NA, D/T S13413/1.

28. *Irish Press*, 5 July 1947; *Dáil Debates*, 2 July 1947, Vol. 107, 608–9, 661–2, 735–9.

29. Joe O'Flanagan to de Valera, 12 June 1944 and 7 July 1947, NA, D/TS13413/A; *Irish Times*, 7 and 12 July 1947. For other reactions, see *Evening Mail*, 12 July 1947; *The Leader*, 12 July 1947; *Irish Independent*, 18 July 1947.

30. *Sunday Press*, 4 March 1951; Report of Fianna Fáil Dower House Committee, 11 June 1953, NA, D/T 13413/A; Senator Kissane to Department of Taoiseach, 5 Aug. 1953. A variation on the idea surfaced in 1958 with a call for flats to be built on farms, and in 1959 when there was a call for 'dower duplexes'. *Irish Press*, 10 Apr. 1958; *Irish Times*, 12 Nov. 1959; *Irish Independent*, 10 May 1960.

31. F.W. Stock, 17 Jan. 1944, NA, D/T 13413/A.

32. J.F. Glynn, 4 Jan. 1944.

33. R.M. Duncan to Land Commission, 1 Jan. 1944, NA, D/T 13413/1. Duncan's impression was accurate. Daughters of large farmers, especially those with a dowry, were more inclined to marry the salaried or professional classes. Dower House Report, p. 12.

34. M.J. Curley, January 1944.

35. Letter by Hilda Tweedy and A.D. Sheehy Skeffington, *Irish Press* 26 Apr. 1948. See NA, CAB S14/249A/1. For a more extensive account of the Commission, see my article, 'The dream gone bust: Irish responses to emigration 1922–60', in O. McDonagh and W.F. Mandle, (eds), *Irish-Australian Studies*, Australian National University, Canberra, 1989, pp. 318–43. For the Irish Housewives' Association, see Hilda Tweedy, *A Link in the Chain: The Story of the Irish Housewives' Association 1942–1992*, Attic, Dublin, 1992.

36. It is still possible that the records of the Commission will be found. Only a small file exists among the Cabinet papers (Cab S14/249A). Some valuable copies of Commission Papers are in the Arnold Marsh collection in TCD

Manuscripts Department. These were examined by me in 1988. However, when I sought access more recently for the purposes of this research, I was told by the Archivist that they are now in storage and will not be available for the foreseeable future.

37. Rural Survey: County Clare, Marsh Papers, TCD, MS 8301, SSI, p. 17.
38. Marsh Papers, SSI, pp. 16–17 and 30–1.
39. Marsh Papers, SS4(b), p. 2; *Irish Times*, 1 Feb. 1949.
40. *CEOP*, pp. 150–1.
41. *Bunreacht na Héireann*, Dublin, 1937; M. Moynihan, ed., *Speeches and Statements by Eamon de Valera 1917–73* Gill and Macmillan, Dublin, 1980, pp. 326–7; P. Travers, 'Irish responses to emigration', p. 323.
42. For the debate on the constitution, see Yvonne Scannell, 'The constitution and the role of women', in B. Farrell, ed., *De Valera's Constitution and Ours*, Gill and Macmillan for RTE, Dublin, 1988, pp. 123–35; Mary Clancy, 'Aspects of women's contribution to the Oireachtas debate in the Irish Free State, 1922–37', in Maria Luddy and Cliona Murphy, eds, *Women Surviving: Studies in Irish Women's History in the Nineteenth and Twentieth Centuries*, Poobeg, Dublin, 1989, pp. 206–32; Mary McGinty, 'A study of the campaign for and against the enactment of the 1937 Constitution', unpublished MA thesis, University College Galway, 1987.
43. *Irish Press*, 11 May 1937.
44. *Irish Press*, 11, 12, 13 May 1937; *Irish Independent*, 12 May 1937.
45. W.G. Hassard to de Valera, 22 May 1937; Louie Bennett to de Valera, 18 May 1937; D. Macardle to de Valera, 21 May 1937. See also various letters in the NA, D/T file, Women: Position under Constitution, 1937, S9880.
46. Gertrude Gaffney, 'A woman's view of the constitution', *Irish Independent*, 7 May 1937.
47. Gertrude Gaffney, 'A woman's view of the constitution'.
48. Cahill to de Valera, 23 May 1937; J.J. Walsh to de Valera, 15 May 1937, NA, D/T S9880; B.B. Waters, letter to *Irish Times*, 22 May 1937.
49. S.A. Roche to Mr O Muimhneacháin, 23 Nov. 1939; Memorandum by W.R. O'Hegarty, 1 Nov. 1939, 'Women in Garda Siochána', 1938–58, NA, D/T S16210.
50. Minister's Brief for Dáil Question, 9 Nov. 1954; Department of Justice Memorandum, September 1957, NA, D/T S16210.
51. For a good recent discussion of Irish immigrant integration in Britain in the last two generations, see *Economic Implications*, pp. 161–214.
52. See address by Peadar O'Donnell to Symposium on Emigration, Dublin, May 1954, *Irish Press*, 10 May 1954.
53. Gertrude Gaffney, *Emigration to England: What You Should Know; Advice to Irish Girls*, *Irish Independent*, Dublin, 1937.
54. *Irish Press*, 23 Apr. 1948; Pastoral letter by Dr Lyons of Kilmore, February 1948, *Irish Press*, 9 Feb. 1948.
55. Maureen married an Irishman who became an alcoholic and beat her. She left him and brought up three children by herself. Two are now attorneys and one is a college lecturer. (Unpublished interview with author.)
56. *Economic Implications*, p. 83; *CEOP*, p. 323
57. M. O'Briain, 'Irish immigrants in London', unpublished M. Phil thesis, the City University, London, 1981; cited in J. Rudd, 'The emigration of Irish women', *Social Studies*, IX, 1987, pp. 1–11.
58. Pedraza, p. 303; *Economic Implications*, p. 160.
59. Unpublished interview with author.

8 Listening and learning: experiences in an emigrant advice agency

Kate Kelly and Tríona Nic Giolla Choille

Introduction

Emigration is an issue which touches everyone in Ireland — individuals, families and communities. We all have friends, relatives and neighbours who have left Ireland. We have all been affected by their enforced departure. We have all witnessed how families and neighbourhoods have been devastated by the exodus of young people. It would be an unusual family that had not seen at least one of its members emigrate within living memory. Opinions about emigration are, therefore, coloured by personal experience.

This chapter is also coloured by personal experience, the experience of years of providing information, advice and counselling to Irish people planning to emigrate. It speaks of contemporary Irish emigration during the time the authors were employed as Information Officers with *Emigrant Advice* an emigrant advisory agency, from 1985–92. As it is based on personal experience, no attempt has been made to be objective. During the years the authors were employed in Emigrant Advice we listened to every theory, idea, opinion about emigration's causes, effects and solutions; we talked to journalists, academics, researchers, students and emigrants about our perceptions of the current wave of emigration and we were the sounding-board for all these people who came in contact with the agency. Now, it is our turn to tell it as we saw it.

But first, a brief word about ourselves, where we worked and the background to emigration in Ireland during that time.[1]

Emigrant Advice

Emigrant Advice is an information, advice and counselling service for people planning to emigrate. It provides practical information on accommodation, employment prospects, welfare rights and entitlements and useful contacts and addresses. It also provides a counselling service whereby intending emigrants can explore the whole process of emigration.

Although emigration is an integral part of Irish history, the reality of leaving — leaving home, friends and family, of going from somewhere you
belong to somewhere new where you may not understand the language,
accent or culture — is not common knowledge. Most of the emigrants we
saw had not had an opportunity to discuss with anybody their feelings
about leaving, about *having* to go, about *having no choice*, about arriving
somewhere new and settling in or their feelings about coming home. There
was little space for them to look at these issues dispassionately because of
the pervasive myths which abounded about emigration: 'there's plenty of
jobs/money/opportunities over there', 'travel broadens the mind', 'sure, lots
of emigrants fly home to Ireland every weekend from London' and 'sure,
you'll all come back home with your skills and languages and set up businesses here'.

The basic brief of the agency, therefore, was to provide information,
advice and counselling so that people could make informed choices about
whether or not they wanted to emigrate.

During the time we worked there Emigrant Advice was also engaged in
two other major areas of work. The first was the provision of an educational
service to schools and youth and community groups around the issue of
emigration. The second was the raising of public awareness of the causes of
emigration and its effects and impact on individuals and communities. The
educational work was, of necessity, limited by the lack of resources, both
human and financial, available to the agency as well as the daily pressure to
provide an information, advice and counselling service on a drop-in basis
to all callers to the agency. Raising public awareness about the issue of
emigration was also inhibited by the pressure to provide other services, and
by the agency's unwillingness to enter into conflict with politicians and
statutory agencies.

Emigrant Advice was not a new organisation but one which had a long
history. It was originally set up in 1942 by the then Archbishop of Dublin,
John Charles McQuaid. At that time it was known as the 'Emigrant Section
of the Catholic Social Welfare Bureau'. At the opening of the agency Dr
McQuaid said:

> I have entrusted to you, as your chief activity in the beginning, the care of
> emigrants, especially women and girls.[2]

Reflecting the climate of the times, the functions of the Emigrant Section
were:

— to put emigrants in touch with Catholics at their destination;
— to make enquiries as to whether or not the proposed employment in
  Britain was suitable for Catholics;
— to secure proper facilities for emigrants to fulfil their religious duties;
— to provide for their social welfare in new and often difficult surround-
  ings.

The emigrant's local parish priest would send details of the intending emigrant to the Catholic Social Welfare Bureau which would then contact the local parish priest in England, notifying him of the new arrival. In addition, Legion of Mary volunteers travelled on the trains to Dun Laoghaire, which was the departure point for boats going to England, and spoke to emigrants, collecting information and addresses which were subsequently sent to the local parish priests in Britain, who were in turn asked to confirm the arrival of the emigrants.

With the decline of emigration during the 1970s the Emigrant Section was wound down. With the resumption of large-scale emigration in the 1980s a new response was called for. Emigrant Advice was the response of the Dublin Diocese. The new service was launched in 1987 in city centre premises and was available five days a week, free of charge, to all callers. However, the agency operated under a number of limitations which restricted its activities and effectiveness.

Emigrant Advice and the Irish voluntary sector

Emigrant Advice was a voluntary organisation under the auspices of the Catholic Social Services Conference and the Dublin Diocese. As part of the Irish voluntary sector it was confronted with the same difficulties which bedevilled many of the organisations in this sector. The most chronic of these difficulties was funding. Funding for most voluntary agencies in Ireland is generally short term, *ad hoc* and inadequate; the situation Emigrant Advice found itself in was no different from that experienced by other groups. Emigrant Advice never managed to secure adequate, long-term funding which would have enabled it to plan a programme of work. The *only* funding available for emigration services was provided by the DION committee which operated within the Irish Department of Labour. The DION committee was set up to administer and disburse funds to emigrant welfare groups *in the United Kingdom*. It had no brief to fund services in Ireland. In recognition of the reality that there was *no funding source* for emigrant agencies in Ireland and of the role which Emigrant Advice played in Ireland, the DION Committee made an annual token award to the agency to fund pre-emigration services in Ireland.

Emigrant Advice also suffered in relation to funding in that it was able to raise money for specific projects, e.g. to publish information leaflets, or to produce an educational pack for schools and colleges, but it was never able to secure funding which would allow it to plan on a long-term basis or to employ staff on a more secure footing. This was unsatisfactory both for the staff concerned and for the agency. The agency's ability to plan and execute a work programme to deal with a major national crisis was severely curtailed by its funding difficulties.

Emigrant Advice: a diocesan agency

Emigrant Advice was a diocesan agency under the auspices of the Catholic Social Services Conference and the Dublin Diocese. As a diocesan agency Emigrant Advice's primary focus was on the welfare of the individual emigrant. This meant that throughout the period covered by this chapter, 1985–92, priority was given to maintaining the information, advice and counselling service. Secondary to this was educational work with schools and youth groups. Concentrating on the welfare aspects of the work left little time to address the political issues it raised.

Statutory relationships

Emigrant Advice had close links with the Department of Labour and FAS, the national training agency. The Department of Labour was responsible for emigrant services and allocated funds for such services through its DION committee. Money distributed by the DION committee was intended to fund emigrant services abroad only. An exception was made for Emigrant Advice in recognition of the role it played in providing a pre-emigration service. This funding, though welcome, was never very much nor very secure. FAS over the years provided some limited information to intending emigrants and also regularly referred individuals and groups of young people to Emigrant Advice for information and advice. During its time Emigrant Advice negotiated with the Minister for Labour, the Department of Labour and FAS in attempts to gain more secure funding for its work. Emigrant Advice was reluctant, therefore, to become involved in public criticism of the very agencies from whom it was seeking funding when issues arose from its work which related directly to public policies and practices. Nevertheless, Emigrant Advice was the only organisation in Ireland to concentrate, full-time, solely on the issue of emigration.

The nature of the work, face-to-face counselling on a drop-in basis, meant that we were privy to the views and attitudes of literally thousands of intending emigrants from all parts of Ireland — despite being based in Dublin one-third of the queries we dealt with were from outside that city. In addition, the work we did with schools and with youth and community groups around the country meant that we saw the effects of emigration and heard at first hand how people felt about it.

This then was the background to Emigrant Advice and our daily routine. But what about the broader context in which we worked? How was this new wave of emigration from Ireland seen by the rest of the country?

Emigration — what emigration?

During the early 1980s claims were made by various Irish centres in London that emigration was on the increase. These claims were based on the number of new arrivals from Ireland they were meeting daily in their work. In March 1986, in a speech made at the annual Bishops' Congress on emigration, the then Minister for Labour, Mr Ruairi Quinn, TD, the government minister with responsibility for emigrant services, said there was no evidence of an increase in emigration. He said it was currently running at 9,000 per annum. In April 1986, the census figures were published – they showed that 31,000 people had emigrated in the previous year. Up until then, arguments had raged about the accuracy of the figures being quoted by all sides in the emigration debate. Voluntary agencies in Ireland and Britain consistently came up with figures which were considerably greater than those compiled by statutory agencies. The voluntary groups maintained on the basis of their day-to-day experience and long-standing involvement with emigrant issues that they were in a position to judge more accurately the extent of emigration.

The battle about figures in America was exacerbated by the presence of large numbers of 'illegal' or out-of-status Irish people. During the 1980s, many Irish people, especially young people, who had failed to find employment in Ireland, travelled to America on holiday or student visas and eventually stayed on as their visas expired. Their numbers were variously estimated as ranging from 50,000 to 200,000 people, depending on who was counting; government ministers opted for the lower figure and voluntary agencies for the higher one. With the publication of the census figures the arguments about the numbers ceased and the extent of the problem was recognised. It was apparent that large-scale emigration had resumed. Newspaper headlines screamed about this fact. Figures increased annually throughout the 1980s to reach a peak of 46,000, in 1989.

Emigration was an immensely sensitive, political issue. In Irish popular culture emigration had very strong negative connotations; popular imagination recalled the spectre of nineteenth-century emigration, of Irish people being forced to flee their native land to go to the New World, never to return; at best these emigrants could hope to survive the journey; at worst they would die *en route*. It was only during the 1960s and 1970s that emigrants began returning to Ireland in significant numbers on holiday or to live. The decades following Irish independence were also marked by steady rates of emigration and it has continued unabated right up to the present day. Ireland as an independent state had simply failed to provide sufficient employment for its people, a fact which embarrassed the politicians. Indeed, much of the economic development which has taken place was predicated on a certain level of emigration.

The resumption of mass emigration took place against a background of rising unemployment and an economic policy that was obsessed with fiscal rectitude. Creating a climate for investment, by lowering interest rates and inflation, was the main objective. If this 'climate' could be created, the theory went, then jobs would follow. They did not.

That modern-day emigration was not the same as the emigration of the past was an often repeated sentiment. During the 1980s new picures of emigration began to be presented by certain sectors of Irish society. Sections of the media, the business and academic communities, began to cite the benefits of emigration for the individuals concerned and also for Irish society in general. Irish young people were getting great opportunities to travel, to work abroad, to live in different societies, to broaden their horizons and to develop new skills and gain new experiences, we were told; Irish society would undoubtedly benefit when these young people returned, as return they would, we were told; emigration was not the same today as it had been years ago when people went away and were never seen again; these days with modern telecommunications and good travel infrastructure throughout the world no emigrant need be any further away than a couple of hours journey from Ireland, they said. Sure, you could travel as quickly from Munich to Dublin as you would from Dublin to Donegal, they said. These were no longer poor, undernourished emigrants we were sending to the New World on coffin ships, we were told; these were our new Europeans — bright, well-educated and sophisticated and we should be proud of them.

This image of our young European emigrants was at variance with our experience of intending emigrants; the majority of those we met were neither well-educated nor keen to go. Most were angry at having to look for work abroad: they wanted to stay in Ireland. Those who did have third-level qualifications often ended up working in exactly the same sectors of the economy as those who had emigrated in the 1950s.[3]

However, this new picture of emigration is best exemplified by quoting from a speech by the then Minister for Foreign Affairs, Mr Brian Lenihan,

> What we have now is a very literate emigrant who thinks nothing of coming to the United States and going back to Ireland and then on to Germany and back to Ireland. Emigration is not a defeat because the more Irish emigrants hone their skills and talents in another environment, the more they develop a work ethic in a country like Germany or the US, the better it can be applied in Ireland when they return. After all, we can't all live on a small island.[4]

This statement created a furore because it was the first time that an Irish politician had stated openly that emigration would continue to be a reality for years to come. Most politicians had hitherto publicly condemned emigration as a tragedy for the country whilst welcoming it privately as solving an otherwise intolerable unemployment problem. This ambivalence was reflected in the media. Reporting of emigration issues was a strange mixture of the 'triumphs' of our successful emigrants and the tragedies of our 'problem' emigrants — of the mass of emigrants who fitted into neither category we heard relatively little, if anything at all. If emigrants were having a hard time abroad — as eventually it had to be acknowledged they were — they were the cause of their own problems. They had not prepared adequately or they had not brought enough money with them. Indeed much of the response to emigration was to look elsewhere for solutions. Politicians travelled all over the world to show concern and solidarity with Irish emigrants — to Boston, New York, London, Paris and Munich. They promised funds for Irish Centres in these countries, they negotiated links between FAS (the Irish national training agency) and Manpower (now the Employment Service) in Britain, special courses for migrants in London, additional visas for Irish emigrants in the United States and most recently they established FAS offices in mainland Europe with the first office opening in Holland in the summmer of 1992. All the solutions offered had one common characteristic — they located the source of the problem *outside Ireland*. Few politicians located the problem *in Ireland* or tackled any of the issues identified by emigrant groups as contributing to the increase in emigration.

Such issues included the following:

— the dearth of information services throughout Ireland which would enable Irish people to make informed decisions about emigration;
— the inadequate level of funding for those voluntary agencies trying to provide such information services;
— the need to include a module about leaving home on the curriculum of all post-primary schools;
— the need to have a strategy for job creation in Ireland;
— the connections between low pay, poverty and emigration;
— the narrow based taxation system which imposed a high burden of tax on the PAYE sector;
— the large volume of repatriated profits made by multinational companies in Ireland and their failure to invest profits in job creation here.

In their failure to tackle any of these issues, the proffered solutions exhibited the nature of the dilemma faced by Irish politicians and statutory agencies. Whilst recognising the reality of emigration and the fact that it reduced significantly the numbers of the unemployed they were wary of seeming to publicly advocate emigration. Hence the unwillingness to fund emigrant services adequately in Ireland; providing resources for such services would be tantamount to advocating emigration, or so they feared it would be perceived.

Throughout the 1980s, voluntary organisations provided emigrant advice services on a shoe-string. Irish politicians showed little interest in the needs of emigrants prior to their departure. Showing concern about our emigrants was fine as long as it did not cost any money. Showing concern abroad might even garner a few much-needed votes at the next election. The depth of our concern about emigrants and our desire to bring them back home was recently shown to be quite shallow. With deep recession in both Britain and the United States, emigrants started returning to Ireland; what welcome have they got? We are told that the reason for the increase in the unemployment figures and the reason why our spending on Social Welfare payments is so large is because all these emigrants are returning! They are the scapegoats for failed economic policies.

What we brought with us

Given the amount of double-think and mythology surrounding Irish emigration it was inevitable that our own personal histories and feelings would influence our thoughts about our work. We give a brief outline of our backgrounds which will help explain why we say what we do and what influenced us.

Tríona Nic Giolla Choille

I finished college in the mid-1970s when there were jobs available in Ireland — during the decade when there was net immigration, when AnCo (the national training agency, now FAS) was offering inducements to emigrants to return home. I didn't have to consider going although emigration was there — it was 'part of what we are' (a popular advertising slogan at the time which promoted Irish butter), part of being Irish. At school everybody had to read a book called *Dialann Deorai* (The Emigrant's Diary); it was on the syllabus for the Leaving Certificate Examination. It was the story of a man who emigrated in the 1950s and went to work as a navvy on the buildings in Britain. We also had to read another book about an Irish man who had emigrated to America and went prospecting for gold in the Klondike; we never thought about it too much then, it just seemed like all the emigrants were men. Women never figured too much in those books. It was only much later that I realised that women were also leaving in large numbers but weren't included in the story of emigration that we were told.

Working in Emigrant Advice raised ambivalent feelings for me. A good day's work was often judged as one in which you counselled the maximum number of people on how best to leave the country, how to apply for visas, etc. The more people we saw the better according to the agency, because it meant that many more people were prepared for the realities of life 'over there'. But to me it meant incredible sadness for people who *had* to leave, who had *no choice* but to go; it also meant anger and rage at the politicians who failed to deal with the causes of emigration. There was also a great deal of sadness that the young people who should have been here working for social change would be working elsewhere and would in reality only return in very small numbers. There was also a frustration which was to do with working in an agency which concentrated primarily on the welfare and information needs of emigrants, which were impossible to meet given the resources of the agency, and concentrated less on the political dimensions raised by the issue of emigration.

There were also huge demands made on us personally in terms of spending days seeing people who were anxious and/or desperate to leave Ireland. Most had high expectations of emigration and equally high expectations of us and the help which we could offer. We frequently had to dash those expectations and aspirations with consequent upset to the people involved.

You also had moments when you began to wonder if you should go too!

So many people were leaving that there were moments when you wondered if you wanted to be here after they had all left. I remember we were particularly conscious of this during the Donnelly Visa Programme; it seemed as though everybody had applied for one and we began to think, well, maybe we should just send in an application form as well!

Emigration was all-pervasive — you couldn't just shut the door on it after work. It was there all the time — when you were out with friends, with family, neighbours: when you went on holiday you were conscious of the effects emigration had had on the different parts of the country you visited, the desolation in many communities during the year and the brief regeneration during the summer and Christmas holidays. You were conscious of it all the time!

Kate Kelly

I'm second-generation Irish. Three generations of my family have emigrated — all to Britain — my parents went back and forth across the Irish Sea twice. My upbringing was English — I wasn't particularly aware of being Irish — I was more conscious of being Catholic, that was a real oddity in my neighbourhood. At school most of us were of immigrant stock — Irish, Polish, Italian or Spanish.

I came to Ireland in my early twenties. I thought working in Emigrant Advice was highly ironic — me telling people born and reared here how to leave! It was also the first time I became aware of emigration — the history of Irish emigration, how it affects individuals, communities and Irish society, realising that the typical 'emigrant behaviour' that I read about could be applied to *my family*, that this was a broader thing than my own family history. It raised all sorts of ambivalent feelings and questions of belonging, roots — identity if you like.

It was also difficult because most of the people we saw were the same age as me — which added to the irony but made me feel as if I should be going too!

I remember the first time I heard someone say that more Irish women than men had emigrated — I thought that can't be right, she's got it wrong. This was something totally new — finding out things like that was like painting in the blanks — it gave me a sense of having a past.

During our time working in Emigrant Advice we were conscious of the absence of information about women's emigration. When we started preparing a handbook on emigration for women we became acutely aware of the lack of information and material about women's experiences of emigration. It is generally assumed that the experience of emigration is the same for both women and men. This assumption has only recently been addressed by a number of publications which document women's experiences and feelings about emigration.

We propose, in this chapter, to look at the experiences of Irish women during the 1980s, based on our experience of working in Emigrant Advice, and to highlight some of the issues we encountered which have not received sufficient attention.

How many Irish women have emigrated?

There are no accurate statistics available on emigration. There are *net migration* figures which are the difference between the projected natural increase in population, i.e. the number of births minus deaths, and the actual number of people in the country enumerated during a census. These figures give us some indication of the numbers who emigrate but they are not definitive. We do not know, for example, how many women emigrate to Britain each year because there are no formal entry requirements and so no way of counting the number of people entering the country. Even where there are passport and visa controls, as with the United States of America, we will only know of those who have gone through the legal procedures: we know nothing of those who have gone 'illegally'. Therefore, much of what is written about emigration is based on inadequate statistical data and the anecdotal evidence of those who have emigrated.

At the very least we know that more people have gone than we know of and that throughout the history of emigration from Ireland women have gone in numbers that equal the numbers of men. Most of the women who have gone in recent times are, like those who went before them, young, between 18–25 years old, single and will have travelled by themselves.

Where have Irish women gone?

A glib, but true, answer is everywhere. The traditional, popular destinations are Britain, particularly London, and the USA, particularly Boston and New York. Up until recently these were still the most popular destinations for Irish women, despite the increasing difficulties involved: for example, the introduction of legislation in the USA, the 1986 Immigration Reform Bill, was designed to curtail the employment of 'illegal aliens' by imposing penalties on employers who hired workers who did not have proper documentation. Recession in both the USA and Britain has made finding work that much harder. Irish women also emigrated, in lesser numbers, to Australia, Canada and Europe. Throughout the 1980s Europe was sold as the 'new' destination for Irish emigrants, where there were unlimited possibilities if you could speak a language. Not many could and the number of people emigrating to European countries remained relatively small throughout the decade.

Why have they gone?

The reasons why Irish women emigrate today are very similar to the reasons why Irish women emigrated in the past — unemployment, lack of suitable job and career opportunities and what could loosely be termed social reasons.

Unemployment has gradually increased throughout the 1980s to reach a total of 291,200 or 21 per cent of the work-force in October 1992.[5] This total does not, however, reflect the true extent of unemployment in Ireland. Many women are ineligible for unemployment benefit or assistance because of their marital status and therefore do not 'sign on' or register for unemployment benefits. They would not be included in the official unemployment figures. Access to training programmes or work experience programmes is often dependent on signing on for minimum periods, e.g. six months, twelve months etc. Therefore, many women are excluded from such opportunities. With such a high level of unemployment in Ireland, emigration has often seemed like the only opportunity.

Even where there are work opportunities, it is often not the kind of work that would allow for a decent standard of living or advancement of any kind. Recent research published by the Irish Congress of Trade Unions has shown that women workers are concentrated in the low-paid sectors of the economy, i.e unskilled and part-time work.[6] State-funded childcare or work place crèches do not exist to any significant extent in Ireland, which again limits female participation in the work-force.

Another reason for emigration, coupled with the lack of employment at home, was direct recruitment of Irish workers by other countries experiencing labour shortages; advertisements for nursing vacancies in the USA, Britain and the Middle East were common in the job pages of Irish newspapers. Young Irish women were also recruited by employers from other countries seeking to take advantage of Ireland's unemployment crisis; we refer to the plethora of small classified advertisements in the evening papers in Ireland seeking childminders or au pairs to work for American families. These advertisements offered wages and conditions which seemed very attractive to young Irish women, especially those who had been unemployed for some time or those who were very anxious to go to the USA. What they offered in practice was illegal entry into the USA and cheap labour for American families. Many found the conditions and wages they experienced on arrival to be quite different from those promised.

While lack of work was the main reason women emigrated, some also left for what could be termed 'social reasons'. This meant a variety of reasons connected with social policies and the type of society which Ireland represented. They included families and single-parent families leaving to seek housing — often under the illusion that housing in Britain was of a higher quality and easier to obtain than here. The fact that they were likely to end up in B&B accommodation, if they were lucky, or be sent home if they were not, was incomprehensible to most. Women leaving to escape domestic violence was also another social reason for emigration and a classic example of the 'exporting' of Irish problems.

Others left because of the particular social and moral climate which had evolved during the 1980s. This climate was perceived as being an excessively repressive one, dominated by the Catholic Church and obsessed with sexual morality. The intolerant nature of the society was exhibited during the two divisive referendum campaigns held in Ireland during the 1980s. The 'Abortion Referendum' in 1983 concerned the insertion of a constitutional prohibition on abortion into the Constitution. The 'Divorce Referendum' sought the removal of a constitutional prohibition on divorce from the Constitution. The first proposal was adopted and the second defeated. The defeat of the Divorce Referendum in particular convinced many young people especially that Ireland was an intolerant, narrow society and that change would come only very, very slowly. Many decided that they simply did not want to wait for that change to take place. Women we spoke to in Emigrant Advice told us that they could not stay in a country where there was so little tolerance of difference or dissent; this lack of tolerance of difference impacted directly on women's lives whether they were married or single, divorced or separated. Others directly affected by an obsession with sexual mores were gay men and lesbian women who left rather than 'come out' in Ireland.

While the above outline gives some understanding of why women emigrate, we believe it is far more compelling to listen to the voices of women, giving a litany of reasons for leaving, one after the other. Our experience, when working with Emigrant Advice, was that the same reasons were cited, day in and day out, and the words 'I have to go' began to sound like a mantra.

PHILOMENA from Dublin, aged 22 years:
I have to go — I haven't worked for two years, there's nothing going on here.

ANNETTE, aged 20 years, just finished a secretarial course:
I've signed on with all the agencies — I've been for some interviews and I haven't got anything — if I don't get something soon I'll have to go away.

MARTINA, from Carlow, unemployed:
I came up to Dublin to get some information — there's no jobs at home so I'm thinking of going to London.

TERESA, 18 years, unemployed for six months:
I'm going to do childminding in New York. I got the job out of the paper, I can't get anything here so I'll have to go.

CHRISTINE, 26 years, just finished her Masters Degree:
I can't find any work in Dublin and there's no point in going home—you can't live on grass, can you?

MOIRA, 23 years, working in a low-paid job:
I graduated a year and I've spent a year working in a restaurant—I can't take any more of this so I'm going to the States—it's got to be better than this!

LORRAINE, 27 years, from the West of Ireland:
I've just finished another FAS course; and ended up with nothing at the end of it; it makes me mad to be put through the hoops—made to do courses when there's no chance of a job at the end of it. So I'm off to England—it can't be any worse there than it is here!

What happens to Irish women when they go?

The feeling of *having to go* was a recurrent one. The women we spoke to felt they had *no choice* if they wanted more from life or even if they wanted the basics from life. Coupled with this feeling of the lack of choice was the equally strong feeling that things *had* to be better elsewhere.

The situation in which many Irish women found themselves, especially in relation to employment, was such that they needed to believe, for their own sense of hope and survival, that things were better elsewhere. However, research which had been carried out 'elsewhere' showed that the situation was rarely as good as they had hoped. Such research showed that Irish women end up working in the same sectors of the economy in which their female predecessors worked. Even where they have skills and/or education they are often employed in jobs that do not reflect the level of training or education that they have attained. Research in London found that

> Irish women are doubly invisible in London. As members of an ethnic minority their existence is frequently unrecognised and as women whose work is scattered in various homes, hospitals and offices their contribution to London's economic and social life is largely ignored. Yet they compriese 10 per cent of all women in London ... their employment in particular sectors, notably nursing, catering and cleaning ... virtually underpins the day-to-day functioning of the city.[7]

Even though recent emigrants left with more qualifications than previous generations, this has not made finding work to match their skill or training any easier in Britain:

> Young Irish women are among the best educated in London, though this is not often reflected in their employment status. Many are apparently unable to find jobs reflecting their education and skills.[8]

In the United States a survey carried out by the *Irish Voice* newspaper found that Irish women were doing the same jobs in 1987 as their predecessors had done 150 years previously, i.e. 54 per cent of them were employed as homehelps or au pairs and 39 per cent earned less than $300 per week.[9]

In Europe, a new destination for Irish emigrants, a similar tale was told. A survey of Irish people in Paris found women concentrated in 'female' occupations — 62 per cent of those surveyed were female; 72 per cent of these were working as teachers, nurses, secretaries or au pairs.[10]

The fact that emigration may not be better than staying in Ireland as far as work was concerned was something that could not be contemplated too much. Many women who contacted Emigrant Advice had almost given up hope in Ireland. Because emigration was seen as a solution to problems, what had sustained them in the period before they came to us was the expectation that things just had to be better somewhere else, anywhere else in fact. They did not expect to hear that things could be worse elsewhere.

Nor did they anticipate the changes that emigration would bring in a personal sense. Young women had no knowledge of the history of female emigration from Ireland nor of the experiences of the thousands of Irish women who had gone before. Thus, each new generation of women had to find out all over again that emigration leads to huge personal changes.

As far as the practicalities of leaving were concerned most women were fairly well-informed and well prepared. They knew, for instance, that finding accommodation in advance, if at all possible, was essential. They knew also that they would have to pay a considerable amount for accommodation; the amount they actually had to pay often came as a shock, as did the deposit they would be expected to pay in advance. Their expectations of employment were often unrealistic; they expected to be able to secure employment quickly and expected it to be employment which would enable them to live a decent life; they were shocked to find that many of the jobs available would not pay enough to enable them to eat, pay rent and buy the other essentials of life. In general, though, these young women were well prepared and checked out in advance what they needed to know, and what they needed to bring with them in the way of identification and references.

However, what few women prepared for or anticipated was how emigration, leaving everything that was familiar — family, friends and a familiar environment — would impact emotionally. For most of these young women the time they emigrated was also the first time they left home to live independent lives. Some acknowledged that they were anxious, some that they would miss their families and friends and others believed that they could cope. But the difficulties they encountered having emigrated were evident from phone calls we received from concerned friends and relatives, seeking advice on their behalf.

One woman rang to say 'my friend is in New York — well, she's living outside New York — she's got work but she's got no one there with her — she's so lonely, how can she get to meet people?' Another woman rang to say her sister had got a Donnelly Visa but 'she's in this hillbilly place — it's not what she expected — she's been there three weeks and she hasn't unpacked yet. She was on the phone last night in tears — is there somewhere she can go for help?'

Many women found that they missed the very things they had emigrated to escape — and that was quite a shock! They missed the routine of Sundays, of always knowing the family would be there and that the same things would be done every Sunday, usually in the same order.

One woman, Miriam, had prepared quite well for emigrating to Germany but when she got to Munich airport, it suddenly hit her: 'I remember thinking, oh no, everyone speaks German here — I hadn't thought about that at all'.

The obvious trauma of arriving in a new country was compounded by the fact that women do not have the traditional networks of support that men have had and still do have — the pubs, the Gaelic Athletic Association(GAA) and the building sites. One of the annual reports of one of the Irish Centres in London states: 'They (Irish women) do not seem to be visible in terms of requests for advice and help from Irish Centres in London'.[11] This is also reflected in the annual reports of other centres which consistently record lower numbers of women than men calling to them. What seems to happen is that they prepare better for the process but that they bear the uncertainty about the results of their decision to emigrate on their own.

Ann, in Germany for two years, tells: 'I didn't go home for Christmas the first year because I knew if I did I wouldn't come back — the second Christmas I went home I cried when I came back'. Ann has now been to university in Germany, having learnt German since her arrival; she now works in a job she would not have been able to get in Ireland. A decision to stay and hard work in the personal sense has resulted in opportunities not available at home.

While immediate reactions to arriving somewhere can be traumatic, at least they can be understood as being in response to tangible changes, i.e. changes in accents, size of city, going from being part of a family or community to being on your own. What can be more difficult to deal with are the more subtle forms of cultural behaviour, those that are not so obvious, such as what is and is not acceptable behaviour, the national sense of humour and the way in which work and social life are organised. It is these subtleties that may take years to understand; not understanding them will make life that much harder and the sense of being an outsider that much stronger. Settling in and adapting to a new environment takes much longer than most emigrants anticipate — years rather than months. The type of personal issues that emigration raises in the long term are those which often force an appraisal of where you came from and where you are going. They can be seen in the degree to which emigrants choose to assimilate into the society of which they are now a part — whether they see themselves as staying for life or returning to Ireland at a later stage — and how these choices affect their ability to function effectively in their country of destination. Some choose to go 'native' and adopt the mores and attitudes of the culture or society they have come to; others seek out all things Irish — Irish bars, dances, masses and clubs — as a more effective way of dealing with being in a new place.

For Irish women such choices are partly imposed by the ease or other-wise of forging a social life for themselves. Ellen discovered when she went to live in Germany: 'It's really easy to make Irish friends — there are so many Irish people here that you don't really have to have German friends; I've tried to make a few (German friends) to see how people live here. But I hate the idea of being in an Irish ghetto'. Being in an 'Irish ghetto' can bring regrets as Bernie found out: 'I made the mistake the first year of just being with Irish people all the time; I wasn't learning the language, I wasn't getting to know the people, the culture, the country; we just went out together all the time, to the cinema — English cinema, of course'.

Being part of the Irish community abroad has pros and cons — for some it offers security but for others the Irish community represents many of the reasons they may have decided to leave, i.e. it imposes the same restrictions and upholds the same values that some women sought to escape. Many of the groups and organisations which Irish emigrants set up embody the same views and attitudes towards women which were dominant in the society the women had left, e.g. the Catholic Church and the Gaelic Athletic Association.

Una has lived for three years in the USA:

> A lot of people come over here and go straight into the all-Irish communities and that's a great sense of security, you've your own kind telling you what to do and what not to do. But those communities are made up of Irish people, some of whom feel they're there because they have to be and there's nothing for them to come back to so they become very embittered. Others are so angry at having had to leave that they want nothing to do with Irish groups over here — they just want to disappear into the American communities here and forget that they are Irish. But generally the Irish tend to stick together over here.

Another feature of Irish life abroad is its emphasis on family life. Social activities, especially in Britain, tend to be family-orientated, thereby excluding many single women. For those who do not fit into the church, GAA or pub-type activities there are precious few alternatives.

Adapting to another country for young, single women, is no easy task; indeed the whole process of emigration, the decision to leave, going and starting a new life, takes its toll in ways that many would not foresee. The fact that they may be leaving Ireland for the rest of their lives was incomprehensible — almost all women expected to come back at a later stage in their lives.

Older women

If this is the view of young women who after all have the rest of their lives ahead of them, what then of the older, single woman forced to emigrate at a stage in her life when the reality of what she is about to do is abundantly clear? Older female emigrants were a small but significant group who availed themselves of the Emigrant Advice service; most were in their mid-fifties upwards and were either widows or carers where the person(s) they were caring for had died, or were housekeepers whose employer had died. Their livelihoods had always been dependent on someone else and when that person died they found they had little or no means and no chance of finding similar work here or any work at all at their age.

Mary's story illustrates how older women fared and shows the parallels between their experience and that of their younger counterparts. Mary, aged 56, had cared for her mother for 25 years. She had never worked outside the home. She had one brother and two sisters who were all married with families of their own and who had had little direct involvement in the care of their mother. When her mother died Mary found that she was not entitled to any social welfare income; she could find no suitable employment and could not afford the upkeep of her home. Reluctant to ask for help from her immediate family, whom she felt would not be in a position to offer much help, she decided to emigrate. Her aim was 'to go to England and find a job as a companion or a housekeeper or something that will keep me going and give me somewhere to live'.

As was the case with the younger generation of women, Mary's belief that things would be better anywhere other than Ireland was as unshakeable as theirs, but her expectations were much more limited. She was not necessarily looking for a well-paid job with prospects but just something that would give her the basics, especially accommodation. Given her total lack of work experience and skills it is hard to imagine that Mary would succeed in her aim.

Unfortunately, one of the frustrations of advising women about emigration was that once they went we rarely heard what happened to them. As previously noted women do not appear as frequently as men in the statistics of Irish advice centres as having sought help; those women who seek such help are in the 18–30 age-group. It is virtually impossible to know what happened to older women like Mary and others, who were leaving after a lifetime spent in Ireland, often in one small part of Ireland, with no skills, no relatives abroad, very little money and an aspiration only to find basic shelter and companionship. It may have worked out or it may not, as in Sarah's case.

Sarah was 50 years of age and single. She had spent a number of years in Birmingham before returning to Ireland some years previously. At the age of 50 she found her situation hopeless — she was living in council housing in an area she did not like, she was unemployed with no skills and found that it was impossible to get work. Living in poverty she was convinced that she would have been better off if she had remained in Birmingham where she also had local authority housing. She had had much better housing in Birmingham than she now had in Dublin, so she started making determined enquiries into the possibilities of returning to the accommodation she had left. After about a year of negotiating with the council, an arrangement was made whereby she could return to Birmingham to be housed by the council; during this year of waiting she had made enquiries about going to London or Liverpool or Manchester, 'anywhere so long as I don't have to stay here — I have to get out of here — I can't stand it — I don't care where I end up'. Sarah went to Birmingham. Six months later, she returned: 'It wasn't like I remembered, it had all changed — it was worse than here', was all she would say. This demonstrates the classic emigrant dilemma: not having decided a long time ago where she was going to make her life, Sarah was caught between her memories of Ireland as being better than England and, on returning to Ireland, finding that it was not quite what she had remembered; then England took on a more favourable memory which soon turned to disenchantment when faced with the reality.

For older women, the reasons for emigrating may be similar to their younger counterparts in that it is often, on the surface, for economic reasons — no job, no money and no future. But the reason why they are in this situation, at their stage of life, has as much to do with the traditional role of carer, either to aged or ill parents or to husband and family, and the limitations this has imposed in terms of being able to be financially and economically independent as it has to do with the economic situation in Ireland at present. We note the lack of a support network for women who take on the role of carer or who choose to devote their attention to their families.

'You put the best part of your years into rearing a family and then you see there is nothing here for them'[12]

The majority of emigrants throughout the 1980s were young people aged between 18 and 25 years. Therefore, they will have left parents behind who will grow old without the company of their children and without the enjoyment of becoming involved in the lives of their grandchildren. Women who have made a full-time career of rearing their children are devastated at the loss they have suffered and find it difficult to come to terms with the prospects of a lonely old age. Ann's story illustrates the pain many Irish women have experienced.

Ann's story

Ann is a married woman in her late fifties who has reared eight children. They have all become emigrants, just as she and her husband did in the late 1950s. She has five children living in London, one in Germany, one in Canada and one in the United States. Ann does not work outside the home and has precious little left to do inside it anymore. Her husband is due to retire in two years' time on a small pension.

Ann already has two grandchildren — one in the United States and one in Canada. She has never seen either child — her daughter and son-in-law in the USA are out-of-status (illegal), and therefore cannot travel home without fear of discovery and/or deportation. Her daughter in Canada is married to an electrician who is in the process of setting up his own business. They have recently taken out a large mortgage so they do not see themselves being able to travel home to Ireland for three or four years. Ann's granddaughter will be almost five by then and Ann will not have seen her at all.

Ann has looked for work outside the home but, with in excess of 290,000 people unemployed in Ireland, it will be difficult, if not impossible, for her to find work. She feels her age and her lack of work experience are against her. Ann and her husband Joe are on a limited income but Ann is trying hard to save some money to travel to the USA and Canada to visit her daughters. If she does not manage to save this money by next year she and Joe will use some of their savings to go and visit their grandchildren. Ann's eldest daughter, who lives in Boston, is pregnant and is due to give birth to Ann's third grandchild in 1993. Ann had always thought that she would be around at the time of her grandchildren's births. She had taken it for granted that she would be there for these events, especially for the births of her daughters' children. She had looked forward enormously to being around, helping her daughters, babysitting for her grandchildren, dropping in to see her daughters or, if they were living outside Dublin, going to spend weekends with them. She had always seen herself, as she had seen her own mother, as being around and available to her children and grandchildren. Her mother had often said that she had enjoyed her grandchildren more than her own children, as she had all the pleasure without any of the responsibility. Ann watched while her friends, some of whom still had their children living in Ireland, enjoyed each one of their successive grandchildren.

Ann had two brothers and two sisters; one brother was in England and the other was in the USA. Both of Ann's sisters were living in Ireland, one in Dublin and one in Portlaoise. Between them Ann and her sisters had eighteen children, only four of whom were still living in Ireland — two in third-level colleges, one was unemployed and one was in a temporary, part-time job. Ann and her sisters had hoped that their children would stay in Ireland, had educated them at great cost and personal sacrifice, hoping that they would thereby be able to stay and find employment in Ireland. Indeed, Ann and Joe had come home from England in the early 1970s because it looked as though things were picking up at last in Ireland and they hoped their children might have a future there.

Ann's life was lonely and empty with all eight children gone. Having survived the busy, hectic years when all her children were so demanding, of both her time and the family's resources, she had looked forward to a more restful time when she would have more contact with all her children but not necessarily have them all living at home with her. When her eldest daughter got married, she looked forward with great anticipation to the arrival of grandchildren. But her daughter and husband could not find work in Ireland and emigrated to America.

Ann's three daughters and two sons in London were in close contact and met regularly. Two of the girls were sharing a flat and the three girls often spent Sundays together. She often phoned them at the flat on Sundays, knowing they would all be there together. She felt so lonely after talking to them, wishing they were at home with her, eating their Sunday dinner with her and Joe. Their own Sundays were so quiet now — only Joe and herself for dinner when there had been 10 of them for more than 20 years! Christmas, when they all came back from London and Germany, was hectic — just like old times with constant callers — young people dropping in, staying late and talking till the owls came home! Ann and Joe dreaded the future — getting old together with old friends but without their children and grandchildren around them. They had friends in Dublin all right but they were heartbroken at the loss and pain in seeing all their children leave the country. Joe was due to retire in two years' time. With his lump sum and the proceeds from the sale of their house they were thinking of going to live in London. At least they would be close to some of the children and maybe, in due course, their grandchildren. Five of their children were living in or around the London area and they would be able to see them on a regular basis. They had lived in London themselves for a few years after they got married so it would not be all that strange. They would miss their friends and they would miss Ireland but Ireland had not been able to offer any of their children a future. So they were thinking of becoming emigrants themselves for the second time in their lives.

Ann's experience is mirrored by the experience of many of the families interviewed for a report on emigration prepared by Galway Action on Poverty.[13] This study described the impact of emigration on three areas of Galway city and county. Many of the families had three, four or more children living abroad. For example, Family A had five children, three of whom were living abroad; Family C five children, four of whom were living abroad; and Family I had seven children, all seven of whom had emigrated at one time or another.

All the families interviewed commented on the sense of loss they experienced, 'almost a sense of bereavement'. They also noted the sense of loss experienced by their communities in which a whole generation was missing—the generation between the young children and the middle-aged people. That generation had simply gone away. This was especially marked during the summer months when many emigrants returned, thereby creating the illusion of community again, for a brief period.

This sense of loss has also been frequently aired on Irish national radio in various chat shows, most recently in September 1992, especially by women, who deeply regretted the exodus which had taken place during the 1980s.

Women escaping domestic violence

Securing rights for Irish women has been a long and difficult battle which still continues. Some legislative change and protection was secured only after recourse to the European Court ensured that women's rights were upheld or after the European Community issued a Directive, e.g. On Equal Pay, with which all Member States had to comply within a specified period of time. Rights which women in other European countries take for granted, such as access to contraception, have not been granted to Irish women. With such limited rights and protection, some women are forced to leave to escape from problems that are simply not given any priority in Ireland. This applies particularly to women involved in domestic violence and is an example of the emigration for social reasons which we spoke of earlier.

The campaign to establish the rights of women experiencing domestic violence in Ireland has been a long drawn-out one. Domestic violence has been estimated to affect one in every six Irish women.[14] Women's Aid, the organisation which provides refuges for women wanting to escape violent relationships, was established in Ireland in 1975. Barring Orders, which introduced a limited form of protection for women in violent relationships, were established in 1976 and women were granted the right to civil legal aid, following a successful appeal to the European Court of Human Rights, in 1980.

However, throughout this period women have continued to emigrate, especially to Britain, maintaining the Irish tradition of exporting social problems with which it chooses not to deal at home. Because of the long history of emigration between Ireland and Britain, emigrating to the UK was frequently considered an option for women experiencing domestic violence. Women considered emigration to Britain for a number of reasons:

1. Most families in Ireland will have relatives in Britain. Since 1981 it is estimated that in excess of 300,000 people have emigrated from Ireland; the majority of these have emigrated to Britain. The 1981 British Census estimated that 850,000 Irish-born people are living in Britain. Therefore, there will be many already existing networks of schoolfriends, relatives, friends and neighbours. The prospect of emigrating alone to another country, usually with a number of small children, does not seem so daunting when one can tap into these networks.
2. Women who are considering emigration will already have a certain amount of information gleaned from friends, neighbours, relatives and schoolfriends who have all lived 'over there'. This information will relate to issues such as housing, social welfare benefits, legal aid, education and health care. This information, which may not always be accurate and may be out of date, may, however, inform women's decisions about emigration.
3. Another factor influencing women seeking to escape domestic violence in Ireland is the relative ease of access to the UK. Passports are not required. Therefore, women can leave the country with their children without alerting their spouses/partners as to their intentions. If they had to apply for a passport they would have to get their spouses'/partners' permission to take their children out of Ireland.
4. The relatively low cost of travel between Ireland and the UK is also a factor. Travel is possible by boat (the cheapest possible option) and by air.
5. Women's Aid, which has been in existence in Ireland since 1975, has contacts with the Women's Aid Network throughout Britain. Therefore, women can be referred to another refuge if they need or decide to go to the UK.

Other factors influencing women's decisions to emigrate because of domestic violence include:

— a perception, frequently confirmed by experience, that legal remedies to domestic violence will simply be ineffective;
— difficulties experienced in actually getting access to legal remedies, e.g. many legal aid centres are closed to non-emergency cases; emergency cases do not always include cases of domestic violence;[15] legal aid in Ireland also involves a means test;

— geographical factors — many women feel that Ireland, and especially Dublin, is simply too small and too close-knit for them to live independently and in safety while their spouse/partner is still living here;
— the absence of divorce in Ireland and the difficulties in establishing and in gaining legal recognition for second relationships;
— housing policies — local authorities who are stretched to provide public housing are frequently unsympathetic to the partners of violent spouses who seek housing in their own right.

These are some of the factors influencing women's decisions to emigrate. The following case history will illustrate some of the issues which encourage women who have experienced domestic violence to consider emigration.

Mary's story

Mary is married and has five children, aged two to eleven years of age. She is 28 years of age. She married when she was 17 years old and six months' pregnant. She was not really sure she wanted to get married but her parents had persuaded her. Unmarried mothers were not as common or accepted as much then as they are today. From the day she got married Mary had been beaten by her husband. In the beginning she thought it was because he had had to get married. Then she thought it was the baby's fault. Her first baby had been very unsettled and never seemed to sleep much. She always seemed to be up with him during the night. Her husband used to get very angry about the baby and the racket he used to make. She thought it was hard on him because he had to go to work every day. She did not get much rest either. But it never got any easier. With each of her pregnancies he had become more violent and more vicious. In fact, he seemed to become more violent when she was pregnant. One of her pregnancies ended because he had given her a particularly bad beating when she was just a few months pregnant. He absolutely refused to use any form of contraception. In all she had had seven pregnancies and dreaded the thought of any more. She had her hands full with the five children she had. As the years went by, the beatings continued, but now she was becoming more and more conscious of the effect they were having on her children. She worried about them and their futures. She did not want them growing up thinking this kind of behaviour was normal ...

After a particularly vicious beating, which had taken place in front of her children, Mary decided that enough was enough. She left her husband and went to the Women's Aid refuge in Dublin. But she was terrified he would find her. Dublin was too small to hide in and anyway she did not want to hide any more. The first few weeks she'd been in the refuge she had hardly gone out at all for fear he would see her or one of his family would see her and tell him. And then maybe he would come looking for her.

Mary had a sister, Bernie, in London. Bernie was always at her to come on over. Bernie said she would easily get housing from the Local Authority because she had young children so they would have to house her. The social worker in Dublin did not think it would be quite as easy as that — that she might have to spend some time in a Bed and Breakfast hostel first and that it might not be of the highest standard — they might all have to share a room. But she did not mind; Mary thought she would be quite happy to have all her children with her, safe and on their own; she would look after them now. She had left school at 14 years of age. She had spent two years then training to be a hairdresser but she had to give it up when she discovered she was pregnant. She hoped to get back to hairdressing some day. Maybe if she could get to London and get some decent housing, get the children into schools and maybe a nursery school for the little one, then maybe she could get some kind of a part-time job; maybe mornings only until the kids were older. Mary talked to the social worker a couple of times about going to England and the social worker checked out some of the information for her. She said it would be harder than Mary thought, away from her family and friends. But Mary thought she would be away from him and his family — that would make things easier for a start. She would have her children safe with her and maybe she could start a life for herself now — she was still only 28! It did not matter about the social welfare, sure she had managed for years on very little money from him, she was used to getting by on very little. She would get some peace for herself at last.

She had tried going to the law about the beatings. She had had loads of Barring Orders which were supposed to protect her. But he always ended up getting round her or the police. He had broken all the Barring Orders she had got. They were never much help to her anyway. Putting the Irish Sea between them would be more use to her than all those Barring Orders.

She would miss her family all right but Bernie was over there and she said there were lots of Irish people round where she lived. If she could only just get over to London — it was going to be expensive but if she saved her welfare money and her children's allowance (monthly child benefit payment) then she could just manage it. The only problem was she could not tell the children in case they told anybody and it got back to him; she did not want him coming after her. So, some day soon when she got her welfare money she and the kids would take off and get away from all the trouble and aggravation she had had in Dublin. London just had to be a better place for her and the kids.

Conclusions

Working in Emigrant Advice involved learning about the processes of emigration and especially how women were affected by them. We learnt that much of the history of women's emigration has not been told. The case histories which we discuss here represent experiences which we frequently confronted in our work. Women's experience of emigration has for too long been presumed to be the same as that of men. It is only recently that women themselves have started documenting this history and experience. We have raised a number of issues arising directly from our experience of working in Emigrant Advice:

— the experience of older women emigrating in search of employment;
— women emigrating to escape domestic violence;
— women who are left behind.

These issues have been neglected in the history of emigration to date. It is time for women now to reclaim this history and continue the process of documenting their story.

Notes

1. This chapter draws on material collected during the preparation of our book, on our own unpublished material, and on interviews and reflections. See also our book, Kate Kelly and Tríona Nic Giolla Choille, *Emigration Matters for Women*, Attic Press, Dublin, 1990.
2. *Annual Report, 1956*, Catholic Social Welfare Bureau, Dublin, 1956.
3. *The Irish Voice*, October 1987.
4. Interview with Mr. Brian Lenihan TD, then the Irish Republic's Minister for Foreign Affairs, *Newsweek*, October 1987.
5. *Monthly Report, October, 1992*, Central Statistics Office, Dublin, 1992.
6. *Survey on Low Pay*, Irish Congress of Trade Unions, Dublin, June 1992.
7. *Irish Women in London*, Strategic Policy Unit, London, 1988.
8. *The Guardian*, 2 September, 1987.
9. *The Irish Voice*, November 1987.
10. Piaris Mac Enrie, 'The New Europeans: the Irish in Paris today', in Dermot Keogh and Joe Mulholland, eds, *Emigration, employment and enterprise*, Hibernian University Press, Cork, 1989.
11. Annual Report, 1987, The Irish Centre, London, 1987.
12. Niall Farrell, *Emigration: the Galway experience*, Galway Action on Poverty, Galway, 1991.
13. Niall Farrell, *Emigration: the Galway experience*.
14. 'Violence in the Family, *Sunday Tribune*, 11 October, 1992, p. 11.
15. *Flac News* (Journal of the Free Legal Advice Centre), Vol. 2, No. 4, June–September 1992, p. 1 and p. 4.

9 Breaking the silence from a distance: Irish women speak on sexual abuse

Íde B. O'Carroll

This chapter focuses on what it is like for some young girls to grow up in homes in Ireland where they have been subjected to sexual abuse and how, for Mary, Hanna and Nora, this history of abuse acted as a conscious/unconscious push factor in their decision to emigrate to America—to be 'out of relationship' with their families and country in order to become connected to the self again.[1] My thoughts in this regard are deeply influenced by the work of Professor Carol Gilligan, and the application of her thinking to oral histories of Irish women immigrants is a new dimension to our experience: what I call psychohistory.[2] Also, I will suggest that listening to the history of Irish women immigrants in America not only raises numerous questions about the motivation for migration, but also raises questions regarding the implications of this voicing for young girls and women in an Irish context.

Some of the questions I seek to address in this brief journey are: Why did these women have to leave Ireland to deal with these issues? What does the USA offer that allowed these women to break their silence? What are the consequences of life stories like these for women—sisters, mothers, friends and other survivors? Will these voices from a distance be a catalyst for the women in Ireland to speak, or for the society to listen? Finally, politically what are the implications of a collective listening by an Irish society to a history of sexual abuse?[3]

'Whose voice?'

During the Christmas holiday 1990, I travelled on Aer Lingus, the Irish national airline, from Boston to Ireland. The inflight magazine, *Cara*, had an article on Irish emigration which immediately caught my eye, as my work in America centred on recording the oral histories of Irish women immigrants. The book under review, *Migrations: the Irish at Home and Abroad*,[4] edited by philosopher and media personality Richard Kearney, was a collection of essays by 'important/famous' Irish people—Seamus Heany *et al.* My anger was deep and immediate at this series of articles by men who, as academics and businessmen, found themselves in a position of authority on this experience. My later reading of the actual book confirmed my early suspicions.

'In what body?'

Yet my own experience as an immigrant in America assured me that for the past two centuries the voices of Irish women emigrants to the USA had not been listened to, recorded or published in any comprehensive form. Most of the histories written contained accounts of the male experience only or more general accounts which did not address the lives of Irish women in America. The pattern of female chain migration had gone almost unnoticed but for the work of Hasia Diner and her classic book on the nineteenth-century experience, *Erin's Daughters in America.*[5] My own book, *Models for Movers: Irish Women's Emigration to America*, sought to address the imbalance by presenting the voices of Irish women from the three waves of emigration in the twentieth century: 1920s, 1950s and 1980s. However, the indirect censorship which seemed to me implicit in the book, *Migrations*, confirmed my belief in the need to listen to emigrants' experience of emigration. Further, it made me ask the question—If it is this difficult for emigrants themselves to have their voices heard, and particularly difficult for women emigrants, how much harder must it be for Irish immigrants who carry in their psychic baggage secrets of social taboos? If history had failed to listen and record our experience, how had it silenced other aspects of our story which might be somewhat revealing of a hidden/exported Ireland? This question made me reconsider a theme which emerged during my work with *Models*—Irish women and their childhood/adolescent experience of sexual abuse.[6]

'Telling what story about relationships (from whose perspective)?'

Hanna, Mary and Nora range in age from 28 to 38. They come from three very different counties in Ireland. All of them emigrated in the 1980s during the third wave of emigration from Ireland to America this century.

Growing up in Ireland all three were given very clear messages on the role of women in Irish society.

> Mary: As an adolescent I was extremely unhappy at home and I know my mother went through periods of depression. I came to a realisation that I absolutely hated my father, and I was very angry with my mother for allowing him to do what he was doing — to come home drunk every night at 9.30pm, and then she would make the dinner for him. Or I would have to make the dinner and look after him.

Hanna: When I think of growing up in Ireland I think of my mother. She was tied into the male thing. When my father died and there was a will he gave everything he owned to three sons. She was left out of the picture. She got a life interest in the house she had bought with money left her by relatives in New York.

There was a very explicit message about your place as young girls growing up. We had dinner ready for the lads and we had to feed them. When they were finished we could have our food. My sister Eileen picked potatoes at this farm with my brothers. The boys got ten shillings and she got half a crown, even though she was the best worker.

The sexual abuse experienced by these three women happened within their own homes, with people whom they had considered worthy of trust and love. For some the sexual abuse is interpreted as a junction on a continuum of cultural disrespect and abuse enacted towards women.[7]

Mary: My father would be completely outrageous and sexually inappropriate in my presence. I remember he was very drunk and talking about rape and how there is no such thing as rape, because he had heard a joke in the pub and it was true. I would be disgusted and angry, but not able to say 'You're wrong, that's wrong and you should stop that'. I was in bed one Saturday morning when he molested me.

Hanna: I think it was all abusive. My father derided my mother and degraded her. The only way my mother could think of for birth control was by not sleeping with my father. The times when she was likely to conceive she would stay in another house. That was the scene of my sexual abuse by my father.

Nora: My eldest brother evolved this game whereby he was the bank manager, I was the secretary and my other brothers were the bartender and vet. We would play this game where they sexually molested me when my parents weren't in the house. I was seven when it started. They were always hounding me. I never felt safe in the house. I was totally innocent about sex stuff. If I brought home any friend they would take a go off her too. So, it was never a place I could go to with pride or any sense of warmth and security.

In my analysis I used Professor Carol Gilligan's idea of the *logic of the psyche as a logic of relationships* and how these women might have been in a process of going 'out of relationship' to protect some semblance of themselves in situations which appeared threatening to them.

Teenage girls and adult women often seemed to get caught on the horns of a dilemma: was it better to respond to others and abandon themselves or to respond to themselves and abandon others? The hopelessness of this question marked an impasse in female development, a point where the desire for relationship was sacrificed for the sake of goodness, or for survival.[8]

Could it be possible, that some Irish women deciding to emigrate in the 1980s and at other times we do not know about, were reaching the same conclusion that the young autobiographical Stephen Dedalus in James Joyce's *Portrait of the Artist as a Young Man* did in leaving Ireland to become adult — 'Silence, exile, cunning?'[9] Did their experience of sexual abuse act as a 'push' factor in their decision to emigrate — was the decision to place themselves 3,000 miles away from family and country a logical, protective measure on the part of Mary, Hanna and Nora to protect their sense of self?

Professor Carol Gilligan also suggests several 'truths' to substantiate this connection between the logic of the psyche and a logic of relationships. *'What is unvoiced (unheard or unspoken), because it is out of relationship, tends to get out of perspective and to dominate psychic life.'*[10]

> Mary: I've always had a tendency to depression, very low self-esteem. disappearing into a black hole. There was no speaking out at school. Nobody ever spoke out in my family.

> Hanna: I think it has always been on my mind. When I think of my time in school, I used always to say that I was dirty. Now how did I think I was dirty? It wasn't that I was poorly dressed, it was deeper than that. I felt dirty and I always felt bad.

> Nora: The first person I told about it was a counsellor at school. I remember she got the Department of Education psychologist to come down. Her main concern again was had there been penetration. I was getting a very clear message all along, that unless there was penetration, it really wasn't all that bad. I didn't talk about it again.

Moving from Ireland—the logic of the psyche?

The decision by these women to move from Ireland to the USA may have initially cloaked a desire to remove themselves physically from a world where they each felt silenced in different ways.

> Mary: I remember as a thirteen-year-old thinking if I can just wait it out 'till I grow up and get the hell out of Ireland. I came to America because it was easier. Even being illegal here was better than being in England, which was too close.

> Hanna: It becomes more salient when I'm at home than here, but I do think it is linked to my leaving Ireland because when I look at my family, not one of us nine girls is in Ireland. Out of six sons, four are in Ireland.

> Nora: I saw America as a place of opportunity. I wanted to have some sense of freedom. I didn't know what that meant, but I certainly wanted a physical distance with what I had been involved with. In Ireland if I worked on this stuff I might still have to see my brothers. This was not a conscious decision, it had more to do with my future, with having fun.

In the USA, both Mary and Nora made decisions to enter psychological health programs. Hanna had conducted some work of this nature in Ireland. The recurring need to work on sexual abuse reinforces another Gilligan 'truth' on the logic of the psyche—*'What is known and then not known, disassociated or repressed, tends to return and return and return.'*[11]

Mary: Throughout my life I've always had symptoms of sexual abuse which I now recognise. One was a phobia about bathrooms. Now, I feel secure because I am getting rid of it. The root of my unhappiness was sexual abuse. For the first time I am leaving my past behind. I am dredging it off. It's breaking my heart, and then moving on. There is absolutely no way I would have done this in Ireland.

Hanna: When I tried getting married in Ireland all these feelings of being out of control came up. There was nothing about Paddy that was scary, he has never tried to take control of my life. I decided not to marry him then. At a workshop it all came back when this guy was talking about being sexually abused. Also, I was teaching seven-year-olds and this beautiful little one was in the class. She used to come into me every morning and I would put out my arms and she would just cry. That was another signpost. I made the staff (devise) an intervention program. All this made it known to me.

Nora: I think it's the single most recurring theme — a feeling of being victimised, which is borne directly out of that experience and it has coloured the way that I behave in a lot of situations.

American culture

I then had to ask the question — What was it about the USA that drew these women here? There had to be some attraction to make a young woman consider leaving her native home for an unknown territory. Information from reliable sources had to reassure Mary and other Irish women before her that a life in Boston, New York or Chicago would be in some way more liberating than if they remained at home. Such information was constantly coming to Ireland in letters from Irish women who had emigrated at earlier periods in the nineteenth and twentieth centuries.

I believe American culture supports the notion of the individual over and above the group. The root of this philosophy may be linked to the fact that historically America was/is more puritan/Protestant with an emphasis on values which seek to promote individualism, values which are most closely linked to capitalism, and reaping the harvest of personal investment. Ireland, being predominantly Catholic, struggles/ed with an ethos which elevates the collective good, where looking after the self and personal gain can be viewed with a sense of shame — 'It is as easy for a rich man to go to Heaven as it is for a camel to pass through the eye of a needle.'

Mary: The hardest thing is to be yourself, or learning to be yourself. Allowing yourself to be was very difficult coming from my culture where the group is promoted above all. The individual is not important. It was always a consensus, where to go, what to do, what to think. Which always took the pressure off me, but created this tremendous pressure to conform. Effectively I was silenced by the group.

Nora: In America I was doing a lot of things on my own. It was great, throwing off the old ways and embracing the new. I did enormous work in a counselling group. I could see also that they were believing me here, that it was OK to say it.

In that group I chronicled for the first time in my life the experience of abuse, I actually was writing it.

Historically, in post-colonial, colonised Ireland there is a terrible lack of models of individuals who successfully act for themselves or voice their realities in contradiction to the restrictive Catholic image of Ireland. Indeed, our best creative people from James Joyce to Samuel Beckett, Kate O'Brien and Sinéad O'Connor have had to exile themselves to be heard:

April 26. Mother is putting my new secondhand clothes in order. She prays now, she says, that I may learn in my own life and away from home and friends what the heart is and what it feels. Amen. So be it. Welcome, O life! I go to encounter for the millionth time the reality of experience and to forge in the smithy of my soul the uncreated conscience of my race.[12]

Perhaps then, the words of a woman, Emma Lazarus, on the statue of a woman, Liberty, drew not only Hanna, Mary and Nora, but other Irish emigrants in the hope of opportunity, expression, liberation.

Mary: There's lots of help here. Asking for it was very difficult. It's for me like some terrible admission of deep failure. It's absolutely worth it. In America, I'm learning to be a little more free about sharing what I feel, on the spot, when it is happening, which is directly going against Irish culture.

Hanna: It was easier to think about marriage over here. I think it was choice and control. When we went to get married it was so easy.

Nora: I never used the word incest before I came to America. I've never even attached any label to it because anything that happened to me when I was little was normal. I had placed all this distance between me and Ireland to see clearly the experience of my abuse. It's the best thing I've ever done in terms of turning my life around.

What are the implications of this listening and recording the words of Irish women migrants and their sexual abuse experience as adolescents or young children in Ireland? Will the telling of their stories, albeit from a distance, allow others to speak within an Irish context? And most importantly will it change the way we think about and listen to young and adolescent girls? It is difficult to answer any of these questions as yet. Certainly Ireland is experiencing enormous change with the election of the first woman President of the country, elected by her own admission by *mná na hÉireann*/the women of Ireland. Mary Robinson, a model of individualism, left her party, the Labour Party (in a disagreement over the Northern Ireland Protestant position regarding the New Ireland Forum), and as an Independent won a Presidential election never before fought so vigorously outside party politics. With a woman at its helm, a strong, articulate, clear-thinking individual, elected by women, a shift may come in this apparent continuum of abuse towards women in Ireland.

I lay great emphasis on the new-found power of the collective women's vote. Perhaps the Ireland now emerging is a different one from the one these three women left in the 1980s. When writing of the campaign of this feminist, socialist woman from the West of Ireland Fergus Finlay states:

> Everywhere she went she was listening intently, not trying to impose an agenda, reminding them only when necessary of the limitations on the power of the office (of the President). Because she decided she was going to listen, all these responses made a powerful impact on Mary (Robinson).[13]

Can I hope that as part of this new and opening Robinson Ireland, the voices of those abroad can be heard from a distance, and that in families and within the society as a whole a climate of opinion is fostered where children and adolescents are listened to and respected?[14] Also, can I hope that the women, sisters, mothers, aunts, grandmothers, cousins some of whom must/may have witnessed abuse of this kind may be encouraged to speak out in support? As a consequence then maybe fewer Noras will have to go abroad to conduct work on sexual abuse, but will be encouraged to speak aloud in Ireland. Indeed, many of the women I spoke to expressed a strong desire to return to Ireland, but only if it changed in terms of its atti- tude to women. Mary says 'At some stage I would like to go and try Ireland. There's things about it I miss. I'm more Irish than anything else.' Perhaps she and others like her may not be 'out of relationship' forever.

The experience of emigration is akin to grieving/exile, but is not a disem- powering process. It is rather an empowering process when viewed through the eyes of the women presented here. For the survivors of sexual abuse, the empowerment comes from giving voice to the silenced slices of their upbringing in Ireland, and by doing so laying claim to their entire selves, growing/building/developing on that. For many the process may be through therapy, a phenomenon historically more freely available in the USA than in Ireland, where there is still a stigma attached to it. A tolerance for and encouragement of voicing is important. Therefore, I consider that there is an onus on me to record all aspects of Irish women's experience, especially themes apparently censored or silenced.

In writing this chapter, I evoke the spirits of all the Irish women through- out the centuries who may have moved to the USA seeking a measure of independence and control over their lives/selves. Historically, some of these must also have been survivors of sexual abuse and carried this extra burden with them to the New World. Nevertheless, the women, presented here, succeeded in creating/making/evolving lives for themselves which are markers/beacons to all women who choose to move in their lives. The message we can gain from listening is *misneach*/courage. The lesson I have learned is to continue to listen attentively, record and present the words of Irish women.

Sometimes a woman needs a room of her own and 500 dollars a month, not necessarily to write fiction, but to reassemble the lifeimages/lifewords of her own herstory. Sometimes this room can only be found 3,000 miles away from what Adrienne Rich calls 'that most dangerous place, the family home'.[15]

Notes

1. Mary, Hanna and Nora are just some of the voices of sexual abuse survivors which emerged during the course of my listening to women's histories for the project 'Models for Movers'. Íde O'Carroll, *Models for Movers: Irish Women's Emigration to America*, Attic Press, Dublin, 1990. I must stress at the outset that this presentation is merely one dimension to these women's lives and does not represent the total sum of their experience in Ireland or the USA.

    Sexual abuse of children covers a wide range of sexual behaviour 'from fondling and exhibitionism to forcible rape. Some of the ambiguity in terms can be attributed to the differences in legal definitions ... and the multitude of variations in act, intent and harm'. *Child Sexual Abuse: a Special Report from the National Center on Child Abuse and Neglect*, US Department of Health, Education and Welfare, Washington DC, 1978, p. 21. USA figures vary, though it is conservatively estimated that one out of four girls and one out of seven boys are sexually abused. In Ireland, the *Report of the Child Sexual Abuse Working Party*, Irish Council for Civil Liberties, 1988, considered child sexual abuse 'a range of sexual activities initiated by older persons involving children'. This report confirms that increased awareness of the problem in Ireland has led to greater numbers of reported incidents — 'In 1986 the number confirmed by Health Boards was 274, more than eight times the number confirmed in 1984', ICCL, p. 12. According to Ruth Torode, Trinity College, a member of the Working Party, the Department of Health figures for 1989 give 568 confirmed child sexual abuse cases out of 1,242 reported cases.

2. In 'Outlines of a Relational Psychology', distributed during a course on The Psychology of Adolescence (H-235), Fall Semester, 1990, Professor Carol Gilligan, Harvard University, offers four questions which act as guiders when listening for voice:

    1. Whose voice (who is speaking)?
    2. In what body?
    3. Telling what story about relationships (from whose perspective)?
    4. In what society and culture?

    I will use these questions as markers in my discussion of women's words and in general comments on Irish women and migration to America. Also, see Peter Loewenberg, *Decoding the Past: The Psychohistorical Approach*, University of California Press, Berkeley, 1985, for a discussion on psychohistory.

3. In my discussion of these questions I am influenced by several readings from the plethora of books available on sexual abuse in America. To list but a few — Ellen Bass and Louise Thornton, *I Never Told Anyone: Writings by Women Survivors of Child Sexual Abuse*, Harper and Row, New York, 1983; Ellen Bass and Laura Davis, *The Courage to Heal*, Harper and Row, New York, 1989. Also, Alice Miller's works translated from the German, *The Drama of the Gifted Child*, Basic Books, New York, 1981; *For Your Own Good*, Farrar, Strauss, Giroux, New York, 1983; *Thou Shalt Not Be Aware*, Farrar, Strauss, Giroux, New York, 1984. Finally, the more recent and important revision of Virginia Woolf's life by Louise De Salvo, *Virginia Woolf: The Impact of Childhood Sexual Abuse on Her Life and Work*, New York, 1989.

4. Richard Kearney, ed., *Migrations: the Irish at Home and Abroad*. Wolfhound Press, Dublin, 1990. The book is a collection of papers delivered at a special seminar on emigration sponsored by the Ireland Fund.

5. Hasia Diner, *Erin's Daughters in America: Irish Immigrant Women in the Nineteenth Century*, Johns Hopkins University Press, Baltimore, Maryland, 1983.
6. Other themes also emerged during the course of these discussions. The theme of Irish lesbians and motivation for migration are explored in my paper 'Coming Out to America!: Gay and Lesbian identity amongst Irish immigrants in the USA and the events of the St Patrick's Day Parade, New York City, March 17, 1991', delivered at the American Conference for Irish Studies 1992 annual conference, University College, Galway, July 1992.
7. Judith Lewis Herman and Lisa Hirschman in *Father Daughter Incest*, Harvard University Press, Cambridge, Mass., 1981, argue that the primary motivation in incest is an enacting of 'power and dominance' and male privilege rather than sexual pleasure. More recent work by Charlene Clarke Hine on the motivation for black women's internal migration from the South to the North in post-Civil War America is remarkably similar to my suggestions in this chapter. 'I believe that many Black women quit the South out of a desire to achieve personal autonomy and to escape both from sexual exploitation from inside and outside of their families and from the rape and threat of rape by white as well as by Black males', *Signs*, 14, Summer 1989. I am indebted to Susan Reverby, Director of Women's Studies at Wellesley College, for bringing this article to my attention.
8. Carol Gilligan, 'Teaching Shakespeare's sister: notes from the underground of female adolescence,' p. 6. This paper is a synthesis of the preface and prologue to C. Gilligan, N. Lyons and T. Hanmer, eds, *Making Connections: the Relational Worlds of Adolescent Girls at the Emma Willard School*, Emma Willard Press, Troy, New York, 1989.
9. James Joyce, *Portrait of the Artist as a Young Man*, Penguin, Harmondsworth, 1960, p. 247.
10. Gilligan, 'Outlines of a Relational Psychology'.
11. Gilligan, 'Outlines of a Relational Psychology', Section B. 4.
12. Joyce, *Portrait*, p. 253. All of these writers were censored and banned in Ireland at different times. Ireland has more censorship statutes on its books than any other country in the world other than Turkey and South Africa.
13. Fergus Finlay, *Mary Robinson: a President with a Purpose*, O'Brien Press, Dublin, 1990, p. 35.
14. Recent work by Professor Annie Rogers, Harvard University, on girls and courage is important here — 'If the survival of girls' courage depends upon girls' relationships with women, how can girls heal women so that women may in turn heal girls and prevent the loss of courage in the next generation? When girls speak about feeling abandoned and betrayed by women when they reach adolescence, it is perhaps because they are often abandoned.' 'The development of courage in women and girls', Harvard University Graduate School of Education, 1990, p. 38.
15. Adrienne Rich, *Your Native Land, Your Life: Poems*, Norton, New York, 1986.

Dedication

This chapter is dedicated to my advisor, Professor Annie G. Rogers, Director, The Project on the Psychology on Women and the Development of Girls at the Harvard Graduate School of Education.

10 'I'm myself and nobody else':[1] gender and ethnicity among young middle-class Irish women in London

Mary Kells

My focus

Irish migration to London alone is estimated to be 40,000 per annum.[2] Women constitute 52.9 per cent of all Irish emigration[3] and have outnumbered male Irish emigrants since 1871. There are thus many Irish women in London, yet they are largely invisible in academic studies.[4] Additionally, there are increasingly large numbers of middle-class migrants. In 1986, only 64 per cent of graduates found employment in Ireland,[5] so the need for other graduate employment options is clear.

This chapter focuses on young, middle-class[6] Irish women migrants in London. I have chosen to concentrate on four first-generation women. They are from the North and South, are Protestant or Catholic and in their twenties to thirties. I wish to ask what it means to be an Irish woman in Britain today. For each woman, I therefore consider what 'being Irish' and 'being a woman' means to them.

Methodology

I investigate this from an anthropological perspective. My data have been gathered through participant observation, which, in an urban setting, entails informal meetings with my informants, socialising with and chatting to them over 1–2 years, and latterly, obtaining tape-recorded interviews.[7] It is a qualitative study, concerned with depth rather than numerical breadth.

Plummer notes the continuum between no involvement on the part of the researcher, through being stranger and then an acquaintance, to a friendship role. My involvement with my informants varied, as did their attitude to me, a Northern Irish Protestant. This obviously affects my findings. While researcher-subject interaction can be a source of bias, Plummer suggests that 'to purge research of (such) "sources of bias" is to purge research of human life'. It presupposes a 'real truth' behind the scenes, yet, he says, 'it is precisely through these "sources of bias" that a "truth" comes to be assembled'.[8] It is therefore appropriate to explain the human interaction through which information is derived and I shall do this below.

My larger study involves around 50 informants, men and women. But here I present data in the form of sociological portraits of four women. These portraits can be seen as partial life stories.[9] My choice of women is intended to represent

i.   the variety of religious and geographical groupings my 50 informants come from; and
ii. the considerable individual variety they demonstrated, even within each group.

The women were also selected because they offered in-depth data; this was partly because they were or became, to varying degrees, friends[10] whom I saw frequently.

Theory

The interrelation of ethnicity and gender is complex. Rather than saying ethnicity is mediated by gender, or indeed vice versa, I suggest that each interweaves, neither structurally prior to the other. Of course, in particular situations, one, ethnicity or gender, may be experienced as predominant and, with particular individuals, one may tend to be a more conscious focus than the other, but the two remain closely linked. Other discourses, such as class, also form a part of the tapestry, and to attempt a holistic picture of how my informants see themselves, an endless number of further threads must be included. However, here I am focusing specifically on ethnicity and gender.

Gender identity

What is gender identity? Kessler and McKenna define it as 'an individual's own feeling of whether she or he is a woman or a man, or a girl or a boy', as 'in essence ... self-attribution of gender'.[11] In the West, gender identity is considered crucial, or as Brittan puts it, 'central to a person's biography' (p. 20). Van Vucht Tijssen also suggests that 'the presentation of self to a certain extent is always the presentation of gender'.[12] This vision of the self or subject as centrally constituted by gender is, as Foucault would perceive it, a discourse; that is, it is a historically located set of ideas rather than an ontological truth. The inevitability of the biological differences between male and female is separate from the socio-cultural significations attached to these differences, but the effect of the gender discourse is that these are seen as naturally fused. Womanhood is presented as having a particular essence, with specific characteristics, such as caring, softness, gentleness, emotion, intuition. By contrast, Moore suggests that 'woman' is inappropriate as an analytic category, as 'women' in fact vary so much that the meaning of the term has no cross-cultural homogeneity.[13] If then, gender and womanhood are not fixed and inevitable essences, how are we to understand them? Brittan points out two ways of looking at gender acquisition: proponents of the socialisation thesis see gender identities as consisting of biology + roles, into which one is socialised from childhood; those holding an alternative view, the 'reality construction model' (p. 36), posit gender as something that is 'always subject to redefinition and renegotiation' (p. 37), as something to be accomplished afresh in every social situation. The latter approach recalls Goffman, who presents the individual as a self-dramatist, choosing which aspects of herself to reveal on the stage of her public persona, tuning performances to audiences.[14] This is a particularly helpful approach for my purposes, but socialisation into roles also contains value: it is simply that these roles are not rigid, but rather that this information and learning can be manipulated.

Ethnic identity
This manipulation of identity also applies to ethnic identity. Barth's concept of ethnic category is helpful in stressing the variable content of ethnicity.[15] He suggests that ethnic groups are 'organisational vessels' whose content is subjective and variable. Thus, the content of 'being Irish' is not a unitary matter, but one particular to gender, age, generation, religion, political aspirations and so on. R. Cohen suggests, however, that ethnic boundaries are not necessarily 'as stable and continuing' as Barth suggests, but that they are 'multiple and include overlapping sets of ascriptive loyalties that make for multiple identities'.[16] Ethnicity can thus in itself generate a multiplicity of self-expression. This can be seen clearly in my informants, who share gender, generation and class and still exhibit considerable differences in their perceptions of their ethnic identity.

Ethnicity at its most basic connotes shared cultural heritage. However, opinion on this may vary. There is an interrelation between individual, subjective opinion on whether one is Irish or not, and collective opinion on what constitutes Irishness. Each individual has an opinion of what they think Irishness is and where they stand in relation to this; they also have an opinion on what they imagine everyone else thinks on the matter. For my 50 informants, these two perspectives could differ. There is thus an individual-collective dynamic, which could otherwise be stated as a subjective-objective one (although it could be argued that all opinion is subjective).[17] In addition to this, R. Cohen suggests that ethnicity 'is first and foremost situational' (p. 388). Thus, the individual-collective dynamic is complicated by situational variability. In other words, individuals do not tend to have a fixed and immutable position, but vary their outlook (to varying degrees) according to where they find themselves and, I would add, to what goals they wish to pursue in this position. This certainly holds true for my informants.

Ethnic identity is partly a choice — for white, English-speaking, middle-class migrants in England, it is an identity which can be de-emphasised; it is one whose meaning, like that of gender, can be manipulated to suit different situations and needs.

Discourse

Ethnicity and gender can thus be seen as discourses, ways of seeing 'reality', which are presented as natural and inevitable. What I am doing here is investigating the meaning of the discourses of ethnicity and gender as presented to me by my informants.[18]

While I am looking at discourses, I am also, paradoxically, employing discourses to understand: those of feminism and post-modernism. Let me say a brief word about each. If I define feminism, firstly, as a movement which seeks to question the traditional role and image of women, to highlight female experience and to eliminate sexism, what I am seeking to do in this chapter follows these general aims: I am seeking to listen to women's voices, to enable them to represent for themselves their feelings about and experiences of their gender and ethnicity. Secondly, post-modernism in anthropology, a movement which has connections with feminism,[19] seeks to emphasise difference, to question grand narratives and totalising theory. Lieteke van Vucht Tijssen suggests that it is more than 'a perspective on difference: it is the celebration of playful plurality'.[20] Diversity, in short, is emphasised and enjoyed. In this chapter, rather than presenting a grand theory on women and ethnicity, I reveal four individual, diverse women and let them talk for themselves. So, while my approach is located within rather abstract discourses, I am also investigating concrete individuals. There is a tension between the two — a creative one, I hope.

Being Irish

I shall introduce the four women here, through four sections which look at questions around 'Being Irish'. The first section covers their ethnic (self-) identification, the options in Northern Ireland being Irish, Northern Irish or British and in the Republic, Irish or Anglo-Irish. This section also looks at opinions of things seen as Irish or non-Irish, and what is deemed relevant behaviour relating to such matters.

The second section looks specifically at integration. Brown suggests that 'the concept of integration, implying the merging of parts into a single whole, is rarely found on immigrants' lips'.[21] What do these women say and do regarding integration?

Thirdly, I cover politics. In my fieldwork, I found second-generation informants who considered political 'purity' the most essential aspect of 'true' Irishness. Although this was rejected by first-generation informants, political viewpoint remains significant: the political history of Britain and Ireland produces strong views, especially when that history continues in conflict in Northern Ireland; additionally, in Northern Ireland itself, one is socialised into well-defined political opinions, usually related to a religious camp.

Religion is the fourth section. The majority of my 50 informants felt that the Irish were more religious than the English.

Elizabeth[22]

Elizabeth and ethnicity: being Irish/Northern Irish/British
Elizabeth is a Northern Irish Protestant in her late twenties.[23] She holds a professional post in the English civil service and is unmarried. We met through a mutual friend and saw each other over a period of a year for fieldwork purposes; we continue to meet as friends. I got the impression she enjoyed her 'informant' role, and she often encouraged me to ask her questions.

Elizabeth described her ethnicity in situational terms, saying sometimes she described herself as Northern Irish, sometimes as Irish, sometimes as British. I enquired under what circumstances each would be chosen. Northern Irish was prioritised, but she said she would describe herself as Irish 'if I'm not being very technically astute or very precise', or on St Patrick's Day. She did not mind when others referred to her as Irish; she said: 'I'm not a stickler for detail, but if they ask me where I'm from, I would say Northern Ireland, but I don't mind.' She described Irish people as 'passionate', 'intense', with a sense of fun, and saw herself as having these characteristics; English people she saw as 'impassive'. Here she identifies with Irish when it is opposed to English.

On other occasions she described the Irish as 'them'. When filling in official forms, she would describe herself as British, 'because constitutionally, we are part of Britain', and when abroad, the same, as 'it seems a bit parochial to say Northern Ireland if you're away in Spain or somewhere'; however, in France she would say Irish, due to the 'affiliation' between those two countries. She told me she called herself Northern Irish in England because she wanted to dissociate herself from IRA terrorism. There was thus a closer link in her mind between self-definition as Irish and support for terrorism than between living in Northern Ireland and supporting terrorism. She pointed out that discussing such things in England differed from discussing them in Ireland, and that she would never consider herself Irish in Northern Ireland.

Elizabeth has thus dealt with the clichéd difficulty of the Northern Irish Protestant who sees herself as British in Northern Ireland, but is referred to as Irish in Britain, by calling herself different things in different circumstances. Her choice of ethnic designation relates to whatever is deemed by her as most suitable for her needs in the situation, whether it is the most favourable thing to be, the most accurate, the least damaging, or the least parochial. Her evaluation of each situation renders different goals appropriate and different strategies of self-designation suited to these.[24]

She also distinguished between objective and subjective sides of ethnicity. British was something she was, a *fact*, whereas, Northern Irish was something she *felt*. Glazer and Moynihan point out that ethnicity offers both an interest-oriented and an affective (or emotional) tie.[25] The situational aspect of Elizabeth's self-identification, I suggest, is related to interest. Underneath this, the affective, emotional identification is for her the Northern Irish one, and it is this she talked about most.

Having established the emotional priority of the Northern Irish identity, I asked her what this meant to her. She answered,

> it's coming from a small community where you know a lot of the same places or maybe the same people. It means, inevitably it means this religious divide which, whether you're one or the other. It also means having value in your life, family and ... community, I think. I come from a farming community ... so I find rural communities much more identifiable to my ... *raison d'être*.

I asked questions to try and get more details from Elizabeth on the extent of her Northern Irishness, for example, on Irish traditions. She told me she had won a trophy for Irish dancing as a child; this was surprising to me, as I expected that she would feel alienated from this as a Catholic concern; she liked Irish, 'folky' music, though was not knowledgeable about it; she loved Irish literature, particularly Joyce and Yeats, though also non-Irish writers like Chekhov; she had no knowledge of Irish language[26] nor interest in Irish sport, though she supported Ireland in the World Cup (1990) against England. She carried a British passport (as is usual for a Protestant in Northern Ireland). I asked her which newspapers she read as this can demonstrate where one's interests lie; she named two Northern Irish Protestant papers, the *Belfast Telegraph* and the *Newsletter* and I observed her carrying the *Guardian*, an English paper. She said she would 'occasionally glance' at the *Irish Times*, but would never buy it.

Issues which Elizabeth raised herself differed slightly. She referred to looking Irish, and to people recognising that she was Irish before she even spoke. 'It must be this pale, anaemic skin and the general lack of sophistication,' she suggested. She also spoke of her 'inferiority complex' because of 'where I'm from' and constantly referred to how much she felt at a disadvantage because of her origins. This was particularly relevant in relationships. It was the association with violence in Northern Ireland which she felt upset others, but she also felt inferior to the 'English rose' whom, she thought, English men were seeking. In context, she tended to see herself as lacking in many areas, not just ethnicity. She also spoke often of her family and of visiting home, which she does on every holiday, even long weekends. 'I'm always running,' she said, 'but I love going home to see my family.' She talked fondly of people at 'home', of what they would be doing, and of big days in Northern Ireland, such as 12 July.[27] Many of her concerns are thus in Northern Ireland; she additionally uses Northern Irish phrases to express herself.

Elizabeth's family were a major part of the importance of her identification with Northern Ireland:

> it's just, I mean, I was born there and that's where my family are, so that's why it's important but if ... if I was born in Scotland, I think, sorry, this sounds like a traitor, but I'd probably feel ... because that's where my family were, I'd probably feel attached to it, but because mine are from (name of town), that's where my whole epicentre is.

The 'troubles' were, by contrast, a major part of her negative feelings about Northern Ireland. Because of them, she said she sometimes wished she had been born 'on the other side of the Irish sea', that is, in Scotland.[28] A reason, an understandable reason, for her strong, negative feelings about the violence may be her experience of seeing an acquaintance shot in Belfast. She was called as a witness afterwards and also witnessed a triumphal reaction by Republican students in her university, where she had been involved in Unionist politics. She said she had difficulty sleeping after the incident, that she felt 'sick', and wondered what was the point of politics when the opposition held an armalite in one hand. Paradoxically, it may also explain her once defending 'my people' in a Politics class she attended in London, when loyalist terrorism was the subject. Here she explained that the Protestant people had simply had enough.

Elizabeth stressed negative aspects of her ethnicity repeatedly, but also told me she was 'very proud' of her 'roots'. The affective aspect of her ethnicity, her feelings about it, were thus conflicting. It is clear that her contradictory statements cannot be explained totally in terms of a situational assessment of what is currently appropriate, though this is relevant: there is also an element of emotional confusion or conflict.

It is also important to remember that the situation is not static. Elizabeth did experience changes in self-identification. For example, she said she would never consider herself Irish in Ireland, though she did in Britain. She also felt that her attitude to the political situation in Northern Ireland had changed. Since coming to England, she said, she had 'realised' that the Unionists were too 'intransigent'. She saw things 'more objectively', she suggested, and said she could envisage a United Ireland, when in London. She also celebrates St. Patrick in London. These are not all permanent changes, as back in Northern Ireland she could not continue tolerating the idea of a United Ireland, for example. Again, the situational nature of ethnicity appears alongside a theme of personal development, where change occurs through new experience.

Elizabeth and integration

Elizabeth described as a 'common trait' among Northern Irish the fact that they wished to disassociate themselves from their origins, whereas she valued and retained hers: 'they just don't go home very often and they try to modify their accent', she said. She mentioned one friend in particular she knew who was like this and who did not seem to want to see Elizabeth very often. She insisted, 'I'm not castigating them', but said that trying to lose one's accent seemed false to her, and that 'you have an identity and I feel if you lose that, you might feel uprooted, whereas I cling to mine'. This is despite feeling that 'English people dislike Irish accents' and despite experiencing Irish people being portrayed as stupid. When this happened, she tended to 'play along with it' rather than take offence, she suggested. Elizabeth thus places herself in a different category from those who wish to leave behind things Northern Irish. Instead, she keeps her accent and visits home often, the two criteria she chose as representative of retaining one's ethnic identity.

However, Elizabeth did not use ethnic networks either to make friends or seek accommodation. Rather, she chose a religious network to find somewhere to stay (a Methodist hostel, followed by using a Church of England accommodation board). Only one of her friends was from Ireland (the Northern Irish one mentioned above), the rest English. 'I don't go to any Irish groups like these Kilburn societies or ... Irish clubs. I'm not saying I deliberately don't go, it's just I don't go in my normal routine,' she told me, though also explained that she did not enjoy groups in general. 'And I don't seek out Irish people,' she continued, though on another occasion she said that she *would* seek out Irish people as she would have more in common with them. She was, however, a 'nominal member', as she called it, of Queen's University Club, London. Her flatmate was Scottish; though she had lived with one Northern Irish person, and represented this as positive due to the things they had in common, most of her flatmates had been non-Irish. She said she liked hearing Irish accents, but disliked being introduced to Irish people at parties: 'there's this inbuilt expectation that you'll get on really well, whereas, I mean, you're two very different people with divergent outlooks, so the chances of relating to one another are fairly slim anyway.' This is quite a clear statement on the limitations of ethnic bonding. Elizabeth does not actively seek out Irish companions, yet she retained her accent and her links with Northern Ireland. There are thus different levels and ways of integrating into British society and of remaining apart. 'Integration' is not necessarily carried out on all levels.

Elizabeth and politics
Elizabeth described herself as very interested in politics and pointed to her job, which had political content, and her evening classes in Politics. She described her view of Northern Ireland politics as follows:

> We are part of the majority, so that's our inheritance, we're two-thirds in numerical terms and I do believe the Unionists have their right to maintain the link with Britain until such times as the Roman Catholics have the numerical advantage but at the moment, it's 60 to 40 per cent in our favour ... I suppose I'm on the winning side, I mean from a purely selfish point of view.

She described herself as 'Unionist but ... not ... intransigent', saying she would seek for compromise, unlike the current Unionist leaders. She felt that 'this inheritance thing' was 'secondary' to peace, and that she would 'give up Britishness if it meant peace'. In Belfast, Elizabeth had been involved in Unionist politics, but became disillusioned with this after seeing her friend shot, saying it seemed 'futile'. If she returned to Ireland, she would like to get involved in a peace movement, she said. I asked how she saw the future and she suggested 'some devolved administration at Stormont with nationalist participation'. She felt that 'the Irish dimension' was needed, that is, the involvement of the Republic in discussions. However, she described herself as 'bigoted' and 'biased', 'inevitably, because of my upbringing' and was unsure if she could write an objective essay on Northern Ireland in her Politics class.

Regarding British politics, she described herself as 'centre left' and said she would vote Labour here at the next election.[29] She said she believed in a 'social market economy' and disapproved of 'the protection of the rich and the affluence of the haves and the deprivation of the have-nots' which was characteristic of Britain, though not of Northern Ireland, she felt. She suggested that there was a greater range of issues in British politics, whereas Northern Irish politics were 'rooted in the sectarian divide'.

Elizabeth and religion
Elizabeth's Christianity seemed more important to her than her ethnic upbringing, though she was contradictory about this. It was a potential source of accommodation, flatmates and friends; she felt that Christians were 'more likely to be honourable', and she described it as a 'common bond'. However, most of her friends were not in fact Christian. I asked if this was a problem and she told me 'on the superficial level, Christianity doesn't really enter into it', so it was not a problem. She felt uncomfortable talking about her faith anyway, she said.

Her opinions about her faith changed in the time I knew her. She was brought up in a Nonconformist tradition and visited various churches in England, being unable to find the one she was brought up in. Since the beginning of 1990, she had settled at a church of the Church of England. In July 1990, she told me she believed in God but was not a 'professing Christian', as this involved putting oneself on a pedestal and one shouldn't unless one could stay up there. She espoused 'practical Christianity', like her mother, however, which involved helping people out, for example with community work. She had worked as an auxiliary in a hospital but stopped as it was too tiring. In April 1991, Elizabeth told me that her faith was 'very strong now', that she would 'profess it' and that she went regularly to church.

This gives the impression that her faith deepened while she was in London. However, initially, 'it dived when I came, gradually ... without me knowing it,... I didn't realise how much I was slipping ... then I stopped confessing to be a Christian', she told me. She put this down to 'all the temptations and all the loneliness and that you see all this tragedy in the world and you wonder, is there a God?'. Finding her current church had made a difference and then her faith 'gained strength slowly'. She found it difficult to reconcile her practical Christianity with life in London, however, saying 'you have to be part of this grabbing society; I mean on the underground, you just develop your elbows like the rest of them or else you're left standing waiting for the third train'. She said she tended to use God as 'a crutch' when feeling depressed, but when describing her most depressed point in London, said she 'just couldn't find any answers to prayer'. She felt that 'the borderlines of right and wrong seem to merge here' and she was shocked at how 'materialistic' the society was.

I asked her what being Protestant meant to her and she said,

it means believing in a Union with Great Britain ... It means ... a link with the old Scottish Presbyterians, no matter how tenuous ... and it has this mentality of No

Surrender and a defensive attitude. It's as if you're always on the defensive, trying to hold onto some ... status or land or inheritance. It's as if you're feeling threatened all the time. And it has connotations of Loyalist violence and terrorism and democratic Unionist shouting from the platforms and Bible bashing.[30]

She continued, 'not only is it its own identity, it's also opposite to Roman Catholic', which she saw as a good thing. I asked how much she felt her Protestantism was wound up with her Northern Irishness and she replied, 'well, it's all a cultural inheritance, that from a child, religion and upbringing were all part of your culture and you ... you just grow up like this without realising it'. She felt religion was more a question of cultural identity than of theology in Northern Ireland. I asked how she reacted to the Irish = Catholic cliché. She said as Catholics were in the majority in Ireland as a whole, she wouldn't challenge this. She also said she felt 'more kin to the Irish than the British' because she anticipated that she would be less alienated in the Republic than in England, due to the materialism of the latter. However, she added, 'I don't think about these issues; you're making me think, so these aren't deeply ingrained viewpoints.'

Caroline

Caroline and ethnicity: being Irish/Northern Irish/British

Caroline is from the Republic and was a statistician and lecturer when I met her. She has now moved back to Ireland, to a lecturing post. She is in her thirties and unmarried. We met at the London Irish Women's Centre at an Irish women's writing workshop and met frequently for a year and a half, becoming friends.

Caroline first emigrated to America, then back to Ireland, then to America again, then to London. She compared London and the English with her American experience and constantly compared English and Irish characteristics as if always trying to make sense of her experience in terms of ethnic diversity. She saw herself unproblematically as Irish. When she talked about 'Ireland' and 'Irish', she referred exclusively to the Republic. Northern Irish, she saw as a different category, somewhere between Irish and English. A central issue here was the Protestant work ethic. This distinguished Protestants and the British from the Irish who were more laid back, she felt, but, in Northern Ireland, each had influenced the other, so they were midway between English Protestant and Irish (i.e. Irish Republic) Catholic attitudes. She initially told me that Irishness and Britishness were 'mutually exclusive' and displayed great antipathy to Northern Ireland Protestants. We argued about this. As a researcher, I could say I was challenging her, seeing how deep this attitude went; as a Northern Irish Protestant, I was, however, probably reacting more emotionally.

Later, she modified her views and in a taped interview just before she left England, she said that Protestants could be Irish too. I reminded her of her earlier opinion and she laughed, 'I mean we got over that, didn't we? I mean it took me a long time because that's how you're brought up, you know.' This indicates the relationship between us quite well. I was initially embarrassed that, as an apparently neutral anthropologist, I had in fact changed her opinion, but if I accept that my position as a Northern Irish Protestant affects the situation, it is valuable information: Caroline's antipathy to Northern Irish Protestants was capable of being overcome by friendship, and her views although strong, were not immutable.

Caroline felt that there was such a thing as an Irish psyche. She included Jung's notion of the 'collective unconscious' in this, saying ideas are laid down in the history of a people which influence the individual's present actions and attitudes. She explained her 'knee jerk' reactions, for example the one above, and also her mistrust of the English as belonging to this. For her, being Irish meant much more than the fact that she spent her early years in Ireland or that her family were there: it entailed whole attitudes to life which were very deep and powerful. She felt that there were regional differences across Ireland, however. My bluntness was part of my Northern origin, she said, and she contrasted this to Corkonian evasiveness. The difference between country and town, and farming and non-farming origin was also fundamental, she felt.

I asked Caroline what being Irish meant to her. She responded, 'God, that's a terrible question to ask; I can't answer that', but proceeded to say,

> I guess ... the first thing that would come into my head, like, is that there's a great oral tradition which later turned into a great literary tradition, so I think ... that aspect of the creativity is quite strong in the culture and I think it's a part of most people, that sort of literary impulse. I think Irish people express themselves quite well and they have a good imagination, a creative one.

The oral tradition and literature were favourite topics of Caroline's, and the fact that Irish people expressed themselves so much more poetically than English. She herself wrote poetry. She felt that Ireland being an island was also important: 'I think that makes a difference ... you're never very far away from the sea and I think you're quite close to nature, you know, for that reason ... because nowhere in Ireland is that far from the countryside'.[31] Thirdly, she mentioned religion — 'we suffer from having too much of the church' (this I look at later). She felt aware of her Irishness in London in that 'people don't crack jokes with you ... sort of in the same way ... make you feel that you're not sort of in a culture that you're at home in'. At work, she was considered 'disruptive', and felt that she had to tone down her Irishness there.

She was positive about Irish folk music and the Irish language, offering to teach me the language. Her spoken English was full of Irish idiom and her conversation full of Heaney and Yeats and an Irish play she saw on the television, the great night she had with some Irish people in the pub and a new Irish event she had seen advertised in the *Irish Post*. She constantly compared Irish and English ways. Traditions, history and myths were all different, she said. Initially, she portrayed the Irish as entirely positive and English as negative — curious, imaginative, individualistic versus 'yes men'; good 'crack', friendly, spontaneous and unpretentious versus formal and restrained; passionate versus passionless and 'very controlled'; 'musical' versus 'boring' use of language; relaxed versus uptight. However, this was later modified, as the Irish were also seen as narrow-minded, hypocritical and repressed, and English people as polite and fair, with English institutions better if you had a crisis. Her attitude often seemed to be combative, with Irish-English relations seen as a battle where she had to hold her own.

Caroline and integration

I asked Caroline what integration meant to her and she replied, 'well I think to integrate, you have to have a sense of belonging ... which means you have to identify with, like, what are the ideals in the culture'. In England, in contrast to America, she found it difficult to pinpoint 'the ideal' and thought it depended on class. She said, 'I would have quite liked to integrate because you, I mean ... you always hope like, the place you're going to is going to turn out to be wonderful and beautiful ... and then you find maybe that the things that are there you cannot integrate with them because they're in great conflict to what you've been brought up with.' In America, this had been the case, as fame and success could not be her ideal in life, she said. In England, she felt that if she stayed, she would 'be willing to compromise on ... the ... emphasis on orderliness and politeness and things like that', but not on the work ethic. She felt that returning migrants from England were always 'more subdued' whereas those from America were 'even more noisy than when they went'. Living elsewhere did change one therefore. Her attitude to two of her friends is interesting. One, though divorced, was keeping her husband's (English) name as she thought it would be 'useful' and had dropped her accent and all identification with Irish things. Caroline was horrified by this. Another friend, from Northern Ireland, concealed her accent and her origins except from a select few and Caroline approved. The difference seemed to be motives: the second friend was deceiving the English on the grounds that you could not trust them with the information, which made Caroline laugh, and the first friend was portrayed as despising her origins.

In my experience of her, Caroline attended many Irish groups and sought out Irish people. She read the *Irish Post*, where she saw these events advertised, and the *Irish Times*. She drew my attention to the Irish Network, a group of young, middle-class Irish; she attended Irish poetry-writing workshops; joined an Irish university college association, and spoke very positively of evenings spent in the company of other Irish people. She also attended non-Irish groups, for example a walking group, and sculpture, yoga and guitar lessons. Her regular poetry group was not Irish. Her stated attitude was, 'I think Irish people know how to enjoy themselves better, that's why I'd be inclined more to go to Irish things. They're just more fun.'

She also told me that she tended 'to have had more Irish friends and people with Irish-type connections than English friends'. This was something I had also observed. It contrasted with her attitude in America, when she knew locals instead. In England, she found Irish people easier to make friends with. English people already had their own networks, she said. More than simply not being open to outsiders, however, she felt that English people disliked Irish accents and were not as open as Irish people would be to outsiders in Ireland. She felt that 'you probably have to change your accent and everything ... to ... be accepted by a lot of English people', which she did not plan to do: 'I would feel such a fraud', she said, if she did. She had changed at work, however, she felt, keeping her head down more.

In general, Caroline often gave the impression of being aloof from English society. However, she also described problems in fitting in to a university in Ireland, so ethnic difficulties were not the only ones she experienced. It is interesting that she chose her ethnicity to explain her difficulties in England.

Caroline and religion
Caroline was very much against organised religion. As 'Irish' meant the Republic for her, so 'the Church' was the Catholic Church. Her main criticisms were that it was patriarchal and sexist; it monopolised spirituality, denying any religiosity to those who did not accept its rules; it was repressive, in particular regarding divorce and contraception. She said she had been indoctrinated by organised religion as a child and it consequently gave her 'the creeps'. It was even given as a reason why she would not live in Ireland at one stage. However, it seemed less acceptable for me as a Protestant to criticise, and when I joined with her in criticising holy pictures such as the Sacred Heart, she seemed shocked.

She did, however, attend church in London from time to time. She said she liked the atmosphere of old Catholic ritual, with Latin masses and candles, and the ritualised aspect of Judaism, but was inclined to see herself as having 'spirituality' rather than religion, which involved living so as to enhance one's own and others' humanity, rather than degrade it. She believed that Jesus lived, but so long ago that it was not relevant now; she did not believe in 'miracles and grace', though on other occasions she said she felt miracles were not confined just to Christianity. She once described herself as 'a bit paganistic', saying she believed in nature.

Irish and Northern Irish people were much more bound by the Church, Caroline thought, than the English, even if they emigrated. The English way was more healthy she felt, as religion in Ireland was to the detriment of human relations, whether regarding divorce or 'the war' in Northern Ireland.

I wondered if her antagonism to the Church connected with her family relations. Her relationship with her father was extremely poor and she described him as very involved in the vocabulary and ritual of Catholicism, yet incapable of looking at himself, which she thought should be the first requirement of 'religion'. Her profound distaste for the Church may have originated in her reaction to what she saw as his hypocrisy.

Caroline and politics

Caroline talked often about the situation in Northern Ireland. She was anti-IRA and said she would 'never' get involved with Irish political groups in London as they were all pro-IRA. She joked that she expected me to be surprised that she, as an Irish Catholic, did not support the IRA.[32] She felt it was essential to have a standpoint about Northern Ireland, however, that one could not sit on the fence. Her gut feelings seemed to be anti-Unionist, with revulsion towards the concept of Protestant aristocracy. She thought devolution was the best option, but that the Unionists could not be trusted. When I asked about a United Ireland, she said, 'well I'm sorry ... that there is a division you know ... but if the division is necessary, then it's necessary in order to keep the peace, so I don't think it should be taken away at all costs'. This surprised me as she seemed strongly nationalist on other occasions. She said she would not expect the 'Ulster Protestants' to move into a united Ireland until the Church was divorced from the state: 'I wouldn't move if I were them', she said.

She also told me she had never been very interested in politics in the Republic and that on the whole, people there *were not* interested in politics. This was because the parties were so similar there, she suggested.[33] She found it quite difficult, she continued, how obsessed everyone was with politics in Britain. This too surprised me as she often talked about the political situation in Northern Ireland to me. Perhaps it was British politics she found uninteresting. She was very interested in green issues, however, expressing increasing support for the Green Party.

Alison

Alison and ethnicity: being Irish/Northern Irish/British

Alison is in her early twenties, a Catholic from Northern Ireland, who works in a paramedical profession. She is now, like Caroline, living in the Republic, with her husband, a Northern Irish Protestant. I knew her husband when I was living in Northern Ireland, and Alison less well. I met them less frequently than my other informants as I was embarrassed researching people I knew, and procrastinated. We did, however, have several meetings and one long taped interview, just before they left for Ireland. I taped her and her husband together as I felt asking for separate interviews would be imposing too much, as they were in the middle of organising how to leave London; it also reflects my own discomfort. It is important to note that Alison was talking in front of her husband, apart from a short period when he was out of the room, as this will have affected her answers. The dynamics of the interview were interesting and I reflect on them in the section on relationships. I asked what nationality Alison considered herself and she laughed and said, 'it depends on the situation that you're asked; you decide which one you want to be ... whether you're British or Irish you know; you can be whatever you want to be'. However, she also told me, 'if (people) say you're Irish, if they say are you from

Ireland, I goes no, Northern Ireland, you know, I do distinguish the difference between them and I wouldn't associate myself with being from Ireland'. Like Elizabeth, therefore, she differentiated between 'Northern Ireland' and 'Ireland'. Denigrating the importance of the ethnic question, she continued, 'it's only really something you stick down on a form, basically', and otherwise, 'I don't think you really think about it'. When I asked her what she put on forms, she said it depended where she was sending them: if she was applying to somewhere in the Republic, she would put Irish; for her job in London, she put British. I asked her which passport she had and she said Irish, but explained quickly, 'the only reason I've got that basically is because I was going to America and I could have got a visa much easier ... with it'.

Alison stressed the situational aspect of her ethnicity so much that I doubted it. I wondered how much it was influenced by the fact that the two other people in the room, her husband and I, were both Protestant. In Northern Ireland, calling oneself 'Irish' is a nationalist statement, usually made by Catholics, and calling oneself 'British', a Unionist statement made usually by Protestants. Perhaps she wanted to play down her difference from us. She also described attending Protestant marches on 12 July in Northern Ireland: 'if there was bands going through the town, everybody always went to see them, be it Catholic or Protestant really', which although part of the truth, ignores the conflict that also exists. This playing down of conflict may be what she was doing when she de-emphasised her Irishness. Perhaps her experience of marrying a Protestant also encourages her to play down sectarian positions. And perhaps my upbringing predisposed me to question what she said more than was appropriate.

She referred to other Irish as 'they' and resented it when they expected her to do them favours because of their shared ethnicity. However, she felt there were differences between Irish and English people, and on this question, all my informants placed themselves in the Irish category. She described English people as 'stand-offish', not liking 'to see you drink' and as having 'quite strong views'. However, she described the people she worked with as 'all very friendly and very helpful and easy to get on with' and said English people who offered to do things for you were genuine, whereas, in Northern Ireland, people offer because it is 'expected', not because they want to.[34] English people argued more in pubs, she felt, whereas if Irish people did, it would be 'heated' and come 'to blows'. English society was class-dominated, whereas 'I don't think Irish people have a class'.[35] There were also differences in politics, religion and relationships, which I look at below. It is interesting that Alison did not see Irish as positive and English as negative at all, but both as mixed. Again, this may be part of playing down her attachment to Irishness. She was also inclined to talk of differences being related to big city versus small town characteristics, following her husband's prompting, rather than English-Irish differences. She had been brought up in a small town herself and saw small towns as breeding parochialism and narrow-mindedness and a claustrophobic closeness, but also trust and familiarity. Some of her difficulties in

London she related to living in a city, for example, people's unfriendliness and mistrust.

Alison and integration

Alison told me that she was frequently mistaken for Scottish. I asked her how she felt about this and she said she just agreed, that 'it doesn't make any difference really'. She complained that people often questioned her about where she was from and what religion, and said she let them guess and would either just agree, or agree if they were right. She thus seemed evasive about her ethnicity, but not operating active concealment. She also disliked being questioned on whether she was married or pregnant, so it seems part of a general dislike of nosiness. On the question of prejudice, she spoke of people who think that the Irish 'are a fairly stupid race, basically', but said 'I don't take offence really unless I think someone really means it, you know'. However, she did get annoyed when people corrected the way she said things because it was in Northern Irish idiom, saying 'everybody's entitled to have their own way of saying things'. She saw these people as a 'minority'.

When I asked her about integration, she told me that 'it just happened', without specifying what. However, she also said that at her work 'I just mix with everybody', and 'I didn't want to be clannish with just the Irish people really'. This was not a conscious decision but 'just a matter of my job to get on with everyone ... there's no point in building barriers'. She disapproved of Irish or other ethnic groups who 'keep trying to keep their culture totally, you know, but they, you have to expect to bend the rules slightly'. She felt that there was no Northern Irish culture to hold on to though. Alison was very keen to stress that both she and Paul had not joined any sort of Irish community: 'we haven't gone out of our way to avoid them, but ... we never went to the places to come in contact with them really on a regular basis'. When Paul talked, he referred to an Irish crowd and gave a rather different impression and when they both mentioned places they frequented, they tended to be Irish pubs.

Alison in fact seemed to mix more with Irish people than she claimed. These links were predominantly through her husband, however. Her own choice of friends seemed to be made on a non-ethnic basis. One of her friends was Pakistani, another Northern Irish, and her colleagues, whom she sometimes visited, were mixed. Alison never said she felt more comfortable with people from 'home'; nor did she appear to avoid them. She had not made many friends apart from her husband, so effectively, she mixed a lot with his Northern Irish (Protestant and Catholic) friends, but things were changing here; increasingly, they were going out alone together instead. In Northern Ireland, I had been told by another source that Alison did not like Paul spending so much time with his friends; in London, perhaps her objections were having an effect. When she said she did not mix with other Irish perhaps she was saying what she wanted to happen.

Alison and politics
Alison dissociated herself from Northern Irish politics, saying, 'I just avoid it basically. I wouldn't get involved with it because it's pointless'. She followed Paul in saying it was 'more religion really' than politics. She said she did not have strong views about a united Ireland or other alternatives. British politics were 'much more interesting', she suggested, though she did not elaborate.[36] The fact that British politics were not religion-based seemed central. As a religiously mixed couple, Alison and Paul have extra incentives to leave behind sectarian modes of thinking.

Alison and religion
While her husband talked about his continuing consciousness of Protestant-Catholic labelling, Alison remarked instead on the greater variety of religions in London, giving a sense of things being broader here.

She remarked that church-going was more common in Northern Ireland, but felt that was due to fear of being talked about if one did not attend. Her own church-going had remained similar in London, she and her husband agreed. Catholic churches in London seemed 'a lot more strict', perhaps, she suggested, because they did not have so many Catholic schools to instruct people. People also welcomed her if she was new, whereas in Northern Ireland people did not pay much attention. She claimed to have no preferences on this. Alison had attended a number of Protestant churches with friends, and declared, 'I'm not intimidated by anyone's religion'. The differences were not that great, she felt. On the question of faith, she told me 'I wouldn't say I've a very strong faith but I do *believe*, you know'. She was not more specific. I got the impression she was not given to philosophising about it.

Breda

Breda and ethnicity: being Irish/Northern Irish/British
Breda is in her twenties, from rural Southern Ireland, though having spent five years in Dublin, says she feels more a Dubliner than anything else. She had a Catholic upbringing and is a lesbian. She worked in the media when I met her, with a small Irish firm. We met frequently over a period of three months. She then became anxious about the fact that I was taking notes about her. I left her to contact me and she did not. We both spent time apart in Ireland. A year later, I rang her again and we met a few times. I asked for a taped interview and she refused. I felt antagonism from the lesbians in the London Irish Women's Centre (LIWC) whom I encountered, people Breda associated with, and Breda's suspicion of me seemed part of a pattern which frustrated me. I felt as if I was not the right political hue, either with regard to sexuality, or Republicanism, when I went to the LIWC. Breda seemed more tolerant but also uncomfortable with me, and I felt loath to pursue the meetings after the break.

She said she first became aware of being Irish when she left Ireland. Her image of the typical Irish person was male, middle-aged, middle-class and conservative — her parents' generation, she said. She demonstrated great antipathy to this image. Her experience of her young Irish, male colleagues and their conservative values undermined her hope that things might change.

Her attitude to Irish women was very different. She seemed to see Irishness as having two poles: at the negative end, the male image I describe, which is complacent and 'out of touch with reality'; on the positive end, female, working class and lesbian. She was positive and negative about Ireland too. It was beautiful, but the people were small-minded and the politicians negative, she suggested; she was very positive about Irish culture and literature, though. She also differentiated in class terms, regarding 'yuppie' Irish (and English) with distaste. She saw herself as working class despite having a degree and a postgraduate qualification, as she said her study was grant-aided. She despised 'yuppie' pubs and university association dinners and so on. On one occasion, however, she indicated to me that she would like to overcome her class origins. She later denied this vehemently.

Breda criticised the Irish men she associated with at great length but also described the English she encountered in negative terms: as 'cold', unfriendly, reserved, lacking spontaneity and class-centred. Irish people were contrasted as more friendly and open. It was only in relation to the English that they were seen as united and positive.

When I asked Breda about her identity, she said it was 'personal' and talked about her career plans as fundamental to it, rather than about being Irish.

Breda and integration

Breda's work involved attending Irish events and meeting Irish people. She also lived in a house full of Irish people in North London. What was her attitude to these choices? She was extremely negative about both. She complained of her colleagues, 'they're so Irish! I know I shouldn't say it, but...'. She constantly complained of the sexism and conservatism of the Irish men she worked with and how their attitudes constituted sexual harassment. She said she was fed up with mixing with so many Irish; what she liked about London was the 'variety' of 'ideas' and 'cultures' and that while you might not always like what you came up against, it was certainly varied. However, with living and working with nearly all Irish, she felt she might as well be back in Ireland. Her home she described as merely a roof and four walls; her female flatmates were always cooking big meals for their boyfriends, she complained. In this alone, she was alienated by her sexuality, her vegetarianism and her feminism, none of which were reinforced. These were major ways in which these Irish people did not fulfil aspects of her self.

However, her friends were largely Irish women. She said she did not deliberately seek Irish people out as friends, but they were easier to get to know, more friendly and open than the colder, more reserved English. If she got to know someone and they were Irish, then this was a 'bonus', she said. This contrasts totally with her earlier complaints. It was women, often lesbian, who were her friends, and the groups she attended were Irish women's groups (e.g. photography, football). When she moved jobs she, additionally, did not leave the Irish milieux, but moved instead to work with Irish women. She described the Irish women's network as 'supportive' and 'friendly' and was very enthusiastic about gatherings of this group. She turned to Irish groups when she needed housing, unlike Alison, who approached the non-ethnic Citizens' Advice Bureau.

At the beginning, Breda said she had been determined to avoid all Irish people. She worked in an English atmosphere, temping, where she felt under pressure to play down her Irishness and instead emphasised it; she was very unhappy here and moved to a male Irish working environment and then to a female Irish one. Her contacts seemed to be increasingly with Irish women's groupings. She felt that coming to London had changed her: she was 'becoming like them' and losing her spontaneity. London also made Irish people in general more class-centred, she suggested.

Breda and politics
Breda was angry with the government of the Republic for not directing enough money towards its migrants. She opposed the British legislation which affected Irish people in Britain, specifically the Prevention of Terrorism Act, which she felt was extremely oppressive. Sexual politics were also important to her. She attended the Gay Pride march in London, but complained, interestingly, that the Republican slogan on the LIWC banner was alienating.

Breda and religion
Breda was considered a heathen by her colleagues, she told me. She tended to shock them by saying she was not a Catholic, complaining that Christmas cards were too religious and so on. She rejected the label of 'lapsed Catholic', saying it was holding onto the skirts of the Church, was hypocritical and insulting to the Church.

When she was not comparing herself to other, overtly religious people, however, she stopped describing herself as non-religious. She felt that the more one accepted all facets of oneself, including spirituality, the more whole one became. She also felt that she had absorbed the teachings of religion, and that the central issue was that God is love; everything else was secondary, including her anxieties about representations of women in the Bible. Her beliefs included reincarnation, however, a Buddhist teaching, and that animals have souls (she is thus vegetarian).

Breda's views were thus unconventional. She avoided labels, and seemed open to ideas on spiritual matters, though she was negative about organised religion.

Being a woman

In this section, I look at ideas on gender and sexuality, then at relationships and family. Relationships and family are traditional female concerns and indeed the place of woman as homemaker continues to be enshrined in the constitution of the Republic. I conclude with references to career and other ambitions and values, to attempt a more rounded picture.

Elizabeth

Elizabeth and gender/sexuality
I asked Elizabeth if being a woman meant anything to her, pointing out that it did not have to. She had never volunteered information on this. She replied, 'well, I don't profess to be a feminist but because I inherently believe men and women are equal, so women don't have to shout it from the rooftops'. She continued, 'I think femininity is important... in terms of... well, of being different from men'. As Protestantism's value was partly in its distinctiveness from Catholicism, so woman meant something in contrast to man. She felt that it was important to 'try to look nice and... exude feminine decorum', but felt that she was 'lacking' in these. She spoke of one woman she met, a model, who was 'the epitome of femininity for me', as she was very attractive and had a 'lovely personality'. Elizabeth said she would 'aspire' to this but some mornings she did not even have time to put on lipstick. Her actions and her aspirations were thus divergent, and she felt guilt about this. She was, however, in my opinion, attractive and feminine, but her self-image was low. She was heterosexual, but never discussed her sexuality.

Elizabeth and relationships
Elizabeth very often discussed relationships, which were of central importance to her, lamenting her lack of male friends, and boyfriends. Relationships were more important to her than her career, but less than her family and religion. Where she planned to live was partly dependent on relationships. When I first met her, she declared that she would not leave London as her ex-boyfriend was there, and she continued to be very attached to him. Later on she said she wanted to leave London partly because she had more chance of meeting a boyfriend in Northern Ireland.

As well as influencing where she lived, the subject of relationships affected her friendships, as Elizabeth felt more comfortable with married friends or those with boyfriends. This was because they talked more readily about relationships, she said. Most of her friends were women.

She felt that her Northern Irishness was a disadvantage in relationships, that her last boyfriend's parents had found this negative and that if the relationship had progressed to marriage, there would have been a real problem. She also felt that she would have difficulty attracting men who would aspire to an 'English rose' rather than to her, as I indicated above. She described herself as 'out of my natural environment' and dislocated in England. Apart from negative aspects on her side, she also had difficulty with English men. Over here, she said, a stranger really is a stranger, whereas at 'home', one always knows something about them or their family.

I asked her whom she would consider having relationships with, regarding ethnic origin and religious beliefs. She replied, 'he'd have to be of British origin', though later changed this to 'preferably of British origin, but not categorically so'. She then expanded to 'someone of a white, Commonwealth background', suggesting Southern or Northern Irish or New Zealander as possibilities. I asked if she had to choose between British and Northern Irish which she would prefer and she said Northern Irish. Her reason was that they could both settle more easily in Northern Ireland, or else that when they visited families at Christmas, both would be in Northern Ireland, so it would be easier, and also that they would maybe know the same people and places. She also felt her partner 'would have to be the same religion as me', clarifying this as meaning 'not Roman Catholic'. Her reason was that getting involved with a Catholic 'would hurt my parents so much'.

On the question of whom she actually had relationships with, she saw one man for two and a half years who was English and agnostic. He was Protestant by upbringing. This seemed to be her main relationship. When I asked Elizabeth what her aims for the next 10 years were, she said she wanted to be married with children. Bringing children up in London would be difficult, she suggested, with no family near; she preferred Northern Ireland, though she was anxious about the violence.

Elizabeth and family

The prospect of starting her own family was important to Elizabeth. Her existing family was important also. In listing what was important to her, family came first. She described herself as a 'homebird' and 'abnormally close to my mother', and also 'close' to her brother. Leaving her family after every visit home was always a great wrench. She missed their practical help, for example, when moving house. More generally, the influence of her parents seemed very great. Her mother picks out job advertisements in Northern Ireland for her and advises her which to apply for, advice Elizabeth abides by; her father recommended that she did not apply for a particular job and she accepted this advice too; her mother worried that she spent all her money on rent and that she did not join groups and both these worries were also articulated as Elizabeth's own anxieties. The desire to be with her family and to look after them was a major reason why Elizabeth wished to return to Northern Ireland. She did suggest, however, that she would not expect emotional support from her family while in London, seeing this as futile while she was living at a distance.

Elizabeth's aims and values

I will look here at those values not covered already. The question of where to live, whether to stay in London or move to Northern Ireland, preoccupies

Elizabeth greatly and is an unresolved dilemma. Partly this is a dilemma between living her own life and looking after her parents. Her indecision contributes to a feeling of not being settled here, she suggested.

She was interested in changing careers, perhaps to law, but lamented the length of study required at Queen's University in Belfast. This would curtail her social life, she felt, and therefore her chance of meeting a partner, I deduced, as she was worried about being in her thirties when she finished. She wanted to own her own house as she was tired of flatsharing. She wanted, 'to be near my family or have my own family... and I'd like to travel... and I'd like to write, but those are just private things'. However, she sounded negative about her current life, saying more than once, 'life goes on and you keep perpetuating the same things'.

Caroline

Caroline and gender/sexuality

Caroline was single and heterosexual. She talked often about the differences between women and men, as she did about Irish–English differences. I asked her once if she considered herself a feminist and she said 'Yes, I probably am'; this suggested to me that she did not really think of herself as a feminist, but knew she could be classed that way. She supported women's equality and rights and was angry about sexism and discrimination. Her experience at work was of a male subordinate finding difficulty with taking instructions from her and of male colleagues patronising her. Partly she felt patronised due to her gender, partly due to hierarchical, status snobbery. She felt that working in a male environment was intrinsically difficult.

Men were, she felt, competitive and groups with men which she attended — for example, poetry writing — were spoilt by this competitive atmosphere. Men needed at least five women to bolster them, she suggested once: their wife, secretary and female underlings. Women by contrast not only had to make it alone but were under pressure to diet and look impeccable as well. Men were more ambitious, whereas women tended to underachieve. In general, men seemed very different from her. There were differences between Ireland, America and England, however. She was most positive about America, where she felt she had been treated as an equal at work. In Ireland, she felt there was no job discrimination, but there were other kinds of discrimination: it was impossible to walk into a pub alone as a woman, and the church there was very patriarchal.

On the whole, she proffered a view of male–female battle rather like the Irish–English battle she sometimes seemed to describe. Once questioning why she alienated people, she said she wondered if it was because she was Irish, then wondered if it was because of her gender and the fact that she refused to play male games like many women do in male professions. The issue is not whether she was right or wrong but the fact that she turned to these two agendas for explanation of problems she felt in social interaction.

Caroline was very private about her sexuality and relationships, but complained quite a lot about gay and lesbian sexuality; she had one gay friend and encountered a network of lesbians at the London Irish Women's Centre (LIWC), and also my gay flatmate when she came to visit me. She found the lesbians at the LIWC 'aggressive' which angered her, and she worried that they might assume she was a lesbian too. Regarding gay men, she was mostly antagonistic to public displays of affection and felt these things should be kept very private.

Caroline and relationships

As I said, Caroline was reserved about her relationships. I knew of one four-year relationship with an Irish man with whom she had travelled to America. She referred to other short-term relationships but her sense of privacy was strong and I felt unable to invade it with questions. She was, however, keen to philosophise on whether an Irish or English man was better.

Once she said she did not care which nationality she was involved with, but later, she said that an English man would be a problem as he would have only English friends, so you would be taking on something quite big; also he would side with the English when Irish affairs were reported in the British press and she with the Irish, but she felt they could probably agree to differ and manage on this. On another occasion she complained of the stage Irish man who would be prone to moodiness and drink; she would not want to get involved with this kind of person, she said. On the whole, however, she said she would prefer Irish men because they were 'more open' about their feelings and not repressed like the English. She was positive about the possibility of meeting an Irish man in Ireland when she moved back. They would fit in together more easily and it would be more relaxing.

Relationships were, I think, important to Caroline but due to her sense of privacy, it is difficult to say how important.

Caroline and family

Most of Caroline's family are in Ireland, though one is in America. She sometimes talked of missing them, and part of her reason for living in 'Europe' rather than America was proximity to her parents. She felt that family were good for practical help, 'for when things go wrong', such as lifts to the airport or financial aid.

However, her feelings about her family were much more frequently negative. She was emphatic that she would not turn to them for emotional support, and felt that they tried to constrain her and not accept who she really was. After she had known me for some time, she said the real reason she left Ireland was to get away from her father. Her relationship continued to be very poor with him, which complicated her desire to see her mother.

Caroline's aims and values

Over the time I knew her, Caroline spent much time, like Elizabeth, agonising over where to live. With Elizabeth, the dilemma usually seemed to be

Northern Ireland or London; with Caroline, the options seemed wider. She felt a city or the suburbs would be best and considered Surrey, Liverpool, Wales, Bristol and Scotland as possibilities. She felt that she had been moving too much, however, and that it had a high price, as she was 'terrified' all the time.

The issue of what to do with her life also occupied her. She questioned remaining in the academic environment, and suggested waitressing as an option allowing her time to read and think. She also suggested working with handicapped children, that this would be 'rewarding'. She felt she was not ambitious at all. I got the impression that her whole life was in flux, where to live, what to do, and that these could change at any time. In fact, she returned to Ireland, but to a university job there.

Values she could not understand were the English emphasis on inherited wealth as deserving respect, and the American focus on success. She cared 'passionately' about the environment.

Alison

Alison and gender/sexuality

The questions of Alison's gender and (hetero) sexuality did not seem to be ones which she problematised. When I mentioned that some people felt sexism was worse in Ireland than in Britain, she said,

> You see, I've never... I don't know. Because I've really, I've only been to school and college in Northern Ireland, so really at that age and at that stage, you really don't really come across, I don't think you do anyway, really any sort of... you might, there's... sexist remarks but they're just sort of part and parcel of everyone, you know, it's just part of growing up really... I've never really come across any sort of... sexist... discrimination or anything, really, no.

Alison spoke with much hesitation, obviously about an unfamiliar subject. She had clearly experienced sexism but accepted it as part of life and had no politicised views on it. I did not question her any more about what being a woman meant to her as I felt strongly it was not a topic she naturally considered.

Alison and relationships

My impression was that Alison's relationships were very important to her. Her social life was largely based on Paul and his friends. She often talked about 'we' rather than I; for example, when talking about whether she was Irish or British, she moved from 'you', which she uses in place of 'I', to 'we': 'whatever you want to be yourself, you know, you don't really have to be either one, do we?'; or when talking about how young everyone was at a disco in Northern Ireland, she said, 'we felt like a granny, you know... or granddad'. She seemed to see her identity and her feelings as something joint with her husband and often talked as if representing both of them, even when Paul was saying quite different things on the subject. He, on the other hand, talked much more readily about 'I'. Alison was more inclined to comment on his statements as well and had to be prompted to talk about herself. Paul warned me that Alison would not be good at talking about herself, but I felt that she talked readily enough once started. Paul, however, talked much more and dominated the interview, a situation I tried to redress, but one Alison seemed happy to accept.[37] She was, however, quick to contradict him on occasion. They seemed to have traditional roles, with Alison cooking and cleaning, but her influence in the relationship seemed quite big to me, for example, the way she was changing their socialising patterns, as I perceived it.

One area where Alison's thoughts were clearly not simply echoing or reacting to Paul's, was in relationships. When I asked if they felt there was any difference between English and Irish ways, Alison suggested the area of relationships. She felt that Paul always kept her informed when he went out without her, whereas English men were much more cavalier. English couples, she felt 'lead separate lives': 'like, it's not uncommon for all the men to go out together and stay away, you know, and like the wives wouldn't really think twice about it and... whereas... in Northern Ireland, if your husband stays away for a night, he's obviously up to something'.

She also talked of having her own family. The financial constraints in London made it impossible to have children here, she felt; additionally, city life would not be 'fair on children'. I feel this influenced her decision to move back to Ireland. She criticised the way Irish people asked her whether she was pregnant when she returned, saying 'what relevance does that have to your life!'. I think it had a lot of relevance to Alison, but she simply disliked nosiness.

Alison and family

Alison missed her family, especially initially, as she adjusted to being unable to visit them every weekend. However, she felt that London had changed her and she could no longer tolerate living close to them. She considered herself 'more independent' now, and valuing 'my own privacy'. Partly this may have been Paul's influence as much as London, as his family situation was very different, and he was very critical of what he saw as the claustrophobic closeness of Alison's family.

Alison's aims and values

The question of where to live was important again for Alison and her husband. They were on the brink of moving to Ireland when I taped an interview with them. Alison said Paul's work was more important than hers; he had been made redundant and she felt he would have more luck in Ireland getting work. I think she valued marriage and family more than her job and was thus being less altruistic than she seemed; she described it as 'the perfect opportunity' to go to Ireland on another occasion, to someone who suggested to me that Alison was keen to have children and did not want to do so in London. Alison hoped the move to Ireland would be a permanent one and felt optimistic about it.[38]

Breda

Breda and gender/sexuality

Breda felt that there were distinct female and male characteristics. She said that working in a male environment had made her aware of being a woman, much as her Irishness became meaningful when she encountered English people. What is being a woman to Breda? She felt that women were more reticent and more complex than men. Men were linear, straightforward, with perhaps more clarity of thought. Women were a huge ocean of meanings that they were only beginning to understand. She referred to a playwright who felt that all the power for the future would be from women, that they had unexplored depth. It was important not to idealise, she added, as women could be divisive and unfriendly. She also felt that everyone had both 'male' and 'female' characteristics within them, if you want to call them that, she said, and that the more one was able to accept both aspects of oneself, the more 'harmonious' a person one became. She complained of women accepting sex roles at her work and her house, where they gave to the point of 'self-extinction' and men just accepted it. Her opinion of men was low. At her work, she complained of sexism. For example, her (male) boss suggested that she wear a short skirt and low-cut blouse to functions, which she found very offensive. One of the women staff had left because of the sexual harassment, she said. Irish men were more sexist than English men, she felt. She did have ('unmacho') male friends however, and felt that they gave her a 'different perspective' on things, which she liked. Breda talked about the women's movement, and the importance of having a radical as well as a moderate section. She despaired of certain Irish papers' anti-abortion stances and conservatism.

On the question of her sexuality, Breda said she had been determined not to leave Ireland because of this, as that would be running away. She was happy that London had the biggest lesbian and gay centre in the world, appreciated the supportive network she found here, however, and she attended at least one Gay Pride march. When I told her about the hostility I felt from women at the LIWC, she was surprised, and said it was a pity; she suggested workshops to discuss straight-gay antagonisms. Another time she told me about problems she had with a close female friend in Ireland, who found it very difficult when Breda told her of her sexuality.

Breda and relationships

Breda very rarely talked of relationships, though more often of her sexuality in general. She referred to having hassles with a woman once and that was as much as she ever confided.

Breda and family

She talked little of her family. She had one brother in London, who, to her chagrin, hardly contacted her; the rest were in Ireland. She had never 'come out' to her family and felt that it was a source of tension, as her whole way of life was unknown to them. She abhorred superficialities. Perhaps this was what her meetings with family seemed to consist of; at any rate, she was inclined to avoid seeing them.

Breda's aims and values

Job-wise, firstly, in the short term, Breda was keen to write for the *Guardian*. I got the impression that she wanted to be respected for doing good journalism. She also wanted to change the sexist, conservative attitudes of her colleagues at work. She said she was afraid of getting 'stuck' on this rung of the ladder, however, perhaps one of the reasons why she left this job. In the long term, she wanted to set up a women's newspaper.

Regarding accommodation, Breda was very unhappy where she lived and wanted to find a 'nice' flat of her own where she could be 'creative'. She felt things would really change then. She suggested going to America; she also voiced fears that visiting Ireland would make her want to stay there. Otherwise, she planned to stay in London.

Another aim was to set up a theatre or drama group. Although this has not happened yet, she co-wrote a feminist play with another Irish woman which was shown in a North London theatre.

Breda told me she had a responsible job, a flat of her own, and to people at home, that sounded so grand, yet she had a feeling of 'is that it?' about her life. I got the impression that she was very unhappy and always looking to changes to help her feel better. She was more positive when I last talked to her, however; with her change of job and new play, perhaps things were at last looking brighter.

Conclusions

I will make some general statements, then look separately at ethnicity and gender, before making some final comments.

These women see themselves strongly as *individuals*. Repeatedly in my research, my larger group of informants suggested to me that they would not be relevant to my research as they were not typical of Irish migrants: Elizabeth, for example, described herself as an 'oddball'. Paradoxically, this stress on uniqueness is one of the most common threads in my sample. Alison, saying 'I'm myself and nobody else', complained of always being identified as her father's daughter in her home town. For her, London offered greater opportunity to be an individual. While her behaviour may not have changed dramatically, significant shifts had taken place; for example, her church attendance remained the same, but she now attended through choice, not through fear of being talked about. However, the distinction between rhetoric and action should be made, as my informants' stress on being individuals belongs to the former, whereas regarding ethnicity, actions often prioritised Irish identifications, and thus they had more in common than they realised. It is important to remember that individuals are rooted in a social context, both the one they have left and the one they now mix in. Consequently, their choices are partly dependent on background in Ireland, whether Protestant or Catholic, from North or South. While acknowledging this, actual visions of Irishness, its content and importance, varied considerably, as did views on gender, so individual variation remains important.

An important aspect of self-identification is its oppositional nature. For all four women and most of my wider sample, Irishness was most unified and clear when it was opposed to Englishness. For those who did not originally see themselves as Irish, for example, Elizabeth, this became meaningful and relevant once in England. Alison saw her ethnicity as unimportant, yet clearly articulated differences between Irish and English. On gender, Breda said being a woman first meant something to her when she worked in a male environment, and Elizabeth noted that femaleness took its meaning from opposition to maleness; Caroline also opposed female and male characteristics.

Ethnicity

Irishness in London is not the same as Irishness in Ireland. For one thing, it is more self-conscious, as other people's attitudes and differences lead one to recognise that one is ethnic. Being presented with this, my informants can choose whether to associate with Irish culture or not, either personally or on a group basis. In this context, I found Northern Irish identity to be situational for both the Catholic and Protestant women, determined partly by interest, in Glazer and Moynihan's terms (though other factors such as inherited cultural values and perception of English values are also relevant). This is not the case for the women from the Republic. Here one does not have the choice of Irish, Northern Irish or British. Rather, one may choose Irish or nothing;[39] an Anglo–Irish identity is possible, but is usually open to Protestants rather than Catholics. In my wider group, Irish is easily preferred over a lack of ethnic identity. Breda noted the pressure to assimilate, but reacted by emphasising her Irishness instead. She had begun by wishing to avoid all Irish people, but quickly moved to considerable involvement with them.

It is not appropriate to judge these choices in terms of wholesale acceptance/rejection; Breda, for example, rejects conservative, male Irish culture vehemently, yet is very fulfilled by her connection with female, radical Irish. Here, we are dealing with the notion of integration, and it is clear that no one is following the total integration referred to by Brown. The concept of uneven assimilation is more helpful. For example, living among Irish people is rejected by three of the women, and disliked by Breda, who does it; socialising in exclusively or predominantly Irish circles is practised to varying degrees by each woman, and with differing attitudes: Alison does so but plays it down; Breda does but criticises some experiences of this and praises others, depending on the type of Irish people involved; Caroline is very positive about her Irish friends and activities; and Elizabeth rarely mixes with other Irish. There are other indicators of assimilation: choosing an Irish partner is on the whole favoured, but preferred rather than prescribed. I look at this below; keeping one's accent is also practised and preferred by all. The variation is thus between and within the women: Elizabeth does not socialise with Irish people but is unwilling to change her accent; Caroline loves to socialise with Irish people but does not live with them; she was also quite specific that there were some things she would integrate into and some she would reject.

The content of Irishness is as variable to the women as the question of whether or not it is significant to them *per se*. This relates to their individual experiences: for example, Caroline's experience of psychotherapy may have led to her interest in the psyche and in Jung, and her viewing Irishness from this perspective. Additionally, her poetry writing is important to her and thus she emphasises the creativity of the Irish; Elizabeth's family are central to her and, being located in Northern Ireland, make this important to her; Alison prioritises her family in Northern Ireland, and also her relationship, which being with a Northern Irish man leads her to other Irish contacts; Breda, feeling rejection or else, less strongly, a sense of difference from English people because of her Irishness, and from straight people because of her sexuality, finds most fulfilment with lesbian Irish women. Her preoccupation with conservative views leads her to react against the conservatism of some Irish people. Standard questions about Irish traditions, papers read and so on, did not represent what is really of interest about being Irish to these women, though they do provide useful information. Talking with them over an extended period of time, listening to what they volunteer, I find that the significant aspects of Irishness are for them quite different, as I indicate. It is also important to remember that the post-migration experience is not static, but can involve dramatic change in self-perceptions: for example, Elizabeth seeing herself (partly) as Irish; others finding new configurations of Irishness, such as the lesbian Irish community (Breda), and Caroline's discovery that she could consider Northern Irish Protestants to be Irish.

Moving to Glazer and Moynihan's notion of affective bond, what emotional significance does Irishness have for my informants? Elizabeth felt emotional attachment to Northern Ireland and to her family there; Alison felt a bond with her family in Northern Ireland and her Northern Irish husband, but less so in the more abstract sense to Northern Ireland or Ireland, though she did correct people who said she was from Ireland rather than Northern Ireland; Caroline demonstrated a very emotional attachment to Ireland and her Irishness and her whole sense of who she was related to this; Breda, finally, was emotional about Irishness in passionately rejecting aspects of it and embracing others: both reactions indicate its emotional effect.

I have stressed that there is considerable individual variation in these women's notions of Irishness. However, common categories also emerged which were reckoned to divide the Irish. The North/Republic divide was fundamental, either in the women's explicit statements, or implicitly, with

North or Republic seen as 'other'. Rural/urban division is also significant, mentioned by all four of the women, and more general regional differences were presented by Caroline and also by Elizabeth, who divided Northern Ireland into desirable areas to live and non-desirable: this related to religion and politics, the most obvious dividers in the Irish identity. Sexuality, finally, is seen by Breda and, to a lesser extent, Caroline, as bisecting the Irish community. While the perception of these divisions was shared, they in fact affected individuals in different ways. For Breda, the sexuality split between straight and gay Irish led to polarised views of Irishness as part strongly fulfilling and part strongly repellent. Caroline, not as personally affected by this or other divisions, was more able to see Irishness as unified than any of the other women.

Regarding politics, clearly the political views held by the women vary according to upbringing, but are also open to change: both Elizabeth and Caroline have changed attitudes since coming to London. The importance attached to politics, either Irish or British, also varies, from Elizabeth who studies Politics A Level in an attempt to broaden her knowledge, to Alison, who rejects politics, particularly Northern Irish politics; this relates to the potentially damaging effects further polarisation between Catholics and Protestants could have on her relationship with Paul. Political upbringing is thus rejected by Alison, but contrast Caroline's insistence that one must have a position on Northern Ireland. Sexual politics are espoused by Breda, most strongly, and also by Caroline. British politics are seen as very different by all, though viewed with some interest. Politics in the Republic tend to be seen as unstimulating by all the women. Breda was most motivated here, opposing the Dublin government's attitude to its migrants.

Regarding religion, there is a general sense among my wider group that the Irish are more spiritual than the English. Of these four, the two Northern Irish women practise their religion (one Protestantism, the other Catholicism), Elizabeth talking about it more than Alison; the two women from the Republic strongly criticise the Catholic Church and its patriarchal repressiveness. In the Republic, the Church governs legislation to a greater extent than in the North, but it is also worth noting that the two women from the Republic have the strongest feminist views of the four. Perhaps these developed as a reaction to the Church, or perhaps the reaction to the Church followed feminism. The two do, however, consider themselves as spiritual people.

On the question, finally, of whether being Irish implies being Catholic, Elizabeth accepts this, though she calls herself Irish and is Protestant; Caroline accepted this but changed her mind over time; Alison rejects the whole question of religious differentiation; and Breda was concerned rather to divorce Catholicism from the Irish identity.

Gender

As with ethnicity, the meaning of gender to these women varies considerably, from femininity, Elizabeth's emphasis, to feminism, Breda's viewpoint. Caroline would fall somewhere in between, and Alison emphasised neither. Being a woman was to Alison a private matter, but was expressed as important, in different ways, by the other three. Male and female characteristics were discussed by Caroline and Breda. Elizabeth also felt there was a difference, but talked in terms of women wearing skirts rather than deeper oppositions. Although not keen to discuss gender or its implications, Alison's actions demonstrated an acceptance of traditional roles within her marriage, as she cooked and cleaned for her husband. This was also expressed in her interaction with Paul during the interview, as she tended to submerge her own identity in favour of listening to or talking about him.

Regarding priority of relationships or career, Elizabeth and Alison viewed relationships as more important, and Breda and Caroline talked much more of their careers. Breda and Caroline had more feminist views, but I would also argue that personal experience of family influences attitudes on this matter. Elizabeth and Alison's experiences of family were positive and loving, whereas Breda and Caroline had much more negative experiences. Positive experiences may have led to a desire to replicate this and seek fulfilment within a relationship and family of one's own, whereas negative experiences encourage one to seek fulfilment elsewhere. While Elizabeth prioritised relationships, her involvements were few. This was something she regretted, however. Breda and Caroline were much more private about their relationships, so it should also be noted that they may have been important, but perhaps too difficult to talk about. Sexuality was mostly talked about by Breda and conflicted with her Irishness in that she felt alienated from heterosexual Irish.

On the question of choosing an Irish or non-Irish partner, Caroline preferred Irish; Elizabeth, Northern Irish, though her only relationship known to me was with an English man; Breda stated no preference, though I heard of one relationship with an Irish woman; and Alison was married to a Northern Irish man. Preferences thus seem to be for Irish or Northern Irish partners. The division between North and South is clear here.

The question of where to live was important for all of the women. For Breda, it was the search for a pleasant home environment in London; for the other three, it involved potentially or actually moving out of London. The concern with the domestic environment was thus significant not just for the women with more traditional values, but for all.

To sum up on the importance of both issues for these women, for Breda and Caroline, gender and ethnicity were both strongly important, though Caroline talked more about Irishness and Breda more about gender issues. For Alison and Elizabeth, these were both less important in the abstract. Elizabeth was, however, more inclined to talk about them than Alison, whose disinterest was more extreme. Being Northern Irish was important for Elizabeth, I feel, but she talked about it more in response to my interest than I feel the other two did. Alison did insist that she was Northern Irish, not Irish, so ethnic identification did have some meaning for her. However,

Elizabeth and Alison placed family and relationships, more concrete issues, further up their agendas.

It is clear that religious, political and regional background affect the opinions and choices of these women. It is also clear that they may manipulate and select from these backgrounds, as well as reject aspects of them. This is most evident in the Northern Irish women's attitudes to their ethnicity, but the variability of the women with regard to both gender and ethnicity and their opinions and actions relating to these, demonstrate that very different things have been selected from these discourses by each woman. Background is influenced by personal experiences, encounters and self-development, and London offers wider opportunity for challenge, with a broader range of cultures and values on display than in Ireland. As personal experience is so vital in framing sense of self, it is hardly surprising that I have encountered such variability. My portraiture does justice, I hope, to the richness of this diversity, while attempting to link it to structural factors.

Notes

1. A quotation from 'Alison', one of the four women in this chapter; all names have been changed to protect confidentiality.
2. Action Group for Irish Youth and TIDE Joint report, *Irish Emigration: a Programme for Action*, Adept Press, 1988.
3. M. Lennon, M. McAdam and J. O'Brien, *Across the Water: Irish Women's Lives in Britain*, Virago Press, 1988, p. 21.
4. See B. Walter, *Gender and Irish Migration to Britain*, Geography Working Paper No. 4, 1989, pp. 3–13. Moore suggests, however, that the problem is less one of invisibility and more one of misrepresentation: H. Moore, *Feminism and Anthropology*, Basil Blackwell, Oxford, 1991, p. 1.
5. Lennon, McAdam and O'Brien, *Across the Water*, 1988, p. 27.
6. Only one woman describes herself as working class and her education, to postgraduate level, challenges this definition.
7. It is largely from the tape recordings that my quotations derive, though not exclusively, as I took notes after informal meetings.
8. K. Plummer, *Documents of Life: an Introduction to the Problems and Literature of a Humanistic Method*, George Allen & Unwin, London, 1983, pp. 103–4.
9. Bertaux distinguishes between the life story, or what an informant says about her life, and the life history, where corroborating evidence is provided of the veracity of the account: D. Bertaux, ed., *Biography and Society: the Life History Approach in the Social Sciences*, Sage Publications Ltd., London, 1981, pp. 7–9. NB, I did not approach my informants specifically to obtain life stories, but through more general participant observation, in which this kind of information played a part.
10. On reading this chapter, one of the 4 women, Caroline, remarked that our meetings had involved 'a lot of time listening to each other, giving support, going out a bit etc.'. This seems to me to be a reasonable definition of friendship and illustrates how some of these relationships went beyond a researcher-informant level of interaction.
11. Suzanne J. Kessler and Wendy McKenna, *Gender: an ethnomethodological approach*,

University of Chicago Press, Chicago, 1978, p. 8, quoted in A. Brittan, *Masculinity and Power*, Basil Blackwell Press, 1989, p. 20.

12. L. Van Vucht Tijssen, 'Women between Modernity and Postmodernity', in B.S. Turner, ed., *Theories of Modernity and Postmodernity*, Sage Publications, 1990, p. 161.
13. H. Moore, *Feminism and Anthropology*, 1991, p. 7.
14. E. Goffman, *Presentation of Self in Everyday Life*, 1956.
15. F. Barth, ed., *Ethnic Groups and Boundaries: the Social Organisation of Culture Differences*, George Allen & Unwin, London, 1969, Introduction.
16. R. Cohen, 'Ethnicity: problem and focus in anthropology', *Annual Review of Anthropology*, 7, p. 379.
17. See also A. Cohen, who suggests that ethnic symbols develop from subjective and individual to objective and collective: A. Cohen ed., *Urban Ethnicity*, Tavistock Publications, London, 1974, Introduction.
18. Even if I am lied to, the stories will still contain the ideals by which informants live their lives. See I. Bertaux-Wiame, 'The life history approach to the study of internal migration', in D. Bertaux, ed., *Biography and Society*, 1981, pp. 256–62, for a discussion of how the form in which stories are told can reveal such ideals.
19. See L. Van Vucht Tijssen, 'Women between Modernity and Postmodernity', p. 148, for treatment of this topic.
20. Van Vucht Tijssen, 'Women between Modernity and Postmodernity', p. 162.
21. J. Brown, *The Un-Melting Pot: an English Town and its Immigrants*, Macmillan Press, London, 1970.
22. On reading over this chapter, Elizabeth told me she felt that she had been much more honest and open than the other women and that it felt as if 'we were all playing a game but I was playing it from different rules'. Of course my interaction with the women varied, as did their openness. This, it seems to me, is part of the data.
23. All ages are correct at the time of writing.
24. See Goffman, *Presentation of Self in Everyday Life*, 1956, and L. Holy and M. Stuchlik, *Actions, Norms and Representations: Foundations of Anthropological Inquiry*, Cambridge University Press, 1983, for a discussion of these issues.
25. N. Glazer and D.P. Moynihan, *Ethnicity: Theory and Experience*, Harvard University Press, 1975.
26. Protestants who attend state schools in Northern Ireland are not given the option of studying Irish language; in Catholic schools, it is obligatory. For a Protestant to learn the Irish language would thus require a special effort.
27. When Protestants celebrate the anniversary of the 1690 Battle of the Boyne with bands and Orange Order parades.
28. Her grandfather was Scottish, and her sister moved to live in Scotland, which may be why she considered this as an option.
29. Interestingly, she said she would vote in Britain rather than by postal vote in Northern Ireland as she was 'more established' here than in the 1987 election, when she voted Official Unionist in Northern Ireland.
30. She dissociated herself from the Democratic Unionist aspect of this identity, but not from the rest.
31. On reading this, Elizabeth agreed with Caroline's view of the importance of the sea, saying she had herself 'an innate love of the sea' and that it was 'in my blood'.
32. In responding to this chapter, Caroline denied expecting this. However, as my memory of her stating it is very clear, I retain it, while also noting her subsequent rejection of it. Clearly it would not stand as a general, continuing view.

33. In her written response to this chapter, Caroline noted that she meant people in the Republic were not interested in 'different political systems — communism, socialism, labour, conservative etc'.
34. A view Elizabeth agreed with.
35. Class differentiation does exist in Ireland but my impression from my own upbringing concords with statements made by my informants, that there is more contact between working and middle classes in Ireland than there is among the English or even among the Irish in England.
36. Elizabeth echoed this.
37. See I. Bertaux-Wiame, in D. Bertaux, *Biography and Society*, pp. 256–61, for treatment of the same issues.
38. They have since moved to America, but plan to stay for a limited period of time, then return to Ireland.
39. Passing as English did not appear to be an option for any of my informants, though is more widely reported for migrants of the 1940s–1950s.

Index

The reader's attention is drawn to the indexer's note on page 222 of *Patterns of Migration* Volume 1 of *The Irish World Wide*.

THE REVEREND ARTHUR BROWNE
From the portrait by Copley

(*See page* 82)

Little Pilgrimages

The Romance of
Old New England
Churches

By
Mary C. Crawford

Author of
"The Romance of Old New England
Rooftrees," etc.

Illustrated

Boston
L. C. Page & Company
Mdcccciiii

1904

Copyright, 1903
by
L. C. Page & Company
(Incorporated)

❧

All rights reserved

❧

Published August, 1903

Colonial Press
Electrotyped and Printed by C. H. Simonds & Co.
Boston, Mass., U. S. A.

TO THE
Reverend Philo Woodruff Sprague

AND

Harriett Appleton,

HIS WIFE,

WHO — THE ONE AS INSPIRING PREACHER,

THE OTHER AS SYMPATHETIC COMRADE —

HAVE HELPED ME UNSPEAKABLY,

THIS BOOK IS GRATEFULLY

INSCRIBED

Spires whose silent fingers point to Heaven.
— Wordsworth.

Respect for sacred things and sacred places is inseparable from good breeding. — Washington Irving.

If keeping holy the seventh day were only a human institution, it would be the best method that could have been thought of for the polishing and civilizing of mankind. Sunday clears away the rust of the whole week. — Addison.

Of right and wrong he taught
Truths as refined as ever Athens heard ;
And (strange to tell !) he practised what he preached.
— John Armstrong.

Puritanism, believing itself quick with the seed of religious liberty, laid, without knowing it, the egg of democracy. — Lowell.

CONTENTS

LIST OF ILLUSTRATIONS

LIST OF ILLUSTRATIONS

LIST OF ILLUSTRATIONS

FOREWORD

*T*HIS little volume does not offer a history of the old churches in New England. Interesting and valuable as such a work would prove, far be it from me to attempt to write it. Nor does it seek to present an account of the noble and enduring influence of that splendid body of New England clergy who, before and during the Revolutionary War, rendered such signal service to American freedom. Another and more gifted pen would be needed adequately to record their glorious deeds. The present work is much less ambitious; it merely aims to give the story side of those old meeting-houses and ministers whose names and aspects are more or less familiar to the general reader. If ministers' sons and daughters also have a place here it is because they were bound to be in such a work. And if once or twice space is given to churches and preachers who cannot lay claim to even the one hundred and fifty years of life which passes in this country for antiquity, it is because they seemed to me really to belong in the narrative.

My hope is that the book, while it reiterates the well-known fact that early New England sheltered under its humble parsonage roofs many of the greatest men and women our country has produced, may make clear as well the truth that these parsons were not prigs. It will abundantly have attained its purpose if it shows that colour and adventure, pure passion

and sweet, true love may as often be found
in the life story of the Christian minister
as in that of the dashing hero of swash-
buckling romance.

It but remains to acknowledge with
gratitude the help of those many kind
friends from far and near who have aided
in the preparation of the manuscript, and
especially to thank Messrs. Houghton,
Mifflin & Company, by permission of, and
special arrangement with, whom the selec-
tions from the letters of John and Abigail
Adams are used. Also I have to thank the
Reverend A. V. G. Allen, who kindly
granted the privilege of here incorporating
a generous portion of the correspondence
first published in his " Life and Letters
of Phillips Brooks."

I might add, in explanation of the
change of base which readers of " The
Romance of Old New England Rooftrees "

may observe in the chapter, " The Lost Prince at Longmeadow," that another careful examination of *all* the evidence has led me to change the opinion ventured in the first book concerning the validity of the Reverend Eleazer Williams's claims to the throne of France.　　　　M. C. C.

Charlestown, Massachusetts, 1903.

x

THE
ROMANCE OF OLD NEW
ENGLAND CHURCHES

———•———

A PRE - REVOLUTIONARY
BELLE

" This humble stone,
In memory of
Elizabeth Whitman,
Is inscribed by her weeping friends, to whom she
Endeared herself
By uncommon tenderness and affection.
Endowed with superior acquirements, she was
Still more distinguished
By humility and benevolence.
Let candour throw a veil over her frailties, for
Great was her charity to others.

11

She sustained the last painful scene
Far from every friend,
And exhibited an example of calm resignation.
Her departure was on the 25th of July, 1788,
In the 37th year of her age.
The tears of strangers watered her grave."

ONE could scarcely find a romance more inextricably interwoven with the lives of eighteenth-century New England ministers than that of the woman to whom this stone still stands (though sadly worn) in the old burying-ground at Peabody, near Salem. A mystery for many years, the inscription — and the traditions to which it gave rise — is believed by many to have furnished Hawthorne with the inspiration for the central character in his "Scarlet Letter." Only within the last dozen or so years have we come to know quite certainly that the heroine of the suggestive tablet was the daughter of a well-known Hartford clergyman, and a

12

descendant through her mother from that Stanley renowned as the friend of William Shakespeare.

In a novel called " The Coquette," first published in 1800, by Mrs. Hannah Foster, wife of a minister at Brighton, Massachusetts, the facts of Elizabeth Whitman's curiously checkered career were so entertainingly distorted, and the character of the heroine, called " Eliza Wharton " throughout the book, so maliciously misrepresented, that the novel ran through endless editions, and was in its day second only in interest to the well-known stories of " Clarissa Harlowe " and " Charlotte Temple." In style the three books are indeed very similar, and the character of the seducer of " Eliza Wharton " is undoubtedly modelled upon that of the Lovelace in Richardson's novel. But the book, as has been said, is notoriously careless of the

13

facts in Elizabeth Whitman's life, and its author, though a kinswoman of the girl whose sad story she essays to tell, has put the worst possible construction upon every incident in a career which, full to the brim as it is of mystery, one yet cannot examine and believe sinful.

On her mother's side, as already stated, Elizabeth Whitman was akin to Thomas Stanley, who, when he came to Hartford in 1636, brought with him some curious old Stanley silver and the tradition that he was a descendant of Shakespeare's friend. This Stanley rose to be one of the governor's assistants. And it was his great-grandson, Nathaniel Stanley, treasurer of the Colony of Connecticut, who, in 1750, gave his daughter Abigail in marriage at Hartford to the Reverend Elnathan Whitman, pastor of the Second Church, and one of the fellows of the Cor-

14

THE PRESENT HOME OF THE SECOND CHURCH IN
HARTFORD (1825)

poration of Yale College, — a man distinguished for scholarly traits, the love of rare manuscripts and forgotten books, and whose library at the time of its destruction in 1831 had been for years the envy of our large universities.

Thus Elizabeth Whitman, inheriting all the grace and culture of the Stanley blood, was born into the best society of her State and time. Her mother was a woman of rare intelligence, and of great beauty, her father a man of prominent and significant character; and his family was not of mean origin, for Trumbull, the poet, Wadsworth, the wealthy benefactor of Hartford, Jonathan Edwards, the distinguished theologian, and Joseph Buckminster, afterward renowned as a Puritan preacher of parts, were all his kin.

Very early Elizabeth, being beautiful, lively, and intelligent, attracted to her side

15

the most distinguished youths of the college and the State. She attended the Hartford Dancing Assembly — whose routs began at 6 P. M. — and was a belle in every sense of the word. Her first accepted lover was the Reverend Joseph Howe, of Church Green in Boston, a young man of rare talents, who had been driven from his charge in Massachusetts by the outbreak of the Revolution, and had taken refuge with a party of friends at Norwich, Connecticut. Here his health failed, and as the state of Boston made it impossible for him to return, Elizabeth's father invited him to Hartford. At once he proceeded to fall in love with the beautiful daughter of the house. The match seems, however, to have been made more by the parents of the young lady than by her own wish. But when her lover's never vigorous health gave way under the rigours of a

16

New England winter, she nursed him with tenderness, and for some time after his death mourned him sincerely.

A far more serious grief to her was her father's death, which soon followed, and which entailed for the three daughters and the one young son of the house considerable deprivation on account of poverty. The family should have been wealthy, but William Stanley, Mrs. Whitman's brother, had been persuaded to leave his large property to the Second Church, and so it came to pass that the wife and children of the old minister were seriously embarrassed by the loss of their father's salary.

It was perhaps for this reason that Elizabeth was again urged to marry, and soon became the betrothed of her cousin, the Reverend Joseph Buckminster, whose name and memory is an illuminated page

17

in the history of New England Congrega-
tionalism. Young Buckminster was born at
Rutland, Massachusetts, in 1751. He was
the son of a Puritan clergyman and of a
Puritan clergyman's daughter. Even in
youth the tenets of Calvinism seemed to
him of all-absorbing interest, and while
an undergraduate at Yale College, — a
stage of life usually given to lighter matters, — he experienced "conversion" of
the most thoroughgoing and soul-trying
type.

Certainly a man of this mould could
have had little in his nature to attract the
love of so high-strung and ardent a maiden
as Elizabeth Whitman. But she met him
soon after her father's death, while on a
visit to the family of the president of Yale
College, and he pleaded his suit with all
the earnestness of a deeply sincere nature.
The result was that she made up her mind

18

to accept his hand in spite of many friends
who counselled her against the step. Buckminster was a teacher at Yale at this time,
— he had been graduated in 1770, — and
the companion, though he could scarcely
have been the friend, of Aaron Burr and
Pierrepont Edwards, both of whom were
connections of the fair Elizabeth. Possibly it was the very goodness of Buckminster, strongly contrasted as it must
have been with the lives of these others,
that drew from the minister's daughter
that sweet affection she undoubtedly gave
him.

Unfortunately, however, there was
deeply seated in this man's nature a terrible tendency to hypochondria, from
which any girl of healthful and cheerful
disposition might well shrink. That Elizabeth Whitman was repelled by this trait in
her lover there is small doubt. Moreover,

she must have felt that marriage with him would bind her to a narrow field of duty and demand of her a degree of self-renunciation quite fatal to her best development. In those days marriage with a strong man from whom one differed in one's views of things always meant that the wife's personality must perish.

It was while discussing the pros and cons of this alliance with Pierrepont Edwards, her cousin, — a man whose personal character was, however, as far as possible removed from that of his distinguished father, Jonathan Edwards, the theologian, — that Mr. Buckminster one summer's afternoon surprised Elizabeth in the arbour of the house at New Haven where she was staying as guest, and dealt her an unmanly blow. The tutor had come for his final answer, and finding his fiancée in confidential intercourse with a man whom he hated and distrusted, he retreated in a fit of terrible anger but without speaking a single word.

After waiting a reasonable time Elizabeth wrote to Mr. Buckminster, who seems in the meantime to have accepted a call to Portsmouth, N. H., to tell him the subject of her conversation with her cousin on that fateful day. And she added that she had intended her answer to his suit to be "Yes." The minister's reply was the announcement of his approaching marriage to the daughter of the Reverend Mr. Stevens, of Kittery, near Portsmouth. Naturally Elizabeth said no more.

Buckminster was in 1779 ordained clergyman of the North Church in the old town by the sea. There, three years later, he brought home his wife, and May 26, 1784, his first son — a brilliant lad even in his early youth — was born. Mrs.

21

Buckminster appears to have been a lady of very elegant and cultivated mind, but she died when her child was very young and so disappears from view.

No such peaceful end was, however, to crown Elizabeth Whitman's life. On the contrary, this flower of our Revolutionary New England was to be ruthlessly trampled upon by a fate which has visited few other women so harshly. Not that the loss of her lovers was a blow from which her buoyant nature could not recover. Her letters at this period of her life are those of a light-hearted, fanciful, and altogether healthful woman. One dated May 10, 1779, — the year of Buckminster's heartless desertion, and addressed to a young poet friend, — reads as follows: "I have spent the evening in company before walking half a mile. It is now one o'clock. Judge, then, if I can pretend to find fault with you at present? No, really: I am too tired and too good-humoured; but for your encouragement I will tell you that I have a sheet full of hints and sketches in that way which I have taken down when I felt most disposed to be severe, and I intend to work them into a sort of satire at the first opportunity." [She herself wrote good verse.] "I heard last night from Mr. Dwight that he will soon take a journey to camp. He will certainly either go or return by way of New Haven, so you will be able to consult him yourself. I fervently wish you may, for I know of no person so capable of advising you. I shall depend upon seeing you before you set out on your tour." The "Mr. Dwight" so pleasantly referred to here was the honoured president of Yale, busy about this time in altering Watts's Hymns with Joel Barlow, the

23

good friend to whom this letter is addressed.

This young man was the husband of Ruth Baldwin, with whom Elizabeth had recently been on a visit. The only authentic Elizabeth Whitman letters in existence are those merely friendly ones addressed to the Barlows during this period of our heroine's life, between her twenty-ninth and thirty-second year. She had first met Joel Barlow and Ruth Baldwin, to whom the poet was even then engaged to be married, at a Christmas party in New Haven in 1778. At a game of forfeits, Joel and Elizabeth were ordered to play the part of man and wife for the whole evening. This game they carried out with great spirit, adopting the nine Muses as their children. Melpomene, Barlow's favourite because he was already well-known as a poet, is caricatured in the correspondence

24

which followed between the two friends as
" Quammeny," and his wife is constantly
called in the letters his " second wife," a
playful allusion on Elizabeth Whitman's
part to the Christmas party game.

Because of his poverty young Barlow
had not been welcomed as a suitor by his
bride's family, and the result of this was
that he married Miss Baldwin while she
was away upon a visit, an offence which
remained for many years unforgiven by
the Baldwins. In this unpleasantness the
pair had the keenest sympathy and interest
of Elizabeth Whitman, and at the very
time when she was supposed to be broken-
heartedly lamenting Buckminster's desertion, she was really interesting herself
in the crockery and furniture of the Barlow establishment. The letters that tell
us this were discovered long after both
Barlow and Elizabeth had passed away,

tied together in a packet labelled "Bessie Whitman's Letters" in the handwriting of her correspondent, by Mrs. Caroline H. Dall, a distant cousin of Elizabeth Whitman, and the one writer who has interested herself in defending the fair fame of the beautiful girl.[1]

The Barlows never had any children, but Mrs. Barlow ultimately adopted as her own her stepsister, twenty years younger than herself, — an exquisite creature who enjoyed the distinction of being sought in marriage by General Lafayette.

It is at the next stage of the story that the real tragedy of Elizabeth Whitman's life begins to dawn. She has now reached the age of thirty-six, and, so far as her friends and family know, she is still unmarried. Yet in the background of her

[1] See "The Romance of the Association," by Mrs. Dall.

life hovered an unknown man. That she had linked her fate to that of some one who hesitated to acknowledge her publicly is the only charitable solution of her story's mystery. Mrs. Dall believes that her life had been joined to that of a French officer — probably a man of rank — stationed at Newport, and that the records of the marriage, performed by a Catholic priest, perished long ago in fire. But of this Elizabeth's kindred and friends knew nothing. And the neighbours made unpleasant remarks. One visitor, her cousin, Jeremiah Wadsworth, was often seen about this time leaving her society at what was called " unseemly hours," and in May, 1788, she was reported to have changed at the bank a large quantity of foreign gold. To add to the murkiness of the situation her health faltered, and her spirits were often sadly depressed.

Then there came from Mrs. Henry Hill, of Boston, an invitation to visit her, which, in view of Elizabeth's debility and the comments of the gossips, was very eagerly accepted. So at midday in the spring of 1788 the still beautiful young woman left her home for what proved to be forever. But the stage-coach did not carry her to her friend's house, as her people believed it would. That she took this conveyance has always been known, but where she left it has remained a mystery. In a letter just received from Mrs. Dall I have, however, learned that Elizabeth Whitman's alighting-place was at Killingly, forty-seven miles east of her Hartford home. There she told her story to Mr. Howe, the clergyman of the place, — the brother of that Reverend Joseph Howe to whom she had once been engaged and whom she had tenderly nursed until death claimed him.

28

Both Mr. Howe and his wife were friends of Elizabeth's dead father, and they were very glad indeed to aid her in her sad predicament. She undoubtedly convinced them that it was necessary to keep her marriage secret. And so loyal were they to their promise then made to her that only at this late day, more than one hundred years afterward, does the fact of her visit come out, told to Mrs. Dall by their own granddaughter, and by Mrs. Dall — herself an old lady now — passed over to me. But Elizabeth could not stop at Killingly. She must hasten on to the sleepy little town of Danvers, which was to witness the tragic last act of her life. Apparently she had arranged to meet her husband at this obscure place.

We have long known that it was from Watertown that our heroine drove in a hired vehicle to Danvers. How she reached

29

Watertown was not so clear. But it is now divulged that Mr. and Mrs. Howe drove her in their own carriage so far on her way, a touching service indeed for these good Connecticut folk to render a forlorn woman who, save for death, had been their sister.

It was a bright June day in 1788 which brought to the old Bell Tavern in Danvers a sweet and gracious woman who registered as Mrs. Walker and said she would stay until her husband came. And then the weeks went by as Elizabeth Whitman waited. Meanwhile Mrs. Hill watched anxiously for a guest who did not come, and down in Hartford the poor widowed mother patiently endured the anguish of her child's disappearance and the scandal that people insisted on making out of it.

Gentle and graceful in all that she did, the stranger was soon the admired of all admirers in the little village. She would sit at the south window of her chamber for days at a time watching, ever watching, for some one who came not, whiling away the long hours of the languorous summer mornings with the guitar and her industrious needle. Some of that wondrous skill in sewing which Hawthorne makes one of the attributes of Hester Prynne, the lady of the Bell Tavern certainly possessed. And this skill in needlework, together with her pleasing ways, soon made her a favourite with the women of the town, who, though they were of the strict Puritanical type and faith, sympathized deeply with her as she posted and received letters from one she called her husband and fashioned dainty little garments with her clever needle. But she kept forever locked in her heart whatever tale she might have told.

Frequently she walked from her lodgings to the tranquil Peabody graveyard to muse and silently weep. And the weeks slipped into months. Then one day Elizabeth wrote with chalk the letters E. W. before the door of the inn, but these were erased by some children playing there during the afternoon. At dusk a soldierly-looking man rode by, studied the door, and, failing to note the erased chalk-marks, passed on. As he turned a distant corner, Elizabeth caught sight of him, and, crying, " I am undone," fainted.

A few days later she died of consumption, into which she had lapsed after the birth of a dead child. When asked on her death-bed if her friends might not be sent for, she replied that she should soon go to them. Privately, however, she added to one who waited on her that her death was wisely ordered and was the easiest

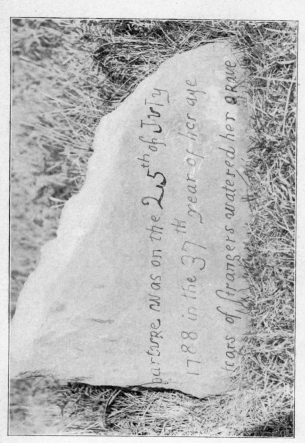

THE TABLET OVER THE GRAVE OF ELIZABETH WHITMAN

solution of many problems. She insisted that her wedding-ring be buried with her, and died expressing a living trust in God's love and mercy. It was only by a brief paragraph in the *Boston Chronicle* that her friends and family learned of her sad and obscure end.

Her funeral was the largest that had ever occurred in the town, the Danvers villagers turning out in great numbers for the ceremony. She was tenderly laid to rest in the beautiful burying-ground she had so often visited, and a few weeks after her death an unknown man erected over her grave a sandstone tablet bearing the inscription we have given. And year after year a mysterious lady and gentleman used to come regularly to Danvers, leave their horse at the tavern to be cared for, walk to the grave, stay there for awhile, return to the tavern to dine, and then go away as quietly and mysteriously as they had come. Every year at the same time they appeared, growing older and sadder each season till both were white-haired and bent. The villagers, though extremely curious about these sad pilgrims, never knew who they were, for they gave no name and no one thought of demanding one. Subsequently, however, it developed that they were Elizabeth's sister Abigail and that young brother of whom the dead woman had once written thus affectionately to Mr. Barlow:

"Do you know, I think my brother improves greatly under your auspices? Let me bespeak your kind attention to him. Form his taste, if you can, to those things you yourself admire, to books and study. Besides, the improving of these afford rational amusement to the mind. These are safe pleasures; but, oh, what deceitful

34

ones lurk in the world to catch the unwary! My poor boy will be particularly disposed to be led astray by these, unless his friends protect him. He is uncommonly influenced by the company he keeps." Surely no grown woman who would write in this noble strain of a young brother could herself have fallen into evil ways as do "the unwary." This "young brother" was known in his later years as an antiquarian, an habitué of the Hartford Athenæum. His sister's tragic death had sobered his gay spirits, for it dealt him a blow from which he could never recover. Abigail lived to extreme old age and never married.

All that is really known of Elizabeth Whitman's life has now been carefully told. But in the story, "Eliza Wharton; or, The Coquette," we have what has come to be regarded as her history. The book was published soon after the last act of the

tragedy it is supposed to rehearse had been
played out, and an utterly specious value
given to its disclosures by the fact that it
was written by the wife of Elizabeth's
cousin. In the book Elizabeth, or Eliza,
as we must now call her, is represented as
a provincial belle, weary of the restraints
of poverty and of the narrow parsonage
life to which she had been born. After
the death of her first lover, Mr. Howe, —
which is made to follow that of her father,
though it really preceded it, — she is sent
to New Haven in search of gaiety and di-
version. Here it is that she is made to
meet for the first time " Major Sanford."
He, the " villain " of the story, is readily
recognized as Elizabeth Whitman's cousin,
Pierrepont Edwards. What the scandal-
mongering public, which seized eagerly
upon countless editions of this crudely sensational novel, quite failed to realize as

they read the story, was that Elizabeth had known her cousin as a family man ever since he was nineteen, — some eighteen years. So any such deception as the book elaborates would have been quite impossible.

In the story the heroine's inquiries into "Sanford's" habits and character pique him into a desire to work her undoing. He therefore makes desperate love to her, and in the midst of his courtship marries another woman for money, and, when married, moves into Eliza's neighbourhood for the express purpose of insulting her with his attentions.

"The Coquette" version has it that Eliza ultimately fell victim to the passion of this cousin, and so places upon the jealousy of Buckminster the worst possible construction. After her fiancé's surrender of her, Eliza is — in the novel — plunged

into dejection and despair, and her letters
— in the novel — are made to show her,
at this time, full of terrible self-reproach.
At that very moment, however, she was in
reality cheerful and light-hearted, as we
have seen from the correspondence with
her friend Mr. Barlow.

As the day of her fatal departure draws
near, the novel represents her confessing
her guilt, confiding in her friend, and writing to her mother. But no confession
passed her lips, and no confidence, of which
we know, was ever given. Concerning her
departure, too, the book is maliciously un-
truthful, for it represents her as carried
away at night by her seducer, unknown to
those who loved her, when, as a matter of
fact, she went off in the regular stage-
coach at high noon with everybody's warm
approval.

This whole story might, indeed, have

been written by a Boccaccio without genius,
so sentimental, heated, and unsavoury is
its general tone. The letters from the villain to the heroine whom he is tempting
are modelled very closely upon those of
Lovelace, and Buckminster (called " Mr.
Boyer " in the book), the very last person
on earth to delight in sentimental talk and
to countenance the intrigues with which he
is associated, is drawn an overbearing as
well as an underbred prig.

Just here it is interesting to learn of
the fashion in which this so-called
" wronged lover " really received the book
that would have defended him. An old
lady, who was his parishioner in Portsmouth, is responsible for the statement that
the minister would never allow anybody to
blame Elizabeth Whitman in his presence.
" I can tell you, too," she said once to
Mrs. Dall, " what happened in this very

room. Just after the book was published,
Mr. Buckminster came to call on my
mother. She was not quite ready to receive him, and probably forgot that a fresh
copy of the novel, just arrived from Boston, lay upon the table.

" When she came down, she found the
doctor thrusting something under the coals
upon the hearth. As he turned round to
greet her with flaming eyes, she saw some
leather covers curling in the blaze.
' Madam,' said he, pointing to the spot,
' there lies your book. It ought never to
have been written, and it shall never be
read, — at least, not in my parish. Bid
the ladies take notice, wherever I find a
copy I shall treat it in the same way,' and
so saying, he stalked out of the room."

Elizabeth Whitman's effects, carefully
examined after her death, failed utterly
to throw any light upon the unknown hus-

band for whom she was supposed to be waiting in the old Bell Tavern. But this letter, written when she was near her end, gives us a hint of her distraught state of mind, in which, however, there was still womanly forgiveness. "Must I die alone? Shall I never see you more? I know that you will come, but you will come too late. This, I fear, is my last ability. Tears fall so fast I know not how to write. Why did you leave me in such distress? But I will not reproach you. All that was dear I forsook for you, but do not regret it. May God forgive in both what was amiss. When I go from here, I will leave you some way to find me. If I die, will you come and drop a tear over my grave?"

Some verses, written about the same time, conclude with this quatrain, her swan-song:

41

" Oh, thou, for whose dear sake I bear
A doom so dreadful, so severe,
May happy fates thy footsteps guide,
And o'er thy peaceful home preside."

Thus we leave the story of Elizabeth Whitman. Though many people have searched, none have been able to find — even in the course of a century during which hundreds of old attics have yielded up long-hidden secrets — any further papers bearing upon the facts of her strange fate. The identity of the unknown man still remains a haunting literary mystery. Many there are who say he was a nobleman, unwilling, after Elizabeth's death, to expose himself to bootless comment by stating the fact and manner of his clandestine marriage. For that there was a marriage all who have sympathetically explored the strange tale insist.

So to-day the lovers of Peabody plight

their troth over the grave of this beautiful woman and swear to be faithful unto death even as she was. And on the stone so strangely put up to her there remains legible only this single last line:

"The tears of strangers watered her grave."

THE WOOING OF ESTHER EDWARDS

SPECULATIONS as to the difference in history which might have resulted from a woman's acceptance of one lover instead of another are always of interest. Particularly is this true when the child of the woman in question turns out to be so curious, so fascinating, and so enigmatic a character as Aaron Burr.

Heredity certainly played strange tricks on itself in the history of the family from which Aaron Burr sprang. We have seen in the story of Elizabeth Whitman that Pierrepont Edwards, son of Jonathan Edwards, the theologian, and Sarah Pierrepont, the heavenly-minded one, was very far indeed from being a child of grace. And the moral lapses of Aaron Burr, born of a high-minded father and a singularly spiritual mother, are too well-known to need more than a passing mention here. The only conclusion to be reached, as one surveys the life of Hamilton's slayer, is that his sad and early bereavement (he was an orphan from childhood) left him so young without a parent's loving direction that one should always pity and never condemn him.

Burr's grandfather — Jonathan Edwards, renowned to this day as the first American author to achieve a European reputation as well as because he is a great theologian — offers to those interested in biography one of the most charming of subjects. It is a source of regret that there is not more to be known of the man

45

himself. The few things that we do know, however, are full of beauty and poetic charm. Born in East Windsor, Connecticut, just two hundred years ago (October 5, 1703), the only son of the pastor of the Congregational Church of that place, Jonathan entered Yale College when only thirteen years of age. After graduation he spent two years in his theological studies, and in 1722, when but nineteen years old, was licensed to preach. For a few months he presided over a small Presbyterian church in New York City, but things were not favourable in the New York of that day to the faith of a Jonathan Edwards, so he soon returned to New Haven to complete his studies.

Then there came into the man's life that affection which has caused him to be so often likened to Dante. For he gained the love of Sarah Pierrepont, of

46

THE REVEREND JONATHAN EDWARDS

whom, when she was a young girl of thirteen, he wrote this exquisite description: " They say that there is a young lady in New Haven who is beloved of that great Being who made and rules the world, and there are certain seasons in which this great Being, in some way or other invisible, comes to her and fills her mind with exceeding sweet delight, and that she hardly cares for anything except to meditate on Him; that she expects after awhile to be raised up out of the world and caught up into heaven; being assured that He loves her too well to let her remain at a distance from Him always. There she is to dwell with Him and be ravished with His love and delight forever. Therefore, if you present all the world before her, with the richest of its treasures, she cares not for it, and is unmindful of any pain or affliction. She has a strange sweetness

47

in her mind and singular purity in her affections; is most just and conscientious in all her conduct; and you could not persuade her to do anything wrong or sinful if you would give her all the world, lest she should offend this great Being. She is of a wonderful calmness and universal benevolence of mind; especially after this great God has manifested Himself to her mind. She will sometimes go about from place to place singing sweetly; and seems to be always full of joy and pleasure, and no one knows for what. She loves to be alone, walking in the fields and groves, and seems to have some one invisible always conversing with her."

Small wonder that this inspired bit has been compared to Dante's rhapsody on his first sight of Beatrice, — then also a young girl like Sarah Pierrepont: " Her dress on that day was a most noble colour, a subdued and goodly crimson, girdled and adorned in such sort as best suited with her very tender age. At that moment, I say most truly, that the spirit of life, which hath its dwelling in the secretest chamber of the heart, began to tremble so violently that the least pulses of my body shook therewith, and in trembling it said these words, 'Behold the deity, which is stronger than I, who coming to me will rule within me.'"

While under the spell of his holy love for "the young lady in New Haven," Jonathan Edwards was invited to become colleague pastor at Northampton, Massachusetts, with his grandfather, the Reverend Solomon Stoddard. And on the fifteenth of February, 1727, when he was a little more than twenty-three years of age, he took up his duty in that important Massachusetts town. The next spring he went back to

New Haven to be married to his lovely
Sarah, now a girl of seventeen, and as
pronounced in her beauty as in her spirituality.

The Northampton in which this young
couple now assumed an important social position stood at the time they came to the
town high among the settlements of the
State. Nearly one-half the area of the province of Massachusetts lay within the borders of the county of which it was the capital. Many office-holders and professional
men of local distinction were settled there,
wealth was being frugally gathered, culture
and refinement prevailed, and the nucleus
of that aristocracy which still survives
was being formed. Naturally, in a village
of this kind the institution of most importance was the church, — only *one,* it is
to be noted, and that the parish over which

the young and spiritually enthusiastic Jonathan Edwards had come to officiate.

" This place," said Edwards, in writing to a friend, " was preëminently, in the respect of conversions, a city set on a hill. People at a distance . . . have been ready to look upon Northampton as a kind of heaven upon earth." And what had been begun under Mr. Stoddard was continued during Mr. Edwards's pastorate, and was celebrated in his writings until the town became famous as the centre of that mighty religious phenomena known in history as the " Great Awakening."

In spite of its previous periodic attacks of religious fervour, the town needed, it was soon discovered, a clarion call back to the necessity of pure life and moral soundness. Edwards and his wife, " endowed with strange sweetness in her mind and singular purity in her affections," were indeed a providential people for this crisis, and they worked a veritable moral revolution in New England and affected a most significant change in the town. In the first revival after the new minister's coming, " upwards of fifty persons above forty years of age, ten above ninety, nearly thirty between ten and fourteen, and *one of four,* became the subjects of the renewing grace of God." Such large numbers of converts were duly received into the church that it numbered at one time about six hundred and twenty members, and included almost the entire adult population. These persons, " with other subjects of grace, in the county of Hampshire, near the banks of the river Connecticut, were turned from a formal, cold, and careless profession of Christianity to the lively exercise of every Christian grace, and the powerful practice of our holy religion,"

52

according to the documents of the time.
And this statement one quite readily accepts, for while Jonathan Edwards's theology had very often the dark and gloomy
colouring peculiar to his time, his preaching was marked by dignity, grace, patience, and a compassion truly Christlike.
Probably it was chiefly his manner, however, which made him what he is confessed
to have been, the greatest preacher of his
age. "His eyes," says one in writing of
him, "were seeing things of which he
talked, and not the people to whom he
spoke. He was calm and pale, he had the
form of an ascetic; rapt and serious in
look, it was his habit to lean upon the
pulpit with marvellous eyes alight, a face
illuminate from within, earnest, confident,
authoritative, with nothing in his vesture
or manner priestly except that his heart

was touched with the feeling of our infirmities."

In his earnest spiritual quest, Edwards
— again like Dante — was constantly
guided by the influence of the woman he
loved. The marriage with Sarah Pierrepont was in every sense an ideal one. As
one studies the life and writings of Edwards one sees evidence on every hand that
in the bewilderment of the " Great Awakening," the preacher depended greatly
on the character and testimony of his wife.
To him was not vouchsafed experience of
those wonderful visions of which others
boasted, and, according to his own statement, it was only in the spiritual exaltation of his wife that he found confirmation
of the truth. Thus after describing the
inner moods of the working of the divine
grace as she had known it, and giving
to the world her religious confessions, he

exclaims, " This could have been no other than the peace of God which passeth all understanding, — the joy of belief which though unspeakable is full of glory."

Of the beautiful family life of the Edwardses we catch several charming glimpses from the diary of the Reverend Joseph Emerson, of East Pepperell, Massachusetts. Ten children, a fair proportion of them girls, had come to bless the union of these two rarely idealistic spirits, and with one of these the Reverend Joseph Emerson fell desperately in love, when in the course of a return journey after Yale Commencement he stayed for a few days at Northampton. Under date of September 17, 1748, we find in Mr. Emerson's journal this, his first reference to the family of his beloved one: " In Wethersfield we met with Mr. Edwards, of Northampton, and concluded to go home with him the beginning of the next week by the leave of Providence. We stopped and dined at Hartford, and called at Windsor upon Mr. Edwards, father to Mr. Edwards of Northampton, where we were overpersuaded to tarry over the Sabbath.

"Sat. 18. Mr. Edwards of Northampton preached A. M. from 1 Tim. 6:19. I preached P. M. Very courteously treated here.

"Tues. 20. Arrived at Northampton before night.

"Wed. 21. Spent the day very pleasantly: the *most agreeable family I was ever acquainted with:* much of the presence of God here.

"Thurs. 22. We set out for home: Mr. Edwards was so kind as to accompany us over Connecticut River, and bring us on our way: we took our leave of him. He is certainly a great man.

56

"Sat. 24. Sat out on our journey: dined at Colonel Willard's at Lancaster; got home to Groton a little after sunset. I have had a very pleasant journey: have not met with any difficulty in travelling above three hundred miles. God's name be praised!

"Sat. Oct. 1. I wrote two letters in the forenoon, one to Mr. Edwards of Northampton, the other to his second daughter, a very desirable person to whom I purpose by Divine leave to make my addresses. May the Lord direct me in so important an affair!"

What answer Mr. Emerson received to his letters the diary does not tell, but one fancies that it was not altogether encouraging. Yet on the principle that faint heart ne'er won fair lady, we find the Pepperell minister soon setting out again for Northampton to plead in person his suit with the girl, then only fifteen years old, who had captivated his fancy. The diary reads:

"Mon. Nov. 7. Sat out some Time before Day on a Journey to Northampton to visit Mistress Esther Edwards to treat of Marriage: got to Worcester comfortably, tho' something stormy: lodged at Mr. Goodwin's.

"Tues. 8. Had a pleasant Day to ride in; got to Cold springs in the Evening: lodged at Mr. Billing's the Minister, where I was very comfortably entertained.

"Wed. 9. Got safe to Northampton: obtained the Liberty of the House: in the Evening heard Mr. Searle preach at an House in the Neighbourhood from, by Grace are ye saved.

"Thurs. 10. I spent chief of the Day with Mistress Esther, in whose Company

58

the more I am, the greater value I have for her.

"Frid. 11. The Young Lady being obliged to be from Home, I spent the Day in copying off something remarkable Mr. Edwards hath lately received from Scotland. Spent the Evening with Mistress Esther.

"Sat. 12. Spent part of the Day upon the business I came about.

"Mon. 14. I could not obtain from the Young Lady the Least Encouragement to come again: the chief Objection she makes is her Youth, which I hope will be removed in Time. I hope the disappointment will be sanctified to me and that the Lord will by his providence order it so that this shall be my Companion for Life. I think I have followed Providence not gone before it."

Yet this Reverend Joseph Emerson was not a lover to be despised. He himself came of a priestly family, and one of his line afterward made Concord as famous as Jonathan Edwards had made Northampton. Though but twenty-four at the time he went forth in the hope of bringing home Esther Edwards as his bride, he had already been to Louisburg as chaplain of Sir William Pepperell's expedition, and had preached for some time in the town he had caused to be named in honour of that doughty warrior. That his love for Esther Edwards, then a maiden of fifteen, had in it something of the exaltation to be observed in her father's love for her mother we cannot doubt. Certainly it was only after repeated rebuffs from the girl and strenuous struggles with himself that this country parson ceased to press his suit, and reluctantly gave up for all time whatever hope he may have cherished that Esther Edwards would tell him " yes."

OLD CHURCH AT PEPPERELL, DEDICATED MARCH
8, 1770, BY PARSON EMERSON

The entries in the diary continue for many months to dwell upon the desire of this godly youth's heart.

" Thurs. Nov. 17. I came home to my lodgings. . . . I was considerably melancholy under my Disappointment at Northampton; concluded notwithstanding, by Leave of Providence to make another trial in the Spring.

" Sat. 19. So discomposed I could not study. I could not have thought that what I have lately met with would have had this effect. The Lord hath put me in a very good school. I hope I shall profit by it.

" Sat. 20. Much more composed. I endeavoured to roll off my burden upon the Lord, and He sustained me. I preached all day from They that are whole need not a physician but they that are sick.

" Mon. Dec. 5. I wrote two letters to

61

Northampton, one to dear Mistress Esther Edwards, who I find ingrosseth too many of my Tho'ts, yet some glimmering of Hope supported my Spirits.

"Frid. 23. I was this day so pressed down under the weight of some peculiar Burdens both of a Temporal and Spiritual Nature, that I could not fix my mind to do anything at all in the forenoon. In the afternoon I attended a private Meeting at Mr. Samuel Fiske's, read a Sermon out of Dr. Watts.

"Sat. 24. Melancholy all day: it seems to be growing upon me. I read a little, but chief of the Day sat meditating on my Troubles. Evening my Burden somewhat lightened. Oh! that I could be thankful: for it almost unfits me for the Service of God or man!

"Sat. 25. Preached all Day from They

that be whole need not a physician, but they that be sick.

" Mon. 26. Went out to divert myself, and visited several of the Neighbours.

" Sat. Jan. 1, 1749. I preached all day from Commit thy way unto the Lord: trust also in him. An extreme cold day, very few people at meeting.

" Sat. 7. Studied all day. Being burdened so much this week, I could not get prepared for the Sabbath until in the Evening.

" Sat. 28. Very much out of order.

" Sabbath 29. Preached all Day from Yea, all who will live Godly in Christ Jesus shall suffer Persecution. Much indisposed all Day.

" Mon. 30. My illness seems to increase upon me.

" Tues. 31. Something better through Mercy: was able to do a little writing.

"Wed. Feb. 1. Something better: wrote two Letters to Northampton.

"Tues. 21. I read all the forenoon: afternoon wrote a Letter to Northampton to send to Mr. Isaac Parker who designs to set out for there tomorrow. Spent the Evening with the Committee who came up from Town to lay out the Common about our Meeting (house).

"Sat. 25. This day being the Anniversary of my Ordination I devoted to Fasting and Prayer. I was obliged to study some not being prepared for Tomorrow. I endeavoured to lay low before God for my many sins, and the many aggravations of 'em. Especially for the short Comings of the Year past. An awful breach of Vows and Promises. I solemnly renewed my Covenant and made Resolutions and Promises. I hoped in the strength of Christ that I would live better, that I

would watch more against sin, and especially against the sin which dost most
easily beset me: I pleaded for Strength to
perform all Duties of my General and Particular Calling. Oh Lord hear my
Prayers, accept my Humiliation, and give
me Strength to keep my Vows for Jesus'
sake. Amen and Amen.

" Sat. March 11. Read something, received a Letter from Mrs. Sarah Edwards
who entirely discourages me from taking a
Journey again there to visit her Sister
who is so near my Heart. I am disappointed: the Lord teach me to profit: may
I be resigned.

" Tues. 21. Very much out of order. I
have a constant faintness at my stomach,
more weak this Spring than usual.

" Wed. 22. Able to study some.

" Mon. 27. My weakness increases upon

me, so I am obliged to leave Pastoral Visits for a Time.

"Sabbath, April 2. I was obliged to preach old Sermons all Day.

"Mon. 3. Rode over to Lancaster. I find riding a service to me under my present Weakness."

And so with a capitalized Weakness that " still continues," ends this interesting old journal found in the Reverend Joseph Emerson's house long after his death, and by one of his descendants now loaned to me.

It is not to be supposed, however, that while this good youth was suffering thus severely from the pangs of disappointed love, things were altogether easy and happy in that family which occupied his thoughts. Mrs. Edwards's journal about this date betrays occasional apprehensions. For though the church at Northampton

PARSON EMERSON'S HOUSE, PEPPERELL, MASS.

was undoubtedly very proud of its gifted pastor and crowds still hung upon his lips, there was brewing just at this time one of those curious church dissensions to be condoned only after the lapse of so many years that one can see both sides of the controversy. Up to the year 1744 Mr. Edwards retained a firm hold upon the confidence and affections of his people. During that year was sown the seed that ripened into hostility and ultimately led to his dismissal.

He learned that a number of the younger members of his church had in their possession licentious books, and he felt that this was a case for discipline. So he prepared and preached a sermon against the sin of light reading, and, after the service, informing the church of what he knew, a committee was appointed to coöperate with the pastor in investigating the hidden sore.

The rub came when the extent of the evil
was ascertained, and it was found that the
sons and daughters of many of the most
respectable families in the place were im-
plicated. Naturally, those young people
whom Mr. Edwards would have dismissed
from the congregation of the righteous because of the lapse involved in reading the
questionable books, became, at this stage,
disaffected toward the pastor. And not
less naturally their parents sympathized
with them. Thus it was that the after
ministry of Mr. Edwards was attended
with but little success.

The occasion of rupture came, however,
when Mr. Edwards opposed the prevailing
custom of admitting to the communion
all baptized persons. His grandfather had
taught — and this example was widely followed in the vicinity of Northampton —
that the Lord's Supper was a channel of

converting grace. But this high sacramentarian view Edwards had distrusted from the beginning, and now after years of study he became firmly convinced that he must refuse the sacred elements to those who would not make a confession of religion. For several years, therefore, there was dissension in the church, and on June 22, 1750, an ecclesiastical council decided by a majority of one that the pastoral relation which had lasted twenty-three years must be severed. Jonathan Edwards was dismissed. Himself, his wife, and his ten children were suddenly deprived of the means of living, and that under circumstances that made it unlikely that he would be again able to practise his profession. Yet that Edwards's position was theologically sound there can be no doubt. Certainly, the practice of later years may be held to have vindicated him.

To the humble post of missionary to the Indians at Stockbridge, this, the greatest living preacher of his day, now cheerfully turned. He had been offered a church in Scotland, but declined the call, preferring to write out in the quiet of the woods the doctrinal works that besieged his brain. So poor was he at this time that he could with difficulty procure the paper necessary to the perpetuation of his thoughts, and parts of his famous "Treatise on the Will" were written on the backs of old letters and on the blank pages of pamphlets. His wife, still beautiful and still saintly, aided by his daughters, all of whom were abundantly gifted, eked out the family income by making lace and painting fans which were sent to Boston for sale.

Esther was at this time eighteen years of age, very lovely to look upon as well as highly talented. Plenty of young men besides the Reverend Joseph Emerson had already sought her hand in marriage, but it was not until two years after the family removed to Stockbridge that there came riding to the door of her humble home a lover who touched her heart. The man who sought her out in the hut on the edge of the wilderness was one of the most renowned and brilliant members of her father's profession. He stayed only three days — this Reverend Aaron Burr — but he made himself so agreeable to Esther Edwards during his visit that after his departure the maiden made no more lace and painted no more fans for the Boston ladies. Rather was she on love-letters and wedding-clothes intent.

This Aaron Burr was not one of those grim-looking persons whose portraits form the repelling frontispieces to the religious

71

books of the pre-Revolutionary period, but
a gentleman whose style and manner would
have graced a court. He had been born
at Fairfield, Connecticut, in 1716, and so
was thirty-seven when he first met the
woman of his choice. For years a schoolmaster and an author, as well as the pastor
of a church in Newark, New Jersey, he
had lately been appointed the first president of Princeton College. He is described
as a man small of stature, very handsome,
with clear, dark eyes of a soft lustre, —
quite unlike the piercing orbs of his son,
— a figure compactly formed but somewhat slender, and with the bearing of a
prince. The fascinating manner and lofty
style of Mr. Burr are frequently mentioned
in the letters of the period. From one of
these letters, indeed, we get this very interesting account of his courtship: " In
the latter part of May the president (of

72

Princeton College) took a journey into
New England, and during his absence he
made a visit of but three days to the Reverend Mr. Edwards's daughter at Stockbridge; in which short time, though he
had no acquaintance with her nor had ever
seen the lady these six years, I suppose he
accomplished his whole design; for it was
not above a fortnight after his return here
before he sent a young fellow (who came
out of college last fall) into New England
to conduct her and her mother down here.
They came to town on Saturday evening,
the twenty-seventh, and on the Monday
evening following, the nuptial ceremonies
were celebrated between Mr. Burr and the
young lady. As I have yet no manner of
acquaintance with her, I cannot describe to
you her qualifications and properties. However, they say she is a very valuable lady.
I think her a person of great beauty,

73

though I must say she is rather too young (being twenty-one years of age) for the president."

Two weeks later this cheerful gossip of a sophomore writes again on the engrossing subject: "I can't omit acquainting you that our president enjoys all the happiness the married state can afford. I am sure when he was in the condition of celibacy the pleasure of his life bore no comparison to that he now possesses. From the little acquaintance I have with his lady I think her a woman of very good sense, of a genteel and virtuous education, amiable in her person, of great affability and agreeableness in conversation, and a very excellent economist. These qualifications may help you to form some idea of the person who lives in the sincerest mutual affections with Mr. Burr."

When Aaron Burr, 2nd, was born (February 6, 1756), the assembly building at Princeton was so nearly completed that the College of New Jersey was able to add a local habitation to its well-earned name. To Princeton, therefore, the president and his family removed late in the year 1756, and it was from this place that Esther Burr wrote this significant description of Aaron, then thirteen months old: "Aaron is a little dirty, noisy boy, very different from Sally almost in everything. He begins to talk a little; is very sly and mischievous. He has more sprightliness than Sally, and most say he is handsome, but not so good tempered. He is very resolute, and requires a good governor to bring him to terms."

That very good governor, his father, who might have made such a difference in the life of this second Aaron Burr, was only a few months later taken out of the world

75

at the early age of forty-two. The labour
of establishing Princeton on a firm foundation had been too much for him, and
so it came about that Esther Burr was,
when scarcely twenty-five, left a widow
with two young children, one three and the
other less than two years old. Her heartbroken letters to her father written about
this time show very clearly how terribly
she suffered in her bereavement, and fore-
shadow her own early death. Scarcely
had Edwards been inaugurated president of the College of New Jersey to
succeed the lamented husband, when both
he and Mrs. Burr died of smallpox. In
the fall of the same year Jonathan Edwards's widow, who had gone to Philadelphia with the intention of conveying little
Aaron Burr and his sister Sarah to her
own home, there to bring them up in careful, godly fashion, was seized with a dread

disease and herself passed to the bourne from which no traveller returns. Thus within a period of thirteen months these children were of father, mother, and grand-parents all bereft. And there was left in the wide world absolutely no one whose chief concern it could be to see that they received no detriment.

A thing almost as beautiful as Jonathan Edwards's youthful rhapsody concerning his child-wife, was his death-bed message to her, — the one woman of his life. It was noticed by those attending him that he said but little. There were none of the raptures peculiar to the " saint of God," no allusions to his books, to the labours of his life, or to the fortunes of the Church. But he spoke to his daughter words thus recorded: " Give my kindest love to my dear wife, and tell her that the uncommon union which has so long subsisted between us has been of such a nature as I trust is spiritual, and therefore will continue forever."

A COLONIAL FRIAR LAURENCE

*A*NY one who should expect to find the life of a mission minister in colonial days altogether prosaic and barren of romance would be greatly astonished upon dipping into the history of the Reverend Arthur Browne, first rector of St. John's Church, Portsmouth, N. H. This parish, alive and prosperous to-day, has been in existence ever since 1732, when right on the present site the "English Society for Propagating the Gospel in Foreign Parts" started its first mission in Portsmouth. In Mr. Browne, "a man of real culture, unpretentious goodness, and eminent worth," was soon found

a leader well fitted for his task. Moreover, Mr. Browne was theologically able as
well as quite unusually democratic in his
views for one of his time and station.
Being born an Irishman and educated at
Trinity College, Dublin, was a good beginning in those days for colonial life in
an aristocratic American centre.

This Reverend Arthur Browne students
and lovers of romance will remember it
was who performed the marriage ceremony
between Governor Benning Wentworth and
Martha Hilton, the aged magistrate's
pretty housemaid. This union was sol-
emnized much against the good rector's
will, but he disliked the match because of
the disparity between the ages of the con-
tracting parties rather than because of the
difference in their rank. In the old record-
book, which visitors to the church may
still examine, the entry of the marriage

in Mr. Browne's own hand is distinguished by no flourish, but has a cramped square inch of room, just like that given to every other couple in a day when paper was scarce and high.

Longfellow has immortalized in his charming poem the tale of this interesting alliance. Young Martha Hilton, idling along the street, ragged and barefoot, was one day rebuked by her mistress of the Stavers' Inn, only to elicit from the maid a toss of the head and the reply that she would yet ride in her own chariot, surrounded by pomp and splendour.

Not very long after it began to look as if Martha's idle prophecy would indeed come true. For upon the death of Governor Wentworth's first wife the girl had gone as housekeeper to the beautiful mansion still standing at Little Harbour [1] and

[1] See "Romance of Old New England Rooftrees."

now occupied by Mr. Templeman Coolidge, who has recently been able by an artistic arrangement of antique furniture to introduce into the ancient interior something of the atmosphere of old-time splendour and luxury which characterized the place in the old days. The portrait of Strafford dictating to his secretary just before his execution, the rare Copley, the green damask-covered furniture, and the sedan-chair were then items sufficiently magnificent, it appears, to tempt Martha Hilton, young and beautiful, into marriage with a man almost old enough to be her grandfather.

This historic event occurred on the sixtieth anniversary of Governor Wentworth's birth. The dinner had been a superb one, the food and wine capital, and the Reverend Arthur Browne was, of course, among the guests, for in those days church

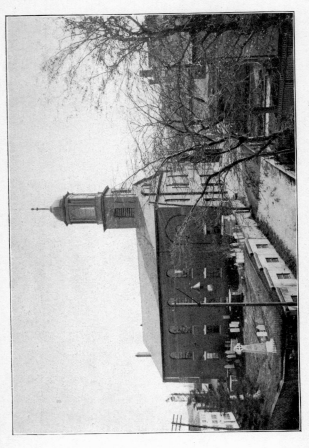

ST. JOHN'S CHURCH, PORTSMOUTH, N. H. (1807)

The first church, built on the same site, was erected in 1732

and state were never far apart, even on occasions when each heartily disapproved of the other.

The grand coup came at the ending of the feast. At a call from a servant, Martha Hilton, now grown to a lovely woman, slipped unnoticed into the room while her lord,

" . . . rising from his chair,
Played slightly with his ruffles, then looked down,
And said unto the Rev. Arthur Browne:
' This is my birthday ; it shall likewise be
My wedding-day ; and you shall marry me ! ' "

Nor did the hesitation of the rector avail, for the impatient governor proceeded to " command as chief magistrate," to the end that the priest could but —

" . . . read the service loud and clear :
' Dearly beloved, we are gathered here.'
And so on to the end.   At his command
On the fourth finger of her fair left hand
The Governor placed the ring ; and that was all :
Martha was Lady Wentworth of the Hall ! "

The date of this interesting event was March 15, 1760, and so it is recorded in the parish register, where the second marriage of the beautiful Martha is also duly set down. For Governor Wentworth did not live long after his romantic espousal, and with what appeared to many most unseemly haste Martha took unto herself a new husband, none other than Michael Wentworth, the governor's brother, then a retired officer in the British army. At this wedding also the Rev. Arthur Browne officiated.

The first rector of St. John's has indeed come down to us as the Friar Laurence of not a few romantic marriages, among them one striking in the extreme. Colonel Theodore Atkinson, Jr., son of that Colonel Theodore whose bread is still served to Portsmouth's poor (of which unique custom more anon) had married a cousin,

84

whose earlier affections had been placed on John Wentworth, Governor of New Hampshire when the Revolution broke out.

In his youth John Wentworth went to England, and it was during his absence that his sweetheart took young Atkinson as her husband. But two years previous to the date one finds set down as the death of Mr. Atkinson, the young Wentworth, now a man, returned. And, what was more, he came back clothed with the dignity of " Governor of the colony and Surveyor of the woods of North America ! "

The windows of this governor's house could be seen from those of Colonel Atkinson, and the gossips of history tell us that signals were often exchanged between the two old sweethearts. Whether or not this is true, Mrs. Atkinson had certainly not forgotten her former lover; for just ten days after her husband's funeral, at

which the venerable Arthur Browne had
duly and decorously officiated, his services
were again required by the lady, but this
time in a happier capacity. Mr. Charles
Brewster, a local historian of the town, has
in his " Rambles About Portsmouth " thus
described the funeral and the ensuing occasion upon which the Atkinson baked
meats did second service:

" The widow was arrayed for the colonel's burial service in the dark habiliments
of mourning, which we presume elicited
an immense shower of tears, as the fount
was soon exhausted. The next day the
mourner appears in her pew at church
as a widow. But that was the last Sabbath of the widow. On Monday morning
there was a new call for the services of
the milliner; the unbecoming black must
be laid aside, and brighter colours, as be-

comes a governor's bride, must take its place."

Rather curiously the bill for the bridegroom's apparel at that hasty wedding in Queen's Chapel (this building the predecessor on the same site of the present church) has come down to us. It follows:

	£	s.	d.
To pair of white silk stocking breeches	1	18	0
To white silk coat, unlined	2	14	0
To a white corded silk waistcoat . .	0	5	0
To a rich gold lace	0	12	0
To gold button and loop, hat recocked, etc.	0	2	0
To three yards queue ribbon	0	1	3

This union of two old sweethearts had unpleasant results for the Reverend Arthur Browne. It may be that he was excited beyond his wont by the despatch with which the late Mrs. Atkinson had consoled herself. Or perhaps he was soliloquizing on the strange turns that confront one in life, and wondering what might happen

next. Be that as it may, he wandered
absent-mindedly down the steps after the
wedding ceremony, and, falling, broke his
arm.

Before leaving the subject of the Atkin-
sons' connection with old St. John's,
mention should be made of the curious custom made possible in this church by the
elder Colonel Theodore's legacy for doling
out a portion of bread each Sunday to the
poor of the parish. Even in this twentieth
century, twelve loaves of bread, known as
" the dole," are thus given away every
Sunday after the morning service. This
bread is placed always on the baptismal
font, at the right of the chancel, and covered with " a fair linen napkin," from
which place the Reverend Henry E. Hovey,
present rector of St. John's, distributes it.

This font is probably the very oldest
object in the building. It is made of por-

phyritic marble of a dull brownish gray, finely veined. It was taken by Colonel John Mason from the French in 1758, at the capture of Senegal, and is undoubtedly African. The tradition is that it had been taken by the French from some heathen temple, and was very old at the time of its capture. Colonel Mason's daughters presented it to Queen's Chapel in 1761. Only in one other church of this country, and that an old parish in Virginia, is the ancient custom of doling out a portion of bread each Sunday to the poor of the parish still kept up. From the income of Colonel Atkinson's bequest about $6,000 has already been expended for this charity, and the original fund remains unimpaired.

One other story of romantic interest is connected with this old parish. This, as recorded by Mr. Brewster, runs:

" Nicholas Rousselet was a man of good

exterior, and when dressed in the official
consular costume, which he wore on public
days, a person to attract attention. Of
his first acquaintance with Miss Moffatt
we have no account, but tradition says that
it was in the Episcopal church during
service hour that the most important
crisis in the courtship transpired.

"Sitting with her in her father's pew,
Mr. Rousselet handed Miss Katherine the
Bible, in which he had marked in the first
verse of the second epistle of St. John,
the words, 'Unto the elect lady,' and the
fifth verse entire, 'And now I beseech thee,
lady, not as though I wrote a new com-
mandment unto thee, but that which we
had from the beginning, that we love one
another.' Miss Katherine, fully compre-
hending the appeal, turned down a leaf in
the first chapter of Ruth, beginning with
verse sixteen, 'Whither thou goest, I

will go; and where thou lodgest, I will lodge; thy people will be my people, and thy God, my God. Where thou diest, will I die, and there will I be buried; the Lord do so to me and more also, if aught but death part thee from me.'"

During Washington's famous visit to New Hampshire, in 1789, just after his inauguration, he went to service at the old Queen's Chapel Parish, now St. John's, and in his diary for that day, November 1, 1789, he wrote: "Attended by the President of the State (General Sullivan), Mr. Langdon, and the marshal, I went in the forenoon to the Episcopal Church under the incumbency of Mr. Ogden."

Tradition tells us that the President was arrayed on this occasion in an elegant complete suit of black velvet, with brilliant buckles. He occupied the old governor's pew, which was framed in red plush curtains, with a heavy wooden canopy over it, bearing the royal arms. In this pew were the two chairs given the parish by Queen Caroline, in whose honour the chapel had been named, and who had presented the parish at the same time with a Bible, prayer-books, and silver service for the communion-table, which last bears the royal arms and is in use at the present day. Trinity Church, New York, and Trinity in Boston were other parishes similarly remembered by gifts of communion silver at this time.

One of these Queen chairs was occupied that Sunday in November, 1789, by the very man who was most responsible for the overthrow of England's power in the New World. And when, less than a score of years afterward, the Chapel was burned (1806), and only one of the two original chairs in the governor's pew remained, tradition patriotically declared that the survivor was the one in which the Father of His Country sat.

In 1791 the parish was incorporated as St. John's, and in 1807 the new church took the same name. It is interesting to learn that Trinity Church, Boston, contributed $1,000 toward the erection of the new building in its need.

One of the unfortunate accidents of the fire of 1806 was the cracking of the historic bell which had begun its career by ringing out peals from the belfry of a French Catholic cathedral in Louisburg, but which had been brought to Portsmouth by doughty Colonel Pepperell, of Kittery, just across the river, after his triumphant capture of the defiant French fortress. But the bell was not beyond repair, and after being recast by Paul Revere, clearly rang forth its tidings of gaiety and gloom for many years. Finally, however, the constant clanging of the tongue so wore upon the metal that in the summer of 1896 the old relic had once again to be taken down and sent to Boston. This time the Blake Bell Company, successors to the Paul Revere Company that had done the same work ninety years before, cast the relic.

Inscribed on the enduring metal of the new-old bell are now these words from the pen of one of the Wentworths, with whose history the church must be forever linked:

> " From St. John's steeple
> I call the people
> On holy days
> To prayer and praise."

And on the rim, besides the motto:

" Vox ego sum vitæ, voco vos, orate, venite," are the words, " My mouth shall show forth Thy praise."

94

Any account of St. John's parish at Portsmouth which should neglect to state that the old Brattle organ, although not used in the church itself, is one of the corporation's most cherished possessions, would necessarily be incomplete. This " instrument " was purchased for the allied chapel in 1836 by Dr. Charles Burroughs, the first settled pastor of St. John's after the rebuilding of the church. It was originally the property of Mr. Thomas Brattle, one of the founders of the old Brattle Street Church in Boston. Mr. Brattle, who was an enthusiastic musician, imported the organ from London in 1713. At his death it was left by will to the Brattle Street Church — " given and devoted to the praise and glory of God in said church, if they shall accept thereof and within a year after my decease procure a sober person that can play skilfully thereon with a loud noise." The will further provided that the organ should go to King's Chapel if not accepted according to the first provision.

The non-compliance of the Brattle Street Church with the condition of the gift would, therefore, seem to have been the gain of King's Chapel, and after remaining unpacked in the tower for some eight months, it was used there until 1756. Then it was sold to St. Paul's Church, in Newburyport, where it was in constant use for eighty years. In 1836, as has been said, it was purchased by Doctor Burroughs for St. John's Chapel, and it is still used in this edifice on State Street, Portsmouth. The case is new, but the old wind-chest and most of the pipes of the original organ remain, and some of the notes are even now of unusual sweetness. According to the "Annals of King's

Chapel," this was "the first organ that ever pealed to the glory of God in this country."

Yet even more interesting than the old church and its chapel on State Street is the parish burying-ground of St. John's. Here rest the remains of the highest and noblest men and women in New Hampshire's colonial annals. For all who served in public position or exercised authority by appointment or permission of the Crown felt in duty bound in those early days to worship at an English church. And from there they were buried.

The Wentworths' tomb is in the centre of the yard, and here, linked with his governor's family in death as in life, repose to-day the remains of the Reverend Arthur Browne, who, in 1773, soon after the death of his aged wife, Mary, — whom

he had married in his native Drogheda
when he was only her father's curate, —
cheerfully laid down his happy, well-
spent life.

COURTSHIP ACCORDING TO
SAMUEL SEWALL

*T*HERE is almost no story of early
New England life that one cannot connect with the Old South
Meeting-House in Boston. The thing that
perplexes is which to choose. For the
building has been the scene of many great
historical crises, during which affairs have
been guided by some of the foremost men
in the annals of our country. Its site
is also famous as that of the home of
Governor John Winthrop, and it was here
that the governor died March 26, 1649.
Subsequent to this event the land was
owned by Madam Mary Norton (wife of

Reverend John Norton), who gave it in trust for ever " for the erecting of a house for their assembling themselves together publiquely to worship God."

The first meeting-house on the spot was a little cedar one, erected in 1669. This stood until 1729, when it was removed to make way for the present structure of brick, built by Joshua Blanchard and dedicated April 26, 1730. In the present building it was some years later (November 27, 1773) that a meeting of five thousand citizens decided that the odious tea should not land; and a few weeks afterward, on December 16th, seven thousand men sat in the church until after candle-light, and, when the messengers returned from Governor Hutchinson at Milton with the word that that official refused redress, a body of them raised the war-whoop at the door and, disguised as savages, rushed

100

THE OLD SOUTH CHURCH, BOSTON, MASS.

from the sacred edifice to Griffin's Wharf, there to celebrate the Great American Tea Party.

Yet it is not of the history of the Old South Meeting-House that I mean to write, for many people have done that interestingly and well. Rather do I choose to twine about the walls of this old building the clinging ivy of one man's life-story, the man selected being Judge Samuel Sewall, the noblest Roman of them all, who, in 1696, stood up manfully in his pew at this church while his confession of wrong in accepting "spectral evidence" during the witchcraft trials at Salem [1] was read aloud by one of the ministers.

It is always of Sewall that I think when I go to the Old South Church — though I know perfectly well that he made his confession in the old cedar meeting-house

[1] See "Romance of Old New England Rooftrees."

which preceded this brick structure — and
that he died just before the present building was dedicated. But I can fancy how
excited he must have grown in his old
age over the elaborate preparations necessary to the erection of so fine a church as
this so long ago as 1730, and I like to
think of the things he must have written
down somewhere about the undertaking, —
in accordance with his lifelong habit of
diary-keeping. Moreover, when all is said,
it was this very place that Sewall frequented and this very spot which he hallowed by that noble confession and by the
sternly kept fast days that followed. The
letters " S. S." on the stone at the north-
west corner may be held to do him fitting
reverence for these brave acts. Here, too,
it was that he was wont to come with his
blooming wife Hannah, the daughter of
Captain John Hull, Mintmaster, and here

that he used to listen with scarcely concealed pride to the sermons of "son
Joseph," of which his famous diary says
so much. It was likewise here that as an
old man he cast sheep's eyes at the women
"in the Fore Seat" eligible to gladden his
desolate hearth. And while walking home
from worship in this place it was that he
weighed, as we shall see, the comparative
merits of the ladies in question.

In Hawthorne's fascinating account of
Samuel Sewall's first courtship occurs this
important sentence: "The mintmaster was
especially pleased with his new son-in-law
because he had courted Miss Betsy out of
pure love and had said nothing at all
about her portion." It is good for us to
remember that passage when we read the
stories of Judge Sewall's later courtships.
For the fact that the first marriage was one
of purely romantic love — even if Sewall

did get his wife's weight in pine-tree shillings when he got her — rather takes the taint of the sordid from the later episodes. There is no need to tell at length the pretty story of Betsy Hull, for it has become a part of American tradition. John Hull, we all remember, had been made mintmaster of the colony and had grown very rich. Then one day a fine young man, Samuel Sewall by name, came courting his daughter, and, meeting the requirements of the situation as to character and education, was readily given the consent of the fair one's fond father. This father had replied to the ardent youth's suit, as a bluff parent of the period well enough might, " Take her, but you'll find her a heavy enough burden." " Yet when the wedding ceremony was over," according to the tale of the Great American Romancer, " the bridegroom was given a surprise which

made him rejoice indeed that the new
Mrs. Sewall was a plump young woman.

"Captain Hull whispered a word or
two to his men servants, who immediately
went out and soon returned, lugging in a
large pair of scales. They were such a
pair as wholesale merchants use for weigh-
ing bulky commodities; and quite a bulky
commodity was now to be weighed in them.

"'Daughter Betsy,' said the mintmaster, 'get into one side of these scales.'

"Miss Betsy — or Mrs. Sewall, as we
must now call her — did as she was bid
like a dutiful daughter without any question of the why and wherefore. But what
her father could mean unless to make her
husband pay for her by the pound (in
which case she would have been a dear
bargain), she had not the least idea.

"'And now,' said honest John Hull to
the servants, 'bring that box hither.'

105

" The box to which the mintmaster
pointed was a huge square iron-bound
oaken chest; . . . The servants tugged
with might and main, but could not lift
this enormous receptacle, and were finally
obliged to drag it across the floor. Captain Hull then took a key from his girdle,
unlocked the chest, and lifted its ponder-
ous lid. Behold! it was full to the brim
of bright pine-tree shillings fresh from
the mint; . . . Then the servants, at Captain Hull's command, heaped double hand-
fuls of shillings into one side of the scales
while Betsy remained in the other.

" ' There, son Sewall! ' cried the honest
mintmaster, when the weights balanced,
' take those shillings for my daughter's
portion. Use her kindly and thank Heaven
for her. It is not every wife that is worth
her weight in silver.' "

Well might Father Hull give to young

STAIRCASE IN COVENTRY HALL, YORK, ME.

Sewall this fortune in pine-tree silver. For the youth was one of the most promising in all the colony, and at Harvard, as in the life of Boston Town, had already made a bit of a name for himself. He came, too, of stock wont to succeed in life. His family were distinguished Coventry folk, and father and son of them had for generations been mayors of the quaint and beautiful city. Coventry Hall, still standing at York, Maine, is modelled after the old home in England. Samuel Sewall himself had been born in Bishopstoke, England, but had early come to this country with his parents, and had been brought up in Newbury. In due time he went to the college at Cambridge, and from that institution he received his bachelor's degree in 1667. In a letter written to his son when Joseph was a grown man Samuel Sewall speaks thus of his college com-

mencement: " In 1674 I took my second
degree, and Mrs. Hannah Hull, my dear
wife, your honoured mother, was invited
by Doctor Hoar and his lady (her kins-
folk) to be with them awhile at Cambridge. She saw me when I took my degree and set her affection on me, though
I knew nothing of it until after our marriage, which was February 28, 1675—76.
Governor Bradstreet married us."

How the youthful parson (for Samuel
Sewall had preached a little before his
marriage, though he entered public life
soon after that event) conducted his first
courtship we have no knowledge. Probably at this stage of his life he confided
to his beloved one rather than to his
diary his fervid emotions. There is indeed a notable lack of entries about the
time of the marriage, and it is only after
he has become a good and solicitous hus-

band that every detail of his and his wife's
life is put down in the quaint old pages
of this book, — which shows us better than
does any other document extant the real
social life of the time.

The births of the many little children
that came to the proud parents, the details
of the husband's wonderful trip abroad,
which occupied most of the year 1688, and
the circuit journeys for the discharge of
his judicial duties, are all constantly referred to in this volume. And there we
can follow, too, the differences in the light-
hearted bridegroom as the years went past
that changed him into the merciless perse-
cutor of the witches.

Then there came a time when child after
child born to Hannah and Samuel Sewall
died in convulsions. The diary abounds in
references to the illnesses of these little
sufferers (who, strangely enough, were one

after another called "Hullie" for the
good mintmaster grandfather), Judge
Sewall seeming to feel that the judgment of
Heaven was being visited upon his children
because he had sent innocent little ones
to death during the Salem trials. So in
January, 1696, he put up his "bill" in
the Old South Meeting-House, and stood
with bowed head while it was read. During the remainder of his life he spent one
day annually in fasting, meditation, and
prayer in remembrance of his sin.

After this the tide of his life turned
for awhile; on September 16, 1713, he had
the great joy of seeing his dear son Joseph,
a fine youth of twenty-five years, ordained
as the colleague at the Old South Church
of Minister Ebenezer Pemberton. The
satisfaction the portly and successful
father took in the sermons of this minister
son inspire some of the most satisfying

pages of the diary, and one likes very much to think of Judge Sewall at this stage of his life, going to the old meeting-house with his dear wife Hannah on his arm, to hear " our son Joseph put up a fine prayer," or " preach a stirring word."

Then came the blow of the man's life, a blow from which he never fully recovered. For I cannot believe that the rather self-conscious old gentleman forever taking his own emotional temperature, so to speak, is Samuel Sewall at his best. But I readily enough forgive him his incessant self-analysis, inasmuch as by reason of it we get the only authentic picture we possess of the way in which the middle-aged wooings of colonial days were conducted.

Judge Sewall's wife Hannah died October 19, 1717. She had been for some time in a decline, aggravated, probably, by some sort of malarial fever; as far

back as July 3d her husband notes that
he has been kept from commencement by
his wife's being taken very sick the night
before. "This is the second year of my
absence from that solemnity."

So with the usual Puritan solemnities
of prayer and fast, the household waited
on this exemplary wife and mother, making her exit. "About a quarter of an
hour past four, my dear wife expired in
the afternoon, whereby the chamber was
filled with a flood of tears. God is teaching me a new lesson — to lead a widower's
life. Lord help me to learn, and be a sun
and shield to me, now so much of my comfort and defence are taken away."

Next day he writes:

"I go to the public worship forenoon
and afternoon. My son has much ado to
read the note I put up, being overwhelmed
with tears."

112

Sewall was sincere with all his great loving heart in his sorrow for this wife of his youth and strong manhood, and he kept her memory in love till his death's day in spite of repeated wooings to argue the contrary. But it was expected, with the rigour of a law in the Puritan land, that widows and widowers should remarry. They all did it, and not to do it was a social offence. Apparently they all helped each other to do it, and for a man in Judge Sewall's social station, there was no chance of escape. Nor, truth to say, did Sewall try to find one. Accordingly, we soon read of his attentions to Mrs. Dennison, — who refused him because he wanted too liberal a settlement, — to Mrs. Tilly, another blooming widow, and even to other ladies of name and position. Mrs. Tilly was his final choice, however, and on October 29, 1719, these two were married, with the usual Puritan festivities, by the judge's son, Mr. Joseph Sewall. The judge was now chief justice of Massachusetts, and had been two long years a widower. Not to make further mention of a lady who, though his wife, seems to us to have been hardly more than a shadow in Sewall's real life, albeit she was an exemplary woman, it may be noted that she died suddenly May 26, 1720.

Sewall's opinion of this wife is in a letter:

" She, my wife, carries it very tenderly, and is very helpful to me, my children, and grandchildren."

After Mrs. Tilly's funeral there is no record of any marital movement on Sewall's part until October 1st — four months only of mourning now! — when he writes:

" Saturday I dine at Mr. Stoddard's;

from thence I went to Madam Winthrop's just at three. Spake to her, saying, my loving wife died so soon and so suddenly, 'twas hardly convenient (seemly) for me to think of marrying again; however I came to this resolution that I would not make any court to any person without first consulting with *her*. [Madam Winthrop.] Had a pleasant discourse about seven single persons sitting in the Fore Seat [of the Old South Meeting-House] Septt. 29 [the Sunday before], viz. Madam Rebecca Dudley, Catharine Winthrop [the lady before him], Bridget Usher, Deliverance Legg, Rebecca Loyd, Lydia Colman, Elizabeth Bellingham. She propounded one and another for me: but none would do, said Mrs. Loyd was about her age."

This conference with Mrs. Winthrop was the first of the many in this the most entertaining colonial courtship of which we have record. Sewall was now sixty-nine and the lady fifty-six, twice married before and with grown-up children.

" Octr. 2. Evening. Waited on Madam Winthrop again; 'twas a little while before she came in. Her daughter Noyes being there alone with me, I said I hoped my waiting on her mother would not be disagreeable to her. She answered she should not be against that that might be for her comfort. By and by came in Mr. Airs, chaplain of the Castle, and hanged up his hat, which I was a little startled at, it seeming as if he was to lodge there. At last Madam Winthrop came too. After a considerable time I went up to her and said, if it might not be inconvenient I wished to speak with her. She assented and spake of going into another room; but Mr. Airs and Mrs. Noyes presently rose up and went out, leaving us there alone.

116

Then I ushered in discourse from the names in the Fore Seat; at last I prayed that Katharine (Madam Winthrop) might be the person assigned for me. She instantly took it up in the way of denial, as if she had catched at an opportunity to so do it, saying, she could not do it before she was asked. Said that it was her mind, unless she should change it, which she believed she could not — could not leave her children. I expressed my sorrow that she should do it so speedily, prayed her consideration, and asked her when I should wait on her again. She saying no time, I mentioned that day Sennight. Gave her Mr. Willard's 'Fountain Opened,' with the little print and verses; saying I hoped if we did well read that book, we should meet together hereafter, if we did not now. She took the book and put it in her pocket. Took leave.

117

Oct. 5. Midweek. Although I had appointed to wait upon her, Madam Winthrop, next Monday, yet I went from my Cousin's Sewall's thither about next Monday about 3. The nurse told me Madam dined abroad at her daughter Noyes, they went to go out together. Gave Katee a penny and a kiss and came away."

" Oct. 6. A little after 6 P. M. I went to Madam Winthrop's. She was not within. I gave the maid 2s. ; Juno, who brought in wood, 1s. After the nurse came in, I gave her 18d. having no other small bill. After a while Dr. Noyes came in with his mother and quickly after his wife. They sat talking, I think, till 8 o'clock. I said I feared I might be some interruption to their business. Dr. Noyes replied presently. They feared they might be some interruption to MY business and went away. Madam seemed

to harp upon the same string, must take
care of her children, could not leave that
house and neighbourhood, etc. I gave her
a piece of Mr. Belcher's cake and ginger-
bread wrapped up in a clean piece of
paper. My daughter Judith I said was
gone from me and I was more lonesome —
might help to forward one another in our
journey to Canaan. I took leave about
nine o'clock."

"October 11th. I write a few lines
to Madam Winthrop to this purpose:
Madam: — These wait on you with Mr.
Mayhew's sermon and an account of the
state of the Indians of Martha's Vineyard.
I thank you for your unmerited favours of
yesterday [she had given him wine mar-
malade, etc.], and hoped to have the happiness of waiting on you tomorrow before
eight o'clock afternoon. I praye God to
keep you and give you a joyful entrance

119

upon the 229th year of Christopher Columbus, his discovery, and take leave, to add, Madam, your humble serv't.

" s. s."

" Sent this day by Deacon Green."

" Oct. 12. In the little room Madam Winthrop was full of work behind a stand. Mrs. Cotton came in and stood. Madam pointed to her to set me a chair. Her countenance looked dark and lowering. At last the work [black stuff of silk] was taken away. I got my chair in place, had some converse, but [she] very cold and indifferent to what [she] was before. [I] Asked [her] to acquit me of rudeness if I drew off her glove. Enquiring the reason I told her 'twas great odds between handling a dead goat and a living lady. Got it off! I told her I had one petition to ask of her: to wit, to change her answer. She insisted on her negative. I gave her

Dr. Preston's ' The Church's Marriages and the Church's Carriage,' which cost me 6s. Sarah filled a glass of wine, she drank to me, I to her. She sent Juno home with me with a good lantern. I gave her 6d., and bade her thank her mistress. In some of our discourse I told her [Madam Winthrop] the reason why I came every other night was lest I should drink too deep draughts of pleasure. She talked of Canary, [I said] her kisses were to me better than the best Canary." Samuel Sewall at sixty-nine evidently knew how to act the gallant.

" Oct. 17. In the evening I visited Madam Winthrop, who treated me courteously, but not in clean linen as sometimes. She said she did not know whether I would come again or no. [He had been five days absent!] I asked her how she could impute inconstancy to me. Give her this day's *Gazette*. Hear David Geoffry's (her little grandson) say the Lord's Prayer and some other portions of the Scriptures. Juno came home with me."

"Oct. 18. Visited Madam Mico who came to me in a splendid dress. I said, It may be you have heard of my visiting Madam Winthrop, her sister. She answered, Her sister had told her of it. If her sister were for it [the match] she should not hinder it. I gave her Mr. Holmes' sermon. She gave me a glass of Canary. Entertained me with good discourse and a respective remembrance of my first wife. I took leave."

This is the lady who, some suggest, would have listened to Sewall's suit more patiently than did her sister. "The splendid dress" in which Sewall notes she came to him, certainly gives one a hint of interest on her part.

" Oct. 19. Visited Madam Winthrop.
Sarah told me she was at Mrs. Walley's.
Would not come home till late. Was ready
to go home, but said if I knew she was
there I would go thither. I went and
found her with Mr. Walley and his wife
in the little room below. At seven o'clock
I mentioned going home; at eight I put
on my coat and quickly waited on her
home. Was courteous to me, but took
occasion to speak to me earnestly about my
keeping a coach. I said 'twould cost £100
per annum. She said 'twould cost but
£46."

" Oct. 20. Madam Winthrop not being
at lecture, I went thither first; found her
very serene with her daughter Noyes, etc.
She drank to me, and I to Mrs. Noyes.
After awhile prayed the favour to speak
with her. She took one of the candles and
went into the best room, closed the shutters,

and sat down upon the couch. She spoke something of my needing a wig. I took my leave."

" Oct. 21. My Son [the parson] and I pray for one another in the old chamber, more especially respecting my courtship. At six o'clock I go to Madam Winthrops. Sarah told me her mistress had gone out, but did not tell me whither she went. She presently ordered me a fire; so I went in having Dr. Sibb's ' Bowells ' with me to read. [This was a book on ' The Discovery of the Union between Christ and the Church.']. A while after nine, Madam came in. I mentioned something of the lateness; she bantered me and said I was later. I asked her when our proceedings should be made public. She said they were like to be no more public than they were already. Offered me no wine that I remember. I rose up at eleven

124

o'clock to come away, saying that I would put on my coat. She offered not to help me. I prayed that Juno might light me home, she opened the shutter and said was pretty light abroad; Juno was weary and gone to bed. So I came home by star-light as well as I could. Jehovah Jirah. The Lord reigneth."

" Oct. 24. As to my periwig I told her my best and greatest friend (I could not possibly have a greater) began to find me with hair before I was born and had con-tinued to do so ever since, and I could not find it in my heart to go to another. She gave me a dram of black cherry brandy and lump of the sugar that was in it."

" Nov. 4. I asked Madam what fashion necklace I shall present her with. She said none at all. I asked her whereabouts we left off last time; mentioned what I had offered to give her [as a settlement];

asked her what she would give me. She said she could not change her condition, and had said so from the beginning."

"Nov. 7. I went to Madam Winthrop; found her rocking her little Katie in the cradle. She set me an armed chair and a cushion. Gave her the remnants of my almonds. She did not eat of them as before, but laid them away. Asked if she remained of the same mind still. She said thereabouts. I told her I loved her, and was so fond as to think that she loved me. The fire was come to one short brand beside the block, which brand was set up on end; at last it fell to pieces, and no recruit was made. She gave me a glass of wine. I did not bid her draw off her glove, as sometime I had done. Her dress was not so clean as sometime it had been. The Lord reigneth."

And so with the one black brand on a

fireless hearth the curtain falls on Sewall's courtship of Madam Winthrop. Soon after he married Mrs. Gibbs.

The rocks on which Sewall's matrimonial venture here split apparently were several. He would not agree to set up a coach, claiming he could not afford it, nor wear a periwig, as Madam wished; he had tried to drive a close-fisted bargain in the marriage settlement, and perhaps had sought to meddle with the status of her slaves. Above all, the lady was, as she said, averse to separation from her kin and grandchildren. So this courtship lapsed, apparently with no ill-will on either side. There are entries in the diary later on which look like willingness on Madam Winthrop's part to leave the door just a trifle ajar; but Sewall went another way. There is one entry, however, of the few more concerning her, made on the

127

Lord's Day, December 6, 1724, which quaintly illustrates the man and the times:

"At the Lord's Supper [in the Old South Meeting-House] Deacon Checklly delivered the cup first to Madam Winthrop and then gave me a tankard. 'Twas humiliation to me and I think put me to the blush to have this injustice done by a Justice. May all be sanctified."

In this precedency of the cup to Madam Winthrop, Sewall evidently saw a slight to his magistracy.

"June 15, 1725. I accompanied my son [the minister] to Madam Winthrop. She was abed about ten, morning. [She was evidently in her last sickness.] I told her I found my son coming to her and took the opportunity to come with him. She thanked me kindly and enquired how Madam Sewall [her successor was already established] did. Asked my son

128

to go to prayer. At coming I said, I kiss your hand, Madam. She desired me to pray that God would lift up upon her the light of his countenance."

The last three entries touching Madam Winthrop are these:

"Monday, Aug. 2d. Mrs. Catharine Winthrop, relict of the Hono. Waitstill Winthrop, Esq., died Æ. 61."

Her former wooer, who was one of her bearers at the funeral, notes: "[She] will be much missed." And after the funeral the old man made a wedding call, "and had good bride-cake, good wine, Burgundy and Canary, good beer, oranges, and pears." So to the very end — he died January 1, 1730, aged eighty — Samuel Sewall enjoyed himself. His career serves indeed to make clear, as does no other chronicle that has come down to us, that a Puritan church-member was not of necessity a long-faced killjoy.   **129**

JOHN ELIOT AND HIS INDIANS

WHEN Dean Stanley came to this country and was asked what places would be of most interest to him, he said: "I want to see the place where the Pilgrims landed and where the Apostle Eliot preached." Our picture shows us the latter — not the same church, of course, but the same site, and itself one of the best surviving examples of the famous New England Meeting-House. Like John Harvard, the founder of the University, John Eliot, the Apostle to the Indians, was educated at Cambridge, England. The birthplace of this remarkable man was the town of Nasing, in

OLD CHURCH ON THE SITE WHERE JOHN ELIOT
PREACHED

Essex, and the year of his coming into the world, 1604. As early as during his student life it is recorded that Eliot had a partiality for philological inquiries, and was an acute grammarian, a turn of mind, we may suppose, which afterward had its influence in stimulating and directing his labours on the language of the Indians. Upon leaving the university, young Eliot engaged in school-teaching. This profession bore early in the seventeenth century the stigma of trade, and, like other trades in England, was looked down upon. Cotton Mather, Eliot's first biographer, labours hard to prove to us that his subject is not to be despised because he once pursued the calling of a teacher — and succeeds in being very amusing in this unnecessary defence.

Eliot, however, early felt stirring within him the desire to leave teaching for the work of a minister of the gospel. In these circumstances, and because he saw that only by self-exile could a parson of his persuasion escape the searching tyranny of Laud, he turned his thoughts to the new western world, where a refuge had already been found by many ministers of whom England had rendered herself unworthy.

Thus it came about that on the third of November, 1631, our young parson Eliot arrived in Boston on the good ship *Lyon,* the same bark upon which the wife and children of Governor Winthrop came over. Mr. Eliot was now twenty-seven years of age, and, though no picture of him at this age is extant, there is reason to believe that he must have looked much as he does in the popular paintings and prints, grave, but gentle rather than Puritanically grim, beardless, and lacking, of course, the wig against which he all his life inveighed.

No sooner had he landed than he found a field of usefulness, and was called to the work upon which his heart was set. When he left England a considerable number of his friends in the old country, who loved him and sympathized in his views, had thought of following him to America, and to them he had given his word that, if they carried that plan into effect, and should arrive in New England before he had formed a regular pastoral connection with any other church, he would be their minister and devote himself to their service. The next year they came to claim the fulfilment of this pledge, and though Boston strove earnestly to obtain Eliot's services, he was true to his bargain, and on the fifth of November, 1632, he began his life tenure of the pastorate of the church at Roxbury.

One other pledge Eliot had made in his

native land. This was an engagement of marriage with a beautiful, sweet-natured English girl, Ann Mountford by name, who seems to have been in every way worthy of his lifelong affection. She, too, followed Eliot to New England, and their union was consummated in October, 1632. Thus John Eliot was, within a year after his first landing in Boston, happily settled in the world, — the vigorous husband of a charming woman, and the gifted and respected head of a thriving church.

Doubtless there came to him at this time of his life many a temptation to pursue the even tenor of his pastoral career, and enjoy, as a man of his nature would have enjoyed, the sweet domesticity of a well-kept home. If he had yielded to this temptation, we should have classed him to-day with Higginson and Phillips, with Cotton and Shepard, with Bradford and Winthrop, as worthy workers in the upbuilding of the Massachusetts Colony. But he would not then have towered, as he does now, above all his contemporaries and above all other preachers ever settled in New England (except, perhaps, the Abbé Cheverus), as a man with the exaltation to see the vision of Indian conversion and the steadfast courage to give his life to that vision's realization.

When our fathers came to the western world they found the wilderness peopled by a race which could not fail to be objects of strong interest apart from any friendly or hostile relations. They had just arrived from a country abounding in all the refinements of the old world; they were suddenly brought into the neighbourhood of a people exhibiting the peculiarities of one of the rudest forms of savage life. But until John Eliot came — and even after he came — there was no thought on the part of the community at large to share with the Indians they encountered on every side the blessings of the gospel and of civilization. Our fathers treated the red men as allies, they treated them as enemies, they sometimes treated them as the beasts of the forest. But whether beasts or men, they always held them to be aliens — not merely aliens in blood and in language, but aliens from that universal empire of God, of which all human races are part. If Eliot's experience with the Indians proves anything, — and I believe it proves much, — it proves that such treatment as he bestowed upon them, had it been ably seconded by all his contemporaries, and energetically extended by those who came after him, would have availed to make the Indian a strong and integral part of our national life. At this late date, after a lapse of nearly three centuries, there would then have been no "Indian problem." And we, as a people, would not have to blush as we do now for our treatment of this sturdy son of the western continent. If Eliot's fellow ministers had given to Eliot's Indians one tithe — aye, one hundredth — of the time that they gave to their theological quarrels, the historian would have had very much less to apologize for in the annals of the Massachusetts Bay Colony.

In one of these famous church agitations Eliot himself, to be sure, was involved. He was one of the witnesses, we are informed, against Mrs. Hutchinson in the synod which met at Cambridge in November, 1637, and condemned that strongly intellectual, but rather too self-sufficient lady.[1] In one other non-Indian

[1] See "Romance of Old New England Rooftrees."

enterprise — but this a creditable one — Mr. Eliot was also engaged about this time. For the first book printed in North America, the Bay Psalm Book, was versified by Eliot, Welde, and Mather.

To return to our Indians. Much discussion and no little variety of statement has been current respecting the religion of the red men. Winslow fell at first into the mistake of saying that they had no religion whatever, but this opinion observation obliged him very soon to change. "Whereas," says he, "myself and others in former letters wrote, that the Indians about us are a people without any religion, or knowledge of any God, we therein erred, though we could then gather no better." As a matter of fact, the religion of the Indians in its general features resembled that of other uncivilized peoples. They recognized the divine power in forms suitable to their rude conceptions. The developments of this sentiment resembled in some degree the polytheism of ancient times. Each part or manifestation of nature was supposed to have its peculiar, subordinate god. There was the sun-god, the moon-god, and so of many other things.

It is interesting here to compare the views on religion of such of the American Indians as are still in a native condition with the views of Eliot's red men. Miss Alice Fletcher, holder of the Thaw Fellowship at the Peabody Museum, Harvard University, who knows more about the American Indian of to-day than almost any other living man or woman, tells me that the Indian's religion has been about as little understood as his use of the totem pole. He believes as we do, she says, in a great overruling power. This power, however, cannot, he feels, come near man

139

save to give him breath. But there are lesser powers, like the wind, and the thunder, and these again have other intermediaries. The nearest approach to the Indians' idea is to be found in that highest conception of the Christian religion, the Immanence of God. In the power of evil the Indian has not much belief. It is man, in his idea, who works mischief.

One other element, and that a very important one, entered into the Indians with whom Eliot had to deal. This was something in the nature of a priesthood found among the New England Indians, an order of men and women called Powaws, the common office of whom was to cure diseases by means of herbs, roots, exorcisms, and magical incantations. This cross between a priest and a juggler was ultimately to present a formidable obstacle to the spread of Christianity; "for," said the Indian,

" if we once pray to God we must abandon our Powaws, and then, when we are sick and wounded, who shall heal our maladies ? "

Eliot's strong faith in the nobility and necessity of his work was sufficient, however, to overcome in large measure even this obstacle, and as soon as his hands were sufficiently held up by the General Court of Massachusetts, he set himself to the task which Bishop Lake, of England, had declared " nothing but old age " prevented *him* from going to America to do. Eliot believed strongly that the Indians were the descendants of the lost tribes of Israel, and his interest in their salvation was naturally greatly stimulated by this belief. But back of all theological ardour was the good man's honest and devoted desire to help these people he found all about him. To this end he set himself to the tremendous task of learning the Indians' language.

"There is," he says, in a letter written in 1648, "an Indian living with Mr. Richard Calicott, of Dorchester, who was taken in the Pequot Wars, though belonging to Long Island; this Indian is ingenious, can read; and I taught him to write, which he quickly learnt. He was the first man that I made use of to teach me words and to be my Interpreter." This man Eliot took into his family, and by constant intercourse with him soon became sufficiently conversant with the vocabulary and construction of the language to translate the Ten Commandments, the Lord's Prayer, and several passages of Scripture into the Indian tongue, besides being able to compose exhortations and prayers in the new language. Eliot's contemporaries well appreciated the difficulty of this, his

142

acquirement, for Cotton Mather remarks
that the " Indian language must have been
growing in unintelligibility ever since the
confusion at Babel." Nothing but the
sustaining influence of an exalted purpose,
one is convinced, could have carried Eliot
through the task of learning such a tongue.
In the annals of literary industry it is
related of Cato that he acquired Greek at
an advanced age, and of Dr. Johnson that
he studied Dutch a few years before his
death. But neither of these feats can
compare in arduousness and nobility of
design with John Eliot's acquisition of
the Indian language, that he might through
this means become Apostle to a neglected
people.

Mr. Eliot's first visit to the Indians was
on the twenty-eighth of October, 1646, at
a place afterward called Nonantum (a
part of Newton, Massachusetts), a spot

which has the honour of being the first
on which a civilized and Christian settlement of Indians was effected within the
English colonies of North America. At
a short distance from the wigwams this
day of Eliot's first visit, he and his party
were met by Waban, a leading man among
the Indians at that place, and were welcomed with English salutations. The
English of the occasion was presumably
furnished by Waban's son, who had some
time before been placed at school in Dedham, whence he had now come to attend
the meeting.

The Indians assembled in Waban's
wigwam, and thither Mr. Eliot and his
friends were conducted. When the company were all collected and quiet, a religious service was begun with an English
prayer. The minister from Roxbury then
began his sermon, taking his text from

Ezekiel 37:9 and 10: "Say unto the wind, son of man, Thus saith the Lord God; . . . Come from the four winds, O breath, and breathe upon these slain that they may live. So I prophesied as he commanded me, and the breath came unto them, and they lived and stood up upon their feet an exceeding great army." Now a very fortunate happening was connected, as it turned out, with the selection of this text, though Mr. Eliot afterward said that he had no thought, when choosing the Scriptural basis for his discourse, that the Indian word for wind was Waban. It was, however, as if he had said, "Say to Waban," and again, "I said to Waban." Naturally the simple Indians took it as especially pleasant that their leader should seem to be commissioned by the white man's Holy Book to do the work he had already begun.

145

The scene at this first "Preaching" is
one of the most interesting and significant
in American history, worthy, certainly,
of the devotion and best work of any
painter. Our Massachusetts artist, H. O.
Walker, has chosen to give us, in the mural
decoration here reproduced, seven figures,
some of them standing and some sitting on
the ground. The younger red men are nude
with the exception of breech-clouts. The
old men and the squaws wear blankets of
dull red or dull green. The braves, of
which there are several fine types, tall and
well formed, with a proud bearing, have
feather head-dresses. Their weapons are
not conspicuously displayed. Most of
them are phlegmatic as to expression. At
the left of the preacher is a brave with
an unusually showy feather head-dress,
standing near the trunk of a tree; and two
or three other figures are seated on the

146

JOHN ELIOT PREACHING TO THE INDIANS
From the painting by H. O. Walker

ground. Eliot himself, standing on a ledge somewhat higher than the level which his audience occupies, is dressed in severe dark gray from head to foot, and is bareheaded. His form is silhouetted against the foaming waters of the river just beyond him. His feet are wide apart, and both arms are extended in an easy gesture of exhortation, the palms of the hands turned upwards. The deep earnestness of the preacher is made sufficiently evident by his pose and the movement of his figure, as well as by the grave and ardent expression of his countenance. The whole group is framed, as it were, by the stems of sturdy trees, the foliage of which, touched by the red and gold of autumn, indicates the season — October. Here, then, was our gifted scholar, educated amidst the classic shades of an English university, exiled from his native land for conscience' sake, a man

147

of high distinction in the churches of New England, standing among the Indians of the forest communicating Christian knowledge. The figure of speech employed in the original narrative of this visit, states that he was " breaking the alabaster box of precious ointment in the dark and gloomy habitations of the unclean."

The matter of that first sermon, which lasted an hour and a quarter, is of decided interest. Mr. Eliot repeated the Ten Commandments with brief comments, and set forth the fearful consequences of violating them, with special applications to the condition of his audience. He spoke of the creation and fall of man, the greatness of God, the means of salvation by Jesus Christ, the happiness of faithful believers, and the final misery of the wicked, adding such persuasions to repentance as he supposed might touch his

148

hearers' hearts. A fairly comprehensive survey of Christian doctrine, it would seem to us.

When the sermon was ended, Mr. Eliot asked the Indians whether they understood what he had said. Many voices at once answered in the affirmative. They were then requested to propose any questions which might have occurred to them in connection with the discourse. To this invitation they responded promptly, some of their queries being amusing in the extreme, and some of such a nature as must have probed the consciences of the English. This part of the conference occupied another hour and three quarters, at the end of which time the Indians affirmed that they were not weary, and requested their visitors to come again. They expressed a wish to build a town and live together, and Mr. Eliot bade them farewell only

149

after he had promised to intercede for them with the Court. After this manner was the most heroic ministry in American annals inaugurated.

A fortnight later Mr. Eliot and his friends repeated their visit to Waban. This meeting was more numerous than the former, and was attended by many children, to encourage whom, Winthrop pleasantly records, Eliot from time to time produced apples and cakes from his pockets. After the sermon there were questions as before, and the meeting closed with a prayer in the Indian language. During the devotional exercise one of the assembly was deeply affected even to tears, a striking illustration, as Converse Francis points out, of Madame de Staël's fine remark, that " To pray together in whatever language and according to whatever ritual, is the most affecting bond of hope and sympathy

which man can contract on earth." The
whole afternoon was spent in this second
visit; and as nightfall approached, Mr.
Eliot and his friends cheerfully mounted
their horses and returned home. On the
twenty-sixth of November and on the ninth
of December other meetings with the Indians were held at Nonantum, conferences
which decided Mr. Eliot to make strenuous
endeavours to procure schools for his pro-
tégés, and to help them in all other possible
ways to civilization and self-respect. He
himself had been a teacher of youth, and it
was his favourite and well-known opinion
that no permanent good effect could be
produced by efforts for the spiritual welfare of the red men unless civilization and
social improvement should accompany such
efforts.

He now aimed to soften, and gradually
to abolish, their savage mode of life, by

bringing them together under some social arrangement. Therefore, with Waban as their head, the Indians formed the plan of a settlement in a grant of land they had received, naming the town Nonantum, which signifies in English rejoicing, " because," says " The Day-Breaking of the Gospell," " they hearing the word and seeking to know God, the English did rejoyce at it, and God did rejoyce at it, which pleased them much; and therefore that is the name of their town."

Not an art of domestic culture was neglected by Eliot in the upbuilding of this interesting community. Not a detail did he fail to consider, not a tool did he neglect to provide, not a want did he disdain to supply. " Like Prometheus in the legend, he not only brought down the fire from heaven, but he used it to lead men out of the wood into the farm and village, and taught his devoted converts how to live as well as how to die, substituting industry for sloth, the plough for the dart, the cloth for the skin, and the steady plenty and comforts of home for the alternate starvation and repletion of the wilderness."

Curious moral questions came to him to be solved, along with spiritual and economic problems. The Indians had been, it seems, exceedingly addicted to gambling, and one of their queries was whether they were bound to pay gaming debts incurred before they were " praying Indians." Mr. Eliot's fashion of extricating himself from this dilemma strikes one as highly ingenious. He first talked with the creditor, urging upon him the sinfulness of gaming, and telling him that, having been guilty in this respect, he ought to be willing to give up half his claim. He then talked with a debtor, reminding him that, though he had sinned in gaming, he had promised payment, and to violate his obligation would be only a further sin; certainly he should be willing to offer half. Which he usually was, having gained release from the other half. With the compromise thus obtained both parties were thoroughly satisfied, and more than ever after that were they disposed to think Mr. Eliot a wise wonder-worker.

It was, however, Natick rather than Nonantum which was destined to be the site of Eliot's most successful colony. This place was chosen because he wished the new Indian town to be more remote from the English than would have been possible at Newton. Besides, Nonantum did not afford room enough for his purpose. He wanted a tract of land where the Indians could be gathered into a large society, furnished with instruction of various kinds, given a form of government, and encouraged to industry, agriculture, the trades, fishing, dressing flax, and planting orchards. He wished to make the experiment under the most favourable circumstances, because he intended to found such a town as might be an example for imitation in future attempts of the same kind, — a model for all the subsequent communities of Christian Indians that might be collected. So, in 1651, the " praying Indians " came together and laid the foundation of a town on the banks of Charles River, about eighteen miles in a southwestern direction from Boston. The place was called Natick, which signifies a place of hills. Thither the Nonantum Indians removed.

The new settlement was to occupy both sides of the Charles River, and one of the first industries undertaken was the building over the stream of a foot-bridge eighty feet long and nine feet high in the middle. The town was laid out in three streets, two on one side and one on the other side of the river. Lots of land were measured and divided, apple-trees were planted, and the business of the sowing season begun. A house-lot was assigned to each family, a circular fort, palisaded with trees, was built, and a large building in the English style erected. The lower part of this was to be used for public worship on the Sabbath and for a schoolroom on other days, while the upper apartment was appropriated as a storehouse and a part of it divided off for Mr. Eliot's own accommodation when he must stay over night at the settlement. The government of this town was largely determined by the Indians themselves, and so well did

156

they observe their own statutes, that for the most peace as well as prosperity reigned.

The next summer another great forward step was determined upon. A church of " praying Indians " was instituted. The manner of this was interesting. A day of fasting and prayer was appointed, the names of the Indians who were to present their confessions sent to the churches in the vicinity, and a large body of people brought together to listen to these statements of religious views and feeling. The confessions were fully written down by Mr. Eliot, who designed them, with an account of the meeting itself, for the information of the London Society for Propagating the Gospel. The resulting tract, entitled " Tears of Repentance," was addressed, when printed, to General Cromwell, and was prefaced with a rather perfervid personal tribute to the Lord Protector. Some of the confessions in this tract charm one by reason of their honesty. One Indian acknowledged that he first became a " praying Indian," not because he understood or cared for religion, but because he loved the English and wished them to love him. This impulse of feeling brought him into a state of mind which resulted in deep and abiding conviction. Further tracts were also sent over to the London Society, but it was not until 1660 that an Indian church was finally formed among the natives of North America. No particular account of the proceedings on this historic occasion have come down to us. We only know that Mr.. Eliot baptized the catechumens and then administered the Lord's Supper. Thus was laid at Natick the foundations

of the first civil and ecclesiastical community of Christian Indians.

Eliot's greatest accomplishment was,
however, to come. From the beginning
of his Indian labours he had had in view
a translation of the entire Scriptures into
the Indian tongue. To this end he had
been intent upon obtaining the best assistance he could command in his acquirement
of the language. As far back as 1649, in
a letter dated July 8th, he had written to
Winslow of his desire " to translate some
parts of the Scriptures " for the Indians.
He considered it as an undertaking demanding the most scrupulous and conscientious care. " I look at it," he said,
" as a sacred and holy work, to be regarded
with much fear, care, and reverence."
The sole cause of delay all these years
had been a lack of the funds necessary
to the printing of this translation. But

a corporation in England now interested itself in the undertaking, and at their expense the New Testament in the Indian language was published, September, 1661, soon after the restoration of Charles the Second. Two years later the Old Testament was likewise published, and to the complete Bible thus resulting was added a catechism, and a translation into Indian of the Old Bay Psalm Book. A copy of the whole work, elegantly bound, was sent to Charles the Second, prefaced by a dedication written with nobility and grace. In this the Commissioners of the United Colonies present their profuse thanks to the king for his royal favour in renewing the charter of the corporation and thus defeating the attempts of its enemies. They assure his Majesty that though New England has not, like the Spanish colonies of South America, gold and silver with which to enrich the mother country, yet they rejoiced to send to the land of their fathers the Bible in the language of the natives, among whom the gospel had been planted and propagated, believing this to be " as much better than gold as the souls of men are worth more than the whole world."

Thus was the Apostle's toil at last crowned with a result which must indeed have gladdened the good man's heart. The Indians had now the whole Bible in a familiar tongue. Not content with preaching to them in their own language, Eliot had brought them the religious store most highly prized in all the world for warning, for instruction, for encouragement, for pleasure. He might reasonably have expected his converts to come to the book. But he did not. Instead, though it was an Herculean task, he took the book to them.

This Indian version of the Scripture was the first Bible ever printed on the continent of America.

For about twenty years the initial impression of the Indian Bible sufficed. Then in 1680 another edition of the New Testament was published, and in 1685 a second edition of the Old Testament appeared which, bound with the latest impression of the New Testament, constituted the second edition of the whole Bible, though there was an interval of five years between the times at which the two testaments respectively appeared. The whole impression was two thousand copies, and in the printing of it the participation of a Christian native, one James [of] Grafton, was notable. The second edition of Eliot's translation of the Scriptures was the last. The printer never was, and probably never will be, again called to set his types for those words so strange and uncouth to our ears. But it is understood that the late Bishop Whipple found Eliot's Bible of great use in instructing the Indians of the Northwest, inasmuch as all the Algonquin tribes speak a kindred language.

This Book of Eliot's is, however, more than a book. When we take the old dark volume into our hands, though we understand not the tongue in which it is written, it speaks to us in another and very beautiful language of the affection which a devoted man cherished for the souls of his fellow men, and supplies a singularly convincing document of such human love as fainted in no effort to bring light to those that sat in darkness.

Scarcely less useful if decidedly less romantic than his Indian labours was Eliot's pastoral career. Few men could have carried on through the length of a lifetime so successfully as did he two distinctly different courses of service. His ministry in Roxbury was never neglected because he was Apostle to the Indians. His church, like his colony, was well ordered. And of his services to the education of American youth we have today an enduring monument in the Roxbury Latin School which he founded.

Mr. Eliot's wife, as has been said, was a woman of many virtues, distinguished alike for gentle piety and cheerful usefulness. Their life together was a long and very happy one, and when, March 24, 1687, she died at the age of eighty-four, her loss smote heavily on the heart of her venerable husband. She who had been bound to him by the strong ties of early love, who had been his solace amidst the arduous toil of his mission, and the soul-sick-ening delays of his translation, had fallen by his side, and he had no wish to live longer. One who was present at Mrs. Eliot's funeral tells us that the Apostle stood with tears fast flowing over the coffin of her whom he had so long loved, and to the concourse of people there gathered said, sadly: " Here lies my dear, faithful, pious, prudent, prayerful wife; I shall go to her, but she shall not return to me."

None the less, Mr. Eliot continued to preach as long as his strength lasted. With slow and feeble steps he ascended the hill on which his church was situated, a hill which is still rather trying to climb. The last sermon which he delivered was a clear and edifying exposition of the eighty-third psalm, and the date of this October 17, 1688. He died May 20, 1690, aged eighty-six years, painfully whispering, " Welcome joy! "

To the last the Indians were his chief interest. Among his farewell speeches is recorded this: " There is a cloud, a dark cloud, upon the work of the gospel among the poor Indians. The Lord revive and prosper that work, and grant it may live when I am dead. It is a work which I have been doing much and long about."

John Eliot lies interred in the Eustis Street Burying-Ground, about ten minutes' walk from the church over which he so efficiently and faithfully ministered. His Bible can be found only here and there in a museum or library. But his story is among the best-known because one of the sweetest of all the romantic tales in our country's history. And Nonantum and Natick will ever be names of beautiful moral meaning in the chronicles of New England.

166

PARSON SMITH'S DAUGHTER
ABIGAIL

*T*HE life of Abigail Adams emphasizes very impressively the truth that in early New England the clergy and their families represented the gentry of the period. Abigail's father was all his life a poor minister. Called from his parish in Charlestown to take charge in August, 1734, of the First Church at Weymouth, his salary at the new parish was only £160 a year, in addition to which the parish munificently settled upon him later the sum of £300, " the latter to be paid £100 annually for three years, all in bills of credit." But if

there was not a large income, there was a
great deal of solid learning and quiet
culture in the little Weymouth home where
was born, November 11, 1744, the beautiful and intelligent girl who was to become
the wife of one President of the United
States, and the mother of another.

As a young girl Abigail Smith did not
enjoy great advantages. Had her health
been better she might have availed herself
of such limited educational opportunities
as were open to girls of her day, but, delicate as she was, her parents thought it
best not to send her away to school. In
a letter written in 1817, the year before
her death, she says, speaking of her own
deficiencies: " My early education did not
partake of the abundant opportunities
which the present days offer, and which
even our common country schools now
afford. I never was sent to any school.

I was always sick. Female education in
the best families went no further than
writing and arithmetic; in some few and
rare instances, music and dancing."

That the parson's sprightly daughter
failed to make the most, however, of such
chances of cultivation as did come her
way, one cannot for a moment believe after
reading her remarkable letters. She seems
to have had a decidedly assimilative mind,
and to have been very well able to obtain
from intercourse with men and women of
attainments whatever they might have to
give. Her grandmother, Mrs. John
Quincy, Abigail tells us, was one of her
most valued teachers. This lady, the
daughter of the Reverend John Norton,
must certainly have had a truly wonderful
mind. In the year 1795, Mrs. Adams tells
her own daughter of the excellent lessons
she received from her grandmother at a

very early period of life. " I frequently think they made a more durable impression upon my mind than those which I received from my own parents. . . . I love and revere her memory; her lively, cheerful disposition animated all around her, while she edified all by her unaffected piety." Again, in another letter to the same person in 1808, she said: " I cherish her memory with holy veneration, whose maxims I have treasured up, whose virtues live in my remembrance; happy if I could say they have been transplanted into my life."

It was probably at one of the pleasant social gatherings at Grandmother Quincy's hospitable mansion that Abigail first met John Adams, the son of a Braintree farmer, who had been born in the quaint old house now in the care of the Quincy Daughters of the Revolution, had been

THE BIRTHPLACE OF JOHN ADAMS, QUINCY, MASS.

sent to Harvard College, had supported himself by school-teaching while studying law in Worcester, and had now returned to Braintree, full of ambition and buoyant manliness, for a short stay preparatory to practising his profession. An illuminating glimpse of the young Adams of this period is afforded by this sample record in his diary: "Rose at sunrise, unpitched a load of hay, and translated two more Leaves of Justinian." He was socially inclined, too, this clever young lawyer-in-the-germ, and with his farm chores and his study he mingled a liberal allowance of chat and tea and jolly visiting at the various Quincy homesteads near his farm. To two of the Quincy sisters he had indeed been greatly attracted before ever he met their cousin Abigail Smith. But these tender emotions were only the forerunners of the deep and sincere affection of his life, which was to spring into being early in the sixties of the eighteenth century, and to grow into a sturdy prop for his manhood and old age.

To John Adams, the farmer's son, marriage with Abigail Smith, the minister's daughter, meant, of course, a decided step upward in the social scale, — clever and gifted as the young man was universally acknowledged to be. In the Weymouth parish, indeed, it was felt that Abigail was not doing so well as she ought in the choice of a husband, and opinions to this effect were freely circulated among the church busybodies at the time of the marriage, October 25, 1764. John's profession, for one thing, was urged against him. According to Puritan ethics, the vocation of a lawyer was unnecessary and unsanctified.

This feeling of his congregation explains a sermon preached by Abigail's father, the

Reverend William Smith, just after the marriage of his second daughter. He was a good bit of a wag, this Weymouth parson, and when his eldest daughter had married Richard Cranch, of whom everybody approved, he had preached upon the text: " And Mary hath chosen that good part, which shall not be taken away from her." Now, immediately after the marriage of Abigail, he outdid himself and rebuked his parishioners in one clever stroke by delivering a fine sermon from the text, " For John came neither eating bread nor drinking wine; . . . and ye say, He hath a devil."

Whether the Weymouth people felt themselves properly rebuked for their coldness to John Adams by this Scriptural attack, we do not know, but certain it is that the young couple began very happily just then their life in the little house close to the one where John had been born, and very soon had friends in plenty flocking to their doors.

The scene of their happy married life is now reverently preserved in many of its antique appointments by the Quincy Historical Society, and is the resort each year of hundreds of pious pilgrims, who delight in the noble simplicity of the venerable old house "where Independence began," and where, July 11, 1767, the little son who was to be Massachusetts' second President, first drew breath.

The very next day after the baby came, good Parson Wibard was called in, and the little child was baptized, as was the practice of the times. In accordance with the request of Grandmother Smith, the boy was named for her father, the aged John Quincy, who then lay dying in his home at Mt. Wollaston near by. Long

THE BIRTHPLACE OF JOHN QUINCY ADAMS, QUINCY, MASS.

afterward President John Quincy Adams wrote of this transaction: " It was filial tenderness that gave the name. It was the name of one passing from earth to immortality. These have been among the strongest links of my attachment to the name of Quincy, and have been to me through life a perpetual admonition to do nothing unworthy of it."

At the time of the little John Quincy's birth, Mrs. Adams was the serene young woman of our picture, lovely, lovable, and carefully domestic. It was indeed a very quiet, happy life which she passed during these years of her early married life. Her husband, to be sure, was not with her so constantly as she would have wished, for he was obliged to go about from place to place, following the circuit, after the custom of lawyers of his time, and even when not away from Massachusetts he

175

practised in Boston, coming to his " still
calm happy Braintree " only for the over-
Sundays. The pathos of these enforced
absences from her husband colours all Abigail Adams's letters. Again and again
she writes of her suffering because removed
from the man to whom she had given her
heart. And he, scarcely less, bewails constantly the tumultuous conditions which
made necessary a life very little domestic.
All this, however, is brought out best in
the documents themselves.

Among the first of the letters from this
devoted wife available to students, is that
dated Braintree, August 15, 1774, sent
to Mr. Adams, who, in company with the
other delegates, had set out to attend the
Continental Congress at Philadelphia.
The lofty tone of the missive is most impressive: " I was much gratified upon the
return of some of your friends from Water-

town, who gave me an account of your social dinner and friendly parting. May your return merit and meet with the grateful acknowledgment of every well-wisher to their country. Your task is difficult and important. Heaven direct and prosper you. . . . I shall reckon over every week as they pass and rejoice at every Saturday evening. . . . Our little ones [other babies had come to play with son John] send their duty to their papa, and that which at all times and in all places evermore attends you is the most affectionate regard of your Abigail Adams." Four days later she writes: " The great distance between us makes the time appear very long to me. It seems already a month since you left me. The great anxiety I feel for my country, for you, and for our family renders the day tedious and the night unpleasant. The rocks and quick-

sands appear upon every side. What
course you can or will take is all wrapped
in the bosom of futurity. Uncertainty and
expectation leave the mind great scope.
Did ever any kingdom or state regain its
liberty, when once it was invaded, without
bloodshed? I cannot think of it without
horror. Yet we are told that all the mis-
fortunes of Sparta were occasioned by their
too great solicitude for present tranquillity,
and from an excessive love of peace, they
neglected the means of making it sure and
lasting. . . . I have taken a great fond-
ness for reading Rollins's 'Ancient History' since you left me. I am determined
to go through with it if possible in these
my days of solitude. I find great pleasure
and entertainment, and I have persuaded
Johnny [the future President] to read me
a page or two every day. . . . The first of
September or the month of September may

be of as much importance to Great Britain as the Ides of March were to Cæsar. I long impatiently to have you upon the stage of action."

The action, however, of that September was in Boston rather than in Philadelphia, as the Massachusetts city was besieged by the enemy. One can scarcely fancy the terrible anxiety to which the absent husband must have been prey when the news of Boston's bombardment reached him. From Philadelphia, September 8, 1774, he writes: "When I shall be at home I can't say, but if there is distress and danger in Boston, pray invite our friends, as many as possible, to take asylum with you." A little later his letter runs: "My babes are never out of my mind nor absent from my heart."

The horrible uncertainty of the mails is again and again the theme of the correspondence between these wedded lovers, and one's sympathy is keenly aroused by such a letter as this of Abigail's, dated Braintree, September 14, 1774: "Five weeks have passed, and not one line have I received. I would rather give a dollar for a letter by the post, though the consequence should be that I ate but one meal a day these three weeks to come. Every one I see is inquiring after you, when did I hear. All my intelligence is collected from the newspaper, and I can only reply that I saw by that, you arrived such a day. . . . This town appears as high as you can well imagine, and if necessary would soon be in arms. Not a Tory but hides his head."

The contrast at this time between conditions in Massachusetts and those in Pennsylvania is very well illustrated by two paragraphs from letters written then by

180

John Adams to his wife. One of these urges upon her the greatest possible attention to the mickles that make the muckle. "Frugality, my dear, frugality, economy, parsimony, must be our refuge. I hope the ladies are every day diminishing their ornaments, and the gentlemen too. Let us eat potatoes and drink water." The other extract runs: "I shall be killed with kindness in this place. We go to Congress at nine, and there we stay most earnestly engaged in debates upon the most abstruse mysteries of state, until three in the afternoon; then we adjourn, and go to dine with some of the nobles of Pennsylvania at four o'clock, and feast upon ten thousand delicacies, and sit drinking Madeira, claret, and Burgundy till six or seven."

Just before leaving this "perpetual round of feasting," which occupied perforce so large a share of his first visit to

Philadelphia, Mr. Adams received two letters which must greatly have delighted his home-loving heart. One of these was written by his seven-year-old son, John Quincy Adams, and runs as follows: "October 13, 1774. Sir, — I have been trying ever since you went away to learn to write you a letter. I shall make poor work of it; but, sir, mamma says you will accept my endeavours, and that my duty to you may be expressed in poor writing as well as good. I hope I grow a better boy, and that you will have no occasion to be ashamed of me when you return. Mr. Thaxter says I learn my books well. He is a very good master. I read my books to mamma. We all long to see you. I am, sir, your dutiful son, John Quincy Adams." The other letter is one of very wonderful beauty, reflecting as it does the loving wife's unselfish determination to surrender all that she holds most dear should her country require the sacrifice. Its date is October 16, 1774, and it begins: " My much-loved friend, — I dare not express to you, at three hundred miles distance, how ardently I long for your return. I have some very miserly wishes, and cannot consent to your spending one hour in town, till at least I have had you twelve. The idea plays about my heart, unnerves my hand, whilst I write; awakens all the tender sentiments that years have increased and matured, and which, when with me, every day was dispensing to you. The whole collected stock of ten weeks' absence knows not how to brook any longer restraint, but will break forth and flow through my pen. May the like sensations enter thy breast, and (spite of all the weighty cares of state) mingle themselves with those I wish to communicate;

for in giving them utterance, I have felt more sincere pleasure than I have known since the tenth of August, the day you went away. Many have been the anxious hours I have spent since that day; the threatening aspect of our public affairs, the complicated distress of this province, the arduous and perplexed business in which you are engaged, have all conspired to agitate my bosom with fears and apprehensions to which I have heretofore been a stranger; and, far from thinking the scene closed, it looks as though the curtain was but just drawn, and only the first scene of the infernal plot disclosed. And whether the end will be tragical, Heaven alone knows. You cannot be, nor do I wish to see you, an inactive spectator; but if the sword be drawn, I bid adieu to all domestic felicity, and look forward to that country where there are neither wars nor rumors of war in a firm belief that, through the mercy of its King, we shall both rejoice there together."

As it fell out, however, John Adams was never to bear arms for his country. His services to the new republic are second to none, but their form was always diplomatic rather than military. Even in the preliminary skirmishes he had no part, for, after passing the winter of 1774 - 75 in Braintree, he set out again for Congress, and thus was absent from Massachusetts even on the eventful Lexington and Bunker Hill occasions. To this latter incident we owe one of Abigail's most picturesque letters, that written on Sunday, June 18, 1775. It begins: " The day — perhaps the decisive day — is come, on which the fate of America depends. My bursting heart must find vent at my pen. I have just heard that our dear friend, Dr. Warren, is no more, but fell gloriously fighting for his country; saying, Better to die honourably in the field than ignominiously hang upon the gallows. Great is our loss. He has distinguished himself in every engagement, by his courage and fortitude, by animating the soldiers, and leading them on by his own example. ‘The race is not to the swift, nor the battle to the strong; but the God of Israel is He that gives strength and power unto His people. Trust to Him at all times, ye people, pour out your hearts before Him; God is a refuge for us.’ Charlestown is laid in ashes. The battle began upon our intrenchments upon Bunker's Hill, Saturday morning about three o'clock, and has not ceased yet, and it is now three o'clock Sabbath afternoon. It is expected they will come out over the Neck to-night, and a dreadful battle must ensue. Almighty God, cover

the heads of our countrymen, and be a
shield to our dear friends! How many
have fallen we know not. The constant
roar of the cannon is so distressing that
we cannot eat, drink, or sleep. May we
be supported and sustained in the dreadful
conflict. I shall tarry here till it is
thought unsafe by my friends; and then
I have secured myself a retreat at your
brother's who has kindly offered me a part
of his house." To this there came back
promptly from Philadelphia the following:
" June 27th. This moment received two
letters from you. Courage, my dear. We
shall be supported in life or comforted in
death. I rejoice that my countrymen behave so bravely, though not so skilfully
conducted as I could wish. I hope the
defect will be remedied by the new modell-
ing of the army. My love everywhere."

The femininity of Abigail crops out

187

deliciously in some of her letters, but she is never petty nor unreasonable. July 5, 1775, she writes: "I have received a good deal of paper from you. I wish it had been more covered; the writing is very scant yet I must not grumble. I know your time is not yours nor mine. Your labors must be great and your mouth closed; but all you may communicate, I beg you would. There is a pleasure," she adds, naïvely, "I know not whence it arises, nor can I stop now to find out, but I say there *is* a degree of pleasure in being able to tell news, especially any that so nearly concerns us, as all your proceedings do. I should have been more particular, but I thought you knew everything that passed here. The present state of the inhabitants of Boston is that of the most abject slaves, under the most cruel and despotic tyrants. Among many in-

stances I could mention, let me relate one.
Upon the seventeenth of June, printed
hand-bills were posted up at the corners
of the streets, and upon houses, forbid-
ding any inhabitants to go upon their
houses, or upon any eminence, on pain
of death; the inhabitants dared not to
look out of their houses, nor to be heard
or seen to ask a question.

"I would not have you be distressed
about me. Danger, they say, makes people
valiant. Hitherto I have been distressed
but not dismayed. I have felt for my
country and her sons. I have bled with
them and for them. Not all the havoc
and devastation they have made has
wounded me like the death of Warren.
We want him in the Senate; we want him
in his profession; we want him in the
field. We mourn for the citizen, the senator, the physician, and the warrior. May

we have others raised up in his room. . . .
I wish I could come and see you. I never
suffer myself to think you are about returning soon. Can it, will it be? May
I ask, may I wish for it? When once
I expect you, the time will crawl till I
see you. It is eleven o'clock at night.
With thoughts of thee do I close my eyes.
Angels guard and protect thee; and may
a safe return erelong bless thy Portia."
Almost all Abigail's Revolutionary letters
are signed by this not inappropriate pseu-
donym.

That the statesman off in Philadelphia
fully appreciated the pluck of his devoted
wife is shown in many of his replies, but
in none more prettily than in this: "It
gives me more pleasure than I can express
to learn that you sustain with so much fortitude the shocks and terrors of the times.
You are really brave, my dear. You are

190

a heroine, and you have reason to be. For the worst that can happen can do you no harm. A soul as pure, as benevolent, as virtuous and pious as yours, has nothing to fear, but everything to hope and expect from the last of human evils."

Very frequently in her letters to Philadelphia Mrs. Adams had inquired concerning Doctor Franklin's share in the deliberations. These queries elicited the following reply, dated July 23, 1775: "Doctor Franklin has been very constant in his attendance on Congress from the beginning. His conduct has been composed and grave, and in the opinion of many gentlemen very reserved. He has not assumed anything, nor affected to take the lead; but has seemed to choose that the Congress should pursue their own principles and sentiments and adopt their own plans. Yet he has not been backward; has been very useful on many occasions, and discovered a disposition entirely American. He does not hesitate at our boldest methods, but rather seems to think us too irresolute and backward. He thinks us at present in an odd state, neither in peace nor war, neither dependent nor independent; but he thinks that we shall soon assume a character more decisive. He thinks that we have the power of preserving ourselves; and that even if we should be driven to the disagreeable necessity of assuming a total independency, and set up a separate state, we can maintain it. . . . This letter must be secret, my dear; — at least communicated with great discretion." Evidently John understood that a woman's secret is always shared with her dearest friends.

The defection of Doctor Church [1] is the topic of several excited paragraphs in

[1] See "Romance of Old New England Rooftrees."

Abigail's letters the following fall. Mrs. Adams writes, October 9, 1775: "You have doubtless heard of the villany of one who has professed himself a patriot. But let not that man be trusted who can violate private faith and cancel solemn covenants, who can leap over moral law and laugh at Christianity. How is he to be bound whom neither honour nor conscience holds?" A few days later she writes again: "What are *your* thoughts with regard to Doctor Church? Had you much knowledge of him? I think you had not intimate acquaintance with him. It is a matter of great speculation what will be his punishment; the people are much enraged against him; if he is set at liberty, even after he has received a severe punishment, I do not think he will be safe. He will be despised and detested by every one, and many suspicions will remain in the minds of people in regard to our rulers; they are for supposing this person is not sincere and that one they have jealousy of." John Adams's reply to his wife's comments reflect the sturdy honesty of the man: "The unaccountable event which you allude to has reached this place and occasioned a fall. I would be glad, however, that the worst construction might not be put. Let him have fair play; though I doubt. The man who violates private faith, cancels solemn obligations, whom neither honour nor conscience holds, shall never be knowingly trusted by me. Had I known, when I first voted for a Director of an Hospital what I heard afterward, when I was down, I would not have voted as I did. Open, barefaced immorality ought not to be so countenanced."

Abigail, as is usual with a woman, has, however, the last word on the subject, and

194

" improves " the occasion by an ethical exordium: " I have been led to think that he who neglects his duty to his Maker may well be expected to be deficient and insincere in his duty toward the public. Even suppose him to possess a large share of what is called honour and public spirit, yet do not these men by their bad example, by a loose immoral conduct, corrupt the minds of youth, vitiate the morals of the age and thus injure the public more than they can compensate by intrepidity, generosity, and honour ? Let revenge or ambition, pride, lust, or profit tempt these men to a base and vile action, you may as well hope to bind up a hungry tiger with a cobweb as to hold such debauched patriots in the visionary chains of decency, or to charm them with the intellectual beauty of truth and reason."

In many of the letters Abigail addresses

John as " her dearest friend," and always in this unique correspondence there is a charming exchange of opinions concerning books and things. Thus, surrounded by household cares though she was, we find the parson's daughter quoting Shakespeare to her absent husband, and he, though oppressed with politics, dropping in turn into Latin verse when that form best expressed his meaning. On one of these latter occasions Abigail observes, with delightful naturalness: " I smiled at your couplet of Latin. Your daughter may be able to construe it, as she has already made some considerable proficiency in her accidence; but her mamma was obliged to get it translated." In the same letter she calls for Lord Chesterfield's Letters, which she has lately heard highly commended. A day or two later she playfully writes: " In the new code of laws which I suppose it will be necessary for you to make, I desire you would remember the ladies and be more generous and favourable to them than your ancestors. Do not put such unlimited power into the hands of the husbands. Remember all men would be tyrants if they could. If particular care and attention is not paid to the ladies," she threatens, " we are determined to foment a rebellion, and will not hold ourselves bound by any laws in which we have no voice or representation." Here, though in jest, spoke our first woman suffragist!

Chesterfield's Letters, however, were not to be hers. " They are a chequered set," the husband in Philadelphia writes. " You would not choose to have them in your library. They are like Congreve's plays, stained with libertine morals and base principles. . . . As to your extraordinary code of laws, I cannot but laugh. We have been told that our struggle has loosened the bonds of government everywhere; that children and apprentices were disobedient; that schools and colleges were grown turbulent; that Indians slighted their guardians, and negroes grew insolent to their masters. But your letter was the first information that another tribe, more numerous and powerful than all the rest, were grown discontented. This is rather too coarse a compliment, but you are so saucy, I won't blot it out. Depend upon it, we know better than to repeal our masculine systems. In practice, you know, we are the subjects. We have only the name of masters, and rather than give up this which would completely subject us to the despotism of the petticoat, I hope General Washington and all our brave heroes would fight; I am sure every good politician would plot."

198

So the letters go on, sometimes playful, often historical, and every now and again fairly throbbing with the passionate longing of husband and wife to be together. In the middle of March, 1777, John writes: "The spring advances very rapidly and all nature will soon be clothed in her gayest robes, reviving in my longing imagination my little farm and its dear inhabitants. What pleasure has not this vile war deprived me of? I want to wander in my meadows, to ramble over my mountains, and to sit in solitude, or with her who has all my heart, by the side of the brooks. The pride and pomp of war, the continual sound of drums and fife as well played as any in the world, the prancings and tramplings of the Light Horse, numbers of which are paraded in the streets every day, have no charms for me. I long for rural and domestic scenes, for the warbling of birds and the prattling of my children. . . ." July 8, 1777: "Next month completes three years I have been devoted to the service of liberty. A slavery it has been to me, whatever the world may think of it. . . . The loss of property affects me little. All other hard things I despise, but the loss of your company and that of my dear babes, for so long a time, I consider as a loss of so much solid happiness. The tender social feelings of my heart, which have distressed me beyond all utterance in my most busy active scenes, as well as in the numerous hours of melancholy solitude, are known only to God and my own soul. How often have I seen my dearest friend a widow, and her charming prattlers orphans exposed to all the influence of unfeeling, impious tyrants! Yet I can appeal to my final Judge, the horrid vision has never for one moment shaken the resolution of my heart."

The indomitable patience, the steady persistence of John Adams's statesmanship at Philadelphia, were quite equalled by Abigail's display of heroic virtues at home. Wisely she ordered the affairs of the household, and saw to the cultivation of the little farm. Over the education of her children she had a watchful eye, and under her care the boy John Quincy early developed conspicuous manliness. The little fellow, when barely nine years old, had fearlessly assumed the duty of "postrider," going on horseback unattended over the eleven long miles of country road which stretch between his home at Braintree (now named Quincy Adams after him) and Boston to fetch and carry the remarkable letters of his remarkable parents.

But now Mistress Abigail is to lose the boy as well as his father. Hardly had the statesman returned from Philadelphia in the fall of '77 than there came the news of his appointment to the Court of France. To all the little family this further separation meant a cruel blow. And after deliberation it was decided that the man child be taken with papa for the sake of the voyage and the education of travel. This wrung the mother's heart, but there is no thought of shirking, for is not a needy country calling its statesman-son to council? It is during the loneliness of the eighteen months which followed the departure of father and son from the beach at Mount Wollaston Farm, close to Norton Quincy's house, that Abigail Adams's letters show for the first time that streak of jealousy which proves her to have been but yet a woman. Because her husband has not

been so lavish of tenderness as in the
Philadelphia correspondence, she reproves
him for "inattention." His answer must,
however, have amply soothed her hurt,
"For heaven's sake, my dear, don't in-
dulge a thought that it is possible for me
to neglect or forget all that is dear to
me in this world. It is impossible for
me to write as I did in America. What
should I write? It is not safe to write
anything that one is not willing should
go into all the newspapers of the world. I
never know what conveyance is safe. God
knows I don't spend my time in idleness,
or in gazing at curiosities. I never wrote
more letters, however empty they may have
been. . . . It would be an easy thing for
me to ruin you and your children by an
indiscreet letter, and what is more, it
would be easy to throw our country into
convulsions. For God's sake never re-

proach me again with not writing. . . . If I were to tell you all the tenderness of my heart I should do nothing but write to you."

John Adams's whole life, in truth, was at this period devoted to the service of the dawning republic. When he returned to Braintree August 2, 1779, after an absence of a year and a half, he was only one week on his peaceful farm before he was sent to draw up the Constitution of Massachusetts, and from that Convention he was obliged again to go abroad, this time to assist in the negotiations for peace. It is pleasant to know that, soon after this, when he was at the Court of St. James as our first minister, Mrs. Adams was able to join him. Thus the Weymouth parson's daughter is seen a matronly beauty of forty, against a background wholly new. From a life of the utmost retirement in a small and quiet country town, she is suddenly transferred to the busy and bustling scenes of the wealthiest city of Europe. Never had an American woman been in like position, for she was the first representative of her sex from the United States at the Court of Great Britain. She passed with grace, none the less, through the ordinary form of presentation at court, and until her husband's return lived becomingly the ceremonious life necessitated by her position. Very glad, however, was she to come back again to America, and gladder still, later on, after serving as "first lady" in the White House, to take up her residence once more in "still, calm, happy Braintree." There she and her husband spent the remainder of their days, honoured by their townspeople, and sought out by the most eminent men of Europe and America.

205

Parson Smith served in the Weymouth parish up to the very time when he died, September 17, 1783, a hoary-headed old man of almost eighty. His church is no longer standing; it seems to have been the fashion to pull down the meeting-house and build a new one whenever the finances of the community warranted the expenditure. But one very interesting temple survives to link the Adamses with our narrative, and that is the imposing edifice provided by John Adams in his will and finished in 1828. Under its portico the remains of the statesman-President and those of his " beloved and only wife " Abigail, who had died some eight years before him, were eventually entombed. Their sarcophagi rest in a square chamber solidly walled with granite and closed with iron doors, and in a similar room adjoining lies the dust of John Quincy Adams beside

THE OLD STONE TEMPLE, WHERE THE TWO PRESIDENTS AND THEIR WIVES
ARE BURIED

that of his wife. Quite lately, in response to urgent demand, the building has been thrown open on certain days to the crowds of historical pilgrims who annually flock to Quincy that they may see the spot sacred to the memory of this greatest of American households.

EAST APTHORP AND HIS PARISH TROUBLES [1]

*B*EAUTIFUL old Christ Church, in Cambridge, may be said to be the godchild, after a fashion, of King's Chapel in Boston. For it was by the rector of the old parish, good Doctor Caner, that, almost one hundred and fifty years ago, this letter was drawn up and sent to the famous Society for the Propagation of the Gospel in Foreign Parts, the body then in charge of the entire missionary activity of the Church of England.

[1] NOTE : The data for this chapter was found principally in "History of Christ Church," Cambridge (1893), by Samuel F. Batchelder.

208

EXTERIOR AND INTERIOR VIEWS OF KING'S CHAPEL, BOSTON, MASS.

" To the Revd. Dr. Bearcroft, Secretary
to the Society for the Propagation of the
Gospel in Foreign Parts:

"Boston, 5 April, 1759.

"Reverend Sir:

"We the subscribers, for ourselves, and in the name and at the desire of a considerable number of families professing the Church of England at Cambridge, Watertown, and places adjacent, humbly beg leave to represent to the Society the difficulties we labour under in regard to the means of public worship, and to entreat their charitable assistance. There is no church nearer to us than Boston, which is from some of us eight, from others ten and twelve miles distant; unless, for shortening the way, we submit to the inconveniences of crossing a large ferry, which in stormy weather, and in the winter

209

season especially, is very troublesome and sometimes impracticable. The Society will easily conceive the difficulty of conveying whole families to a place of public worship at such a distance, and attended by such obstructions. To remedy this, we have agreed to build a Church at Cambridge, which, as it is in the centre, may indifferently serve the neighbouring places, of Charlestown, Watertown, and Newtowne; besides providing for the young Gentlemen who are students at the College here, many of whom, as they have been brought up in the Church of England, are desirous of attending the worship of it. We have also made application to Mr. Apthorp, for whom we have a great esteem, and who is willing to undertake the care of such a church, on supposition we can procure him an honourable support. It is for this purpose, we have presumed to apply to the Society, being sensible that without this kind assistance our attempt would be frustrate. For our parts, we purpose and promise, for ourselves and in behalf of those we represent, to provide a Parsonage house and a Glebe, and to pay annually to Mr Apthorp twenty pounds sterling, if the Society shall think proper to countenance our design, & assist us with such farther provision as may enable him to settle among us. We shall indeed be ready to comply with any farther instructions the Society shall please to communicate, within the compass of our ability; and shall make such authentic instruments for accomplishing what we propose, as the Society shall intimate to be proper. Humbly begging a favourable answer to our request, to take leave to

profess that we are, Rev. Sir, the Societies'
and your most humble servants,

> " Henry Vassal,
> " John Vassal,
> " Thomas Oliver,
> " Robert Temple,
> " Joseph Lee,
> " Ralph Inman,
> " David Phips,
> " James Apthorp."

Hardly was this petition started on its
long voyage across the Atlantic before the
promoters of the enterprise, without waiting for the result of their request, began
their building subscription. One of the
most liberal gifts came from the rector-
elect, the young East Apthorp, who contributed to the fund his salary until he
should enter into active service, — a gift
which, with the increase soon allowed by

the English mission, amounted, for the two and a half years which must intervene before the church should be ready for occupancy, to over one hundred and twenty-five pounds.

East Apthorp was at this time a youth of twenty-six, " ardent, impulsive, inexperienced, confiding, of sensitive feelings and high spirit." He had been born in Brighton, then known as Little Cambridge, his father being Charles Apthorp, a wellknown Boston merchant. Young East as a lad attended the Boston Latin School, whence he proceeded to the English Cambridge to complete his education. The death of his father at the close of the year 1758 recalled him to his native land, and shortly after his return he married Elizabeth, the daughter of Judge Foster Hutchinson. Thus well educated, well born, and well settled in life, this young man was held to be an ideal rector for the new church.

The Society for the Propagation of the Gospel in Foreign Parts (established by King William III. on the sixteenth of June, 1701), had promptly acceded to the request of the Cambridge petitioners. Although it was already supporting in Massachusetts King's Chapel, Christ Church, and Trinity in Boston, St. Michael's at Marblehead, St. Peter's at Salem, St. Paul's at Newburyport, St. Thomas's at Taunton, St. Paul's at Hopkinton, Christ Church at Braintree (now Quincy), and St. Andrew's at Scituate, it cheerfully added the Cambridge enterprise to its list, and appointed as rector the choice of the Cambridge people, with a salary allowance from them of fifty pounds sterling per annum.

In the architect appointed to draw up

ST. MICHAEL'S CHURCH, MARBLEHEAD, MASS. (1715)

plans for the church, the little group of
Cambridge gentlemen were very happy.
For they chose Mr. Peter Harrison, then
of Newport, Rhode Island, who, ten years
before, had designed King's Chapel in
Boston. Mr. Harrison had probably been
induced to come to this country by Bishop
Berkeley,[1] whose story is bound up with
old Trinity, Newport, and he had brought
with him the best traditions of Sir Christopher Wren, who was, at this period, the
leading architectural spirit of England.
He is believed to have worked in the old
country upon the palace of the Duke of
Marlborough, at Woodstock, and upon
other similarly imposing piles. His design for Christ Church has been pronounced a real advance over King's
Chapel. From its first erection the edifice
has been considered by connoisseurs in

[1] See " Romance of Old New England Rooftrees."

architecture one of the best constructed churches in New England. In general appearance it is not greatly changed to-day from the original design, and its beauty of line and stateliness of aspect has inspired many a poet, not the least of them Oliver Wendell Holmes, who wrote:

> " Our ancient church ! its lofty tower,
>   Beneath the loftier spire,
> Is shadowed when the sunset hour
>   Clothes the tall shaft in fire ;
> It sinks beyond the distant eye
>   Long ere the glittering vane,
> High wheeling in the western sky,
>   Has faded o'er the plain."

The corner-stone of the church seems to have been laid rather more than a year after the subscription was begun. On this occasion, a stately ceremony, doubtless, Sir Francis Bernard, Bart., the recently appointed governor of the province of Massachusetts Bay, was present. The stone bore the following inscription, probably from the pen of the learned Mr. Apthorp:

" Deo. Æterno.
Patri. Filio. Spiritvi. S.
Hanc. Ædem.
Sub. Avspiciis. Illustriss. Societatis.
Promovendo. Evangelio.
In. Partibus. Transmarinis.
Institutæ.
Consecrabant. Cantabrigiensis.
Ecclesiæ. Anglicanæ. Filii.
In.
Christianæ. Fidei. et. Charitatis.
Incrementvm
A. D. MDCCLX.
Provinciam. Procurante.
V. Cl.
Francisco. Bernardo." [1]

[1] Under the guidance of the most venerable Society founded for Propagating the Gospel in Foreign Parts, the inhabitants of Cambridge, members of the Church of England, dedicated this house of worship to the Eternal God, Father, Son, and Holy Ghost, for the increase of Christian faith and charity, in the year of our Lord 1760, the Honourable Francis Bernard being governor of the province.

The opening service of the church was held on October 15, 1761, a large and not altogether enthusiastic congregation being present. For in the pews might have been noticed an astonishing proportion of the old Orthodox inhabitants of Cambridge, who had come out full of curiosity and distrust to witness the initial proceedings of an organization that had brought into their midst the very elements of popery and confusion from which their forefathers had thought to free themselves forever. Cambridge had gotten on for almost one hundred and thirty years with the stern creed, the bare meeting-house, and the uncomfortable doctrine of the dissenters, and it felt itself doing very well. So many silent scoffers, one may be sure, were seated in Christ Church on the day of that first service. The sermon was " On the Constitution of a Christian Church," and the ruddy-faced, strenuous young rector delivered it with great unction from the picturesque wine-glass pulpit, to rows of high, square box pews, well filled by gentlemen in cocked hats, laced coats, and white silk stockings, accompanied by ladies in flowered silks, high-heeled shoes, and all the other outward and visible signs of the fashion of 1761. If he noticed the unbending outsiders he gave no sign, for he was very happy.

And then, having removed his vestments and received the congratulations of the proprietors, who paid him the delicate compliment of requesting that he print his discourse, Dr. East Apthorp walked joyously out of the church, across the Common, to his own comfortable and well-kept home. For while the church had been in process of erection the young clergyman had built himself the stately mansion of Georgian architecture which is to-day still standing (10 Linden Street), and which is known all over Cambridge as "the Bishop's Palace," even under its modern disguise of Apthorp Hall, a college dormitory. Only by the addition of a deforming third story (built when Mr. John Borland came in possession of the house, the better to accommodate his domestic slaves), is the building changed on the exterior from its original appearance. The interested visitor may yet enter its wide hall with the elaborate staircase balustrade, may yet admire the stately proportions of its rooms, and the wealth of hand-carving on cornice and mantel, may yet gaze in astonishment at the intricate patterns of the quaint delft tiles in the fireplace where Doctor Apthorp warmed his hands after his homeward walk that long-ago Sunday.

CHRIST'S CHURCH AND "THE BISHOP'S PALACE,"
CAMBRIDGE, MASS.

To-day these signs of wealth and taste excite only our admiration, but a hundred and forty years ago their principal effect was to increase most unpleasantly the distrust with which the establishment of a Church of England Society in Cambridge had from the first been regarded. It was believed in all sincerity that the Episcopalians would now endeavour to impose their form of faith upon the very people who had come over to the new country to escape such traditions. To the Reverend Dr. Jonathan Mayhew it was plain that " a certain superb edifice near Harvard College was even from the foundation designed for the palace of one of the humble successors of the Apostles." And those were days when people said very plainly what they thought.

Thus it came to pass that very soon, under stress of the attacks, both open and cov-

221

ert, which were aimed at him, the face of the young rector of Christ Church became lined with anxiety. He began to realize what had been the meaning of his old college chum, the Bishop of Bristol, when he wrote him: " I need not urge to you the consideration of the situation in which an Episcopal clergyman finds himself in your parts, and of the great circumspection which it requires." Mr. Apthorp, in his innocent desire to add still another noble specimen of colonial architecture to the buildings already in Cambridge, had been very far from " circumspect," as it proved. He soon found popular feeling running so high that he was moved to publish his views on the Establishment in a pamphlet entitled " Considerations on the Institution and Conduct of the Society for the Propagation of the Gospel." And this step was his undoing.

222

As has ever been the case, the challenge was eagerly met by the controversialists spoiling for a fight. Doctor Mayhew published an acrimonious reply, and the war of the pamphlets raged fiercely on. Doctor Apthorp, who has come down to us as a most mild and Christian gentleman, suffered very keenly during this controversy. The position in which he had been placed was a singularly trying one; "though actuated by the best motives," to use his own words, "and a desire to do such service as he could to the Church of England and his country, he had sustained as rude a storm as perhaps ever beat upon a person of his station."

The end of it all came soon. In a press notice of the time one reads: "Boston, Sept. 13th, 1764. (Thurs.) Monday last sailed from hence the *Hannah,* Captain Robert Jarvis, for London, in which the

Rev. Mr. East Apthorp, Missionary for Cambridge, . . . and several other persons went passengers."

The alleged excuse for this summary retreat was the settlement of urgent private affairs in England, but shortly after reaching London Mr. Apthorp resigned his Cambridge mission and took up residence for the remainder of his life in a land where bishops were respected rather than ridiculed. In his adopted country he received the recognition his talents deserved, was appointed Vicar of Croydon, and in 1790 was actually offered a bishopric — Kildare — which he, however, refused on account of his failing health. His last years were spent in his university home, the English Cambridge, and he lies buried in the chapel of Jesus College, with the following inscription composed by himself upon his tombstone:

" East Apthorp, S. T. P.,
Hujus collegii nuper alumnus et socius,
Ædis Cathedralis S'ti Pauli prebendarius.
Decessit in fide die XVI. Aprilis.
MDCCCXVI. Ætatis LXXXIV.
Expectans misericordiam
Domini Nostri Jesu Christi
In vitam æternam." [1]

The bitter and distrustful feeling
against Episcopacy somewhat subsided
after Mr. Apthorp's departure from Cambridge, but for three years Christ Church
had no settled rector. Then in June,
1767, the Reverend Winwood Serjeant arrived in Cambridge and took charge of
the mission. It was during his happy eight
years of ministry that the William and
Mary communion service, still in use, was
presented to the church by Governor

[1] East Apthorp, professor of divinity, a former
graduate and fellow of this college, prebend of St.
Paul's Cathedral. Departed in the faith April 16,
1816, aged 84, looking for the mercy of Our Lord
Jesus Christ unto eternal life.

225

Hutchinson, the successor of Governor Bernard. But these peaceful days were not long to last, for the clouds of the American Revolution had already begun to loom large. In a letter dated March 12, 1774, Mr. Serjeant writes: " The populace are almost daily engaged in riots and tumults. On the 7th inst. they made a second destruction of thirty chests of tea. Political commotions run extremely high in Boston; if not suppressed soon, the whole province is in danger of being thrown into anarchy and confusion." Three months later: " Boston is in a terrible situation, and will be much more so if they do not submit to government before fall; the poor will be most miserably distressed and the town will be absolutely ruined."

This must have been one of Mr. Serjeant's last letters as rector of Christ Church, for his ministry soon came to an untimely end. Already the proprietors of the church had found Cambridge too hot for them, Major John Vassal, John Borland (the purchaser of the " Bishop's Palace "), and others of the Tory aristocrats having early in the summer abandoned their homes and sought in Boston the protection of the King's forces. Thomas Oliver, to be sure, remained till September, and left his home (now Elmwood, the James Russell Lowell place) only when an armed mob appeared in front of the house and wrung from him his resignation as president of the council. But after that he, too, sought perforce the hospitality of General Gage.

While we have no actual proof that the Reverend Mr. Serjeant was subjected to violence while in Cambridge, a letter written (probably from Newburyport) in the August of 1775 would indicate that his house also had been attacked: " Families, however inoffensive," he writes, " suspected to retain any loyal principles, were treated with the utmost insolence and rigour. I was obliged to retreat with my family fifty miles into the country to Kingston, in New Hampshire, where I was in hopes of meeting with a peaceful retirement among rural peasants, but my hopes were soon disappointed. The restless spirit of fanaticism renders unintelligent minds more licentious and ferocious. I found it necessary to remove to Newbury, where I hoped to be protected from the insults of the common people. I have lost not less than £300 in household furniture and books destroyed and pillaged." All the rest of the Serjeants' family history is, indeed, sad and pitiable. But it is not exceptional. The Episcopal clergy frequently suffered much in Revolutionary times because of their loyalty to the mother country.

With the history of Cambridge during, as well as before, the Revolution, the Christ Church parish is intimately bound up. "The Bishop's Palace" served both as headquarters and barracks for General Putnam and his Connecticut troops till about the time of the Battle of Bunker Hill, and after the surrender of Saratoga it became the residence of Burgoyne. As for the church itself, it supplied quarters for Captain John Chester's Connecticut troops, soldiers who blithely melted into rebel bullets the Tory organ pipes, and felt themselves quite at liberty to do as they would with other more sacred churchly relics presented by the English Establishment.

Yet Christ Church was to acquire one share of Revolutionary prestige more in

229

keeping with its divine origin. For here it was that on New Year's Eve, 1775, General Washington held service, Colonel William Palfrey reading the prayers. Washington, like most Southerners of his day, was a good churchman, but during the first months of his stay in Cambridge he had worshipped, partly from policy and partly from necessity, in the "meeting-house" then under the care of Doctor Appleton. In the middle of December, however, Mrs. Washington arrived in Cambridge, and very soon orders were given to prepare the *church* for divine service, hasty repairs being made, tradition tells us, at the expense (with a kind of fine irony) of Judge Lee, the only Tory proprietor whose loyalty to George III. was of sufficiently mild a brand to render his continued residence in Cambridge without danger.

The courteous white-haired sexton, who for many years now has been the guardian of Christ Church, points out with pride, for the benefit of visitors, the exact spot which the General and Mrs. Washington hallowed by their presence, that eventful Sunday in 1775. The pew which succeeds the old pew is opposite the third pillar from the door as one enters, and to it still clings, of course, an odour of sanctity. And properly enough, too. That American must indeed be dead of soul who is not thrilled at the thought that Washington prayed in that very spot for the liberty we now enjoy.

In a letter to his wife, Colonel William Palfrey, the acting clergyman at that New Year's service, thus described his performance of the office that fell to him:

"What think you of my turning parson? I yesterday, at the request of Mrs.

Washington, performed divine service at the church at Cambridge.

" There was present the General and Lady, Mrs. Gates, Mrs. Custis, and a number of others, and they were pleased to compliment me on my performance. I made a form of prayer, instead of the prayer for the king, which was much approved.

" I gave it to Mrs. Washington at her desire, and did not keep a copy, but will get one and send it to you."

The prayer, which was undoubtedly prepared with a view to use as a substitute for the petitions in behalf of the king, incorporated in all Church of England services, was as follows: " Oh Lord our Heavenly Father, high and mighty, King of kings and Lord of lords, who hast made of one blood all the nations upon earth, and whose common bounty is liberally bestowed upon thy unworthy creatures; most heartily we beseech Thee to look down with mercy upon his Majesty George the Third. Open his eyes and enlighten his understanding, that he may pursue the true interest of the people over whom thou and thy Providence hast placed him. Remove far from him all wicked, corrupt men and evil counsellors, that his throne may be established in justice and righteousness; and so replenish him with the grace of thy Holy Spirit that he may incline to thy will and walk in thy way.

"Have pity, O most merciful Father, upon the distresses of the inhabitants of this western world. To that end we humbly pray Thee to bless the Continental Congress. Preside over their councils, and may they be led to such measures as tend to thy glory, to the advancement of thy true religion, and to the happiness and prosperity of thy people. We also pray thee to bless our provincial assemblies, magistrates, and all in subordinate places of power and trust. Be with thy servant, the commander-in-chief of the American forces. Afford him thy presence in all his undertakings; strengthen him that he may vanquish and overcome all his enemies; and grant that we may in due time be restored to the enjoyment of those inestimable blessings we have been deprived of by the devices of cruel and bloodthirsty men, for the sake of thy son, Jesus Christ Our Lord. Amen."

Of other services which Washington attended in Christ Church, record is lacking. There has always been a tradition that he worshipped there regularly, but it is quite probable that in tactful concession to the views of the main body of the army, he

234

attended instead the services at the "meeting-house," there to listen to the Reverend Mr. Leonard's preaching to the troops.

Rather curiously, it was after the real storm and stress period of Cambridge had passed, and after the church had ceased to be a barracks, that the main damage to the building was done. It has been said that General Burgoyne occupied "the Bishop's Palace." This was, of course, after his capitulation on October 17, 1777, at the time when the British and Hessian troops, forty-two hundred strong, were assigned to Cambridge as their prison ground.[1] The artillery of the captured troops was parked on the Common at this crisis, in front of Christ Church, and the barracks built for the besiegers of Boston were now occupied by her vanquished foes. Naturally, there was a great deal of dis-

[1] See "Romance of Old New England Rooftrees."

235

order among the demoralized and idle Hessians, and, as a result of this, one peculiarly unhappy incident occurred. This was the shooting, in June, 1778, of Lieutenant Richard Brown of the Twenty-first Regiment (one of the English prisoners), by a stupid sentry.

Brown was driving down Prospect Hill, Somerville, and had lost control of his horses, when a raw country lad, standing guard at the foot of the slope, challenged him to halt and show his pass. Inasmuch as it was impossible to do this, Brown merely pointed to his sword (which he retained by the terms of the surrender as one of Burgoyne's officers), to indicate his rank and privilege. At this, the sentry, whether ignorantly or wilfully will never be known, ran up to the carriage and shot the Englishman through the head. The affair caused great excitement, and the unfortunate lieutenant's funeral, on June 19th, was the one service ever held in Christ Church in which English officers and soldiers, German officers, and not a few Americans prayed to God together. Lieutenant Brown, according to a contemporary account, was "entombed in the church at Cambridge with all military honours," his coffin being added, it is believed, to the nine Vassal caskets which occupy the vault beneath the church. It was on the occasion of this funeral, and because of the indignation aroused by the incident related, that the most severe damage that the building received during the war was done. Ensign Anbury, an eyewitness to the affair, tells us in his "Travels" :

"I cannot pass over the littleness of mind and the pitiful resentment of the Americans in a very trifling circumstance

[for] during the time the service was performing over the body [at the tomb in the cellar?] the Americans seized the opportunity of the church being open, which had been shut since the commencement of hostilities, to plunder, ransack, and deface everything they could lay their hands on, destroying the pulpit, reading-desk, and communion-table, and, ascending the organ loft, destroyed the bellows and broke all the pipes of a very handsome instrument." Thus, in a burst of fury which certainly reflects little credit upon the innate reverence of the Cambridge patriots, ended the Tory term of Christ Church.

The building was now little better than a ruin, and the congregation was as completely shattered as the church. All through the eighties the edifice remained desolate and neglected, but in 1790 it was reopened by the Reverend Doctor Parker, of Trinity, Boston, his sermon (July 14th) being on the text, " Now, therefore, ye are no more strangers and foreigners, but fellow citizens with the saints and the household of God; and are built up upon the foundations of the Apostles and the Prophets, Jesus Christ himself being the chief corner-stone; in whom all the building fitly framed together groweth into a holy temple in the Lord." In the prayer used on this occasion remembrance was made of the fact that he who was now supreme civil authority had fifteen years ago, when newly invested with highest military honours, prayed for his country in Christ Church.

It was not, however, until another quarter-century had elapsed that Christ Church really recovered from the blow of the Tory dissolution. Then (in 1824) a committee was appointed by the Diocese of Massachusetts to solicit subscriptions for repairing the building. By their exertions upwards of three thousand dollars were obtained, of which three hundred were given by Harvard College, many of the Episcopal undergraduates of which (then, as now) attended service in the quaint old edifice. During the summer and autumn of the following year the church was thoroughly repaired, and a number of changes made in its interior. No long and prosperous terms of rectorship are, however, to be noted until the Reverend Nicholas Hoppin, D. D., assumed, in 1839, the charge of the parish. Mr. Hoppin served faithfully and acceptably for no less than thirty-five years, during which time the church was enlarged, and its work greatly strengthened. It was during Mr. Hoppin's time, too, that the one hundredth anniversary of the opening of the church was celebrated with much ceremony. The day (October 15, 1861) was a remarkably fine one, and fifty clergymen, as well as an immense congregation, were present to listen to the fine historical sermon preached by the rector.

On that glad occasion the peal of the Harvard Chime, presented to the church by a committee of University graduates, first rang out on the still Cambridge air. These chimes are operated from the ringing-room in the second story of the tower, where the old-fashioned system of a frame, into which the ends of the bell-ropes lead, is in use. There are thirteen bells in the set, and each bears in Latin a portion of the " Gloria in Excelsis." From the outset the Chime has been regarded as a common object of interest and enjoyment for the whole city, and because of its intimate connection with the University, it has been rung, not alone on church days, but also on all festivals and special occasions of the college. Thus the music of Christ's sweet-toned bells has for more than forty years now been associated in the minds of Cambridge students with all that is most beautiful in the life of their Alma Mater, and through this medium the oldest institution in Cambridge has become identified with the oldest church.

A FAMOUS TORY WIT AND DIVINE

THE Hollis Street Church is now
the Hollis Street Theatre. But
the exterior walls of the building
are the same as those put up in 1810
when the third meeting-house was here
erected on the site which, since 1732, had
been the church " at the south part of
Boston." The original house of worship
was dedicated by the Reverend Doctor
Sewall, of the Old South Church, and the
first minister settled there was the Reverend Mather Byles, a Tory wit and
scholar. Doctor Byles's salary began at
£3 10s. a week, but it was gradually increased from year to year until, in 1757,

it reached £11 per week. So for more than forty-four years he served his people acceptably. Then the Revolution dawned, and in the crisis resulting Doctor Byles's course was such as to bring him into marked disfavour. He was therefore tried in the church, the specific offences instanced against him by his parishioners being: " (1) His associating and spending a considerable portion of his time with the officers of the British army, having them frequently at his house, and lending them his glasses for the purpose of viewing the works erected for our defence; (2) That he treated the public calamity with lightness; (3) Meeting before and after service with a number of our inveterate enemies at a certain place in King Street called Tory Hall; (4) That he prayed in public that America might submit to grate Britain."

244

THE REVEREND MATHER BYLES

The Tory doctor was dismissed August 14, 1776, and in the following May was denounced at town meeting. Being there convicted as a man "inimical to America," he was sentenced to imprisonment with his family in a guard-ship, and condemned to be sent in forty days to England. The sentence was afterward commuted to confinement in his own house, and a sentinel was placed before his door.

Very amusing stories have come down to us of this imprisonment of Doctor Byles, "the great Boston wit." At one time during his imprisonment in his own residence at the corner of Nassau and Tremont Streets, he required, we read, to have an errand performed. No one was at home for the time being and so, interviewing the sentinel, he asked permission to absent himself for a little while. But this permission was not granted. Thereupon he requested the sentinel to do the errand for him, offering to do the duty of guard until he should return. This favour being granted, Doctor Byles shouldered a musket and for half an hour or more marched back and forth before his own door, greatly to the amusement of his neighbours. After a time the guard was withdrawn, and again replaced. Alluding to this fact, Doctor Byles observed that he had been "guarded, regarded, and disregarded."

When the British finally left Boston, and the people returned from the towns round about where they had taken refuge, they began, of course, to put things to rights. Then it was that the Hollis Street Society "prepared to deal with Doctor Byles," and, calling a meeting of the male members, sent for that clergyman. The scene was rather a desolate one. Nothing

246

was left in the church, which had been used as a barracks, but the pulpit and stove. The brethren assembled in one of the galleries and awaited with some trepidation the doctor's appearance.

Soon he entered, arrayed, we are told, in " ample flowing robes and bands, a full bush wig, newly powdered, surmounted by a large three-cornered hat." With long strides he mounted the pulpit, hung his hat on a nail, and took his seat, saying, " If ye have aught to say, say on." Far up in the gallery a little man, with a small voice, arose to prefer charges against the doctor. " Louder, louder! " exclaimed the latter, and again he repeated, " Louder! " After listening for some time to the charges, he exclaimed, " False! False! and the Hollis Street people know that it is false! " and, seizing his hat, he rose and departed, leaving the

247

brethren to settle the affairs in the best way they could.

In spite of the fact that Doctor Byles and his family remained Tories till their dying days, the gifted minister and wit was not disregarded by all his patriot friends. In his later years Franklin, who had been one of his youthful companions, renewed his intimacy with him. Almost the latest writing preserved from the doctor's pen is indeed the following brief letter to the Great American Philosopher:

"Boston, 14th May, 1787.

"Sir: — It is a long time since I had the pleasure of writing to you by Mrs. Edward Church, to thank you for your kindly mention of me in a letter that I find was transmitted to the University of Aberdeen [this institution had, in 1765, conferred on Doctor Byles the degree of

D. D.]. I doubt not whether you ever received it, I seize this opportunity of employing my daughter to repeat the thanks which (but under great weakness by old age and a palsy) I aimed to express in that letter. Your Excellency is now the man that I early expected to see you; I congratulate my country on having produced a Franklin, and can only add, I wish to meet you where complete felicity and we shall be forever united. I am, my dear and early friend, your most affectionate and humble servant,

" M. BYLES."

Doctor Byles enjoyed, too, the distinction of a correspondence with Pope, his letters to that celebrated writer evincing a keen appreciation for his works. A very beautiful copy of Pope's Odyssey came to the doctor as a result of this admiration.

This sturdy old Tory's ruling passion for the *bon mot* was strong even in death. It is related of him that just before he expired (July 5, 1788) his intimate friend, Bishop Bowker, called to see him; and as he entered the room and approached the bedside of the dying man, the doctor by lifting his finger signified that he wished him to bend over and place his ear near to his lips. This the bishop accordingly did. Then Doctor Byles whispered, "I have almost got to that land where there are no bishops." His friend, who seems to have been quite his match, replied quickly, "I hoped, doctor, that you were going to the Shepherd and Bishop of Souls." The story seems almost ill-timed, but it certainly reveals a serenity that not even the shadow of death could disturb.

Doctor Byles left a son and two daughters. This son, — another Tory of course, — got into trouble during the Revolution with his church also, that church being none other than the Old North on Salem Street, from which the lanterns were hung on the eve of the nineteenth of April. This second Mather Byles, graduated at Harvard in 1751, had been duly ordained a Congregational clergyman like his father, and was for some time pastor of the church in New London, Connecticut. But in 1768 he became an Episcopalian, and was called to Boston, where he was rector of Christ Church until just previous to the Revolution. Thus for a term of years Doctor Mather Byles, Sr., a Congregational minister, presided over the Hollis Street Church, while Doctor Mather Byles, Jr., his son, preached the opposing creed at the other end of the town.

Doctor Byles's two daughters, Catherine

and Mary, never married, and they continued to the end of their life to reside in the old family mansion on Nassau Street, and to cherish their Tory predilections. Their house was filled with antique curiosities and memorials of bygone days. They took a special delight in "drinking their tea off a table at which Franklin had partaken of the same beverage." "Blowing their fire with a bellows two hundred years old," was another source of great satisfaction to them; and they seemed to live for years amidst recollections of the happy past. From a curious old volume, "Sketches of History, Life, and Manners in the United States. By a Traveller," we get this entertaining description of a visit paid in 1823 to the Misses Byles:

"I sought them out and found them in an old decayed wooden house at the foot of a Mall [Common]. The house (which

must have seen a century at least) stood
in a luxuriant grass plat, with two beautiful horse-chestnut-trees growing near the
door: the whole was enclosed by a decayed
wooden paling, which communicated with
the street by a small gate with a wooden
latch. Upon opening the gate I was
within a few steps of the door; but by
the looks of the house, the old rotten step
at the door, the grass growing through it,
not a trace of human footstep to be seen,
and the silence that pervaded the moulder-
ing mansion before me — I imagined it
could be no other than a deserted house.
I knocked at the door, however, and an
elderly female opened it immediately; I
inquired for the ladies of the house; she
replied that she was one of them, and that
her sister was sick. Upon my saying something about my paying my respects to
them, she very coldly invited me to walk

in. The house looked something better inside. . . . Among the three or four old chairs in the parlour was one which appeared to be the monarch of the rest. It was curiously carved, wholly of wood, with a straight high back, upon which was mounted the English crown, supported by two cherubim. This chair of state is carefully placed under the portrait of their father. . . .

"Miss Byles appeared to be about seventy-five years of age. . . . I drew a few sentences from her, the amount of which went to show that she was a warm lover of the British crown and government, and that she despised the country she was in. She said the Americans had her father, herself, and her sister up in the time of the Revolutionary War, treated them ill, imprisoned her father, and suspended him from preaching; came very

254

near sending the whole of them off to England just because her father prayed for the king! . . ." On the accession to the throne of William IV., one of the sisters, who had known the sailor king, during the Revolution, addressed to him a congratulatory epistle, assuring him that the " family of Doctor Byles never had renounced and never would renounce their allegiance to the British crown." The elder sister died in 1835, the younger, Mary, in 1837. It had long been one of the comforts of these forlorn spinsters that not a creature in the States would be any better off for what they left behind them. This indeed proved to be the case, for their modest little estate passed, as they had carefully arranged it should, into the possession of relations in the Provinces. The history of Boston, it seems to me, affords few more pathetic and pictur-

255

esque bits than the little glimpse given us
by the " Traveller " above quoted, of these
prim old ladies, cultured and polished,
though somewhat eccentric, cherishing for
sixty years after the public denunciation
of their father as a Tory the political
prejudices for which he had suffered.

One other minister of the Hollis Street
Church, the Reverend John Pierpont, poet,
Abolitionist, and divine, — the grandfather of John Pierpont Morgan, — is
conspicuous in the history of the parish
as a pastor possessed of opinions he refused to abandon. Mr. Pierpont came to
the church in 1818, and for fifteen years
was a very popular pastor. Then he, too,
began to develop views — anti-slavery
ones — to which a portion of his parish
was bitterly opposed. He was invited
to resign, but declined. A sharp correspondence between him and the standing

committee of the church ensued, the matter
being finally referred to an ecclesiastical
council, which, after hearing the charges
against Mr. Pierpont, dismissed them and
exonerated him. Meanwhile, his salary
was withheld, and he sued the society for
it. It was only after he had obtained judgment in the Supreme Court and secured
payment of his claim that he voluntarily
resigned, and the warfare ended. This
was in 1845. Until 1859 Mr. Pierpont
was engaged in the regular ministry over
various Unitarian churches, but when the
war broke out in 1861, he became chaplain
to the Massachusetts regiment. His increasing infirmities compelled him to retire, however, and the rest of his life was
employed in the Treasury Department at
Washington, arranging its decisions, a
work for which he was well fitted, because
he had been bred a barrister and had aban-

doned the profession only when compelled to the step by scruples of conscience. Mr. Pierpont's hymns combine in a remarkable way terseness and tenderness. One of these, written for the opening of the Independent Congregational Church, in Barton Square, Salem, Massachusetts, December 7, 1824, is very well known both in this country and England:

" O Thou, to whom in ancient time
    The lyre of Hebrew bards was strung;
Whom kings adored in songs sublime,
    And prophets praised with glowing tongue;

" Not now on Zion's height alone,
    Thy favoured worshippers may dwell,
Nor where at sultry noon Thy Son
    Sat weary, by the patriarch's well:

" From every place below the skies,
    The grateful song, the fervent prayer,
The incense of the heart, may rise
    To heaven, and find acceptance there.

258

"To Thee shall age with snowy hair,
    And strength and beauty, bend the knee ;
And childhood lisp with reverent air,
    Its praises and its prayers to Thee.

"O Thou, to whom, in ancient time,
    The lyre of prophet-bards was strung, —
To Thee, at last, in every clime,
    Shall temples rise and praise be sung."

"To Thee shall age with sleepy hair
And strength and beauty bend the knee,
And childhood lisp with reverent air
Its praises and its prayers to Thee.

"O Thou, to whom, in ancient time,
To Thee. . . . .
. . . .

WHEN A FRENCH EXILE WAS BOSTON'S BISHOP

*J*UST one hundred years ago (September 29, 1803) the first Catholic temple in the city of Boston was erected on Franklin Street, and five years later, in 1808, St. Patrick's Church, the first Catholic meeting-house in the State of Maine, was built at Damariscotta Mills. The fact that both these edifices came into being through the efforts of one man, a French exile, who was afterwards a prince of the Church, renders their history of decided interest. The country church, much of the material for which was brought from Europe, is still standing

260

ST. PATRICK'S CHURCH, DAMARISCOTTA   CHURCH OF THE HOLY CROSS, FRANK-
MILLS, ME. (1807)   LIN ST., BOSTON, MASS. (1803)

Two churches built by Bishop Cheverus

midway between Damariscotta Mills and the village. Originally the pews here were only rough benches hewn from the trees of the forest, but now the furnishings are modern. As for the Cathedral of the Holy Cross, the modern successor, though on a different site, of the first Catholic church in Boston, — it covers more than an acre of ground and is generally called one of the most imposing church buildings in New England. Only the personality of Bishop Cheverus and the faith of the Church he so loved connect these two widely dissimilar structures.

The career of John Louis Anne Magdalen Lefebvre de Cheverus, — to give his name in full, — born at Mayenne, France, January 28, 1768, is full to the brim of colour and interest. Bred up in a very pious household and early sent to the college of his native place, he received, when only twelve, the tonsure at Mayenne, and began his studies for the priesthood. Meanwhile the troubles of the French Revolution were beginning to cast their shadow before. When M. de Cheverus was ordained, December 8, 1790, — in the twenty-third year of his age, — it was at great personal risk. For to accept holy orders at that time was to court persecution, confiscation, imprisonment, and martyrdom from the fierce tyrants rising up in France to destroy both church and state, and deluge the fairest of lands in the blood of its noblest citizens. Undaunted, however, by the calamities that were hastening upon his country and his religion, the young priest repaired at once, after taking orders, to his native city, and assumed the public exercise of the holy ministry as assistant to his uncle, the venerable Curé de Cheverus. At the same

time he received from the Bishop of Mans
the honour of being a canon in his cathedral. Soon, however, he was called upon
to take the oath of the Revolution, which
he firmly resisted, and, resigning his
place, exercised the holy ministry in
private. Thus his father's house became
at once his prison and his chapel. But
he was not destined to remain long in the
little town he called home, for, making his
escape in the June of 1792, he proceeded
to Paris. Naturally, the lynx-eyed members of the Committee of Vigilance speedily found him out in that troubled centre,
and made his life a far from comfortable
one.

Then was passed the resolution of the
twenty-sixth of August, which condemned
to banishment those priests who had not
taken the constitutional oath. This was
M. de Cheverus's opportunity. The mas-

sacres of the second and third of September had already taken place, and he had gone free only by being concealed for several days in his own chamber. The decree of banishment seemed to him, therefore, almost a providential means of escape, and, disguising himself, he sailed as speedily as possible for England, where, though a stranger in a strange land, he soon found friends and a means of support as teacher of French and mathematics in a boarding-school. Here, through the necessary intercourse with his pupils, he acquired a good knowledge of English, and was thus quite ready to accept the invitation which came to him in 1795, to share with the Abbé Matignon, then officiating at Boston, labour in that new and fruitful vineyard.

To M. de Cheverus this call to a foreign field, which embraced all New England and the Indian tribes of Penobscot and

Passamaquoddy, offered a glorious opportunity to do the work he so loved. He therefore made over his patrimony to his brothers and sisters in France, and sailed at once for the new world. "On the third of April, 1796," says the chronicler, "he arrived safely at Boston, where he was received by M. Matignon as an angel sent from heaven to his aid."

Naturally the Boston of that day was inclined to be none too cordial to these exiled French priests. The English colonists had brought with them to the new country all the religious prejudices of their native land, and Massachusetts had long been filled with men of a great variety of religious sects which, though in doctrine differing widely from each other, were united on one point, hatred of all things Catholic. Never were such ministers weary of declaiming against the

Church of Rome, which they represented as an impure assemblage of idolaters, and condemned as the new Babylon in the Apocalypse.

To found a Catholic church in a country where such a state of feeling existed seemed almost a hopeless enterprise. But M. Matignon and M. Cheverus happily hit upon the one and only way of gaining ground, — that of exhibiting lives so genuinely Christlike that men must perforce honour the religion they served. " A new and touching sight was then witnessed in Boston," we read; " two men, examples of every virtue, living together as brothers, without distinction of property, with no difference of purpose or of will; always ready to yield to each other, to anticipate each other in rendering most polite and delicate attentions; possessing in truth but one heart and one soul; filled with the same desire, that of doing good; the same inclinations, those which pointed to virtue; and the same love of whatever is good, upright, and charitable." The Boston *Monthly Magazine,* in its issue for June, 1825, said, in speaking of them: " Those who witness the manner in which Abbé Matignon and Abbé Cheverus live, will never forget the refinement and elevation of their friendship; it surpasses those attachments which delight us in classical story, and equals the lovely union of the son of Saul and the minstrel of Israel."

One story will illustrate the effect of such living. After M. Cheverus had been in Boston for a year, a Protestant came to him and said, very frankly: " Sir, I have studied you closely for a whole year; I have watched all your steps and observed all your actions; I did not believe that a minister of your religion could be a good man. I come to make you the reparation which honour demands. I declare to you, that I esteem and venerate you, as the most virtuous man that I have ever known."

The universal confidence which M. Cheverus had inspired soon brought him into new and inconceivably multiplied relations. Protestant ladies from the highest ranks of society came to open their hearts to him and ask his advice. One of these having said to him one day that it was the doctrine of confession which more than anything else would to her prove an insuperable obstacle to the acceptance of the Catholic religion, M. Cheverus replied, with his delightful smile: "Madam, you really have not so great a repugnance to confession as you think; on the contrary, you seem to have experienced its necessity and its value, since, for a long time, you have confessed to me without knowing it.

Confession is nothing more than just such disclosures of the troubles of conscience as you have been pleased to make to me in order to receive my advice."

This remarkable visitor from overseas was early able to perceive that if the religion he represented were to obtain in Boston the respect he believed should be accorded it, the Catholic clergy, besides living Apostolic lives, must be as well versed in what the world called learning as in sacred knowledge. For himself, therefore, he zealously pursued those studies ever held in high honour in Boston. He made himself master of the arrangement, construction, and etymology of the English language, he read all the most distinguished works that language has produced, and he further kept himself *au courant* with the modern literatures of other lands. An attentive and discriminat-

269

ing observer of society, he had been quick to remark the high estimation in which human learning and those who possessed it were held in the city of his adoption, and the general taste for literary acquirements even among women. Accordingly, he so cultivated himself that the extent and variety of his information soon connected him with all the learned men of Boston, the literary societies of the city sought him as a member, and it is very interesting to learn that he was a powerful instrument, with the other leading Bostonians of the day, in founding the Boston Athenæum, to which he even gave many books from his own library.

The account given by his biographer, J. Huen-Dubourg, — from whose enthusiastic " Life " most of our facts are drawn, — of the good bishop's missionary journeys among the Indians in the

270

Penobscot and Passamaquoddy regions, is full of interest and colour. M. Cheverus found these people, we learn, almost wholly admirable. In one place they had kept intact for fifty years the faith delivered to them by the Jesuits who first brought Christianity to their section. M. Cheverus discovered these natives by chance one Sunday morning singing the well-known chant associated with the royal mass of Dumont, and at the sight of the black gown all the assemblage uttered cries of joy and delight, ran to meet him, called him father, and placed him on a bearskin, their seat of honour. Soon he learned the language of the tribe, and became their highly esteemed spiritual leader. Thus it was that he built the church between Newcastle and Damariscotta to which reference has already been made.

One very remarkable anecdote of these Indian converts has come down to us. Soon after the death of Louis XVI. — who was led to the scaffold by his own subjects, and in the presence of sixty thousand of them sacrificed to the revolutionary frenzy — the news of the sad affair was brought to the Indians by some English travellers. The red men could not credit the story. The French missionaries who had preached to them, and M. Cheverus, himself, whom they so respected, had represented to them that France contained a people honourable and generous, an idea not to be reconciled in their minds with the extraordinary tale of the English travellers. One of the native chiefs, therefore, sought the truth from their spiritual head: "Father," he began, "we know you do not lie; tell us, then, how this is. The English say that the French have put their king to death; this is impossible; it must be to make us hate the French that they broach this falsehood."

M. Cheverus, greatly embarrassed how to answer this question, tried to explain that it was not the French nation, but rather some mad men who had temporarily gotten the upper hand, who put the king to death, adding that all France disowned the Revolutionists, and regarded their crime with the deep horror and execration that it deserved. Still the Indians were unappeased. "Ah, my father," replied the chief, much moved, "but I no longer love the French since this is true. It was not enough to disclaim this crime; they ought to have thrown themselves between the king and his assassins and have died rather than suffered his person to be touched. Why, father," he added, "it is as if one should come to kill you while among us and we should allow you to be killed. Should we not then be guilty? We are better than the French; for we would all be killed to save you."

To the very end of his stay in Boston M. Cheverus, both as priest and bishop, was accorded the most remarkable honours. At the dinners to which he was invited, and where sometimes thirty ministers of various sects would be present, he was always asked to say the blessing, which he did, making the sign of the cross and pronouncing the customary prayers of the Catholic Church. When President John Adams visited Boston and was tendered a magnificent banquet by the city, M. Cheverus was placed at one side of the distinguished guest. The President was greatly impressed by this mark of respect paid to a Catholic priest in a city where, only a few years before, all of the hated belief had been treated with scorn. He remarked, therefore, to M. Cheverus that he was as astonished to see him, a Catholic priest, there occupying the place of honour on his right, as to reflect that he himself was being honoured in Boston as President of the United States. The first subscriber to the Catholic church which M. Cheverus soon built on Franklin Street, Boston, opposite old Theatre Alley, it is interesting to note, was President Adams. With this name at the head of the list, subscriptions naturally came in very readily, and on the twenty-ninth of September, 1803, the building was dedicated by Bishop Carroll, of Baltimore, under the name of the Church of the Holy Cross.

On November 1, 1810, the abbé was raised to the dignity of a bishop in the cathedral at Baltimore by Archbishop Carroll. But this increase of power made no difference whatever in the style of the good man's life. It is said that he even continued to split his fire-wood himself. And, as before, his ministrations to his beloved Indians went on. Only with difficulty, however, was he able to remain thus humbly in the New England of his adoption. When Archbishop Carroll died in 1815, great pressure was brought to bear upon Bishop Cheverus to induce him to take the higher office. He replied, however, that the church at Boston needed him most, which was indeed the truth, for after the death of his good old friend, Abbé Matignon, in 1818, the place he had to fill was bigger than ever.

But the happy relation between Boston and Bishop Cheverus could not go on indefinitely. His health had become sadly impaired by his rigorous life and the severe New England winters, a fact which

276

all his friends observed with great sorrow
and which caused one of them — a French
ambassador to the United States just returning to his own country — to apprise
Louis XVIII. of Bishop Cheverus's great
worth, and to ask that monarch to recall
the exile to his native See of Montauban.
This was accordingly done, — to the great
distress of the Bishop of Boston. With
what grace he could, he declined the king's
kind offer, and there went to Paris with
his letter a petition in which more than
two hundred Protestants, as well as the
body of Catholics in Boston, begged that
their bishop be permitted to remain with
them. "If the removal can be referred
to the principle of usefulness," they wrote,
"we may safely assume that in no place
nor under any circumstances can Bishop
Cheverus be situated where his influence,

whether spiritual, moral, or social, can be so extensive as where he now is."

All this, however, was of non-avail. By return mail the king commanded Bishop Cheverus to return to France and there take charge of the Diocese of Montauban. Evasion was no longer possible. To leave Boston was to the good bishop like partial death, but the physicians had just declared that his health could not endure another winter in this severe climate, so the recall was perhaps providential after all. The bishop himself regarded the day of his departure as the day of his death. Before it arrived, therefore, he wished, according to his own expression, " to execute his will."

The church, the episcopal residence, and the convent which he had built, he bequeathed, therefore, to the diocese. All the rest of his possessions he distributed among his ecclesiastics, his friends, and the poor. As he had come to Boston a poor man, he chose to depart poor, with no other wealth than the same trunk which he had brought with him twenty-seven years before. The universal regret expressed at his departure is indicated by this quotation from the Boston *Commercial Gazette* [Protestant] of September 22, 1823: " This worthy dignitary of the Roman Catholic Church has been with us nearly thirty years, and during this period he has enjoyed the confidence and respect of all classes of people. The amenity of his manners as a gentleman, his accomplishments as a scholar, his tolerant disposition as a religious teacher, and his pure and apostolic life, have been our theme of praise ever since we have known him. We regret his departure as a public loss."

This description of Bishop Cheverus as

General Oliver remembered him in Boston seems very happy: "The last time I saw him was as he passed up Franklin Street clad in a black suit, with buckled shoes, stockings, small clothes, long vest and full coat of the fashion of the day, all of black, his face beaming with thoughtful kindness, and his whole bearing that of a dignified and saintly minister of good." To this may well be added a few sentences written by Doctor Channing: "We have seen [in the metropolis of New England] a sublime example of Christian virtue in a Catholic bishop. We have observed this man declining in great degree the society of the cultivated and refined that he might be the friend of the ignorant and friendless; leaving the circles of polished life, which he would have graced, for the meanest hovels; bearing with a father's sympathy the burdens and sorrows of his large

BISHOP CHEVERUS

spiritual family; charging himself alike
with their temporal and spiritual concerns;
and never discovering, by the faintest indication, that he felt his fine mind degraded by his seemingly humble office.
This good man, bent on his errands of
mercy, was seen in our streets under the
most burning sun of summer and the
fiercest storms of winter, as if armed
against the elements by the power of charity. He has left us; but not to be forgotten."

The bishop embarked from New York,
October 1, 1823, and in his native land
was received with all possible honour and
joy. Through the trying Revolution of
1830 he bore himself with such dignity
as not to forfeit the respect even of those
who differed from him, and soon afterwards he was elevated, upon the suggestion
of the king, to a place in the College of

Cardinals. He accordingly received the red hat February 1, 1836. In this exalted position he lived only a short four months, for on Sunday, July 7, 1836, after officiating at several churches of his episcopal city, he sank down in the evening with utter prostration from an attack which was the beginning of his short last illness. So it is as the Bishop of Boston rather than as a Prince of the Church that history to-day remembers him. Plenty of prelates have been imposing cardinals, but New England has had only one Bishop Cheverus.

THE OLD CHURCH ON THE GREEN, LONGMEADOW, MASS.

THE LOST PRINCE AT
LONGMEADOW

*T*HE first meeting-house to be built
at Longmeadow, a beautiful old
town on the Connecticut River,
not far from Springfield, Massachusetts,
was erected in 1714, and that same year
the Reverend Stephen Williams, who had
been taken captive with his father's family
in the sack of Deerfield,[1] was ordained
minister of the parish. For sixty years
he served the community here, his round
of parish duties being interrupted only
by work as chaplain in the Louisburg
expedition of 1745, and on other occasions,

[1] See "Romance of Old New England Rooftrees."

and by his missionary interests in the Indians. This last concern of his had arisen very largely from his solicitude for the children of his sister Eunice, who, it will be remembered, had steadily refused to return with her family to New England and to the faith of her fathers, preferring the Roman Catholic religion and an Indian chief. To Stephen Williams, as to all the rest of the family, this apostasy on Eunice's part was a deep and abiding sorrow.

So it was, perhaps, that he might compensate in a measure for his sister's "error" that the minister of Longmeadow laboured so zealously to cultivate the virtues of Protestant Christianity in the little town to which he had been called. In June, 1767, the "old church on the green" of our picture was begun by him, and the work of building the same was steadily carried on under his superintendence until, in April, 1769, this meeting-house was dedicated. Then Stephen Williams was gathered to his fathers, being buried in the summer of 1772 from the church he had struggled to achieve. His chosen successor was the Reverend Richard S. Storrs, Doctor Williams's grandnephew. And during Doctor Storrs's ministry it was that quite another Williams came to Longmeadow, and, by his connection with the town and its meeting-house, furnished an excuse for the introduction here of a Longmeadow chapter. For the romance of the Reverend Eleazer Williams, believed by many to be Louis XVII. of France, is far and away the strangest and most fascinating story in all New England history.

If you search the Longmeadow town records you will find repeatedly mentioned there the name of Deacon Nathaniel Ely, who figures in the local history as agent in the " Important Business " of making Longmeadow " the oldest child of the state." [The precinct was the first to be incorporated as a town after the signing of the Treaty of Peace, September 3, 1783.] Deacon Ely had married the grand-niece of Eunice Williams, and he was a worthy and intelligent, though uneducated, man. Until he was thirty years of age he had worked on his farm and enjoyed uninterrupted health. Then his whole family was suddenly attacked with sickness, and his mother and three children swept at once to the grave. He likewise was very ill at this time, and he vowed that if he recovered, " his future life, health, property, and everything dear on earth should be consecrated to God." For this reason, as well as because he was

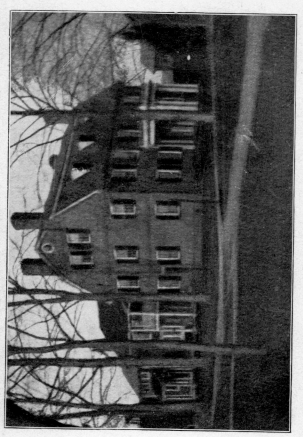

DEACON ELY'S HOUSE, LONGMEADOW, MASS.

greatly interested in the conversion of the Indians, he early offered to bring up the children of his squaw kinswoman. Always, however, his offers had been refused. His surprise was therefore quite as great as his delight when, in 1800, Thomas Williams, Eunice's grandson, brought to him his two boys, Eleazer and John, to be educated.

It has come down to us in local tradition that from the first the Longmeadow folk noted the curious difference both in appearance and in mental aptitude between these lads. John, the younger, only seven, was every whit an Indian. He stayed in Longmeadow a few years, and then went back to his own people scarcely changed at all by his contact with civilization. Eleazer, however, exhibited no Indian characteristics. Neither in form, feature, nor bearing, was he in the least

287

a red man. He was eager for study, and by 1810, in spite of repeated illnesses, had read six books of the Æneid, several orations of Cicero, was going through the New Testament in Greek, and was anxious to begin Hebrew. This precocity may be held to indicate previous culture. Indeed, Mr. Ely, as well as others in the village, seems to have been early informed that Eleazer was an adopted and not a real son of his Indian parents. People generally believed the boy to be the son of some French Canadian family of standing. Always the deacon used to say, however, that Eleazer Williams was born to be a great man, and that he intended to give him an education to prepare him for his rightful station.

It was in 1800, as we have said, that Eleazer Williams arrived at Longmeadow; in 1803 he began to follow the example of Deacon Ely and to keep a journal. This practice he continued with occasional short interruptions for the rest of his life, and from the resulting journal it is that we get the most interesting light obtainable upon the development of his character. This record shows that from the outset civilized life was natural to him. There is every token that education came to him as a recovery.

The religious strain in the lad was, however, marked from the first; as early as the year 1802 he was greatly affected by a sermon preached in the old meeting-house by Mr. Storrs in the course of a great revival. His conversion at this time was hailed by his friends with great rejoicing, as the object of his education was to prepare him for missionary work. In pursuance of this high end Mr. Ely began the next year to beg money in Eleazer's behalf from certain local missionary societies. That it was in 1803 that the deacon first made such applications is believed to be significant. For when the lad was converted to Protestantism, it is surmised, the remittances for his support were no longer forthcoming.

In 1804 Thomas Williams and his wife visited the two boys at Longmeadow, and the great contrast between Eleazer and his reputed relatives awakened anew the curiosity and interest of the neighbourhood. In May of the same year, Mr. Ely, being in Boston with Eleazer, made application to the Legislature for pecuniary assistance in carrying on the boy's education, and he received a grant of three hundred and fifty dollars to help fit the lad for missionary duty among the Indians. Even thus early, it will be perceived, there was a very general feeling that this boy was an unusual person raised up for a great work. Yet the degrees by which he was removed from his Longmeadow friends had not up to this time been even suspected.

Perhaps it was first in the May of 1806, when Mr. Ely and Eleazer, being in Boston, attended the Catholic church of the Abbé Cheverus, that there broke upon the boy's consciousness a hint that he might be really very different from those among whom he lived. Deacon Ely must have been a particularly good example of the close-mouthed Puritan. He gave as his excuse for attending the church in question his love of music, but that he should have gone at all to the service of a communion to which he was by birth and training bitterly opposed, is remarkable. And that he should have stayed afterwards to talk with the priest about Eleazer, is to be accounted for only in one way. Unfortunately, no record of the conversation with Bishop Cheverus has come down to us in Deacon Ely's journal, a diary so painstaking in its description of every-day farm work and commonplace happenings that one must believe its silence concerning this quite unusual incident to have been intentional. We do know, however, that Eleazer was introduced to the Abbé Cheverus as an Indian youth studying for the ministry. And we know further that the good abbé, though his interest in Indian missions was tremendously keen, did *not* question his caller concerning his life in the forest, or his desires to be of spiritual aid to the red men. On the contrary, he quite ignored this obvious topic, and asked the boy about the practice of the Indians in adopting French children, and whether he had ever heard of a boy being brought from France and left among them. The Abbé

Cheverus was himself a devoted Loyalist, an exile from France, as we have already seen, because of his political adherence to the cause of the martyred king. There seems little doubt that he suspected Deacon Ely's handsome charge to be none other than the Dauphin of France.

It is now generally admitted by even the most cautious students of history that there exists abundant and very strong evidence in favour of the theory that the Dauphin Louis XVII. did not die in the Temple. The physicians acknowledged, soon after the event, that they could not testify to the identity of the dead child with the Dauphin; several other persons in the Temple positively asserted that the child who died was not the Dauphin; the police were ordered to arrest on the highways of France any persons travelling with a child of the Dauphin's age, as

there had been an escape from the Temple;
the royal family rejected at once the heart
of the child who died in the Temple; the
name of the Dauphin was omitted in the
religious services ordered by Louis XVIII.
in remembrance of the royal victims of
the Revolution; the grave supposed to
contain the body of the Dauphin, in the
Cemetery of St. Marguerite, was utterly
neglected; the Duchess d'Angoulême asserted on her death-bed that her brother
was not dead, and demanded that he be
found and restored to his heritage. Along
with all these facts are to be placed the
interesting links in the chain by which a
wholly disinterested historian, the Reverend John H. Hanson, was able to pro-
claim in *Putnam's Magazine* for February, 1853, his astounding story that
Louis XVII. of France had been found
in the person of the Reverend Eleazer

Williams, at that time a devoted missionary to the Indians, living in Green Bay, Wisconsin.

In 1795, we learn, a family of French refugees, consisting of a gentleman and lady and two children, a girl and a boy, arrived in Albany, New York, and stayed there for a short time. The adult couple were called Monsieur and Madame de Jardin, but they did not appear to be husband and wife, the man acting rather as attendant upon the other members of the family. The boy, apparently about ten years old, was called Monsieur Louis, and the curious thing about him was that he did not seem to notice any one nor to be aware of what was passing around him. Still it was perfectly obvious to all who saw the little family that Monsieur Louis was regarded as the important member of the group. Several ladies who could speak

French called upon Madame de Jardin, and to one of these she confided that she had been maid of honour to Marie Antoinette, and was separated from her on the terrace of the palace before the imprisonment in the Temple. In speaking of affairs in France Madame de Jardin became much agitated, and with tears streaming down her cheeks she played and sang the Marseillaise. After a time the de Jardin family left Albany, and their new acquaintances never heard of them again. Very soon after their disappearance two Frenchmen, one of them a Catholic priest, having in charge a sickly and apparently imbecile boy, came to Ticonderoga, near Lake George, and left the boy in charge of an Iroquois chief, a half-breed, named Thomas Williams, whose grandmother was the Eunice Williams of the Deerfield raid. A half-breed Indian chief, who witnessed the transfer, heard the two strangers tell Thomas Williams that the imbecile boy was French by birth. While there is, of course, no positive proof that the Monsieur Louis of the Albany family was the same boy left with Thomas Williams, the circumstantial evidence pointing to their identity is strong.

For some time the health of the adopted lad was extremely delicate, but an outdoor life, plain food, and the simple remedies furnished by his Indian protectors proved admirable means for the upbuilding of his impaired physique. His intellect, however, continued deranged until, during one of his annual excursions to Lake George, where Thomas Williams went each year to hunt, he fell from a high rock into the water and cut his head severely against a stone beneath the surface. He was taken up insensible, and had no recollection afterwards of the accident; but the shock awakened his benumbed faculties, and his mind resumed its normal activity, though his memories of the past were still spasmodic and confused. The same half-breed chief who saw the boy when he was brought to Williams, was a witness also of this accident and of its happy effect.

Scarcely had Eleazer attained the condition in which impressions and people must have stamped themselves with particular clearness upon his memory than he was visited by two strangers, one of whom was a Frenchman, elegantly dressed, and wearing powdered hair. This man embraced the lad tenderly, wept over him, talked earnestly to him with tears and endearments, and tried very hard to make him understand what he had to say. Eleazer, however, could no longer follow a conversation in French, though when he had been brought to the Indians French was the language that he spoke. The next day the two strangers came again, the splendid gentleman in the ruffled shirt calling the little lad *" pauvre garçon,"* and examining with care the traces on his knees and ankles of what one must believe to be the tumors from which the child had suffered terribly during his confinement in the loathsome Temple under the care of the brutal Simon. When the stranger went away he gave the boy a gold piece. Thomas Williams, however, was anxious only to know whether Eleazer understood what the gentlemen had said to him. Upon being assured by his foster-son that the whole proceeding was utterly incomprehensible to him, he seemed greatly relieved.

A few days after this visit Eleazer, who slept in the same room with his reputed parents, overheard Thomas Williams urging his wife to give her consent to a request which had been made to them to allow two of their boys to be sent away from home for education. She objected on religious grounds, but finally said: " If you want to, you may send away the strange boy; means have been put into your hands for his education; but John I cannot part with." This remark made Eleazer suspect that he did not really belong to the family, but the impression soon passed away, as such impressions do from the minds of children.

The sensation which the coming of the boys produced in the quiet village of Longmeadow we have already seen. Everywhere Eleazer was called " the plausible boy," by reason of his charming and graceful manners. In his chat with the other lads he used sometimes to tell them that he remembered noble edifices, beautiful gardens, gorgeously furnished apartments, ladies and gentlemen in splendid attire, troops on parade, and he himself lying on a rich carpet with his head on a lady's silk dress. Other images of painful form likewise thronged his mind. Once he spoke of the scars on his forehead, and said the sight of them in the glass always brought up distressing thoughts upon which he could not bear to dwell.

The death in 1808 of Mr. Ely, Eleazer's first friend and benefactor, was a great grief to the lad. But it served to bring abruptly to a close the first scene of his civilized life in America. For he had now made friends for himself on all sides, and had quite determined to be a missionary to the people among whom he had been placed as a child. He remained at Mansfield and Longmeadow, therefore, only

till December 22, 1809, when he was put
under the tuition of the Reverend Enoch
Hale, of Westhampton, Massachusetts,
with whom he stayed till the month of
August, 1812, though during a great portion of this time he was absent on journeys
to various places, engaged in surveying the
missionary field. His equipment for the
work which he had elected was in many
ways remarkable, and on the breaking out
of the War of 1812 he was speedily recognized by the American government as the
person best fitted to prevent the Indians
from taking up arms against the United
States, and was accordingly appointed
General Superintendent of the northern
Indian Department with a secret corps of
army scouts and rangers under his command. In this capacity he served very
effectively. But when peace was established he devoted himself again to the

study of theology, and after mature deliberation resolved to join the ministry of the Protestant Episcopal Church instead of remaining in the Congregational communion with which he had been so long connected. This change in his opinions and purposes, while it did not cause any hard feeling among his early friends, greatly hampered him financially, because he was now, of course, forbidden by delicacy to accept any of the missionary funds heretofore placed at his disposal by the Congregational bodies. All his life, however, he continued to be interested in the old church at Longmeadow, where he had first embraced the Christian faith. Miss Julia Bliss, of that town, writes me that she distinctly remembers hearing him preach there once, and was greatly impressed by his courtliness of manner, as well as by his able discharge of the clerical function.

In July, 1822, Eleazer Williams removed from New York to Green Bay, Wisconsin, where land had been provided for an Indian settlement. And in this remote place it was that the Prince de Joinville, eldest son of King Louis Philippe, sought him out when he came to America in 1841, and made the extraordinary disclosure that gives us our romance. One of the prince's first inquiries upon setting foot in the country was whether a man named Eleazer Williams lived among the Indians of Northern New York. After considerable investigation he learned that the person he was seeking was an Episcopal missionary at Green Bay, Wisconsin, and for further information he was advised to consult Mr. Thomas Ogden, a prominent Episcopalian of New York City.

At the request of the prince Mr. Ogden wrote to Mr. Williams (who was then at Hogansburg, New York, engaged with several other persons upon important business connected with Indian affairs), and told him that the Prince de Joinville was in the country and wished to see him before returning to France. A meeting was thereupon appointed at Green Bay, and Mr. Williams left his business unfinished and started directly for the West, while the prince took the route through Canada, leaving Boston, where he was being entertained, very suddenly and mysteriously to pursue the journey. Naturally, Mr. Williams was greatly surprised at the summons to meet the prince, but he supposed the visitor wished to consult him concerning Indian affairs, upon which he was a

305

recognized authority, and he therefore
made all haste to keep the appointment.

He had expected to meet the prince at
Green Bay; but on arriving at Mackinac
he heard that the royal party was expected
there that day, and he decided, therefore,
to connect at once with his distinguished
visitor. Soon the steamer came in sight,
salutes were exchanged, flags were displayed, and crowds gathered, — as they
always have and probably always will in
this inconsistent democracy, — for the
purpose of gazing upon a representative
of royalty. On landing, the prince and
his retinue went to visit the famous rocks
about half a mile from the town, and the
steamer waited for them. But while they
were gone, the captain sought out Mr.
Williams, assuring him once more that
the prince was very anxious to see him.
The two then embarked on the same vessel,

and in due time Mr. Williams was brought face to face with the Prince de Joinville.

On seeing the missionary, the scion of the King of France started with involuntary surprise; his manner betrayed great agitation of feeling; he turned pale, his lip quivered, and it was only by the exercise of tremendous self-control, half a dozen onlookers testified later, that he was able to greet the supposed Indian with conventional civility. Mr. Williams was greatly surprised and mystified by the prince's manner, the more so when he was invited to take the seat of honour at the private table of the royal party. This distinction he however declined, and it was not until the afternoon that the acquaintance was resumed. All that day and the next the two talked about the relations between France and America at the time of the Revolution, and about the sad fate

of Louis XVI. On arriving at Green
Bay, the prince invited Mr. Williams to
accompany him to his hotel, but the missionary excused himself, saying that he
must go to his own home. [He had married, some twenty years before, a wife of
French extraction, by whom he now had
several children.] Before leaving Mr.
Williams promised, however, to return in
the evening, — so urgent had the visitor
been, — and thus no time was lost in getting to the matter of importance in hand.

When Mr. Williams came back to the
hotel the prince received him alone in his
chamber, and at once opened the interview
by saying that he had a communication
of vital interest to both to make, but that
since the matter deeply concerned several
other people, he must, before going further, receive the missionary's promise that
the secret he was about to divulge should

not be revealed. At first Mr. Williams objected to pledging himself without knowing the nature of the information he was to receive. But after some discussion he consented to sign his name to an agreement not to repeat what the prince was going to tell him, *provided* that no harm to other persons should follow from his silence.

This being done, the prince told him at once that he was not a native of America, but was born in Europe, a son of a king. He further presented a document written on parchment in double columns of French and English, which he invited Mr. Williams to read. He then left the room.

Scarcely knowing whether his eyes made out aright the mystifying words, the missionary then perused the imposing document spread before him, an official paper

from which he learned that he was
himself the son of Louis XVI. and rightful
King of France under the title of Louis
XVII. He learned also — and this must
have burned itself torturingly into his
reeling brain — that he was requested to
abdicate all his rights and titles in favour
of the reigning king, receiving instead a
princely establishment, either in France or
in America, together with the restoration
of the private property of the royal family,
confiscated during the Revolution, or
fallen afterwards into other hands.

Long and painful were the hours which
the simple, conscientious Christian minister passed alone in that hotel room at
Green Bay, going over his duty to his
family and to himself as he faced that
astonishing parchment. Very clearly he
saw that the prince's father was indeed,
as he said, the choice of the people

THE DAUPHIN OF FRANCE
(LOUIS XVII.)

THE REVEREND ELEAZER WILLIAMS

of France, and, therefore, in all probability, rightful king. Likewise unmistakable was the fact that he, Eleazer Williams, could never by himself prove the truth that the parchment asserted. Yet, on the other hand, he could not consent of his own free will to barter whatever inherent rights he might have in the throne of France. After earnest thought, therefore, he made known to the prince his irrevocable choice of truth and honour. He told the visitor from overseas that he would not for any consideration whatever give up his own rights and sacrifice the interests of his family. He told him further that, as he had placed him in the position of a superior, he must assume that position and express his indignation at the conduct of the Orleans family, one of whose members was guilty of the death of the murdered king, while another

311

wished to deprive him of his inherited rights. When Mr. Williams declared his superiority in rank, the prince stood in respectful silence. The next day the subject was resumed, but Mr. Williams gave the same answer. As the prince went away, he said to the missionary: "Though we part, I hope we part as friends."

For seven years then the matter slumbered. Mr. Williams made no attempt whatever to bring his claim to the attention of the public, nor did he talk to any of his many friends about the subject of the prince's visit. Only to the pages of his journal did he confide the thoughts which haunted and distressed him. The pressing duties of active life soon cast into the background those few hours of awakened feeling which seemed in the retrospect like a bewildering romance, and, but for the startling intelligence communicated to him in 1848 from the death-bed of one Bellanger, the whole matter might never have come to the ear of the public. But Bellanger asserted as a dying confession that he had assisted in the escape of the Dauphin from the Temple, had brought him to America, placed him among the Indians, and that he [the Dauphin] was now a missionary to the Oneidas, under the name of Eleazer Williams. A Boston newspaper, the *Chronotype,* got hold of the matter, and published a communication on the subject, April 18, 1848.

From this slight beginning the news gradually spread, exciting occasional discussion but not creating general interest until, in the autumn of 1851, the Reverend John Hanson, an Episcopal clergyman, happened to see an article in a New York daily paper wherein it was stated that there were strong reasons for believing that Eleazer Williams was indeed the son of Louis XVI., one of the reasons being his remarkable resemblance to the Bourbon family. Mr. Hanson's curiosity was at once awakened by this, and he resolved to make further investigations. Soon afterwards he accidentally met Mr. Williams while travelling, and by his sympathetic interest in the man and his ability to make him see that the very terms of his promise to the Prince de Joinville left him free to disclose the substance of the interview, won from the now almost distraught clergyman the whole curious story.

The tale of Mr. Hanson's search for additional evidence that Eleazer Williams was indeed Louis XVII. supplies one of the most interesting volumes the last century has produced. This clergyman seems

to have recognized from the first Mr.
Williams's unfitness to cope with the difficulties of the question. On this account
he himself determined to do everything in
his power to bring the truth of the matter
to light. In 1853, as has been said, he
embodied his researches in an article published in the February number of *Putnam's Magazine,* and entitled, " Have We
a Bourbon among Us ? " This paper
created immediate and widespread interest
among readers on both sides of the water.
A marked copy was, of course, sent to the
Prince de Joinville, and, as was to be
expected, that nobleman denied the whole
story. In spite of the witness of several
trustworthy persons, he alleged that he had
not sought out the Reverend Eleazer Williams, asserted that he had met him only
by chance, and stated further that what
conversation he had had with him was alto-

gether devoted to Indian matters. The reader who cares to follow the details of this very interesting controversy is referred to the volume " The Lost Prince," written by Mr. Hanson and published by the Putnams in 1854. For still further information one may see that very readable book, " The Story of Louis XVII. of France," written by Elizabeth E. Evans, who is herself one of the Williams family. Affidavits from physicians to show that Eleazer Williams had about him none of the physical traits of the Indian, but possessed many of those accredited to the Bourbons, of his foster-mother to prove that he was indeed an adopted child, of men who witnessed the Prince de Joinville's agitated recognition of Eleazer Williams, of Frenchmen who asserted that they were fully persuaded that this man was the lost Dauphin, of two eminent portrait painters, Chevalier Fagnani and Mr. Muller, who had painted the Bourbon kings, are all given in this very interesting work. Fagnani first saw Williams in a crowded room, and, after observing him for some time, replied to the question, "Well, what do you think of this being a Bourbon?" "I don't think at all; I know!" That the Dauphin was indeed brought to America seems now to be very well established. So eminent a man as Citizen Genet said of the matter as early as the year 1818, in the course of an evening party, where his remarks were overheard by several trustworthy witnesses: "Gentlemen, the Dauphin of France is not dead, but was brought to America." M. Genet further informed the company that he had believed the Dauphin was in Western New York.

One cannot indeed carefully examine

the evidence without being convinced of
the truth of Eleazer Williams's high
claims. It is impossible to believe that
this man could have romanced to the extent that the circumstances must have
necessitated. Moreover, he never once
tried to make capital out of his story.
Further, the mental as well as the physical
characteristics of Mr. Williams curiously
correspond with those the Dauphin
would probably have exhibited had he
been alive and in such a position after
a complicated career. Those who remember Mr. Williams at Longmeadow bear
constant testimony to his charm of manner,
his interesting conversation, and his unusual courtliness of address. But they
further say that his judgment in matters
of self-interest was weak. Though fluent
and eloquent in diction, his ideas were
not always well assorted. And he seemed

318

to have no proper sense, as a man with
that horrible childhood in the Temple
might very well not have had, of the steps
necessary to establish his identity.

The traces of that fatal blight which
fell upon his infancy became more and
more perceptible as the years passed, and
though he had been a brilliant and promising youth, he was only fairly successful
in middle age. This was not at all to be
wondered at, for after the revelation of
his birth Eleazer Williams seemed to have
no rightful place among his fellow men.
Ignored by his royal kin across the sea,
regarded as an impostor by many
of his brother-ministers, separated from
his supposed Indian relatives through
their recognition of his alien ancestry,
unfitted alike for the position to which
he was born and for the work which
circumstances had imposed upon him, —

319

surely few human beings have occupied a more anomalous place in society.

If this mystery of the Bourbon prince had come to light in 1903 instead of fifty years ago, it would probably have met with a far different reception. Certainly one cannot believe that we of to-day would suffer the rightful heir to a foreign throne to pour out his life in missionary service without paying him even the stipend that such service ordinarily commands. But this is what happened to Eleazer Williams. Though he had rendered very valuable aid to the country in its Indian troubles, his contributions to the solution of that tremendous problem were never properly appreciated. And though there is no question whatever of his simple, sincere, lifelong devotion to the cause of Christ, he never received an adequate salary or the cordial coöperation of his fellow min-

320

isters. He died August 28, 1858, at Hogansburg, New York, — where for four years he had been spending the greater part of his time, engaged in missionary work, while his family remained at their home on Fox River, Green Bay, — the same Mr. Hanson who had so zealously exploited his cause having here built a house for his use. The house has now been turned into the Epiccopal parsonage of the place. His grave in the cemetery at Hogansburg is marked by a headstone erected by his son, and bearing his name and the date of his death.

The true story of the two puzzling lives here traced will probably always remain an unsolved historical puzzle. But to those who are inclined to follow their intuitions and their sympathies rather than to be eternally skeptical of things, it is sufficiently

clear that the young man who was " converted " in the old Longmeadow church
in 1802 was indeed none other than Louis
XVII. of France.

THE REVEREND JOSHUA YOUNG'S CHURCH,
BURLINGTON, VT.

THE OSTRACISM OF AN
ABOLITIONIST

*T*HOSE of us born in New England
since the Civil War have so carefully been taught that the North
was ever Abolitionist in its attitude, that
it is with not a little shock that we learn
of such a case of persecution for opinion's
sake as that of the Reverend Joshua
Young, D. D., who was driven from his
parish at Burlington, Vermont, because he
officiated at John Brown's funeral.

Doctor Young is still living in a pleasant little town near Boston, and one day
he intends to tell in full the story of his
relation to the Abolition movement. Mean-

while, I give the account of this minister's connection with John Brown as he himself, a serene white-haired octogenarian, with vivid recollections of the past, recently gave it to me. At first I found him rather reluctant to open anew the old wound of his social ostracism because of sympathy with the cause of the blacks. "They are rather ashamed now up in Burlington at the way I was treated," he said, "so why go over it all again?"

But when I told him that the rising generation would not and could not believe that New England had ever failed to live up to the lofty anti-slavery sentiments with which we have been taught to associate her, unless the details of such stories as these are made more clear, his interest in a modern rehearsal of the half-century old drama was enkindled, and he speedily brought out his "John Brown Book" —

one of the most significant scrap-books it has ever been my privilege to examine — the better to retrace with me the various steps that led to his forced resignation of his charge as pastor of the Congregational Unitarian Church, at Burlington.

"From the beginning," said Mr. Young, "I was an Abolitionist. As early as my college days (I was graduated from Bowdoin with the class of '45) I had given my sympathies to the cause of the blacks. And always I admired John Brown as the noblest of men. But the ministry was the work to which I had decided to devote myself, and so, after leaving the Harvard Divinity School in '48, I went at once to what was then known as the New North Church, on Hanover Street, there succeeding as pastor Francis Parkman. This building is still standing, but it is now a Roman Catholic Church.

325

"In 1850, after the fugitive slave law was passed, obliging the return of slaves who had escaped to free States, I witnessed the shameful rendition of Anthony Burns in accordance with that law, and I saw Thomas Symmes similarly sent back into servitude. For eleven years I was a member of a vigilance committee, and I sheltered many escaping slaves in my house on Unity Street in the North End. By this I made myself liable to a fine of one thousand dollars or imprisonment. The house was the second on the right of Unity Street from Charter Street, and the slaves well knew that if they could get to me I would help them. And it was just the same at Burlington, where I was known as station keeper of the underground railway to Canada.

"At Burlington I was not far, of course, from North Elba, where John

JOHN BROWN'S HOME, NORTH ELBA, N. Y.

Brown's family had, in 1849, been settled
on a farm by the sturdy Abolitionist. If
you've read any life of John Brown, you
must know how pure was his devotion to
the cause for which he died, and how
strong was the grip his personality and
example had upon the spirits of young
Abolitionists. He himself had been intended for the ministry, you remember,
and all his life long he was a religious
man, filled with the spirit of the Old
Testament desire to right the wrongs of
the oppressed even at the cost of his own
and his opponents' lives. In his family
life he was Puritan and patriarchal, con-
ducting family worship, ruling his children firmly, instructing them at his knee
and singing hymns to them, not at all the
kind of man, you see, that his enemies
make him out. Though he was head-
strong, he was humane and kind, and

327

Frank Sanborn, of Concord, who knew
him well, even tells of seeing him weep
at a performance of Schubert's 'Sere-
nade.' This, and the fact that he taught
a singing-school for a time at North Elba,
shows whether he was or was not the brutal
creature his enemies believed."

But here let us review — as I was
obliged to before I could fully appreciate
Doctor Young's interesting story — some
of the facts of John Brown's life. This
and a glimpse into his cabin at North
Elba will help us to get into the spirit
of the narrative. Up in that rough Adi-
rondack home of his, Brown's favourite
books numbered not only the "Pilgrim's
Progress," but a "Life of Napoleon," not
only Baxter's "Saint's Rest," but the
"Life of Oliver Cromwell." His daughter
has told us that though he loved all of
the Bible he cared especially for the story

of Gideon. This sheds light upon subsequent events. Undoubtedly he aspired to do for the blacks what Gideon did for the children of Israel.

Brown's ideal seemed first to express itself in definite action when, in September, 1855, he went to Kansas, whither his sons had preceded him. To his wife and children at North Elba he wrote picturesque accounts of his journey, and in one of the letters there is a tender allusion to the skill with which Oliver, the young son who had accompanied him, brings down the chickens used for meat, as the party travels in their rude caravan wagon.

Brown's purpose in making this journey was, of course, to try to establish an anti instead of a pro-slavery majority in Kansas. Contrary to the pledge of the Missouri Compromise, the Kansas-Nebraska Bill provided that the question of slavery in that State should be determined by those who should settle there. Consequently it was a rush to see which side should colonize first. The Emigrant Aid Company, of New England, was sending many settlers into Kansas with the object of outnumbering and outvoting the proslavery settlers, and over these John Brown acted as a kind of captain and leader.

The Free State people were at first altogether inclined to be quiet and law-abiding, but the Missourians became so high-handed in their acts, and so deliberately rode across the line into the Territory to vote fraudulently, to shoot and to rob, that the New England friends of the settlers from the North soon began to send down rifles, the better to advance the cause they had so near their hearts.

Brown bestirred himself promptly

against the Missourian invaders, and in December, 1855, was made captain of a band organized to resist a raid on the Free State town of Lawrence. On this first occasion the raiders were repulsed, one of Brown's men being killed.

It was not, however, until the next spring that Brown struck his stinging blow at the raiding Missourians. His own life and that of all his followers was in danger, and it seemed to him that it was absolutely necessary to show fight to the men who were terrorizing the neighbourhood. So, getting together a small party, he went, on the night of May 24, to the shores of Pottawatomie Creek, and calling the pro-slavery leaders out of their beds, he directed the execution of five of them.

This fearful deed sent a thrill of horror through the entire country. But Brown seems not to have had the smallest doubt that he was directed by Providence in his act. There is a story that, after the terrible night, he called his followers and his captives together for divine worship in his camp, and raised to heaven in fervent invocation hands to which still clung the dried blood of his victims. His son discredits this — at least, the " dried blood " part.

Evidently Doctor Young, however, wished to be assured that Brown did not personally partake in this awful piece of work, for one of the most interesting autograph letters to be seen in his " Brown " book is the following, obviously in reply to an inquiry of his:

" NORTH ELBA, N. Y., Dec. 27, 1859.

" THE REVEREND JOSHUA YOUNG — *Dear Sir:* — Your letter to my mother was

THE REVEREND JOSHUA YOUNG

received to-night. You wished me to give you the facts in regard to the Pottawatomie execution or murder, and whether my father was a participator in the act. I was one of his company at the time of the homicides, and was never away from him one hour at a time after we took up arms in Kansas. Therefore I say positively that he was not a participator in the deed.

" Although I should think none the less of him if he hàd been, for it was the grandest thing that was ever done in Kansas. It was all that saved the Territory from being run over with drunken land pirates from the Southern States. That was the first act in the history of our country that proved to the demon of slavery that there was as much room to give blows as to take them. It was done to save life and strike terror through their wicked ranks. I should like to write you more about it, but I have not time now. We all feel very grateful to you for your kindness to us. Yours respectfully,

"SALMON BROWN."

Terrible as the deed undoubtedly was, it seems to be quite true that it was this that saved Kansas to the free States, for Brown's men, a mere handful, were soon able to do deeds out of all proportion to their strength — witness the battle at Osawatomie. And ere long it was recognized that slaves could not be held in Kansas. After that the climax came on apace.

John Brown's daring plan to raid Harper's Ferry was first disclosed to his Northern friends February 22, 1858, at the house of Gerrit Smith, in Peterboro, New York. Frank Sanborn, of Concord, and Colonel Thomas Wentworth Higginson were both present at this conference, and they used every possible argument to dissuade Brown from his desperate and obviously ill-fated undertaking.

Hour after hour the men talked and contended, Brown answering volubly every objection presented. When they protested that it was utterly hopeless to undertake so vast a work as war with the whole South upon such slender means, the indomitable captain replied: " If God be for us, who can be against us ? " In truth, it seemed to be John Brown's rebellion. So, promising to raise what money they could to help, the Massachusetts Abolitionists returned home. And Brown, after a brief visit to the family at North Elba, went to Canada to enlist the support of the negroes who had taken refuge there.

Then he took up a residence in Virginia, and elaborated his plans for the raid.

In all the world's history there is recorded nothing more audacious than this determination of Brown's to precipitate war upon the slave States by seizing the United States arsenal at Harper's Ferry. It was a desperate and a fatal step from the start. Brown's own sons disapproved of it, and all his followers tried to turn him from it. But at this stage, if not before, the Abolitionist was a fanatic, determined to die if need be in the cause he had espoused. It is asserted that Brown preached to a band of simple believers in the little Dunker Chapel just before starting out on his raid. And then he and his handful of men silently and swiftly captured one of the arsenal buildings.

A picturesque incident of the raid was

the way in which Brown took possession
of a famous sword captured with Colonel
Lewis Washington, a descendant of George
Washington's brother. This sword was one
which Frederick the Great, of Prussia,
had sent as a gift to General George Washington, and which Lewis Washington had
inherited. Brown took it and carried it
proudly until he was himself made a
prisoner. So effectively did his manner
make its impress upon Colonel Washington that that gentleman had at first no
doubt at all that the wearer of his an-
cestral sword was the important head of
a large force instead of a trebly outlawed
leader of scarcely a score of men.

All the morning of October 17th there
was scattered fighting, the militia having
promptly, of course, come to arrest the
unknown white man called "Captain
Smith" who was attempting to stir up a

negro insurrection. Finally, having lost many of his men, Brown barricaded himself in the engine-house, all the time, as he directed the men, giving them orders not to shoot when they could possibly avoid it. His last words to his men, before leaving on this desperate errand, indicate, indeed, as nothing else does, the spirit in which the attempt was made: " And now, gentlemen, let me press one thing on your minds. You all know how dear life is to you, and how dear your lives are to your friends; and in remembering that, consider that the lives of others are as dear to them as yours are to you. Do not, therefore, take the life of any man if you can possibly avoid it; but if it is necessary to take life in order to save your own, then make sure work of it."

Of course the arrival by train from Washington of a company of United

States marines, headed by Colonel Robert Lee and Lieutenant J. E. B. Stuart, both of them afterwards famous as Confederate generals, quite settled the question of fighting. Moreover, scarcely any of Brown's men were by this time alive. Stuart it was who, coming into the engine-house with a light under a flag of truce to parley, exclaimed, on seeing Brown: " Why, aren't you old Osawatomie Brown, of Kansas, whom I once had there as my prisoner ? "

" Yes," said Brown, " but you did not keep me." This was the first intimation that the Harper's Ferry people had of Brown's identity.

Arrest, trial, and conviction for " treason and conspiring and advising with slaves and others to rebel, and of murder in the first degree," followed swiftly after Harper's Ferry. Only six days were neces-

sary to bring in the verdict of conviction.
All the way through the prisoner was calm
and self-possessed, and refused to plead to
insanity, which, when his lawyer urged it
for him, he called "a miserable device."
Very often, indeed, he said to those about
him: "I think that my great object will
be nearer its accomplishment by my death
than by my life."

He was hanged at Charlestown, Virginia, December 2, 1858, his last recorded
act as he went to the gallows being a
tender kiss bestowed upon a negro child.
He would have no religious services at
the execution, because all the available
clergymen were pro-slavery men.

The day of the execution, Doctor Young
recalls, meetings were held for and against
Brown's cause all over the country. The
excitement ran very high, and so turbulent
was the popular feeling that the mayor of

Philadelphia would not give Mrs. Brown permission to let the body, which had been given over to her, receive undertaking attention in that place. Here it was that the false casket episode was enacted.

"That happened in this way," said Doctor Young, when I asked him about this part of the funeral journey. "Only the swiftest possible passage of the body through Philadelphia could ensure peace, the mayor believed. But the mob was there. So to divert them a tool-box in the car was substituted for the coffin, a deerskin thrown over it, and policemen called to bear it to a waiting cart. These officers removed their hats and reverently bore the box on their shoulders out from the car to the cart. Of course, when the cart started off the crowd followed. Then the true coffin was taken to another station and sent on through to New York, the entire trip taking five days.

"As soon as I learned that the body was to be brought to Brown's home for interment, I said to my wife: 'I shall go over to that funeral.'

"'Joshua,' she replied, 'is it wise?'

"'It may not be wise,' I answered, 'but I am going, just the same.'

"An Abolitionist friend, Mr. Bigelow, a young man like myself, agreed to set out with me. It was our intention to join the funeral party at Vergennes, fifteen or twenty miles from Burlington. But we arrived there too late to connect with their train, and we had to go on all night as best we could through a terrible winter storm. We reached North Elba about nine o'clock in the morning, having had nothing to eat for more than twenty-four hours.

"The burial was at one o'clock, and,

342

INTERIOR VIEW OF TRINITY CHURCH

JOHN BROWN, AND HIS GRAVE AT NORTH ELBA, N. Y.

though I had come as an Abolitionist
friend and admirer of John Brown,
rather than as a clergyman, it happened
that I was the only minister there. I
was told that it would greatly please the
family if I should perform the last rites
and make a prayer. This I did.

"Wendell Phillips was looking after
Mrs. Brown, who, very naturally, quite
broke down when the remains had been
escorted from the rough cabin house to
the grave near the great bowlder beside
which Brown had asked to be buried, and
as she stood there, sobbing and overcome
with her grief, I whispered to her for
consolation that sublime text from St.
Paul: 'I have fought a good fight, I have
finished my course, I have kept the faith:
henceforth there is laid up for me a crown
of righteousness, which the Lord, the
righteous judge, shall give me at that day.'

" When I took up the Burlington paper the next day, I found myself attacked with terrible fierceness for using this text over John Brown's body. And this was but the beginning of the veritable persecution I experienced. Six of the most prominent families of my parish retired at once from the church, and it looked as if my professional prospects were to be ruined for life.

" One of the most cutting snubs I received was at a social function, a reception to a bride, to which Mrs. Young and I had been invited before the funeral. Quite naturally, when I saw a group of ladies with whom I had been on intimate terms, as a popular pastor is on intimate terms with the prominent women in his congregation, I stepped up to them and made some pleasant remark or other.

" Quick as a flash they turned away

from me without speaking. At first I
hardly knew what to make of it. But I
soon saw that the coldness of the assembly
was for my benefit, and, as quickly as we
could, Mrs. Young and I went home. The
treatment we received at that reception
was but a hint of what was to follow.
Door after door to homes where we had
been welcome guests were shut against us.
My parishioners cut me on the street. The
feeling was that I had disgraced myself
and the church and all my fellow ministers
by officiating at the funeral of one whom
they regarded as a felon and a traitor. It
would seem as if a clergyman should be
immune wherever he might have performed the sacred rites of his holy office,
but business interests were imperilled by
the slave insurrections, and politically as
well as commercially the excitement ran
very high.

"It was soon necessary for me to leave Burlington. While I was not actually driven out of my parish, I was ostracized socially, and made to feel that, for the good of the church, I must go. I was thirty-six when I left the parish in Burlington, and went out into the world, not knowing whither. For a time it seemed as if I must give up the ministry, but eventually I was called to another charge, and since my life has gone on as smoothly as most lives do. My 'persecution,' as people call it, is only interesting (if it has interest) as a side-light upon New England character in the early '60's, and as an example of what may come into the life of an honest minister."

THE REVEREND PHILLIPS BROOKS

THE IDEAL MINISTER OF THE AMERICAN GOSPEL

*I*T was Oliver Wendell Holmes who said of Phillips Brooks, "I believe he is to stand as the ideal minister of the American gospel, — which is the old world gospel, shaped, as all gospels are, by their interpreters, by the influences of our American civilization." This masterly interpretation of Brooks's life was made when he was in the height of his career as rector of Trinity Church. To the parish as well as to the minister, therefore, may well enough be accorded the credit of powerful formative influence in the evolution of latter-day American Christianity.

347

The history of the first edifice called
Trinity Church began in 1728. In the
April of that year steps were taken toward
the formation of a third Episcopal church
in Boston "by reason that the chapel
(King's Chapel) is full, and no pews to
be bought by newcomers." Land was
accordingly purchased at the corner of
Summer and Hawley Streets, and it was
arranged that a church should be built
thereon "most conducing to the decent
and regular performance of divine service
according to the rubrick of the Common
Prayer-Book used by the Church of England as by law established." The movement developed slowly, and it was six
years before the corner-stone of the proposed building was laid, though the church
was soon organized under the name of
Trinity Church, and services were begun.
On April 15, 1734, however, sufficient

subscriptions having been secured, the corner-stone was laid by the Reverend Roger Price, of King's Chapel, as commissary of the Bishop of London. Then without further delay the building was erected, a wooden structure ninety by sixty feet, and thirty feet high. On August 15, 1735, the house was opened for worship, the Reverend Addington Davenport, brother-in-lay of Peter Faneuil, being chosen first rector.

The parish seems to have become speedily prosperous. After the death of Mr. Davenport, the Reverend William Hooper, who had been pastor of the West Congregational Church (now the West Church Library), was chosen to be the rector. Mr. Hooper had left the Congregationalists because of his desire to enlist in a church of greater breadth than was the West Church of that date, and his ordination was made

349

especially impressive from the fact that he went to England for it. In 1747 he came back in full orders, took charge of the parish immediately, and retained it for twenty years — till, in 1767, he fell suddenly dead as he was walking in his garden.

Trinity Church alone, it is worth noting, stood for the Episcopacy in Boston during the Revolutionary War; it was always open for worship, keeping alight the endangered fire of the old faith. To be sure, the rector, Doctor William Walter, fled to Nova Scotia when Boston was evacuated by the British, but Doctor Samuel Parker, who had been his assistant, nobly filled the place left vacant, and by his calm and dignified behaviour made possible the holding of the hated Church of England service even in those troublous Revolutionary times. Doctor Parker had the tact to omit the prayers for the king, concluding that " it would be more for the interest and cause of Episcopacy, and the least evil of the two, to omit a part of the liturgy, than to shut up the church." And this good sense it was which saved the Episcopacy to post-Revolutionary Bostonians. When General Washington was in Boston, in 1789, to pass the Sabbath, he went to Trinity Church in the forenoon to hear Doctor Parker preach.

In 1804 this faithful rector was chosen Bishop of Massachusetts. He died the same year. But before his death another ministry, which was destined to be long and influential in the history of Trinity, had begun, for John Sylvester Gardiner, who had been chosen assistant minister in 1792, was then made rector. He served for twenty-five years, in the course of which the Anthology Club, which grew into what is now the Boston Athenæum, was organized in his home. He was succeeded by Doctor Doane.

But the time had come when the old church building, which had stood almost a hundred years, no longer satisfied the people. The proprietors, therefore, voted, in 1828, to take down the venerable structure and to build a new one. This second church, known to-day as Old Trinity, was finally consecrated by Bishop Griswold, November 11, 1829. Doctor Hopkins, Doctor Wainright, Doctor Watson, Bishop Clark, Doctor John Cotton Smith, Doctor Mercer, Doctor Potter (now Bishop Potter, of New York), and Bishop Eastman, were the succeeding rectors who antedated Phillips Brooks as ministers here.

It was on Sunday, October 31, 1869, that America's greatest preacher began his ministry in Boston. The new rector brought with him from Philadelphia, where he had been serving under Doctor Vinton, tremendous enthusiasm for his work, and very soon Trinity Church was crowded to the doors by those who came from far and near to "hear Phillips Brooks preach."

The new rector was but thirty-three, a bachelor, and in the height of that manly beauty which men, as well as women, have ever so greatly admired. From the first, of course, the young ladies of old Trinity Church made the minister very welcome to their homes, as is the fashion of young ladies toward ministers. But neither then nor at any future time was the name of Phillips Brooks linked with that of any woman. To be sure, vague rumours of a romance left behind in Philadelphia followed him throughout his life, and helped those who needed help to account for his

continued celibacy. The fact patent to all,
however, was that he gave always to
Trinity Church the single-hearted devotion
another might have given to a wife. From
the beginning of his rectorate Boston
seemed in a fair way to go mad over the
young preacher. Soon Trinity Church
had exceeding difficulty in looking after
the throngs that came. The sexton, Mr.
Dillon, strove in vain to meet an emergency so wholly unlike anything he had
hitherto known in his long administration.
He tried to sort the people who presented
themselves for admission. " Dillon once
came to me in the vestry-room," said Mr.
Brooks, in speaking of the matter to a
friend, " to tell me of a method he had
devised to reduce the numbers who sought
admittance to the church. ' When a young
man and a young woman come together,
I separate them,' he explained, and he

354

expected me to approve the fiendish plan!"

The journalists of the day found this new preacher exceedingly good "copy." One of them writes as follows of a Sunday service: "The old building seems the fitting place of worship for the solid men of Boston. There is an air of ancient respectability about it. . . . The deep, roomy pews, thoughtfully padded, seem adjusted for sleeping, and though seven can sit comfortably in them, if you humbly ask for the fifth seat in some of them, beware of the lofty look and high-bred scorn which seems to say, ' Are not the galleries free to negro servants and strangers? . . . I shall have to let you in, I suppose. Take that prayer-book and keep quiet; service has begun. Don't you see Mr. Brooks?'

"Yes, we do see the Reverend Phillips

Brooks, a tall, stout, powerfully built man, with smooth, boyish face and very near-sighted eyes, which, nevertheless, by the help of glasses, seem to search you out in whatever dark corner you may be hidden. He is reading the service with a thin voice and rapid, breathless, almost stuttering delivery, and yet with a certain impulsive and pleading earnestness that carries even Congregationalists onto their knees, and takes them to the throne of grace."

The young people, especially of the more cultivated class, ran after Mr. Brooks as no Boston minister before or since has ever been run after. Without being able to analyze it, all his hearers felt the man's magnetism. Very soon the preacher rose to the place of foremost citizen of Boston, his native town. His presence at every civic solemnity or function seemed indispensable to its completeness. Often the boy in the man was greatly amused at the deference paid to him; and often he would drop, almost perforce, from the pedestal upon which adoring Bostonians had placed him. It is related that in February, 1871, when he was present at the meeting in Music Hall, which ultimately resulted in the Boston Museum of Fine Arts, he spoke with singular ingenuousness of what he had gained as a boy in the Boston Latin School from the old room which contained the wonderful casts of the Laocoon and Apollo, and this simple speech doubtless helped very greatly in the erection of the fine building in Copley Square.

One of Mr. Brooks's boyhood ideals had been to be a famous lecturer. But now that he was a man he would have none of any profession except the preacher's. Mr. Redpath, of the famous New England Lyceum, wished to conduct a lecture course for him as much as the editor of the *Atlantic Monthly* wished to make him a literary man. But both invitations he declined. Whatever he did from the time of his coming to Boston he did as a preacher.

One of his letters speaks very beautifully of his joy in this work: "The old round of parish duties which I have gone to afresh every autumn for twelve years has opened again, and I have been rather surprised at myself to find that I take it up with just as much interest as ever. I suppose that other men feel it of their occupations, but I can hardly imagine that any other profession can be as interesting as mine. I am more and more glad I am a parson." (September 25, 1871.)

Mr. Brooks's occasional comments on Boston institutions were very amusing. Under date May 30, 1872, he writes: "I

358

am getting up a sermon for the Ancient and Honourable Artillery Company, one of the queer old Puritan organizations before which every Boston minister preaches sometime in his career, and is not thoroughly initiated without." At the time of the Peace Jubilee, he writes: " It is a terrible week in Boston. The Jubilee is going on with flash and bang all the time. It's wonderful what a row this Jubilee is making. I like to see a crowd, and expect to enjoy this very much, but it is all very funny and sensational — and the primness and classicism of Boston turns up its stiff nose at it."

When the new rector first came to Boston, he took rooms at 34 Mt. Vernon Street, but because of scanty sunlight he soon transferred himself to the Hotel Kempton, on Berkeley Street, where he entertained an increasing host of friends.

For some time before this (1872) there had been thought of a new and larger Trinity. Under date of June 11th we find the preacher writing: "We have chosen Richardson, of New York, for our church architect — the best of all competitors by all means. He will give us something strong and good." So when the church on Summer Street was well-nigh destroyed in the Boston fire, the catastrophe was hardly so appalling as it would otherwise have been. But to Trinity's rector it was none the less a good deal of a blow, as we see from his letters of that period: "The fire began about eight o'clock Saturday evening," he wrote to a friend, November 12, 1872, "and hour after hour it went on growing worse and worse. Street after street went like paper. There were sights so splendid and awful as I never dreamed of, and now the desola-

OLD TRINITY CHURCH, SUMMER STREET, BOSTON,
AFTER THE GREAT BOSTON FIRE

tion is bewildering. There was hard work enough to do all night, and though much was lost, something was saved. Old Trinity seemed safe all night, but toward morning the fire swept into her rear, and there was no chance. She went at four in the morning. I saw her well afire, inside and out, carried off some books and robes, and left her. She went majestically, and her great tower stands now as solid as ever, a most picturesque and stately ruin. She died in dignity. I did not know how much I liked the great gloomy old thing till I saw her windows bursting and the flame running along the old high pews.

"I feel that it was better for the church to go so than to be torn down stone by stone. Of course, our immediate inconvenience is great, and we shall live in much discomfort for the next two years. We have engaged the Lowell Institute, a lecture-hall that seats a thousand people, and shall begin service there next Sunday." And according to the journals of the day his sermon in Huntington Hall the following Sabbath was full of an onward and upward sweep, of life through death — the lesson of the fire.

The erection of the new Trinity Church was a matter very near Brooks's heart. During his next few summer vacations abroad his thoughts hovered constantly over the work that was to result in the noble edifice on Copley Square with which his name must be forever linked. To Mr. Robert Treat Paine, one of his letters about this time confides his intense interest in the work:

"Tours, France, Aug. 4, 1874.

"Dear Bob: — And how's the new church? I dreamed of it when I wrote

THE PRESENT TRINITY CHURCH, BOSTON, MASS.

to you from London, and now I dream
of it again, slowly rising, course on course.
I shouldn't wonder if the robing-room were
done up to the eaves, but I would give
much to step out of the hotel and look in
the gorgeous moonlight at that blessed lot
on the Back Bay."

And again, " How many things I have
coveted for the new church. There was a
big mosaic at Salviati's that would glorify
our chapel."

It is probable that the supreme beauty
of Trinity Church is due very largely
to this constant thought of its rector concerning it. Mr. Brooks was not an architect, but he had travelled much and made
himself very familiar with historic
churches in the countries he had visited.
His desire to combine with whatever
should have place in a Protestant church

363

all that was of human and enduring significance in the earlier methods of Christian architecture resulted in the imposing structure that marks the highest attainment of American church architecture. Inside as well as out the endeavour was to secure the best our country could produce. Decorated by artists, as distinguished from artisans, the church was indeed a noble whole when, February 9, 1877, it was consecrated by the Bishop of the Diocese.

In a letter to Mr. Paine written the day after the consecration, Mr. Brooks expressed with exquisite tenderness his feeling for the new Trinity: " I wish I could tell you, my dear Bob, something of what yesterday was to me, and of how my deep gratitude and love to you mingled with the feeling of every hour. May God bless you, is all that I can say. The church would not be standing there, the beautiful and stately thing that it is, except for your tireless devotion. . . . Many, many happy years are before us if God wills, and when we leave the great dear thing to those that come after us, we shall be near one another, I am sure, in the better life. . . . P. B."

The rector of the new church had now returned to Boston to live in a fashion befitting his station. His father and mother had given up their house on Hancock Street, and had gone to North Andover to reside in the old Phillips homestead, where they had been married fifty-four years before. Their son had tried hard to persuade them to stay with him, but they preferred their own home, and he himself now set up housekeeping at 175 Marlborough Street, taking into his employment the servants who had lived with his mother.

The next summer we find him at a house

in Hingham, from which quiet little town he goes to Boston every Sunday to preach. " I never had such a profoundly quiet summer as I am having now," he writes to a friend. " I am here in a queer little cottage on an obscure back bay of Boston harbour, where there is nothing to do, or, at least, where I do nothing, no sailing, no fishing, no riding, no walking. Nothing in the world but plenty of books and time and tobacco."

Phillips Brooks's first call to a bishopric came when he was fifty. His former home, Philadelphia, then did its best to win him back in this higher capacity, but he would not listen to the plea. His love for Boston seems indeed to have so grown with his growth that the thought of leaving the place where the strong work of his young manhood had been put in was positively painful to him. From California he writes

366

Mr. Paine, under date of June 1, 1886:
" . . . I have had a lot of correspondence
about that episcopate in Pennsylvania.
There was no moment when I thought of
going. How could I, so long as I dared
to believe that you all still wanted me to
stay in Boston? Will you tell me honestly
and truly and like a friend when you
think it is best for me to go away?" Ere
long, however, came the call to be Bishop
of Massachusetts, a call not to be gainsaid.
All the important newspapers had for a
long time been naming Mr. Brooks in this
capacity, and again and again it was said
that only his election could put the Episcopal Church where it should be in New
England life.

The convention met on the twenty-ninth
of April. Mr. Brooks was not present, but
the moment the vote had been taken there
was a rush from the hall where the con-

vention was sitting to the study of the Trinity Church rectory, on Clarendon Street, to tell him the news. He heard it, however, without elation. For he realized that this was the beginning of the end. His letters no longer have the joyous note of boyishness. Being a bishop seems from the first to have weighed upon his spirits. Meanwhile, however, all the world sent congratulations; he was hailed as bishop, not only of the Protestant Episcopal Church, but of Massachusetts. A letter from James Russell Lowell shows well the feeling:

"DEAR DOCTOR BROOKS: — Though I do not belong to the flock which will be guided by your crook, I cannot help writing a line to say how proud I am of our bishop. Faithfully yours,

"J. R. LOWELL."

THE HOUSE ON CLARENDON STREET, WHERE PHILLIPS
BROOKS LIVED AND DIED

That the newly chosen bishop looked forward with no little dread to the new life one soon sees in his letters. To Mr. Paine he writes from North Andover, August 17, 1891: "My dear Bob Paine: — There are six weeks before the awful day comes which sends me bishoping to the far confines of the State. I dread the pageant of that day, but it will soon be over." And to Mr. Newton, rector of the church at Pittsfield: "It will break the shock a little to have one of my earliest visits to your church, and will let me feel as if I had not wholly said good-bye to the old life. *You don't know how I cling to it.*"

The consecration of Bishop Brooks, October 14, 1891, was a State and civic as well as an ecclesiastical event. Long before the hour of service Copley Square was crowded with people anxious to share in some measure in the great affair. Only on the sad day of his funeral, a little over two years later, did a larger throng ever gather in that Boston square.

The end came quickly. A short two years of full life as Bishop of Massachusetts, and then a cold, a brief illness, and the passing of his spirit. His last public address was at the Woodland Park Hotel, Newton, on the occasion of a choir festival. Five days after he was dead. The funeral was held, of course, in the Trinity he had helped to build and had loved as few men love anything. From eight o'clock people of all classes thronged the church to look for the last time upon his peaceful face. The whole city was in mourning. The stock exchange and all the shops were closed. When the service within the church was over another was said in the square for the vast crowd of people who completely filled the open space. Harvard men then bore the body to the hearse, and the procession to Mt. Auburn by way of the bishop's Alma Mater began.

Of memorials to Massachusetts's bishop there are many in and about Boston, but the recent announcement that the great St. Gaudens statue of the preacher is to be architecturally connected with Trinity Church proves that this $100,000 statue, the funds for which were given by all the people of the country, will be his final and supreme memorial. And fittingly. For above and beyond all the other things that Phillips Brooks was, he was rector of Trinity, — Preacher to the People in that house of God he had in so true and high a sense builded for Boston.

THE END.

INDEX

373

INDEX

INDEX

375

INDEX

INDEX